EVEREST

EVEREST

Eighty years of triumph and tragedy

Edited by
Peter Gillman
Assisted by Leni Gillman

Foreword by
Tom Hornbein

THE
MOUNTAINEERS

Published in North America by
The Mountaineers
1001 SW Klickitat Way, Suite 201
Seattle, WA 98134

Published in Great Britain by Little, Brown and Company

First edition published in Great Britain and the United
States of America in 1993 by Little, Brown and
Company

Compilation copyright © Peter Gillman Ltd 1993, 2000

The moral right of the author has been asserted.

Library of Congress Cataloging-in-Publication Data
A catalog record for this book is available at the Library
of Congress.

ISBN 0-89886-780-0

Designed by Wilson Design Associates
Picture research by Audrey Salkeld and Peter Gillman
Printed and bound in Spain by Book Print, S. L.

Quote in Thomas Hornbein foreword from a Calvin and
Hobbes cartoon by Bill Watterson. © 1995 by Bill
Watterson. Used by permission of the Universal Press
Syndicate. All rights reserved.

See pages 236–7 for copyright details and original
publication of extracted material.

Cover: *Sunset on Everest's South-west Face,
photographed by Galen Rowell from the peaklet, Gokyo
Ri (17,989ft/5,483m).*

Page 1: *The North Face of Everest under heavy post-
monsoon snow, photographed by Roger Mear.*

Page 2: *The long and winding trail: in Doug Scott's
photograph, taken during his 1987 attempt on the
North-east or Pinnacles Ridge, Rick Allen (foreground)
and Sandy Allan toil through heavy snow near the top of
Bill's Buttress at 23,200ft/7,072m. Scott and his
colleagues reached the First Pinnacle at around
26,000ft/7,925m, with the summit still 3,000 feet
beyond.*

CONTENTS

'THE FINEST CENOTAPH IN THE WORLD' 1921–1939

'ED, MY BOY, THIS IS EVEREST' 1951–1969

'ALL THE WORLD LAY BEFORE US' 1970–1979

'A DREAMLIKE SENSE OF DISBELIEF' 1980–1989

'A BLEND OF FASCINATION AND HORROR' 1990–2000

CLIMBING EVEREST: THE COMPLETE LISTS

FOREWORD

All things change. And so it is with Everest. For one, since we were there in 1963, it's gotten two meters higher (thanks to the new measurements made by Bradford Washburn and his global satellites). For another, and this has evolved since the first edition of this book appeared in 1993, there is what one anthropologist has referred to as the 'Everest boom'. Everest tee shirts have been long a presence but the arrival of coffee cups and other mementos cannot be far away. Now the 'Big E' is hot, fueling the aspirations of a wealthier and more vigorous fringe of those known as adventure-travelers. It's no longer the private preserve of seasoned, self-sustaining mountaineers. Everest has become a more social mountain, subject, like the world we wanderers are escaping from, to crowding and queues. Thanks to the miracles of modern communication, even armchair mountaineers can savor the experience in near real-time, unburdened by the discomforts of altitude and cold and the appreciable risk of not coming down alive. Much of the mystery has gone.

The changes, at least with the sharpened perspective of hindsight, come as no surprise. As has been the case with all other attractive mountains – the Matterhorn, Rainier, Kilimanjaro, Denali – guided climbing on Everest was inevitable, and if Dick Bass had not claimed the honor of being the first paying client to reach the summit in 1985, someone else soon would have.

It's all so different from when Mallory and Irvine and their famous companions made those first tentative steps across the North Face in the 1920s and 1930s, when Ed Hillary and Tenzing Norgay finally reached its summit in 1953, and when Willi and I found ourselves marveling as the sun set on a spring day ten years later. What I remember most of those twenty minutes at the top of the earth was our closeness to each other and to those who had gotten us there, a vast aloneness so far from home, and the lateness of the hour with miles still to go. I feel blessed to have been born at the right time and to have had the fortune to have been on this highest mountain when being there was still a lovely, way-out-there adventure. A bit of my soul is saddened that our human affair with Everest has moved beyond this lonely stage to that of 'men jostling in the street'.

Those who would mourn the change may seek solace (and escape) in this paraphrase of the famous last line in Maurice Herzog's *Annapurna*: 'There are other Everests in the lives of men.' But I choose not to bemoan too much this evolution. One reason is that doing so won't alter anything. Mainly, though, it's because for me change, with its mix of better and worse, is precious. Change, and its companions, uncertainty and risk, kindle our aspirations:

'Change,' as Calvin opined to Hobbes, 'is invigorating. If you don't accept new challenges, you become complacent, lazy! Your life atrophies. New experiences lead to new questions and new solutions. Change forces us to experiment and adapt. That's how we learn and grow.'

There you have it, and change is what this new edition of Peter Gillman's superb anthology of Everest in writings and photos is about. I have treasured my copy of the first edition, particularly as the book became such a collector's item that personal copies had a tendency to disappear. A visual journey through the incredible history told here, written and photographed by those who made it, is about as glorious as an armchair Everest adventure can be. Peter Gillman places each step of this historical journey with caring insight into the bigger picture of how mountains age in their relationship with humankind. Enjoy the journey. And avoid the crowds.

Tom Hornbein

Tom Hornbein

Tom Hornbein, with his companion Willi Unsoeld, made the first ascent of the West Ridge of Everest in 1963. A poll in August 2000, when Hornbein was 69, ranked him as the American Climber of the Century.

Opposite: *Everest from the west: in Chris Curry's photograph, taken from 23,442ft/7,145m Pumori in Nepal, the West Ridge is seen in profile, between the sunlit North Face and the South-west Face, in shadow. Entering the picture, bottom right, is the Khumbu Glacier and Icefall, leading to the Western Cwm, the key to the first ascent by a British expedition in 1953.*

INTRODUCTION

I first became aware of Everest's power to inspire when I was eleven. In the autumn of 1953 I was among the schoolchildren taken to watch *The Conquest of Everest*, the film of the triumphant British first ascent. The sequence which held that potentially unruly cinema audience most spellbound was cameraman Tom Stobart's epic upwards pan from the snow-covered floor of the Western Cwm to the corniced Summit Ridge.

Stobart's shot often returned to me as I luxuriated in my task of compiling the first edition of this book. It served as a reminder of the odds its contributors faced, from the prewar pioneers who struggled to within a thousand feet of the summit, to their latterday counterparts, forging routes of increasing audacity. I felt special admiration for the photographers, determined to take pictures in the most hostile of environments.

I was still collecting material when I saw Everest for the first time, rising serenely from the great brown plateau of Tibet. Afterwards my task seemed to have become harder, the problem being what to omit from the hundreds of extracts, articles and photographs I had gathered. In the end I made a selection of the old and the new, familiar icons and unpublished material which I hope conveyed the awe I felt 40 years before.

Since the first edition of this anthology appeared in 1993, an editor's task has become even more complex. The nature of Everest mountaineering has changed dramatically, above all with the advent of commercial expeditions intent on placing more and more people on the summit. The disasters of 1996 brought home the dangers of the new mountaineering, while the discovery of the body of George Mallory in 1999 served as a counterpoint, evoking the daring and innocence of the first attempts. At the same time, almost unnoticed, mountaineers have continued to search for new routes on this greatest of peaks. I have aimed to represent all aspects of the new Everest in this revised edition, mixing familiar texts and stories with others which have been barely celebrated outside their own countries. The new edition also reflects the continuing research into the mountain's history, with new photographs and documents emerging to remind us that Everest, as always, retains its power to surprise.

Peter Gillman

Galen Rowell's photograph (right) *shows Everest from the Pang La, the 17,200ft/ 5,243m pass 40 miles to the north in Tibet. Clearly visible is the North Face, bisected by the Norton (or Great) Couloir. To its left the North Ridge rises diagonally to join the North-east Ridge at 27,630ft/8,422m.*

A HOUSEHOLD WORD

Sir George Everest, the son of a London solicitor, was Surveyor General of India from 1830 to 1843. He married in 1846, when he was 55, and had six children. He was knighted in 1861 and died in 1866. It was Everest's successor, Andrew Waugh, who proposed naming the world's highest mountain after him as a tribute to his pioneering work in mapping India. There were objections to Waugh's proposal, mostly on the grounds that a local name should be used instead. But Waugh won the argument and the name Everest was officially adopted by the Royal Geographical Society in 1865, just one year before Everest died.

It was in 1808 that the British began the process which was to locate and name the world's highest mountain. It was undertaken by the India Survey, staffed by army officers charged with providing reliable maps to help the British maintain their rule in the era of the Raj. Their goal was to survey the entire Indian sub-continent, and it was a formidable task.

The survey officials began by laying out a series of triangular grids which would eventually cover the whole country and provide a series of fixed points on which to base their maps. They were also plotting the Great Arc of India, a no less ambitious project by which they hoped to be able to calculate the true shape of the earth, suspected of being flattened at the poles rather than a perfect sphere.

With their calibrated chains and measuring rods, their great theodolites so heavy that they had to be carried by 12 men, the survey teams gradually worked their way north. By the 1830s they had reached the foothills of the Himalayas. Across the border into Nepal, they could glimpse snowy peaks rising beyond lines of intervening ranges, although for much of the time they were obscured by cloud.

The British already suspected that these distant peaks were the highest on earth. Infantry officers had been encouraged to map the territories they visited, and in 1803 Captain Charles Crawford, a trained surveyor, compiled several maps while posted to the British residency in Kathmandu. One, based on his own observations and measurements, showed 'the valley of Nepal', the first formal map of the region. A second, compiled from reports of 'merchants, religious mendicants and other travellers', depicted the entire kingdom of Nepal, and showed a line of peaks named as 'the snow mountains', with one marked as 'highest in the range'.

Crawford's findings had particularly intrigued the Surveyor General himself, Lt Col Robert Colebrook, who had already seen the 'snow peaks' from some 150 miles away. In 1807 Colebrook saw them again from near the Indian town of Gorakhpur: 'a scene which for grandeur can scarcely be rivalled – every part of the stupendous range appeared to be covered with snow.' Colebrook calculated that two of the mountains were at least five miles high, putting them above any peak in the Andes, then considered the highest

range. 'If that is the case,' Colebrook concluded, 'they must be the highest mountains in the known world.'

The surveyors of the 1830s were equally impressed by what one termed these 'stupendous pinnacles' and resolved to establish just how high they were. To their dismay, all further northward travel was barred. The obstacle stemmed from Nepal's suspicion of British intentions: as an autonomous state which had escaped British rule, it was determined to remain that way. It had expelled the British resident in 1803 and, so a British diplomat observed, 'nothing will dissuade the Nepalis from the belief that topographical surveys, geological examinations and botanical collections are either the precursors of political aggression, or else lead to complications which end in annexation.' The surveyors sought permission on several occasions to cross into Nepal but were turned down.

The British were thus compelled to make their observations from the Terai, a tract of country parallel to the Himalayas south of Nepal. They began by marking out a new series of base lines, interspersed with observation posts, 30 feet high,

To measure heights as accurately as possible, Everest deployed giant theodolites weighing up to 1100lbs and needing 12 men to carry them. In 1849 survey officer James Nicolson used this theodolite to observe what was then known as peak 'b' from distances of more than 100 miles. Nicolson's sightings established that the peak was the highest in the world.

built from mud bricks. Conditions were hideous: part-covered in jungle, the Terai was subject to torrential rain and malaria was rife. Of five successive survey officers, two died and two were forced to retire through ill-health. The fifth contracted malaria too and a stretcher party set off to carry him to hospital in Darjeeling, but he died before it arrived.

Undaunted, the British team began detailed observations of the great Himalayan peaks in 1847. The difficulties remained immense. The distances were enormous, up to 150 miles between the observation stations and the peaks. The weather restricted work to the final three months of each year, when the clouds which habitually obscured the peaks were most likely to clear. But they persevered, and in November the Surveyor General, Andrew Waugh, made a series of observations from Sonakhoda at the eastern end of the range.

One of the peaks which most interested Waugh was Kangchenjunga, hitherto regarded as most likely to be the world's highest peak, and for which the surveyors were already using a version – Kanchanjinga – of the local Nepalese name. Beyond it, some 140 miles away, Waugh sighted another snow-covered mountain which looked higher still. One of Waugh's officials, John Armstrong, saw the same snowy summit – 'perceptible but rather indistinct' – from further west, and called it peak 'b'. Afterwards Waugh wrote that the observations of the peak 'indicate an altitude higher even than that of the great Kanchanjinga . . . but on account of the great distance the observations require further verification from a station less remote.'

Waugh sent a survey officer to the Terai in 1848 to obtain closer sightings, but peak 'b' remained hidden by clouds. The following year he dispatched another officer, James Nicolson, who made two observations over a distance of 118 miles from Jirol station before the cloud closed in again. Taking the largest theodolite, Nicolson headed east and in two months obtained 36 observations from five different stations, the closest 108 miles from the peak.

Although Nicolson did not yet know it, he had just completed the observations which were to establish peak 'b' as the highest mountain in the world. But a hiatus occurred. When the rains came, Nicolson withdrew to a town near Patna on the River Ganges where he was due to make the calculations based on his sightings. His raw data were impressive: he had obtained an average height for peak 'b' of around 30,200 feet, and although that made no allowance for light refrac-

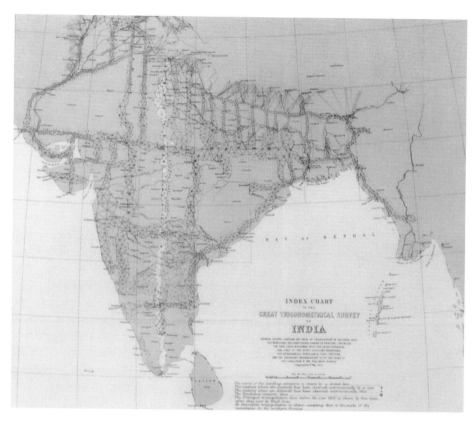

tion, which exaggerated heights, it placed it substantially higher than Kangchenjunga.

However, Nicolson was in no position to claim that he had just discovered the world's highest mountain, as he had no idea what heights his colleagues might have obtained elsewhere. Then he too was struck down by malaria, and had to be invalided home. Only in 1854 did Andrew Waugh begin work on Nicolson's figures at the survey headquarters in Dehra Dun. One of Waugh's assistants, Michael Hennessy, had given new designations to the peaks, based on Roman numerals: Kangchenjunga was Peak IX, peak 'b' became Peak XV.

Waugh and his staff spent almost two years on their calculations, wrestling with the problem of refraction which was notoriously difficult to calculate, particularly as they had no idea what allowances to make for temperature and barometric pressure over the enormous distances of Nicolson's sightings. They were also concerned in case the vast gravitational pull of the Himalayas had distorted their equipment. But in March 1856 Waugh finally announced his findings in a letter to his deputy in Calcutta. 'I am now in possession of the final values of the peak designated XV,' Waugh wrote. 'We have for some years known that the mountain is higher than any hitherto measured in India.'

Waugh then gave the crucial figures: Peak IX, Kangchenjunga (now known to be the world's

The officials of the British India Survey covered the country with a series of triangular grids to give them fixed points on which to base their maps. Starting at India's southern tip in 1808, they gradually worked their way north, taking 30 years to reach the Himalayas – known to the early mapmakers as the 'snow mountains'.

third highest mountain – the second is K2) was 28,156 feet; Peak XV was 29,002 feet. It was, Waugh concluded, 'most probably the highest in the world.'

There remained the question of what the highest peak should be named. Partly to deflect the accusation that it was merely an appendage of British rule, the survey had been anxious to preserve local names: hence its use of Kangchenjunga – 'the Five Treasure-Houses of the Snows' – and other names such as Dhaulagiri, 'the White Mountain'. But for Peak XV – so Waugh now argued – no obvious name existed.

There was in fact a plethora of existing names. Best-established was Chomolungma, which had been current in Tibet for several centuries and had appeared on a map published in Paris by the geographer D'Anville in 1733. Based on information from Tibetan lamas which was passed on by Jesuit missionaries in Peking, D'Anville's map rendered the name as Tschoumou-Lanckma, Tibetan for 'Goddess Mother of the World', clearly indicating the reverence accorded to the mountain. The name had echoes of another Tibetan phrase, Lhochamalung, which meant 'the district where birds are kept' and had been used from around 650 AD, when the early Tibetan kings had the birds in the region fed at their own expense. There were

at least three other candidates, including Devadhunka and Chingopamari, which were well-known in the ancient literature of Nepal, and Gaurisankar, although that turned out to be the name of another mountain.

Despite the claims for Chomolungma, Waugh was set on another name entirely. With some sophistry, he argued that since there were so many local names it would be invidious to choose any of them, and proposed instead that Peak XV should be named after his predecessor as India's Surveyor General – George Everest.

Everest had first arrived in India in 1806. Born in London, he was then a 16-year-old artillery cadet set on a career as an army officer. After a spell in Java he returned to India where he was appointed chief assistant to William Lambton, the current Surveyor General. When Lambton died in 1823, Everest took charge of the Great Trigonometrical survey, rising to become Surveyor General in 1830. He also completed the Great Arc of India, and it was he who had supervised the building of the giant theodolites vital in obtaining the decisive measurements of the Himalayan range, including Peak XV itself.

To Waugh, Everest was the obvious candidate after whom Peak XV should be named. He had set exacting standards for his officials but he too had

The British India Survey continued its work into the 20th century. The picture, right, taken in 1904, shows officials taking zenith observations: the British officer at the telescope is observing a star, calling out readings which are noted by his assistant at the table. The observations helped fill in the map of India which began with the triangulations of the Great Trigonometrical Survey.

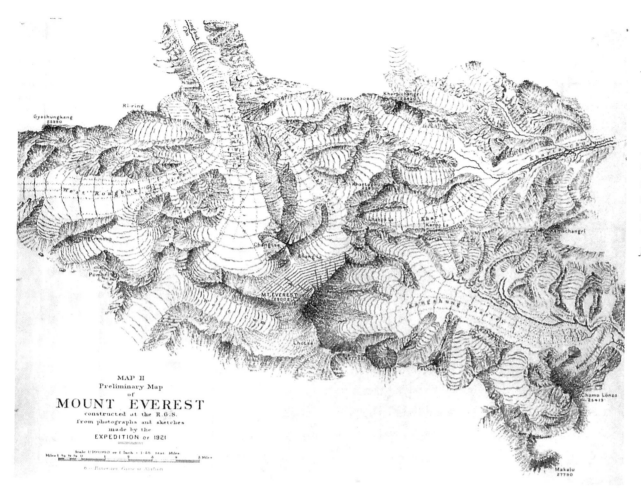

MAP II
Preliminary Map
of
MOUNT EVEREST
constructed at the R.G.S.
from photographs and sketches
made by the
EXPEDITION of 1921

fallen victim to India's unforgiving climate, being invalided home in 1825. He had returned to India in 1830, extending the Great Arc northwards and building new observatories. His first request to survey inside Nepal in 1840 was turned down, and he returned to Britain three years later.

Waugh was well aware that in nominating the name Everest for what he termed 'this noble peak', he was selecting what was bound to become 'a household word'. Waugh judged that Everest deserved such a privilege, 'in testimony of my affectionate respect for a revered chief, and to perpetuate the memory of that illustrious master of accurate geographical research'.

Waugh's proposal caused immediate controversy, with the renowned Schlagintweit brothers, three adventurers and explorers from Germany, among the objectors. Even Everest himself demurred. He had been among the most insistent that the India Survey should use local names, and told the Royal Geographical Society in 1857 that his name could not be pronounced by 'the native of India', nor could it be written in Hindi. But Waugh was not to be deterred. He set up a committee which duly disposed of the Schlagintweit's objections and backed Waugh's choice. Finally, in 1865 – just one year before

Everest himself died – the Royal Geographical Society officially adopted Mount Everest as the name of the world's highest mountain.

While Waugh was keen to commemorate the name of Everest against other deserving claims – and Chomolungma is increasingly used today – his own reputation deserves to be perpetuated. His calculation of Everest's height, 29,002 feet, based on observations made in the face of such intractable problems, remained the agreed figure for almost 100 years. In the 1950s Indian surveyors established a new chain of triangles into Nepal, going nearer to the mountain than the Victorians and establishing higher observation points. Their new figure of 29,028 feet/8,848 metres was less than 0.1 per cent higher than Waugh's.

Even with new survey methods the old figures have held. The most recent calculations were made by the eminent US cartographer, Bradford Washburn. On 5 May 1999, US climbers and Sherpas placed Global Positioning System equipment on the summit which produced a new figure of 29,035 feet/8,850 metres. Washburn announced the new height in Washington in November 1999. 'We all have immense admiration and respect for the achievements of the 19th century pioneers,' Washburn said.

The cartographer's art was consummated in this superb 1:50,000 map compiled by Bradford Washburn of the Boston Museum of Science. A renowned geophysicist and photographer, Washburn based his map on his aerial survey and on satellite images. It was drafted by the Swiss Federal Office of Topography and published by the US National Geographic Society in 1988. In 1999, after overseeing the project to place GPS equipment on the summit of Everest in order to obtain a more precise measurement, Washburn produced a new edition of the map (partly reproduced, above) showing the revised height of 29,035 feet/8,850 metres.

THE SPOTLESS PINNACLE OF THE WORLD

In 1903 the British government dispatched a top secret mission to Tibet. Led by Colonel Francis Younghusband, its aim was to secure favour with Tibet's leader, the Dalai Lama, in a bid to prevent Russia from occupying a country from which it could threaten Britain's rule over India. Attempts at negotiations failed and Younghusband marched on Lhasa, beating back attacks by Tibetan forces en route. The British finally achieved their goal in a treaty signed in September 1904.

Among Younghusband's staff, and accorded the rank of Joint Commissioner, was the intriguing figure of J. Claude White. As Britain's political officer in Sikkim, White had considerable experience of the tangled politics of India's north-east frontier, and was fascinated with what he termed 'the mysterious, unknown land of Tibet'. In his account of the mission, Younghusband portrayed White as the quintessential exile; he and his wife were devoted to their garden in Sikkim, finding 'a never-ending interest with all the English flowers – narcissus, daffodils, pansies, iris – in the spring'.

Younghusband did not mention another of White's interests – photography. White took to Tibet a cumbersome plate camera with which he recorded a remarkable series of photographs. Some captured scenes of daily life which had so enthralled him; others clearly had a more practical purpose, showing roads, passes and river-crossings – landmarks of strategic interest to the British.

Whether from his personal interests or wider British aims, White also photographed Mount Everest, doing so from the fortress town of Kampa Dzong, 94 miles to the north-east. Precisely when is not clear: the photograph is now in the Curzon Collection in the India Office archives in London, dated 1904. But both White and Younghusband were first in Kampa Dzong in July 1903, Younghusband later describing how he could see from his tent 'the first streaks of dawn gilding the snowy summits of Mount Everest, poised high in heaven as the spotless pinnacle of the world'.

It was not the first photograph of Everest. The Workmans – Fanny and Bill, the American travellers and adventurers – had photographed it from Sikkim, as had the Italian Vittorio Sella,

'Poised high in heaven': in Claude White's photograph, taken from Kampa Dzong during the British mission to Tibet of 1903–4, Everest, with the East or Kangshung Face prominent, is the snow-covered peak at the centre of the range. The two highest peaks to the left are Chomolonzo and Makalu.

during a journey with the British explorer Douglas Freshfield in 1899. But it appeared as a distant lump in these pictures, and there was still confusion over its name. White's photograph was the first to capture its inspirational grandeur, rising clear above its neighbours as Younghusband described.

After the mission, White returned to the north-east frontier. The mountain state of Bhutan was added to his territory, bringing him continuing delight in 'scenery unparalleled anywhere in the world for magnificence and grandeur'. Although when he returned to Britain White wrote a book – *Twenty-one Years on the North-East Frontier* – about his service in Sikkim and Bhutan, he included not a word about the mission to Tibet, clearly still regarded by the British as too sensitive a matter. He died in 1918.

'THE FINEST CENOTAPH IN THE WORLD'

1921-1939

THE DREAM OF EVEREST

The members of the 1921 reconnaissance expedition were the first to pursue the dream of Everest, so graphically described by George Mallory in a letter to his wife Ruth. Front row, left to right: Mallory, Wheeler, Bullock, Morshead; back row: Wollaston, Howard-Bury, Heron, Raeburn. (The ninth man, Alexander Kellas, died during the approach march.)

Pages 16–17: The photograph was taken on 26 April 1924 by Noel Odell at the Pang La, the high pass 35 miles north of Everest, to the left of the frame, with its snowy plume blowing from the summit. Scrutinising their goal are Sandy Irvine, right, and George Mallory, centre in white hat. The 'cenotaph' remark was made by Howard Somervell after Mallory and Irvine's deaths.

The first person to publicly raise the question of climbing Everest was the surgeon and mountaineer Clinton Dent. In his book *Above the Snowline*, published in 1885, Dent drew comparisons with polar expeditions to assert that since matters of supplies, expense and risk had not hindered Arctic explorers, there was no reason why they should prove insuperable to Himalayan mountaineers. Dent, who had studied the effects of altitude on balloonists and believed that the problem could be solved through acclimatization, concluded: 'I do not for a moment say that it would be wise to ascend Mount Everest, but I believe most firmly that it is humanly possible to do so; and, further, I feel sure that even in our time, perhaps, the truth of

these views will receive material corroboration.'

The first full-scale British expedition to the Himalayas came when Martin Conway climbed a 22,600 foot peak near K2 in the Karakoram Range in 1892. Duly encouraged, Dent wrote an article for *Nineteenth Century* magazine entitled: 'Can Mount Everest be climbed?' and several British explorers and climbers took up the challenge. Chief among them was a Gurkha officer, the Hon. Charles Granville Bruce, who had taken part in Conway's Karakoram venture and now suggested an Everest expedition to Francis Younghusband, who was to lead the celebrated mission to Tibet in 1903–4. Younghusband was enthusiastic. During a reconnaissance trip into western Tibet after the Lhasa treaty was signed, two of his officers came within 60 miles of Everest from the north, close enough for them to conclude that the North Ridge offered a clear way to the summit.

From that moment all attempts to organise expeditions to Everest became mired in the unforgiving politics of the region. The chief obstacle was the Secretary of State for India, one John Morley, who blocked all bids out of 'consideration of high Imperial policy', and probably personal animosity towards the mountaineers besides. The nearest any westerner came to Everest in the next ten years was an illicit foray into Tibet by the British adventurer and photographer Captain John Noel in 1913 with his skin and hair darkened as a disguise. He too came within 60 miles of Everest from the east and obtained one magical glimpse of its top 1,000 feet, a 'glittering spire of rock fluted with snow'. To Noel's bitter disappointment – he later blamed the high wind 'which prevented proper exposures' – he was unable to obtain a photograph.

Noel was among a group who started to plan an attempt on Everest in 1915, backed by the Alpine Club and Royal Geographical Society. After a hiatus caused by the First World War, their efforts resumed in 1918. Noel described his Tibetan journey to the RGS in 1919, although at an RGS meeting the following year, the former Gurkha Lieutenant, Charles Bruce – now Brigadier General Bruce – warned how little about the mountain was known. 'We have a distant view of its northern ridge, far the most promising part of the mountain that has yet been seen,' Bruce declared. 'It however causes one to think; there are evidently portions of it which are steep, and we have to think out the camps. Very much will depend on what the ridge usually is. Will it be ice, or firm snow, or soft snow? This last is terrible at great heights.'

In January 1921, taking due heed of Bruce's warnings, the RGS and the Alpine Club formed a Mount Everest Committee to launch an expedition with nine members and costing £4,000. Once again the politicians objected – this time for fear of disturbing Japan – but the Everest Committee stuck to its guns and by April 1921 the expedition was on its way to Darjeeling. Its aim was, first and foremost, to find a route up Everest. If possible, it was to climb the mountain as well, although if it failed, that task would be taken up by a full-scale expedition the following year.

The expedition leader was an army officer, Lieutenant Colonel Charles Howard-Bury, a traveller of independent means who owned an estate in Ireland and a string of race-horses, and who had made several exploratory trips into the Himalayas some 20 years before. The most charismatic figure was George Mallory, another Great War veteran and former school-master with socialist leanings and impressive literary talents.

The expedition faced difficulties from the moment it left Darjeeling in May. Their supplies and equipment were carried on Army mules, but these proved to have such poor stamina that they had to be replaced with hill mules and yaks. The climate was exhausting, with heat in the morning, a dust-laden wind by midday, and bitter cold at night. The expedition's food was rudimentary and gastro-enteritis was rife.

Under the strain, relationships between the more strong-willed members began to fracture, with Howard-Bury and Mallory forming a particular dislike of each other. Mallory described his leader as 'too much the landlord with not only Tory prejudices, but a very highly developed sense of hate and contempt for other sorts of people than his own'. The culminating misfortune came when the senior doctor, Alexander Kellas, a man in his fifties, died of a heart attack brought on by exhaustion and dysentery. Mallory meanwhile was plunged into further bouts of depression. 'I sometimes think of this expedition as a fraud,' he later wrote to a friend. 'The prospect of ascent in any direction is almost nil.'

By early June the expedition was little more than 50 miles from Everest. It had passed Kampa Dzong, from where Claude White had obtained his famous photograph, and was at the edge of the territory explored at the time of the Younghusband mission. Mallory noted: 'We are just about to walk off the map.' On 13 June, after entering a spectacular landscape of limestone cliffs and gorges, Mallory and a colleague, Guy Bullock, decided to climb a cliff above the Yaru Gorge in the hope of obtaining a view of Everest. It seemed a frail chance, as the Himalayas were shrouded in cloud. Later, in a letter to his wife Ruth, Mallory described what he had seen. Gone are the frustrations and doubts; in their place is the rapture of the moment when he and his companions became the first westerners to observe Everest in its full awesome glory.

'We were able to make out almost exactly where Everest should be; but the clouds were dark in that direction. We gazed at them intently through field glasses as though by some miracle we might pierce the veil. Presently the miracle happened. A whole group of mountains began to appear in gigantic fragments. Mountain shapes are often fantastic seen through a mist; these were like the wildest creation of a dream. A preposterous triangular lump rose out of the depths; its edge came leaping up at an angle of about 70 degrees and ended nowhere. To its left a black serrated crest was hanging in the sky incredibly. Gradually, very gradually, we saw the great mountainsides and glaciers and arêtes, now one fragment now another through the floating rifts, until far higher in the sky than imagination had dared to suggest the white summit of Everest appeared. And in this series of partial glimpses we had seen a whole; we were able to piece together the fragments, to interpret the dream . . . '

Within a few weeks, having completed their demanding walk from Darjeeling, Mallory and his colleagues were also to become the first mountaineers to attempt to fulfil that dream.

WE HAVE ESTABLISHED THE WAY

by George Mallory

After the long trek across the Tibetan plateau, the 1921 reconnaissance expedition arrived at Tingri, 40 miles from Everest, in late June. While the surveyors went about their task, George Mallory and Guy Bullock explored the glaciers, cols and peaks on the northern and eastern approaches. For Mallory, it was the opportunity and dream of a lifetime. After serving as an artillery officer during the First World War, he had become increasingly frustrated with his career as a schoolmaster, resigning to take part in the 1921 trip. Mallory was an imaginative writer who was keen to explore the emotional core of his experiences as well as to record the details of the reconnaissance. He did so in the stream of letters he dispatched to his family and friends, above all to his wife Ruth, whom he had married on the eve of the war. In this composite account of the search for a route to the summit, most of the extracts are taken from his letters to her.

28 June

First camp under Everest: This is a busier life than might be imagined even on an off day. It is after 9 pm and I have only just finished my lengthy but necessary despatch to Howard-Bury, and I shall have to be up at 5 am . . . I'll tell you about Everest in my next letter. Suffice it to say that it has the most steep ridges and appalling precipices that I have ever seen, and that all the talk of an easy snow slope is a myth.

We are completely cut off from civilization here. There is a monastery quite close to us; it's rather convenient as supplies come up the valley for the monks and we can arrange for fuel to come for us with theirs, so we shall probably keep the base camp here for some weeks. It's a fairly sheltered spot and just near a beautiful little spring, but the wrong side of the valley for the morning sun. Everest is just a little east of south from us.

Yesterday we made a first mountaineering expedition, started at 3.25 am with five coolies; one and a half hours to the terminal moraine of the glacier; 5.45, crossed a torrent with difficulty; then across a flat basin to the end of the glacier, which is covered with stones and made of enormous hummocks; bore across to the true left bank of the glacier and worked up a dry stream bed. Breakfast at 7 am near a great stone, just as the sun hit us. An hour's fast walking brought us to a corner where a glacier comes in from the west. We worked round this corner and up on to a shelf on the mountainside.

I found it pretty hot on the glacier; there is no doubt the sun tends to take the heart out of one, but not unbearably so. I must confess to a degree of tiredness after the glacier work which I have never quite reached in the Alps, but in all I was very pleased with myself from a physical point of view. My darling, this is a thrilling business altogether. I can't tell you how it possesses me, and what a prospect it is. And the beauty of it all!

Now Good Night and God bless you. Why aren't you lying where Guy Bullock is so that I could kiss you Good Night! Come close to me at least in spirit dearest – as you shall be all night.

6 July, climbing Ri-Ring

An early start at 4.15 am, straight up the stony slopes above our camp. After about an hour's going, I took some photos of Everest and some of his neighbours, all looking magnificent in the early sun. It was about 2,500 feet to the crest of our ridge: Bullock and coolies rather tired at this point;

40 minutes' halt and some food. Roped up for snow towards 8 am. A long upward traverse to a snow col, where we halted, 9.30 to 10.10.

From this point we had to follow a long snow ridge and then rock and snow. Two coolies dropped out here, and the other three after an hour and a half more. Bullock and I plugged on, climbing now and then little steep bits of slaty rock, treading carefully along snow crests, occasionally cutting a few steps in ice to reach the arête again after a short traverse. Our interest was partly in what we saw, partly in the sheer struggle of getting on. We moved very slowly, keeping up muscular energy and overcoming lassitude by breathing fast and deep. It was a colossal labour. We reached the top at 2.45. The aneroid, which reads about 400 feet low, registered 23,500. After a week at our camp I consider this a good performance – a rise of 5,500 feet in the day. I have no doubt when we get better acclimatised and start from a higher camp we shall be able to go a great deal higher. It is a remarkable fact about mountaineering here, so far as our experience goes, that the descent is always very tiring. It is only possible to keep oneself going by remembering to puff like a steam-engine.

19 July, to the col between Lingtren and Pumori

An exciting walk. I so much feared the cloud would spoil all. It was just light enough to get on without lanterns after the moon went down. At dawn almost everything was covered, but not by heavy clouds. Like guilty creatures of darkness surprised by the light, they went scattering away as we came up, and the whole scene opened out. The North Ridge of Everest was clear and bright even before sunrise. We reached the col at 5 am, a fantastically beautiful scene; and we looked across into the West Cwm at last, terribly cold and forbidding under the shadow of Everest. It was nearly an hour after sunrise before the sun hit the West Peak.

But another disappointment: it is a big drop, about 1,500 feet down to the glacier, and a hopeless precipice. I was hoping to get away to the left and traverse into the cwm – that, too, was quite hopeless. However, we have seen this western glacier and are not sorry we have not to go up it. It is terribly steep and broken. In any case, work on this side could only be carried out from a base in Nepal, so we have done with the western side. It was not a very likely chance that the gap between Everest and the South Peak could be reached from the west. From what we have seen now, I do not much fancy it would be possible, even could one get up the glacier.

28 July, to Kharta

I have been half the time in ecstasy. My first thought on coming down was that the world was green again. A month had made all the difference to the appearance of the hillsides. As we have come down lower, and nearer to the Arun valley, the appearance of greenness has steadily increased. We have crossed two passes on the way, and we have slept near two clear bubbling streams; and all that we have seen of snow mountains has been of interest, but none of that counts with me. To see things grow again as though they liked growing, enjoying rain and sun – that has been the real joy.

I collected in a beautiful ramble a lovely bunch of wild flowers. The commonest were a pink geranium and a yellow potentilla and a little flower that looked for all the world like a violet but turned out from its leaf to be something quite different; and there was grass of Parnassus, which I love, and in places a carpet of a little button flower, a brilliant pink, which I think must belong to the garlic tribe. But most of all I was delighted to find kingcups, a delicate variety rather smaller than ours at home, but somehow especially reminding me of you – you wrote of wading deeply through them in the first letter I had from you in Rome.

7 August, to the summit of Kartse

We walked for about three-quarters of an hour by candlelight up a moraine. Even before the first

George wrote assiduously to his wife Ruth, an architect's daughter, during his three Everest expeditions. They met in Godalming, Surrey, where George was teaching at Charterhouse school, in 1913, and fell in love on a trip to Venice with Ruth's family at Easter, 1914. They married on 29 July, on the eve of the First World War, when George was 28, Ruth 22. They had three children: their two daughters, Clare and Berry, were born during the First World War, when George spent 16 months on the Western Front; their son John was born in 1920.

glimmer of dawn, the white mountains were somehow touched to life by a faint blue light – a light that changed, as the day grew, to a rich yellow on Everest and then a bright grey blue before it blazed all golden when the sun hit it, while Makalu, even more beautiful, gave us the redder shades, the flush of pink and purple shadows. But I'm altogether beaten for words. The whole range of peaks from Makalu to Everest far exceeds any mountain scenery that ever I saw before.

Then we plugged on over the glacier, well covered with fresh snow, till we took off our snow shoes and for the first time the party (four coolies) found themselves on steep rocks – not a very formidable precipice, but enough to give us all some pleasure. The rocks took us to a pass which was our first objective. Below on the far side was a big glacier but we couldn't yet see whether it led to the North Col of our desire.

We had already taken time to observe the great Eastern Face of Mount Everest, and more particularly the lower edge of the hanging glacier; it required but little further gazing to know that almost everywhere the rocks below must be exposed to ice falling from this glacier; that if, elsewhere, it might be possible to climb up, the performance would be too arduous, would take too much time and would lead to no convenient platform; that, in short, other men, less wise, might attempt this way if they would, but emphatically, it was not for us.

We now wanted to see over a high ridge to the col itself. The next section was exceedingly steep. Bullock thought it would prove impossible, and it was stiff work; I had a longish bit of cutting in good snow. We then reached a flat plateau, put on snow shoes, and hurried across to the far edge. The party then lay down and slept in various postures while I took photographs and examined the North Peak through my glass. It was clearly visible down to the level of the col, but no more than that – so that, though the view was in many ways wonderful, the one thing we really wanted to see was still hidden. Eventually I asked for volunteers to come on to the top, and two coolies offered to come with me. It was only a matter of 500 feet, but the snow was very deep and lying at a terribly steep angle. One coolie refused to come on after a time; the other struggled on with me.

And then suddenly we were on the summit. As the wind blew rifts in the snow I had glimpses of what I wanted to see, glimpses only, but enough to suggest a high snow cwm under this North-east Face of Everest, finding its outlet somehow to the north. It is this outlet that we have now to find – the way in and the way up. We are going back to the valley junction, the glacier stream we left, with the idea that at the head of one of its branches we shall find the glacier we want.

17 August, to the Lhakpa La

When we started at 3 am, our hope was to reach our snow col while the snow was still hard, in four or five hours from the camp. It was a dim hope, because we knew fresh snow had fallen. After a few steps on the glacier, we found it necessary to put on our snow shoes – blessed snow shoes in that they save one sinking in more than a few inches, but a dismal weight to carry about on one's feet on a long march.

We reached the col at 12.30 pm. Apart from a couple of hours on snow-covered rocks above the icefall, this time was all spent in the heavy grind on soft snow. It is no use pretending that this was an agreeable way of passing time. Once we had regained the glacier from the rocks and eaten breakfast at about 8.15 am, we were enveloped in thin mist which obscured the view and made one world of snow and sky – a scorching mist, if you can imagine such a thing, more burning than bright sunshine and indescribably breathless. One seemed literally at times to be walking in a white furnace. Morshead, who knows the hottest heat of the plains in India, said that he had never felt any heat so intolerable as this. It was only possible to keep plodding on by a tremendous and continually conscious effort of the lungs; and up the steep final slopes I found it necessary to stop and breathe as hard as I could for a short space in order to gain sufficient energy to push up a few more steps.

The clouds of course hid the peaks when we got there, but in the most important sense the expedition was a success: we saw what we came to see. There, sure enough, was the suspected glacier running north from a cwm under the North-east Face of Everest. How we wished it had been possible to follow it down and find out the secret of its exit! There we were baffled. But the head of this glacier was only a little way below us, perhaps 700 feet at most; and across it lay our way, across easy snow up into the other side of the cwm, where the approach to the North Col, the long-wished-for goal, could not be difficult nor even long. And so, whatever may happen to the glacier whose exit we have yet to find, we have found our way to the great mountain. In such conditions as we found it, it cannot of course be used; but there it is, revealed for our use when the weather clears and the snow hardens.

1 September, Advance Base

I wonder how many damp sunless days we shall wait here before the weather clears – it is due to clear at the beginning of the month, but I don't much believe in these changes by calendar; every day it delays puts off my meeting you again dear; and also I think decreases our chance of climbing the mountain by shortening the days and increasing the cold by nights. Dear love, how I want to be with you again! What good times we'll have and how much we shall have to tell each other . . . And I want to see the children, dear souls, more than you might think. I don't think I knew before how much they are a part of life. You must tell them that Daddy thinks of them and loves them. What can I bring them home from the East? I must look round the bazaar in Calcutta . . . And now Good Night, sweet love, my near-faraway one.

15 September

Pour out your pity, dearest, pull it up from your deep wells – and be pleased to hear that I read myself agreeably to sleep, and slept, slept bountifully, deeply, sweetly from 9 pm to 6 am and woke to see the roof of my tent bulging ominously inwards and a white world outside. It was easy enough to make out that conditions for climbing were entirely hopeless. Every visible mountain face was hung with snow, incredibly more so than

The 1921 expedition leader, Charles Howard-Bury, took a series of photographs with a panoramic camera as the expedition probed for a route on to Everest. This picture, formed by joining two of Howard-Bury's shots and sadly damaged since, was taken at the crest of the Lhakpa La, the pass which the expedition first reached on 18 August. Before them, at last, lay the route to Everest. At far right, front, in the photograph is the East Rongbuk Glacier, which leads to the North Col, the dip in the skyline ridge, to the left of the black cliffs. Rising leftwards is Everest's North Ridge, culminating in its junction with the North-east Ridge. The summit lies unseen beyond the apex of the ridge, a mile or so further on.

when we last were there three weeks ago. The glacier presented an even surface of soft snow and everything confirmed what everybody had previously said – that it was useless to attempt carrying loads up to our col until we had a spell of real fair weather.

I ordered the whole party to pack up and go down. We were still pulling down tents and covering stores when the clouds came up with a rush and the sizzle of hard-driving snow was about us again. We sped down the hillside, facing wind and snow, down the long valley, dancing over the stones half-snow-covered and leaping the grey waters of many streams, and so at length to the humpy grass in the flat hollow where the big tents are pitched . . .

Just now we are all just drifting as the clouds drift, forgetting to number the days so as to avoid painful thoughts of the hurrying month. For my part I'm happy enough; the month is too late already for the great venture; we shall have to face great cold, I've no doubt; and the longer the delay, the colder it will be. But the fine weather will come at last. My chance, the chance of a lifetime, I suppose, will be sadly shrunk by then; and all my hopes and plans for seeing something of India on the way back will be blown to wherever the monsoon blows. I would willingly spend a few weeks longer here, if only for the sake of seeing Everest and Makalu and the excitement of new points of view. I would like to undertake a few other ascents, less ambitious but perhaps more delightful. And it will be a loss not to see again that strangely beautiful valley over the hills, and the green meadows dominated by the two greatest mountains.

Of the pull the other way I needn't tell you. If I picture the blue Mediterranean and the crisp foam hurrying by as the ship speeds on to Marseilles or Gibraltar where I shall expect to see you smiling in the sunshine on the quayside – my dear one, when such pictures fill my mind, as often enough they

do, I'm drawn clean out of this tent into a world not only more lovely, more beautifully lit, but signifying something.

17 September
Wonder of wonders! We had indication that the weather intended to change. We woke and found the sky clear and remaining clear, no dense white clouds drifting up the valley, but a chill wind driving high clouds from the north. I had a good walk yesterday with Morshead and Bullock and we were rewarded by a beautiful view of Everest. Today Morshead, Bury and I started at 2 am to ascend a snow peak on the boundary ridge between this valley and the next one to the south. We had a glorious view, unimaginably splendid – Kangchenjunga and all the higher mountains to the East were standing up over a sea of fleecy cloud: Makalu straight opposite across the valley was gigantic, and Everest at the head of the valley – very fine too. But the snow was in bad condition and it's not melting as it should; above 20,000 feet or so it was powdery under a thin crust and it was impossible to get along without snow shoes, and if it doesn't melt properly on the glacier we might as well pack up our traps at once. In addition to this cause of despair, Morshead was going badly and I must admit to feeling the height a good deal. I'm clearly far from being as fit as I ought to be. It's very distressing, my dear, just at this moment and altogether my hopes are at zero.

After ten weeks' exploration, culminating in a frustrating three weeks pinned down by bad weather, Mallory believed he had found the way at last. His goal was the North Col, on Everest's North-east Ridge, which he believed would open the way to the summit. On 22 September he and his colleagues crossed the Lhakpa La and descended to pitch their tents on the Rongbuk Glacier, ready to attempt to reach the col - and perhaps even to push on for the summit - the next morning.

---

23 September
After a late start and a very slow march we pitched our tents on the open snow up towards the col. It might have been supposed that in so deep a cwm and sheltered on three sides by steep mountain slopes, we should find a tranquil air and the soothing, though chilly calm of undisturbed frost. Night came clearly indeed, but with no gentle intentions. Fierce squalls of wind visited our tents and shook and worried them with the disagreeable threat of tearing them away from their moorings and then scurried off, leaving us in wonder at the change and asking what next to expect. It was a

The map (right) *shows the journeys described by Mallory in these extracts. He and Bullock also went to the head of the middle spur of the Rongbuk Glacier in their bid to find a route on to the North Col, and along the Kangshung Glacier, where they concluded that the East or Kangshung Face was 'emphatically not for us'. The final key was reaching the Lhakpa La, where they saw that the North Col could be reached via the head of the East Rongbuk glacier.*

cold wind at an altitude of 22,000 feet, and however little one may have suffered, the atmosphere discouraged sleep. Again I believe I was more fortunate than my companions, but Bullock and Wheeler fared badly. It was an hour or so after sunrise when we left the camp and half an hour later we were breaking the crust on the first slopes under the wall. We had taken three coolies who were sufficiently fit and competent, and proceeded to use them for the hardest work. Apart from one brief spell of cutting when we passed the corner of a bergschrund it was a matter of straightforward plugging, firstly slanting up to the right on partially frozen avalanche snow and then left in one long upward traverse to the summit. Only one passage shortly below the col caused either anxiety or trouble; here the snow was lying at a very steep angle and was deep enough to be disagreeable. About 500 steps of very hard work covered all the worst of the traverse and we were on the col shortly before 11.30 am.

By this time two coolies were distinctly tired, though by no means incapable of coming on; the third, who had been in front, was comparatively fresh. Wheeler thought he might be good for some further effort, but had lost all feeling in his feet. Bullock was tired, but by sheer will power would evidently come on – how far, one couldn't say. For my part I had had the wonderful good fortune of sleeping tolerably well at both high camps and was now finding my best form; I supposed I might be capable of another 2,000 feet, and there would be no time for more. But what lay ahead of us? My eyes had often strayed, as we came up, to the rounded edge above the col and the final rocks below the North-east arête. If ever we had doubted whether the arête were accessible, it was impossible to doubt any longer. For a long way up those easy rock and snow slopes was neither danger nor difficulty. But at present there was wind. Even where we stood under the lee of a little ice cliff it came in fierce gusts at frequent intervals, blowing up the powdery snow in a suffocating tourbillion.

On the col beyond it was blowing a gale. And higher was a more fearful sight. The powdery fresh snow on the great face of Everest was being swept along in unbroken spindrift and the very ridge where our route lay was marked out to receive its unmitigated fury. We could see the blown snow deflected upwards for a moment where the wind met the ridge, only to rush violently down in a frightful blizzard on the leeward side. To see, in fact, was enough; the wind had settled the question; it would have been folly to go on. Nevertheless, some little discussion took place as to what might be possible, and we struggled a few steps further to put the matter to the test. For a few moments we exposed ourselves to the col to feel the full strength of the blast, then struggled back to shelter. Nothing more was said about pushing our assault any further.

29 September

My dearest Ruth,

This is a mere line at the earliest moment, in the midst of packing and arrangements to tell you that all is well. It is a disappointment that the end should seem so much tamer than I hoped. But it wasn't tame in reality; it was no joke getting to the North Col. I doubt if any big mountain venture has ever been made with a smaller margin of strength. I carried the whole party on my shoulders to the end, and we were turned back by a wind in which no man could live an hour. As it is we have established the way to the summit for anyone who cares to try the highest adventure.

I had plenty of reserve personally and could have carried on another 2000 ft anyway with ease had the conditions been favourable. As it is we have established the way to the summit for anyone who cares to try the highest adventure; and I don't much regret having failed to beat a record, as we could have done easily enough had fortune favoured us. Now homewards, with all speed.

Oliver Wheeler, pictured with his plate camera and two of his local assistants, was both an expert surveyor and an accomplished mountaineer. From Canada, where he had climbed in the Rockies, he was one of the six-man party, led by Mallory and including three Sherpa porters, which reached the North Col on 24 September, thereby establishing that it offered a route to the summit.

THE 1922 PANORAMAS

Even 75 years after the first Everest expeditions, fresh research discoveries were being made. In 1999 the Everest historian Audrey Salkeld unearthed a remarkable series of panoramic photographs from the archives in the basement of the Alpine Club in London. They depict events and landscapes from the 1922 expedition, conveying the immensity of the undertaking on a new and breath-taking scale.

The Mount Everest Committee records show that the panorama camera was purchased for £50 early in 1922 and so replaced the model used by Charles Howard-Bury in 1921 (see pages 22-23). The new camera had a clockwork lens that could rotate through

180 degrees, painting its image through a slit onto a long strip of negative. The equipment was heavy and cumbersome, requiring a large wooden tripod like the one depicted on page 25, and would have been carried by Sherpa porters and/or packhorses.

It is not known who took the photographs, although two of the most likely candidates are John Noel, the official expedition photographer, who took part in both the 1922 and 1924 trips, and the Australian George Finch, an accomplished photographer in his own right. The photographs were astonishing in their scope, recording the expedition's passage from the jungle of eastern Tibet and across the great Tibetan plateau, with scenes of overnight camps below such fortress towns as Shegar Dzong. Once at Everest, the camera was hauled along the East Rongbuk Glacier and carried as high as the North Col, capturing the challenge facing the climbers as never before. Two of the newly found photographs are shown below.

In an image reminiscent of Napoleon's retreat from Moscow, the 1922 expedition makes its way across the windswept Tibetan plain north-east of Everest. In a letter home, George Mallory described a blizzard which struck as they neared Kampa Dzong, freezing his fingers so that he could hardly write.

The tiny tents of Camp II were pitched beside the East Rongbuk Glacier at 19,800ft/6,035m. Expedition member John Morris and a line of porters appear dwarfed as they descend a mound of moraine into the camp.

THE TORTURES OF TANTALUS

by George Finch

The first full-scale expedition to Everest was like a moonshot of its day. The climbers who arrived in the Rongbuk Valley in April 1922 after their six-week trek across the Tibetan plateau were venturing into the unknown, uncertain of the effects of altitude, and with clothing and equipment rudimentary by today's standards. The first summit attempt met near-disaster when three climbers lost their footing on an ice slope and George Mallory held them on his rope. The second came on 25 May, when a party of three set off from the North Col. They consisted of Geoffrey Bruce, a Gurkha officer and nephew of the expedition leader Charles Bruce, who had never climbed before; his regimental aide, Tejbir Bura; and the Australian-born George Finch, who ranked with Mallory as one of the most accomplished mountaineers on the expedition.

O n 24 May, Captain Noel, Tejbir, Geoffrey Bruce, and I, all using oxygen, went up to the North Col. Bent on a determined attack, we camped there for the night. Morning broke fine and clear though somewhat windy, and at eight o'clock we sent off up the long snow-slopes leading towards the North-east Shoulder of Mount Everest, 12 porters carrying oxygen cylinders, provisions for one day, and camping gear. An hour and a half later, Bruce, Tejbir, and I followed, and, in spite of the fact that each bore a load of over 30lb, which was much more than the average weight carried by the porters, we overtook them at a height of about 24,000 feet. They greeted our arrival with their usual cheery, broad grins. Leaving them to follow, we went on, hoping to pitch our camp somewhere above 26,000 feet. But shortly after one o'clock the wind freshened up rather offensively, and it began to snow. Our altitude was 25,500 feet, some 500 feet below where we had hoped to camp, but we looked round immediately for a suitable camping site, as the porters had to return to the North Col that day, and persistence in proceeding further would have run them unjustifiably into danger. This I would under no circumstances do, for I felt responsible for these cheerful, smiling, willing men, who looked up to their leader and placed in him the

complete trust of little children. As it was, the margin of safety secured by pitching camp where we did instead of at a higher elevation was none too wide; for before the last porter had departed downwards the weather had become very threatening. A cheerful spot in which to find a space to pitch a tent it was not; but though I climbed a couple of hundred feet or so further up the ridge, nothing more suitable was to be found. Our

George Finch, 34 in 1922, was something of a maverick who was never fully accepted by the British mountaineering establishment. Born in Australia, brought up in Switzerland, he was turned down for the 1921 reconnaissance and not invited in 1924. As well as writer and photographer, Finch was a pioneer of mountaineering equipment. He rejected the Alpine clothing recommended for the 1922 team and, as shown left, designed his own jacket from balloon cloth with a quilt lining filled with eiderdown.

Breakfast at Base Camp; the 1922 expedition ate impressively, their supplies ranging from basic items such as cans of Heinz spaghetti to tinned quails truffled in pâté de foie, reserved as a morale-booster for exhausted climbers. Seated left to right: expedition doctor Arthur Wakefield; John Morris; the expedition leader, General Bruce; Karma Paul, the local interpreter; Geoffrey Bruce, nephew of the expedition leader; an unnamed Gurkha; and Edward Norton, one of Mallory's three partners on his summit attempt. The picture was taken by the official expedition photographer, John Noel.

porters arrived at 2 pm, and at once all began to level off the little platform where the tent was soon pitched, on the very edge of the tremendous precipice falling away to the East Rongbuk and main Rongbuk Glaciers, over 4,000 feet below. Within 20 minutes the porters were scurrying back down the broken, rocky ridge towards the snow-slopes leading to the North Col, singing, as they went, snatches of their native hillside ditties. What splendid men! Having seen the last man safely off, I looked to the security of the guy-ropes holding down the tent, and then joined Bruce and Tejbir inside. It was snowing hard. Tiny, minute spicules driven by the wind penetrated everywhere. It was bitterly cold, so we crawled into our sleeping-bags, and, gathering round us all available clothing, huddled up together as snugly as was possible.

With the help of solidified spirit we melted snow and cooked a warm meal, which imparted some small measure of comfort to our chilled bodies. A really hot drink was not procurable, for the simple reason that at such an altitude water boils at so low a temperature that one can immerse the hand in it without fear of being scalded. Over a *post-prandium* cigarette, Bruce and I discussed our prospects of success. Knowing that no man can put forward his best effort unless his confidence is an established fact, the trend of my contribution to the conversation was chiefly, 'Of course, we shall get to the top.' After sunset, the storm rose to a gale. Terrific gusts tore at our tent with such ferocity that the ground-sheet with its human burden was frequent-

ly lifted up off the ground. On these occasions our combined efforts were needed to keep the tent down and prevent its being blown away. Although we had blocked up the few very small openings in the tent to the best of our powers, long before midnight we were all thickly covered in a fine frozen spindrift that somehow or other was blown in upon us, insinuating its way into sleeping-bags and clothing. Sleep was out of the question. We dared not relax our vigilance, for ever and again all our strength was needed to hold the tent down and to keep the flaps of the door, stripped of their fastenings by a gust that had caught us unawares, from being torn open. We fought for our lives, realising that once the wind got our little shelter into its ruthless grip, it must inevitably be hurled, with us inside it, down on to the East Rongbuk Glacier, thousands of feet below.

And what of my companions in the tent? To me, who had certainly passed his novitiate in the hardships of mountaineering, the situation was more than alarming. About Tejbir I had no concern; he placed complete confidence in his sahibs, and the ready grin never left his face. But it was Bruce's first experience of mountaineering, and how the ordeal would affect him I did not know. I might have spared myself all anxiety. Throughout the whole adventure he bore himself in a manner that would have done credit to the finest of veteran mountaineers, and returned my confidence with a cheerfulness that rang too true to be counterfeit. By one o'clock on the morning of the 26th the gale reached its maximum. The

When the 1922 expedition had to ford a river during its approach march, Arthur Wakefield (centre in picture) removed his walking boots, while Howard Somervell (left) took off his shorts as well. George Mallory (right), a long-time enthusiast for skinny dipping, clearly felt no inhibitions.

wild flapping of the canvas made a noise like that of machine-gun fire. So deafening was it that we could scarcely hear each other speak. During lulls we took it in turns to go outside to tighten up the tent more firmly with our Alpine rope. It was impossible to work in the open for more than three or four minutes at a stretch, so profound was the exhaustion induced by this brief exposure to the fierce cold wind. But with the Alpine rope taking some of the strain, we enjoyed a sense of security which, though probably only illusory, allowed us all a few sorely needed moments of rest.

Dawn broke bleak and chill; the snow had ceased to fall, but the wind continued with unabated violence. Once more we had to take it in turns to venture out and tighten the guy-ropes, and to try to build on the windward side of the tent a small wall of stones as an additional protection. The extreme exhaustion and chill produced as a result of each of these little excursions were sufficient to indicate that, until the gale had spent itself, there could be no hope of either advance or retreat. As the weary morning hours dragged on, we believed we could detect a slackening off in the storm. And I was thankful, for I was beginning to wonder how much longer human beings could stand the strain. We prepared another meal. The dancing flames of the spirit stove caused me anxiety bordering on anguish lest the tent, a frail shelter between life and death, should catch fire. At noon the storm

once more regained its strength and rose to unsurpassed fury. A great hole was cut by a stone in one side of the tent, and our situation thus unexpectedly became more desperate than ever.

But we carried on, making the best of our predicament until, at one o'clock, the wind dropped suddenly from a blustering gale to nothing more than a stiff breeze. Now was the opportunity for retreat to the safety of the North Col camp. But I wanted to hang on and try our climb on the following day. Very cautiously and tentatively I broached my wish to Bruce, fearful lest the trying experience of the last 24 hours had undermined his keenness for further adventure. Once again might I have spared myself all anxiety. He jumped at the idea, and when our new plans were communicated to Tejbir, the only effect upon him was to broaden his already expansive grin.

It was a merry little party that gathered round to a scanty evening meal cooked with the last of our fuel. The meal was meagre for the simple reason that we had catered for only one day's short rations, and we were now very much on starvation diet. We had hardly settled down for another night when, about 6 pm, voices were heard outside. Our unexpected visitors were porters who, anxious as to our safety, had left the North Col that afternoon when the storm subsided. They brought thermos flasks of hot beef tea and tea provided by the thoughtful Noel. Having accepted these most

This picture, taken by Finch, shows his climbing partner Geoffrey Bruce trying out the expedition's rudimentary oxygen equipment. Although some expedition members were sceptical about using supplementary oxygen, regarding it as cumbersome, unreliable, or improper, Finch was in no doubt. After he and Bruce had used it during a frightening night at 25,500ft/7,772m, when they struggled to breathe, Finch declared that it had saved their lives. Bruce's clothing was typical of its day, from his pith helmet to his puttees, a primitive form of gaiter.

gratefully, we sent the porters back without loss of time.

That night began critically. We were exhausted by our previous experiences and through lack of sufficient food. Tejbir's grin had lost some of its expanse. On the face of Geoffrey Bruce, courageously cheerful as ever, was a strained, drawn expression that I did not like. Provoked, perhaps, by my labours outside the tent, a dead, numbing cold was creeping up my limbs – a thing I had only once before felt and to the seriousness of which I was fully alive. Something had to be done. Like an inspiration came the thought of trying the effect of oxygen. We hauled an apparatus and cylinders into the tent, and, giving it the air of a joke, we took doses all round. Tejbir took his medicine reluctantly, but with relief I saw his face brighten up. The effect on Bruce was visible in his rapid change of expression. A few minutes after the first deep breath, I felt the tingling sensation of life and warmth returning to my limbs. We connected up the apparatus in such a way that we could breathe a small quantity of oxygen throughout the night. The result was marvellous. We slept well and warmly. There is little doubt that it was the use of oxygen which saved our lives during this second night in our high camp.

Before daybreak we were up. Putting on our boots was a struggle. Mine I had taken to bed with me, and a quarter of an hour's striving and tugging sufficed to get them on. But Bruce's and Tejbir's were frozen solid, and it took them more than an hour to mould them into shape by holding them over lighted candles. Shortly after six we assembled outside. Some little delay was incurred

in arranging the rope and our loads, but at length at 6.30 am, soon after the first rays of the sun struck the tent, we shouldered our bundles and set off. What with cameras, thermos bottles, and oxygen apparatus, Bruce and I each carried well over 40lb; Tejbir with two extra cylinders of oxygen shouldered a burden of about 50lb.

Our scheme of attack was to take Tejbir with us as far as the North-east Shoulder, there to relieve him of his load and send him back. The weather was clear. The only clouds seemed so far off as to presage no evil, and the breeze, though intensely cold, was bearable. But it soon freshened up, and before we had gone more than a few hundred feet the cold began to have its effect on Tejbir's sturdy constitution, and he showed signs of wavering. Bruce's eloquent flow of Gurumuki, however, managed to boost him up to an altitude of 26,000 feet. There he collapsed entirely, sinking face downwards on to the rocks and crushing beneath him the delicate instruments of his oxygen apparatus. I stormed at him for thus maltreating it, while Bruce exhorted him for the honour of his regiment to struggle on; but it was all in vain. Tejbir had done his best; and he has every right to be proud of the fact that he has climbed to a far greater height than any other native. We pulled him off his apparatus and, relieving him of some cylinders, cheered him up sufficiently to start him with enough oxygen on his way back to the high camp, there to await our return.

After seeing him safely off and making good progress, we loaded up Tejbir's cylinders, and, in view of the easy nature of the climbing, mutually agreed to dispense with the rope, and thus enable ourselves to proceed more rapidly. Climbing not very steep and quite easy rocks, and passing two almost level places affording ample room for some future high camp, we gained an altitude of 26,500 feet. By this time, however, the wind, which had been steadily rising, had acquired such force that I considered it necessary to leave the ridge and continue our ascent by traversing out across the great Northern Face of Mount Everest, hoping by so doing to find more shelter from the icy blasts. It was not easy to come to this decision, because I saw that between us and the shoulder the climbing was all plain sailing and presented no outstanding difficulty. Leaving the ridge, we began to work out into the face. For the first few yards the going was sufficiently straightforward, but presently the general angle became much steeper, and our trials were accentuated by the fact that the stratification of the rocks was such that they shelved outward and downward, making the securing of adequate footholds difficult. As I led out over these steeply

Geoffrey Bruce (ahead) and George Finch on the North Col. Carrying 30lb loads, they set off from the col on 25 May to make their summit attempt. Accompanied by Bruce's regimental aide, Tejbir Bura, and supported by 12 Sherpas who carried supplies to Camp V, they were, Finch wrote, 'bent on a determined attack'.

Frost-bitten and exhausted, Bruce (left in foreground) is assisted by Sherpas as he descends to Camp II on 28 May, following his failed summit bid with Finch (right, with scarf) and Tejbir Bura. 'We were deplorably tired,' Finch wrote. 'Knees did not always bend and unbend as required. At times they gave way altogether.' They had reached a record height of 27,300ft/8,321m before turning back. 'Ours were truly the tortures of Tantalus,' wrote Finch. 'Weak from hunger and exhausted by that nightmare struggle for life, we were in no fit condition to proceed.'

sloping, evilly smooth slabs, I carefully watched Bruce to see how he would tackle the formidable task with which he was confronted on this his first mountaineering expedition. He did his work splendidly and followed steadily and confidently, as if he were quite an old hand at the game. Sometimes the slabs gave place to snow – treacherous, powdery stuff, with a thin, hard, deceptive crust that gave the appearance of compactness. Little reliance could be placed upon it, and it had to be treated with great care. And sometimes we found ourselves crossing steep slopes of scree that yielded and shifted downwards with every tread. Since leaving the ridge we had not made much height although we seemed to be getting so near our goal. Now and then we consulted the aneroid barometer, and its readings encouraged us on. 27,000 feet; then we gave up traversing and began to climb diagonally upwards towards a point on the lofty North-east Ridge, midway between the shoulder and the summit.

Soon afterwards an accident put Bruce's oxygen apparatus out of action. He was some 20 feet below me, but struggled gallantly upwards as I went to meet him, and, after connecting him on to my apparatus and so renewing his supply of oxygen, we soon traced the trouble and effected a satisfactory repair. The barometer here recorded a height of 27,300 feet. The highest mountain visible was Cho Oyu, which is just short of 27,000 feet. We were well above it and could look across it into the dense clouds beyond. The great West Peak of Everest, one of the most beautiful sights to be seen from down in the Rongbuk Valley, was hidden, but we knew that our standpoint was nearly 2,000 feet above it. Everest itself was the only mountaintop which we could see without turning our gaze downwards.

The point we reached is unmistakable even from afar. We were standing on a little rocky ledge, just inside an inverted V of snow, immediately below the great belt of reddish-yellow rock which cleaves its way almost horizontally through the otherwise greenish-black slabs of the mountain. Though 1,700 feet below, we were well within half a mile of the summit, so close, indeed, that we could distinguish individual stones on a patch of scree lying just underneath the highest point. Ours were truly the tortures of Tantalus; for, weak from hunger and exhausted by that nightmare struggle for life in our high camp, we were in no fit condition to proceed. Indeed, I knew that if we were to persist in climbing on, even if only for another 500 feet, we should not both get back alive.

The decision to retreat once taken, no time was lost, and, fearing lest another accidental interruption in the oxygen supply might lead to a slip on the part of either of us, we roped together. It was midday. At first we returned in our tracks, but later found better going by aiming to strike the ridge between the North-east Shoulder and the North Col at a point above where we had left it in the morning. Shortly after 2 pm we struck the ridge and there reduced our burdens to a minimum by dumping four oxygen cylinders.

The clear weather was gone. We plunged down the easy, broken rocks through thick mists driven past us from the west by a violent wind. For one small mercy we were thankful – no snow fell. We reached our high camp in barely half an hour, and such are the vagaries of Everest's moods that in this short time the wind had practically dropped. Tejbir lay snugly wrapped up in all three sleeping-bags, sleeping the sleep of exhaustion. Hearing the voices of the porters on their way up to bring down our kit, we woke him up, telling him to await their arrival and to go down with them. Bruce and I then proceeded on our way, met the ascending porters and passed on, greatly cheered by their bright welcomes and encouraging smiles.

But the long descent, coming as it did on the top of a hard day's work, soon began to find out our weakness. We were deplorably tired, and could no longer move ahead with our accustomed vigour. Knees did not always bend and unbend as required. At times they gave way altogether and forced us, staggering, to sit down. But eventually we reached the broken snows of the North Col, and arrived in camp there at 4 pm. A craving for food, to the lack of which our weakness was mainly due, was all that animated us. Hot tea and a tin of spaghetti were soon forthcoming, and even this little nourishment refreshed us and renewed our strength to such an extent that three-quarters of an hour later we were ready to set off for Camp III. An invaluable addition to our little party was Captain Noel, the indefatigable photographer of the expedition, who had already spent four days and three nights on the North Col. He formed our rearguard and nursed us safely down the steep snow and ice slopes on to the almost level basin of the glacier below. Before 5.30 pm, only 40 minutes after leaving the col, we reached Camp III. Since midday, from our highest point we had descended over 6,000 feet; but we were quite finished.

That evening we dined well. Four whole quails truffled in pâté de foie gras, followed by nine sausages, left me asking for more. The last I remember of that long day was going to sleep, warm in the depths of our wonderful sleeping-bag, with the remains of a tin of toffee tucked away in the crook of my elbow.

THE LAMA'S TALE

In the third month of the Tibetan year once again a group of 13 Britishers with 100 coolies and 300 pack-charges pitched their camp in front of the mantra house and stayed one day. The representative from the authorities at Ding-Ri [Karma Paul, interpreter to all British expeditions of the 1920s and 1930s] also came as guide and assistant. He said to me: 'The best thing would be to meet the leaders and all their servants or at least the principal sahib. There is no means of avoiding it.'

I said, 'If one meets one heretic there is no point in keeping all the others back'; but I was feeling very sick.

The next day I greeted the General, three other sahibs and their interpreter. The leader gave me a photo of the Dalai Lama and a length of gold brocade with a ceremonial scarf. I had tea and rice-with-curds served.

'Where are you going?' I asked.

'As this snow peak is the biggest in the world, if we arrive on the summit we will get from the British government a recompense and high rank,' he said.

I replied, 'As our country is bitterly cold and frosty, it is difficult for others than those who are devoted to religion not to come to harm. As the local spirits are furies, you must act with great firmness.'

'Thank you. As we shall also come under the Lama's protection, we trust you will allow us to collect a little brushwood for firewood. Moreover we won't harm the birds and the wild animals in this area. I swear we have no weapons apart from this little knife.'

After saying this, they took their leave. According to the custom of the country, I had conveyed to them a carcass of meat, a brick of tea, and a platterful of roasted wheat flour. After they had left, they established a big camp near the mountain. They stayed about a month and a half. Making use of instruments such as iron pegs, wire

ropes and crampons they strove to ascend the mountain.

They climbed with the most extreme difficulty. Two sahibs got frost-bitten feet. Meanwhile the others climbed on ahead. When they had reached about a third of the way up the mountain, one day, with a roar, an avalanche occurred and some men were projected over the cliff face. Seven or eight coolies died. The leader of the expedition sent 15 silver coins with a request to say prayers for the dead. I was filled with compassion for their lot who underwent such suffering on unnecessary work. I organised very important dedications for the dead.

At the time of the yearly prayer-dance five sahibs and many coolies arrived back. They took photos of the dance, etc. I asked them to stay the night. The following day I met eight sahibs and all the servants. The leader started by saying, 'Previously I sent money with a request for a special prayer for the seven coolies who died. Just now I sent rice and a cook-box for the Shel-rdzong representative. Did they arrive?'

I asked, 'Are you not weary?'

'Me? I'm all right. A few men died,' he replied, and was a little ashamed.

I gave him a wooden tubful of breads and a new gold and copper image of Tara; I resolved to pray for his

The chief Lama of Rongbuk Monastery, who received the 1922 expedition on 30 April. Although he viewed the climbers as 'heretics', he supplied them with meat and tea. Expedition leader Charles Bruce found the Lama 'full of dignity', with an 'intelligent and wise face' and an 'attractive smile'.

conversion to Buddhism. Then, as he left, as is the custom in Tibet, he took off his hat and said: 'Be seated, be seated,' and so saying went away.

After that, learning that there remained much roasted barley flour, rice and oil, etc. in the places where the Britishers had stayed near the mountain, about 20 youngsters passed by secretly at midnight and arrived at the base of the mountain. From a cleft in the scree, seven bears came out. At first one man caught sight of them; after that they all saw them and in a great panic they all ran away. When they came back they asked: 'Is not this inauspicious sight terrible and will not our lives be harmed?'

I said, 'It is a sign that at the moment the guardian spirits of the valleys are not pleased. But if we do our prayer rituals in order, no harm will come.'

From the Chronicles of the Lama of Rongbuk Monastery, 1922.

THE PHOTOGRAPHS OF NOEL ODELL

In the mountaineering world, the geologist Noel Odell was long known as the man who took the last photograph of Mallory and Irvine before they left on their doomed summit attempt in June 1924 (see page 47), and as the last person to see them alive. During the 1990s it emerged just how fine a photographer he was.

When Odell died in 1987 his grandson Peter was given his collection of photographs and the silver nitrate negatives from which the prints were made. Silver nitrate negatives are particularly fragile as they can spontaneously combust during the normal printing process. Odell joined forces with the American climber and photographer Ed Webster, and technician Steven Gilmore, to make a series of new prints at the Photo Craft darkroom in Boulder, Colorado. With the aid of a special 'cold' enlarger, around 80 of Odell's 160 negatives were

Noel Odell (above) *photographed George Mallory* (right) *as he undertook one of his beloved skinny dips, this time in Sikkim at an early stage of the 1924 expedition's approach march.*

As shown in Odell's photograph, the 1924 expedition camped beside the Yaru Chu river at Tinki Dzong, spending two days there before resuming the six-week trek to Everest.

printed, and the result was a revelation.
Here was a stunning record of life on the 1924 expedition, framed by Odell's sympathetic view of his colleagues and their efforts to climb the highest mountain. His sense of landscape was spectacular and his ability to empathise

with his subjects was manifest.
It was especially appropriate that the new prints should result from Anglo–US teamwork, since Odell played a significant role in the development of US mountaineering. A geology lecturer at Harvard in the late 1920s, he joined

a team of young US climbers, including Charlie Houston, to attempt Nanda Devi in 1936, Odell reaching the summit with Bill Tilman. On Odell's death, Houston hailed him as 'generous, mild and modest – a lovely companion'.

Expedition leader Edward Norton (left in photograph) dictates a dispatch for The Times *to Geoffrey Bruce who is seated at the typewriter at Camp I, sited at the junction of the Central and East Rongbuk Glaciers.*

Odell accompanied Sandy Irvine (seated right) and George Mallory on an initial foray up the East Rongbuk Glacier in May 1924, both men heavily protected against the sun. Two Sherpas are resting against the large ice pinnacle in the left of Odell's shot.

TWO FRAIL MORTALS

by T. Howard Somervell

The second summit bid of the 1924 expedition was made by Edward Norton, who had taken over as expedition leader when Charles Bruce fell ill with malaria, and Howard Somervell, a surgeon who had remained in India after 1922 to run a missionary hospital. On the first attempt, George Mallory and Geoffrey Bruce established Camp V at 25,200 feet/7,780 metres on the North Ridge. On 2 June, Somervell and Norton left the North Col with six porters, passing Mallory and Bruce on the way down. Climbing without supplementary oxygen, they reached Camp V that evening and prepared for their attempt. As well as writing about their climb, Somervell recorded it on a vest-pocket 'Autographic' Kodak camera, obtaining a remarkable sequence of pictures culminating in the highest photograph yet taken.

Howard Somervell, aged 34 in 1924, was the polymath of the expedition. As well as surgeon, photographer and mountaineer, he was a talented artist and musician with a love of literature. He and Mallory read Shakespeare to each other in their tent at Camp III.

Norton and I settled down to melt snow for tonight's supper and tomorrow's breakfast, looking out from time to time at our porters bucketing down the mountainside, and far beyond them at a sunset all over the world, as it seemed – from the rosy fingers of Kangchenjunga in the east, past the far-distant peaks of mid-Tibet, separated from us by several complete ranges of mountains, to Gaurisankar and its satellites in the west, black against the red sky. I remember a curious sensation while up at this camp, as if we were getting near the edge of a field with a wall all round it – a high, insuperable wall. The field was human capacity, the wall human limitations. The field, I remember, was a bright and uniform green, and we were walking towards the edge – very near the edge now, where the whitish-grey wall said: 'Thus far, and no farther.' This almost concrete sense of being near the limit of endurance was new to me, and though I have often felt the presence of a Companion on the mountainside who is not in our earthly party of climbers, I have only on this single occasion had this definite vision of limitation. With it I went to sleep, and slept remarkably well, though I woke up at 5 am with my extremely sore throat even worse than before, and with the unwelcome announcement by Norton that the cork had come out of the thermos flask and there was nothing for it but to melt some more snow and make more coffee.

So it was 6.40 am before we started, taking with us a few cardigans, a thermos flask of coffee and a vest-pocket Kodak: nothing else save ice-axes and a short rope.

The ground over which we started was easy but trying; scree, which slipped while we were trying to mount it, and rocks, which provided simple scrambling. It was intensely cold, but ahead of us we saw a patch of sunlight, and strained every nerve to reach this and get warm. There was one broad patch of snow across which Norton chipped steps, and once over this the slippery scree ended and we climbed for the rest of the day on rocks – easy rocks, though all the ledges sloped outwards and many of them were covered with small stones which made one feel rather insecure. The sun, however, was kind to us, and cheered us on our way. Even the wind was not so bad as it had been the day before. We had, in fact, the best possible weather conditions; if only we had not started on our climb already a couple of invalids, emaciated and enfeebled by the bad weather of the last few weeks.

About 700 or 800 feet above our camp the effects of height seemed to assert themselves quite suddenly. From going 300 feet or so of vertical height in an hour, we suddenly found ourselves cut down to little more than 100. From taking three or four breaths to a step we were reduced to having to take ten or more. Even then we had to stop at frequent intervals to get our breath. As Norton said in the account he wrote afterwards: 'Every five or ten minutes we had to sit down for a minute or two, and we must have looked a sorry couple.' The

imaginative reader must not picture a couple of stalwarts breasting the tape, but a couple of crocks slowly and breathlessly struggling up, with frequent rests and a lot of puffing and blowing and coughing. Most of the coughing, and probably most of the delay, came from me; Norton was, as ever, infinitely patient, and never so much as suggested that I was keeping him back. Finally, as we approached the level of 28,000 feet, the summit being only half a mile away or less, I felt that, as far as I was concerned, it was hopeless to continue. I told Norton that he had no chance of the summit with me. My throat was not only extremely painful, but was getting almost blocked up – why, I knew not. So, finding a suitable ledge on which to sit in the sun and pull myself together, I told Norton to go on. If the remainder of the mountain was as easy in general angle as what we had already done, there was no particular danger in climbing it alone; we two had not yet used the rope at all.

So, at 28,000 feet, I sat down and watched Norton. But he, too, was not far from the limit of his endurance, and after proceeding for some distance horizontally, but not a hundred feet in vertical height above me, he stopped in the big couloir, looked at the rocks around its tip (which

are rather steeper than we had thought) and turned back. Soon he was shouting to me to come on and bring a rope, as he was beginning to be snow-blind and could not see where to put his feet. So I went on and joined him, not forgetting to put a specimen of the rock from our highest point in my pocket. We roped up. Norton went down first and myself last, ready to hold him if at any time he slipped owing to his failing eyesight.

We sat down for a bit and worked out our chances of reaching the top – 900 feet above us, nine hours of climbing at our present rate, including the difficult bit that was just above Norton when he was at his nearest point to the summit, where two climbers, properly roped up, were essential for success and safety. Obviously, we could not get up to the top before midnight, and we realized that, in the moonless night which almost certainly required a few stops to find the way down, that meant almost certain death by freezing. We had been willing always to risk our lives, but we did not believe in throwing them away, so we decided that we must go down the mountain and own ourselves beaten in fair fight. No fresh snow, no blizzards, no intense cold had driven us off the peak. We were just two frail

The world from 27,000ft/8,230m: Somervell's photograph, one of the series he took during his attempt with Norton, shows the view to the north-west of Everest. The black peak at lower right is Changtse, rising above the central Rongbuk Glacier. The peak in the centre foreground is Ri-Ring, first climbed by Mallory and Bullock on 5 July, 1921. Behind Ri-Ring, running across the frame, is the West Rongbuk Glacier.

The highest photographs on earth: the picture (right) is Somervell's shot of the summit of Everest, taken at 27,000ft/8,230m with the vest-pocket Kodak camera shown above. Norton can be seen bent over his ice-axe as he struggles for breath. Somervell took another picture (far right) of the summit from just above 28,000ft/8,534m. Hardly able to breathe because of the obstruction in his throat, Somervell gave up at this point. But Norton, centre left, struggled on for another 100 feet before giving up. Somervell's photograph remained the highest known to have been taken for the next 29 years.

mortals, and the biggest task Nature has yet set to man was too much for us. Moving slowly and resting frequently, and so far from normal that for the first time in my climbing experience I dropped my ice-axe, we carefully retraced our steps down the rocky ledges, Norton, in spite of his eyes, making no mistake nor slip.

One thing we had plenty of time to survey, and that was the view. In its extent it was, of course, magnificent. Great peaks that had towered over us with their impressive and snow-clad heads a week ago were now but so many waves on the ocean of mountains below us. Except for Everest itself there was nothing within view so high as we were ourselves. The colossal bastion of Cho Oyu and Gyachung Kang was a wall over which we could see the low limestone hills of Tibet, and far away in the distance beyond them a few snowy summits, maybe 200 miles away. Mountain peaks are nearly always at their best when one is below their level: but whilst they lose their individual glory when seen from above, there is an exhilaration about a view of tremendous extent such as was ours that day.

In a country which has the clearest atmosphere in the world, we were lucky in being upon Everest on an exceptionally clear day. We simply saw everything there was to see; the experience of a lifetime, but quite indescribable. At so great a height, one's psychical faculties are dulled, and, just as this amazing extent of landscape failed to give us its full impressiveness, so, when we turned from it to descend, we had but little feeling of disappointment that we could not go on. We realized that it would be madness to continue, and we were somehow quite content to leave it at that, and to turn down with almost a feeling of relief that our worst trials were over.

We called at our camp, and took away a tent-pole as a substitute for my axe. Below this, the going was easier, so we unroped. Alas, that we did so! Somewhere about 25,000 feet high, when darkness was gathering, I had one of my fits of coughing and dislodged something in my throat which stuck so that I could breathe neither in nor out. I could not, of course, make a sign to Norton, or stop him, for the rope was off now; so I sat in the snow to die whilst he walked on, little knowing that his companion was awaiting the end only a few yards behind him. I made one or two attempts to breathe, but nothing happened. Finally, I pressed my chest with both hands, gave one last almighty push – and the obstruction came up. What a relief! Coughing up a little more blood, I once more breathed really freely – more freely than I had done for some days. Though the pain

was intense, yet I was a new man, and was soon going down at a better pace than ever to rejoin Norton. He had thought I was hanging back to make a sketch before the light went completely, and fortunately had not been worried. Shuffling along in the dark with the aid of an electric torch, we at last got into touch with Camp IV, for Mallory and Odell came out to meet us. Though the oxygen they carried for our use was a kind thought, it was not what we wanted at all; but the news they brought of Irvine in the camp below brewing hot tea and soup cheered us up and brought us home in good temper. What a contrast to our arrival in the same camp two years before, with Morshead not far from dying, and no food nor drink for us, nor any living soul nearer than Camp III. This time we entered the camp soon after 9 pm, and within an hour were warmed and fed and asleep.

The height Norton reached after continuing on his own was later calculated as 28,126 feet. He had passed the mark set by George Finch in 1922 and established a record, the highest point achieved by any climber, which lasted until the first Swiss attempt of 1952. Norton was also the first to reach the giant couloir which runs down the face from close to the foot of the summit pyramid, which became known variously as the Norton or Great Couloir.

PURSUING THE DREAM

By Peter and Leni Gillman

George Mallory must have known that if he failed on Everest in 1924 he was unlikely to return. His decision to take part had caused both him and his devoted wife Ruth immense anguish; they had a growing family and he had started a new job in Cambridge. On 28 May he and Geoffrey Bruce set off, without oxygen, on what was supposedly their last attempt, to be followed by Norton and Somervell. But then Mallory schemed a final bid, using oxygen and partnered by Sandy Irvine.

May 28 dawned without a cloud, the still air making Everest seem closer than ever in its majestic upward sweep above the Rongbuk glacier. Somervell and Noel were keen to move off, Noel to get into position to film and photograph the attempts. Despite his fears about the impending monsoon, Norton counselled caution, reckoning that the climbers would benefit from one further day's rest. George took advantage of the delay to write three more letters. He told David Pye that although they were shortly moving off, the 'adventure seems more desperate than ever . . . You'll have good news of me from Ruth, I hope.' He told his sister Mary: 'I'm due to make the first dash with Geoffrey Bruce and arrive at the top 7 days hence – but we may be delayed or caught by the monsoon or anything . . . This party has been badly knocked out but we still seem to have some guts among us I hope.' He wrote to his mother too. 'It will be a great adventure, if we get started before the monsoon hits us, with just a bare outside chance of success and a good many chances of a very bad time indeed. I shall take every care I can, you may be sure.'

From here, barring three notes which he sent down the mountain, there is nothing more to be heard in George's voice. But he was being observed by his colleagues, whose writings and photographs, together with the items found on his body in 1999, help form a picture of his actions and intentions in the last ten days of his life. He and Bruce arrived at Camp III on 30 May. Irvine, who was disappointed at having lost his place in the first summit team, gave George a light rucksack which he had made from one of the oxygen packs. 'Feel very fit tonight,' Irvine wrote. 'I wish I was in the first party instead of a bloody reserve.' On 31 May George and Bruce, together

with nine high-altitude porters, moved up to the North Col. Irvine and Odell, who had been assigned a support role on the North Col, cooked a supper of pea soup, tongue and cocoa.

The next day, 1 June, Irvine was up at 4.30 to make breakfast. George, Bruce and eight porters moved off at 6 am. Although the day had seemed fair, once on the shoulder they were hit by a bitter north-east wind. George was hoping to site Camp

Mallory with his eldest daughter, Clare, at Godalming, Surrey, in 1918. In 1923 the family moved to Cambridge, where Mallory had taken a lecturing job. He agonised over whether to go to Everest in 1924.

V at 25,300 feet but they were 300 feet short when four porters said they could go no further. The others pushed on, finally coming to a halt at 25,200 feet where they pitched two tiny tents on crumbling rocks on the lee side of the north shoulder. Bruce and the Sherpa Lobsang fetched the remaining loads and carried them to the camp. Five porters returned to the North Col, leaving three to carry loads to Camp VI the next day.

The morning brought only disappointment. The weather was still clear but when Bruce tried to rouse the porters, they said they were too tired to carry on. Talking in Nepalese, Bruce did his best to persuade them to continue, but only one would change his mind. Without the porters to help establish a further camp at around 27,000 feet, the attempt was doomed, and the group returned to the North Col.

That same morning, 2 June, Norton and Somervell, together with six porters, had set off from the North Col on their summit attempt. They had been going for about two hours when, to

Mallory wrote constantly to his family and friends during his three expeditions. In 1922 he sent this letter to his daughters Clare and Beridge, then aged six and four; 'John' in the letter is their brother, who was nearly two.

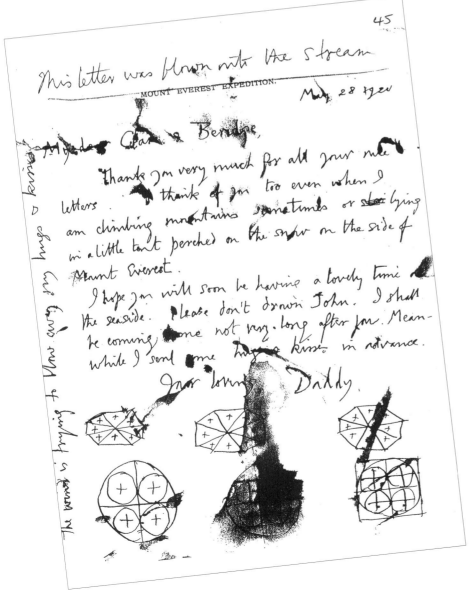

their surprise, they saw George, Bruce and their porters descending towards them. 'Their story was distressingly simple,' Norton later wrote. After they had spent the previous day in exhausting wind, nothing '– not even Bruce's command of the language and well-known influence over these men – would induce any of the porters to go higher'. Somervell added that 'the only thing they could do was to come down, leaving the tents for us, and wishing us better luck with our assault on the mountain. It was a grievous disappointment, and must have been worse for them than for us.'

George and Bruce reached the North Col at midday, where it was Odell's turn to be surprised. George, he said, was both 'disappointed and upset' by the porters' refusal to go on. George then told Odell that he intended to make another attempt with Irvine, using the oxygen apparatus. Irvine, who had just arrived with Hazard and some porters from Camp III, also recorded this decisive moment. 'George decided that I should go down in Hazard's place and prepare apparatus for an oxygen attempt.'

It is not clear precisely when George concluded that his attempt with Bruce was bound to fail, or when he resolved to revert to his original plan for making an oxygen attempt with Irvine. But it was the defining moment of his life. Throughout his mountaineering career he had always pushed as hard and as far as he could, refusing to give up until he was convinced beyond all possible doubt that he had no other choice. Now that the weather remained fair, and he was still on his feet, and he had a willing partner, and there was oxygen equipment at Camp III, he could not renounce his hope of going to the summit. It offered him the supreme opportunity of being the climbing leader who climbed the highest mountain. As he had declared in New York, a climber was what he was, and this is what climbers did; and this was how they fulfilled their wildest dreams.

There was more. If he went back to Ruth with Everest unclimbed, he could face the anguish of wondering whether he should leave her and his children and their home for yet another try. He could not see how he could inflict that on her again. It was only by making another attempt now that he could be true to Ruth and all they had gone through together, and to the ideals of honesty and integrity they had expressed that were embodied in their love.

It was also the only way he knew of redeeming the suffering he had caused Ruth: if he climbed Everest now the conflict at the core of their marriage, the conflict between his dreams and their love, would be reconciled.

THE RIDDLE OF MALLORY AND IRVINE

George Mallory and Andrew Irvine (right) on board the SS California which carried the 1924 expedition to India. Irvine, an Oxford undergraduate and at 22 by far the youngest member of the expedition, was shy in his elders' company. But Mallory soon warmed to him, writing that although he was 'a bit young and hasn't much to talk about' he knew 'a lot about engineering' and was 'one of the best'. Although some of his colleagues were surprised when Mallory selected Irvine as his partner for his final attempt, Mallory had intended to climb with Irvine from an early stage in the trip. It was while climbing in support of Mallory and Irvine on 8 June 1924 that Noel Odell glimpsed them for the last time through a parting in the clouds blanketing the North-east Ridge. But where had Odell seen them? The question was crucial in judging whether they could have reached the summit – but Odell could never be sure. There were further clues to debate through the discovery of Irvine's ice-axe in 1933, and of Mallory's body in 1999.

The fate of George Mallory and Sandy Irvine has always been the most mesmerising of Everest's mysteries. The two men were last seen high on the North-east Ridge of Everest, within striking distance of the summit. To the expectant British public in 1924, their disappearance came as a profound shock, the first notice that mountaineering was a lethal game, even where Everest's heroes were involved. Ever since then, two questions have preoccupied the mountaineering world. Could they have reached the top? And how and where did they die? Although the extraordinary discovery of Mallory's bleached body in 1999 intensified the debate, the mystery is still to be resolved.

The pairing of Mallory and Irvine for the final summit bid of 1924 was an intriguing one. At 37, on his third Everest trip, and the expedition's climbing leader, Mallory was manifestly the senior partner, and it was he who selected Irvine for the attempt. Mallory had been drawn to Irvine from the start, seeing in him a figure with technical skills, particularly with cameras and oxygen equipment, to complement his own more visionary nature. Irvine, a 22-year-old Oxford chemistry student who had rowed against Cambridge in the annual boat race, was as determined as Mallory to succeed. During the trek across Tibet, Mallory had proposed that he and Irvine should make the first attempt using oxygen equipment. But bad weather disrupted the expedition's plans, and instead Mallory was paired with Geoffrey Bruce, reaching 25,200 feet without oxygen equipment. Then came the astonishing effort, again without oxygen, by Norton and Somervell. When they returned to the North Col, the expedition appeared to be over – but then Mallory proposed that he and Irvine, using oxygen, should give it one more shot.

The two men left the North Col at 9 am on 6 June. Two days later, perched in the tenuous shelter of Camp VI at 26,800 feet, they set out for the summit.

In a final note, Mallory declared that the oxygen was 'a bloody load for climbing' but added that they had 'perfect weather for the job'. Climbing in support, some 2,000 feet below, was the geologist Noel Odell, whose view of the mountain's upper reaches was blocked by banks of cloud. At 12.50 pm the clouds magically cleared. In a dispatch to *The Times* which has become one of the epic texts of mountaineering, Odell described what he saw:

The entire Summit Ridge and final peak of Everest were unveiled. My eyes became fixed on one tiny black spot silhouetted on a small

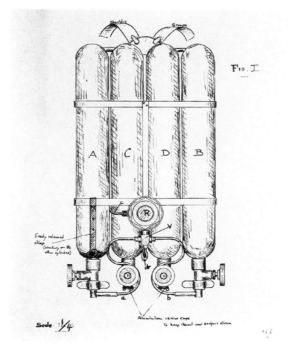

Sandy Irvine had a passion for engineering, and while at school at Shrewsbury had designed a machine-gun and a gyroscopic stabiliser for military aircraft. He became the 1924 expedition's oxygen expert and adapted the equipment to make it lighter and more reliable. Noel Odell's photograph (above) shows him with the modified equipment at Shekar Dzong on 24 April. Irvine had drawn a plan (left) showing how he would invert the oxygen cylinders and reduce the amount of pipework.

In another of Noel Odell's photographs, George Mallory (seated, left) and Sandy Irvine (in pith helmet, right) try out the principal attraction of a rudimentary amusement park in a Sikkim village during an early stage of the long march to Everest. Irvine wrote to his mother that many villages had 'the predecessor to the great wheel at Blackpool . . . most amusing to go round on'.

snow-crest beneath a rock step in the ridge; the black spot moved. Another black spot became apparent and moved up the snow to join the other on the crest. The first then approached the great Rock Step and shortly emerged at the top; the second did likewise. Then the whole fascinating vision vanished, enveloped in cloud once more.

Odell was in no doubt that he had seen his two colleagues heading – 'with considerable alacrity' – for the summit. They were never seen again. Two days later, Odell climbed back up to Camp VI, finding it just as they had left it. He laid out two sleeping bags in the shape of the letter T – the pre-arranged signal to his colleagues below that a catastrophe had occurred. Four days later, with heavy hearts, the surviving members of the expedition cleared Base Camp and embarked on the long journey home.

Ever since then there has been speculation about the significance of Odell's sighting. At first, Odell believed he had seen the two men surmount the Second Step, the prominent buttress at 28,200 feet on the North-east Ridge. As this was believed to be the last major obstacle, Odell concluded there

was 'a strong possibility' that they had succeeded, only to die from a fall or exhaustion and exposure during their descent.

Ten years later, Odell changed his mind. He was swayed by reports from the 1933 British expedition, which found the Second Step a daunting barrier – Percy Wyn Harris described it as a 'dark grey precipice, smooth and holdless'. Odell now doubted whether Mallory and Irvine could have climbed it at all, let alone in the five minutes he had described. Instead he presumed he had seen them on the First Step, some 300 feet lower down – making it far less likely that Mallory and Irvine could have reached the summit before nightfall.

A second discovery in 1933 seemed to clinch the matter. Above Camp VI Percy Wyn Harris found Irvine's ice-axe on the North-east Ridge, some way below the First Step. The consensus was that it marked a fatal slip by one or both of the men during their descent. If so, they must have failed, for they could not have reached the summit from the First Step and returned to the ice-axe site before nightfall. Nor could they have reached the site the following day, as they could not have survived a night out on the mountainside. The mountaineering world, Odell among them, reluc-

In a note written before he and Irvine left Camp VI on 8 June, Mallory advised the photographer John Noel where to look out for them (8 pm is an error for 8 am). Two days earlier Noel Odell had taken the last photograph of Mallory (left) and Irvine as they set off from the North Col.

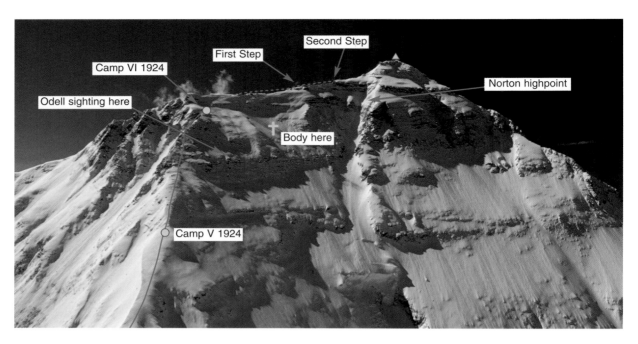

The photograph shows the principal landmarks of the disappearance and discovery. Odell made his last sighting of Mallory and Irvine at 12.50 pm on 8 June 1924 – but were they on the First or Second Step? Mallory's body was found at 26,700ft/8,138m on 1 May 1999. Also shown is Edward Norton's highpoint of 28,124ft/8,572m, which he reached on 3 June.

tantly concluded that Mallory and Irvine must have met their deaths in gallant defeat.

For some 40 years the matter rested there. But then came new generations of climbers and researchers prepared to reconsider the evidence. For a long time the North-east Ridge had been barred to western mountaineers by the Chinese occupation of Tibet. When westerners finally reached the crest of the ridge they found that the Second Step was far less formidable than it appeared from below. They also looked along Odell's sight-path and reported that the Second Step fitted his description, while the First Step was scarcely in view.

One of the most insistent revisionists was the American climber and writer, Tom Holzel. He felt that previous theories had ignored the significance of Mallory and Irvine's oxygen equipment, which would have given them a greater boost than hitherto supposed. Controversially, he also argued that the two men could have split up, enabling Mallory to take the remaining oxygen supplies and reach the summit alone. In 1980, Holzel's interest was intensified when he learned that a Chinese climber, Wang Hung-boa, had stumbled across an 'English dead' on the North Face five years before. Holzel was convinced that the dead Englishman was Sandy Irvine. In 1986, Holzel helped organise an expedition which hoped to find Irvine and even his camera, which could prove whether he and Mallory had reached the summit. Although the attempt was defeated by bad weather, the issue was back in the public domain.

In 1999 came the most momentous discovery of all. Other researchers had taken up the cause, among them a young German historian, Jochen Hemmleb, who was one of the motivators behind a bid by a US expedition, led by Eric Simonson, to search the North Face anew. As is related elsewhere in this book (see page 206), Conrad Anker, who was climbing outside the main search zone, came upon a dessicated body at 26,700 feet on the North Face. At first the US team thought it had found Sandy Irvine; then it realised that the body was that of George Mallory.

In the aftermath of the find, the debate reached fever pitch. There were notes in Mallory's pocket which indicated that he and Irvine intended to carry a full load of oxygen cylinders, which strengthened the case for their success. Against that, Anker, who went on to climb the Second Step without using the ladder left in place by the Chinese in 1975, concluded that it was at the limit of Mallory's capabilities and certainly beyond those of Irvine. But that implied that Odell had not seen them on the Second Step after all. As the arguments raged, the contradictions only seemed to multiply. And how had the two men died? Even that remained unclear. There was a frayed 40 foot length of rope around Mallory's waist, suggesting that it had broken during a fall. But the body was surprisingly undamaged, suggesting that such a fall had occurred not from the site of the 1933 ice-axe find, but from lower down.

Nor had the Americans found a camera, the holy grail. And what of Irvine? Since the Americans had found Mallory, in effect, by looking in the wrong place, there seemed a good chance that Irvine's body – and with it a camera – could still be located. Inevitably plans were laid for a new search, to be conducted in spring 2001. The quest would go on.

THE WRONG MOUNTAIN

The headline says Everest; the photograph shows the distinctive West Ridge of Makalu, Everest's neighbour and the fifth highest mountain in the world. The Times *later corrected its mistake. In the picture* left, *the leading Westland was photographed by the second plane as they reached Everest's summit.*

OVER EVEREST
FIRST PICTURES OF THE HOUSTON MOUNT EVEREST FLIGHT

In March 1933 a new Everest expedition arrived in India. Equipped with two Westland biplanes fitted with plate cameras, its aim was to make the first flight over the mountain and obtain the first aerial photographs.

The Westlands took off from 150 miles south of Everest on 3 April. As the leading pilot, Squadron Leader Lord Clydesdale, headed up to 31,000 feet, his navigator and photographer, Colonel Blacker, saw Everest appear as a 'tiny triangle of whiteness, so white as to appear incandescent'. An immense snow plume was streaming from its crest – the sign of 'a mighty wind raging across the summit'.

Blacker began exposing his plates, some through a floor hatch, others from the open cockpit. 'The scene was superb and beyond description,' he recalled. As the plane approached the South-west Face it hit a downdraught and plunged 2,000 feet.

Clydesdale managed to lift the plane and cleared the summit by 100 feet. It was promptly caught in the snow-plume, ice fragments rattling into the cockpit. As Clydesdale fought for control, Blacker 'crammed plate after plate into the camera, releasing the shutter as fast as I could'.

The results were superb, some shots showing Everest rising above its neighbours, Makalu and Cho Oyu, others revealing the mountain's most intimate rock and snow scenery. The two Westlands touched down after a three-hour flight and the photographs were duly dispatched to *The Times*.

The outcome was somewhat unfortunate. On 24 April, *The Times* published the best of the photographs, the first captioned: 'a vivid impression of the awe-inspiring summit of Everest.' Filling the entire front page, however, was a picture not of Everest but of Makalu. Reports soon appeared elsewhere gleefully pointing out *The Times*'s mistake.

At first Clydesdale gallantly shouldered blame, saying that he might have changed course to Makalu while Blacker was changing a plate, but Blacker was adamant he knew which mountain he had photographed. The newspaper's mistake was corrected at an exhibition of the pictures which opened on 18 May. 'I want to assure everyone,' Blacker joked, 'that we did not go to the Andes'.

MY NASTIEST MOMENT

by Jack Longland

The four British expeditions of the 1930s were dispiriting affairs, beset by rows and battles against poor climbing conditions and heavy snow. The most determined attempt was made in 1933, when three climbers reached around 28,100 feet/8,565 metres, the height achieved by Edward Norton in 1924. It was also in 1933 that Jack Longland, an experienced Alpinist, later a distinguished broadcaster, faced the most alarming predicament of his mountaineering career. On 29 May, Longland, together with two colleagues and eight Sherpa porters, established Camp VI at 27,500 feet/8,382 metres. Longland set off to lead the Sherpas back to Camp IV when the group was hit by a storm.

We gave the party a day's rest, and then at 5 am on 28 May set off again up the weary ridge to Camp V. It is a slow grind up easy rocks and scree – easy, that is, if there's not a wind to throw you off your balance. Scree is always exhausting, for your feet slip back at every step. It's specially beastly above 24,000 feet, when each step needs three or four breaths. We must have looked a strange bunch of asthmatic crocks, but after five hours we had worked our way to the little sloping shelf, and found the tents at Camp V intact.

You don't stay long to admire the view at that height; after seeing the porters safely packed away, we crawled into our sleeping-sacks and started the laborious game of cooking. Cooking is a courtesy title – what we really did was to fill our cooking-pots with snow, and wait for an hour or more till the water grew faintly warm, and we could produce something that was a mockery of soup or tea. At that height even boiling water is not hot enough to scald your hand. Then came an uncomfortable night, trying to keep warm inside double sleeping-sacks with all our clothes on. It must have been cold, because at 5 am when I tried to pour the water out of the vacuum flask that had been filled with lukewarm water the night before, several small pieces of ice came out with it. We found a bitter wind blowing outside, and decided to send the porters back to their tents, then cooked more warm drinks to fortify ourselves for the job ahead. At last, when the wind dropped a trifle and the sun was out, we set off at half-past eight.

We aimed to hit the long East Ridge of Everest near a tower at about 28,000 feet – the 'First Step'. The route took us over great slabs of outward-shelving rock, reminiscent of the tiles of a roof, and mostly coated with new snow and varied by belts of steep scree. We found no flat ledges to rest on, and there were long periods of difficult balancing where we had to depend on the friction of our bootnails against the smoothly sloping rock.

Birnie had to stay behind at Camp V – he'd crocked a leg. So I had to give up the idea of joining Wyn Harris and Wager in their attempt on the summit next day, and concentrate on seeing the porters safely down from Camp VI. On the way up Wyn Harris and Wager prospected the route, while I brought up the rear: but all the porters climbed magnificently, like seasoned mountaineers, on ground where a slip would often have been fatal. The going was treacherous, particularly where the rocks were covered with loose pebbles, and a slither would have been hard to check – and if it *wasn't* it would only have ended when you reached the glacier, 8,000 feet below.

At the end of every 50 minutes we called a ten-minute halt, and I could encourage the most exhausted porters when I had breath to spare to try out my few Nepalese phrases. I was as glad of the halts as they were, though they were carrying 10lbs or more on their backs and we were unloaded. At last, just about mid-day, we struggled up over a steeper band of yellowish rocks, and found a sloping snow-clogged ledge at about 27,500 feet. This was to be Camp VI – but there wasn't even room to pitch our tent until the porters had cleared away the snow and built up a platform of

small stones at the lower edge. Even then the tent sloped drunkenly downwards, and those who slept in it always found the man who had the upper berth slipping down on his companion during the night. Still, there it was – the final jumping-off place for the top, now not much more than 1,500 feet above. Our eight porters had done a magnificent piece of work. They had carried up the highest camp that has ever been pitched, 700 feet higher and nearly a quarter of a mile nearer the summit than a tent had been before – or since.

There wasn't much time for resting – the porters had to be got down to safety at Camp IV before night came. I remember catching a glimpse of the Rongbuk Monastery 10,000 feet below, and thinking how odd it was to see it across those great depths after nearly six weeks' absence. We set off just before one o'clock, after the briefest of goodbyes to Wyn Harris and Wager in their tent, and one final glance towards the summit which looked invitingly close.

I decided not to try and take the porters directly down the steep and slippery slabs by which we had climbed up from Camp V. Looking back, I have never blessed any decision more – if I had decided otherwise I doubt if I should be alive now. Instead we worked along horizontally, following a break in the steep Yellow Band and aiming to hit the top of the main North Ridge, which I thought would be safer for the tired porters to descend. As I was helping them down a steep section just before the ridge, I had a moment to look at the view. You are more than ordinarily stupid at that height – the brain is starved of oxygen, and so neither eyes nor ears nor any of the senses do their job properly. But I told myself that this was the best view I was ever likely to see, and managed to take in the fact that I was seeing peaks that must have been more than 250 miles away; and all the high summits that had looked so proud from Camp IV were now insignificant humps below.

These glimpses of the view had a sudden and

It was Percy Wyn Harris, Lawrence Wager and Jack Longland (centre row) who set up Camp VI at 27,500ft/8,382m on the North Face. The photograph, taken later in the safety of Base Camp, also shows seven of the eight Sherpas who, led by Longland, had fought for their lives after being hit by a storm.

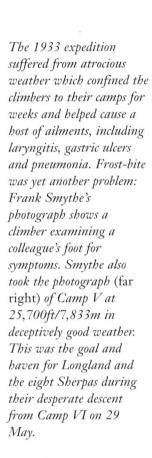

The 1933 expedition suffered from atrocious weather which confined the climbers to their camps for weeks and helped cause a host of ailments, including laryngitis, gastric ulcers and pneumonia. Frost-bite was yet another problem: Frank Smythe's photograph shows a climber examining a colleague's foot for symptoms. Smythe also took the photograph (far right) of Camp V at 25,700ft/7,833m in deceptively good weather. This was the goal and haven for Longland and the eight Sherpas during their desperate descent from Camp VI on 29 May.

nasty interruption. Without any warning that I remember a storm blew up out of the west. There were no more distant horizons – the most I could see was a snow-swept circle of 20 or 30 yards. A mountain storm is always unnerving, but its effect at 27,000 feet on cold and exhausted men is devastating. Worst of all I was responsible for the safety of eight men who had trustingly followed us to this height, and who had somehow to be got safely down to Camp IV. Even worse, we were now at the top of the North Ridge, and the whole length of it down to Camp V was entirely unknown to me, as our diagonal route of the morning had missed it out. That wouldn't have mattered on some ridges, even in an Everest hurricane, for a sharp ridge is easy to follow, even if you can't see more than a few paces. But the North Ridge of Everest is broad and badly defined – you can miss the best way even in calm weather – and here I was trying to collect my

wits and mountaineering experience to follow it correctly when it was all I could do to stagger downhill at all, and when all the rest of my mind was occupied with keeping the porters together, urging on the stragglers, and seeing that they kept away from the steep rocks where a fatal slip might occur.

The snow began to cover the holds on the rocks and give a slippery coating to the patches of scree, and the wind came in terrifying gusts, forcing us to cling or cower against the rocks to avoid being blown bodily away. My snow-goggles soon became useless, choked with snow. I took them off, only to find that eyelids and eyelashes coated up as well, forming an opaque film which had to be rubbed away every few minutes before I could peer out and get a glimpse of the next few yards.

Every ten minutes I called a halt to count up my band and collect them together, and then with a few shouted words of encouragement in what I hoped was Nepalese, off we pushed again, fighting our way down against the bitterly driving snow.

We had a moment's respite in the lee of a small cliff, where we happened on the tattered remains of a green tent. It must have been the old Camp VI from which Mallory and Irvine left in 1924 for their attempt on the summit. For a minute or two the least tired porters rummaged among the wreckage. One brought out a candle lantern and another an electric torch – the kind that worked with a press-button. Even after nine years of storm and cold the torch still worked, so we pushed on rather heartened by these signs of human occupation, many years old as they were.

But the finding of the 1924 tent gave me my nastiest moment. I had a photograph in my pocket on which the position of Mallory's camp was marked. I was going to use it to mark the position of our own new Camp VI for Smythe and Shipton, who were to follow up Wyn Harris and Wager if the first attempt failed. I pulled the photograph out of my pocket and discovered to my horror that Mallory's camp was marked as being not on the main North Ridge, but on a subsidiary spur further east.

This must mean that, in spite of all my care, we were not on the main ridge, and worse still, this second spur ran out on steep ice-slopes overhanging the East Rongbuk Glacier thousands of feet below. If I led the party on to these slopes there was no escape – it would at best mean a night in the open, and to spend a night out at this height, even without a storm, would be fatal.

I had to think desperately quickly – and it was a problem I couldn't possibly share with the porters, though if I went wrong they were equally involved in an unpleasant death. Looking at the photograph again I saw that if we *were* on the wrong ridge, I ought soon to see signs of a steep ice couloir on the left. Equally, if I *wasn't* wrong, that couloir ought not to appear. So the next half-hour or more was full of desperate anxiety, as I peered through the snow expecting and yet hoping not to see that steep funnel of ice on my left. When minute after minute of painful stumbling and struggling with the wind went by and no couloir appeared, I began to hope that the marking of the photograph was wrong and that my mountain experience had led me right. It was a pretty desperate chance – nine times out of ten map or photograph is bound to be right, and the climber lost in a storm is as certainly wrong.

Meanwhile the storm was telling: the more exhausted porters were beginning to sit down, even between our frequent halts. It took a lot of urging to get them to their feet again – it was so much easier to lie down and die! And perhaps they were right – if I really was leading them down the wrong ridge, why not die quietly now rather than after hours of struggle and cold? That was the problem that made these two hours the worst I have spent – worse even than the storm and the effort of fighting on down against it.

All this time I was hoping for some pause in the storm – just a minute of clearer view which would give me a glimpse of the North Peak and a chance of fixing our position. I believe I carried my compass in my gloved hand during most of the descent, but without a single landmark to be seen beyond the driving snow it was as much use as a sick headache. The weaker porters were beginning to sit down more often now. More than once I had to lift a man up and set him going again: anything seemed better than continuing in the face of that unrelenting storm. Still I hoped it was the right ridge – surely, if I was wrong, we ought to have come to the tip of those ice-slopes by now. I don't remember much about the last bit of the descent – it was all slipping and staggering down icy screes and round little snowed-up cliffs. Then suddenly, down through the snow-scud, appeared a little patch of green. I rubbed the ice off my eyelashes and looked again: and it was a tent, three, four tents – the little cluster that meant Camp V and safety, and an end to the tearing anxiety of two hours.

Only two hours of storm – less than three since I'd left Wager and Wyn Harris at Camp VI; but I seemed to have crowded a lifetime of fear and struggle and responsibility into that short time. And it wasn't till a day or two later that I learnt that it was careless marking of the photograph that had made me think that Mallory's camp was not on the main North Ridge.

MIRAGES AT 28,000 FEET

by Frank Smythe

During my solitary climb two curious phenomena were experienced. It is with great diffidence that I describe them, and then only at Ruttledge's [expedition leader] request. I prefer to draw no inferences from them and merely to describe them. The first was one that is by no means unique, and has been experienced in the past by solitary wanderers, not only in mountains but on desert wastes and in polar regions. All the time that I was climbing alone I had a strong feeling that I was accompanied by a second person. This feeling was so strong that it completely eliminated all loneliness I might otherwise have felt. It even seemed that I was tied to my 'companion' by a rope, and that if I slipped 'he' would hold me. I remember constantly glancing back over my shoulder, and once, when after reaching my highest point, I stopped to try and eat some mint cake, I carefully divided it and turned round with one half in my hand. It was almost a shock to find no one to whom to give it. It seemed to me that this 'presence' was a strong, helpful and friendly one, and it was not until Camp VI was sighted that the link connecting me, as it seemed at the time, to the beyond was snapped, and, although Shipton and the camp were but a few yards away, I suddenly felt alone.

The second phenomenon may or may not have been an optical illusion – personally I am convinced that it was not. I was still some 200 feet above Camp VI and a considerable distance horizontally from it when, chancing to glance in the direction of the North Ridge, I saw two curious-looking objects floating in the sky. They strongly resembled kite-balloons in shape, but one possessed what appeared to be squat, under-developed wings, and the other a protuberance suggestive of a beak. They hovered motionless but seemed slowly to pulsate, a pulsation incidentally much slower than my own

Frank Smythe (with Himalayan lily, left) was one of the most prolific writers and photographers of pre-war mountaineering. He took part in all three principal Everest expeditions of the 1930s and in 1933 made a solo attempt on the summit, reaching just over 28,100ft/8,565m on the North Face and equalling Norton's height record from 1924. Smythe climbed without supplementary oxygen and later – in the official expedition account, Everest 1933 *– described the hallucinations which were to become familiar to other climbers at that altitude.*

heart-beats, which is of interest supposing that it was an optical illusion. The two objects were very dark in colour and were silhouetted sharply against the sky, or possibly a background of cloud. So interested was I that I stopped to observe them. My brain appeared to be working normally, and I deliberately put myself through a series of tests. First of all I glanced away. The objects did not follow my vision, but they were still there when I looked back again. Then I looked away again, and this time identified by name a number of peaks, valleys and glaciers by way of a mental test. But when I looked back again, the objects still confronted me. At this I gave them up as a bad job, but just as I was starting to move again a mist suddenly drifted across. Gradually they disappeared behind it, and when a minute or two later it had drifted clear, exposing the whole of the North Ridge once more, they had vanished as mysteriously as they came.

It may be of interest to state that their position was roughly midway between the position of the 1924 Camp VI and the North-east Shoulder. Thus, they were at a height of about 27,200 feet, and as I was at about 27,600 feet when I saw them, a line connecting their approximate position with my position would not bring them against a background of sky, but against lower and distant mountains. It is conceivable, therefore, that it was some strange effect of mist and mountain magnified by imagination. On the other hand, it may have been a mirage.

THE MAD YORKSHIREMAN

by Audrey Salkeld

During the British 1935 expedition, Charles Warren was resting on a rock in the upper East Rongbuk Glacier, waiting for his companions to catch up, when his eyes lit on a boot sticking out of the snow. Beside it was what he took to be the remains of a tent.

'I say,' Warren called, 'there's a perfectly good pair of Lawrie boots and a tent up here.' Only when Warren approached more closely did he see a body lying huddled in the snow. It had to be

Maurice Wilson, dubbed 'the mad Yorkshireman', who had disappeared while making an audacious solo attempt on Everest the previous year.

Wilson had made no secret of his plans. Born in Bradford in 1898, he had served with distinction in the trenches during the Great War, winning a Military Cross at Ypres, and surviving a spray of machine gun fire which had left his left arm permanently weak. He had then embarked on a spell of globe-trotting, including several years in New

Wilson bought his Gipsy Moth, which he promptly named Ever-Wrest, *before he could even fly. His feat in piloting it to India in 1933 was impressive enough but he overreached himself in making a solo bid to climb Everest.*

Zealand. After recovering from a serious illness through a combination of fasting and prayer, he became imbued with a sense of divine purpose which convinced him he could climb Everest. True, he lacked the resources of the previous British attempts; but these would be more than compensated for by his faith and his belief in the power of the human mind.

'When I have accomplished my little work,' he declared, 'I shall be somebody. People will listen to me, and I shall be allowed to do the tests I want on the experimental machine I want to build.' (Beyond Everest lay an even grander project to ascend into the stratosphere.)

Just how Wilson intended to accomplish his feat seemed utterly far-fetched. He bought a second-hand Gipsy Moth which he christened *Ever-Wrest*. With this he intended to fly to Tibet, crash-land on Everest's lower slopes, then step out for the summit. It did not matter that he had never flown a plane or climbed a mountain in his life; he took a holiday in the Lake District and booked a course of flying lessons at the London Aero Club. He tested his nerve by making a parachute jump and to build up his stamina regularly walked from London to Bradford, where his parents lived.

By the spring of 1933, Wilson was almost ready. There was a last-minute hitch when he flew to Bradford to say goodbye to his parents, crashing en route and costing him a three-week delay. Then the British Air Ministry sent a telegram forbidding him to take off. Wilson tore it up and departed. After an impressive solo flight, he reached northern India two weeks later.

Here Wilson had to modify his plans. Having been definitively refused permission to fly over Nepal or Tibet, he sold the Gipsy Moth and headed for Darjeeling. There, early in 1934, he engaged three Sherpas and made his way to Tibet, travelling in disguise and often by night, arriving in the Rongbuk Valley in mid-April.

On 16 April, carrying a 45lb rucksack, Wilson embarked on his attempt. Nine days later, defeated by storms and fatigue, he returned without even

having reached the top of the East Rongbuk Glacier. He remained undaunted. 'I still know I can do it,' he wrote in his diary.

Eighteen days later Wilson tried again. This time two of his porters accompanied him to the traditional site of Camp III near the foot of the North Col. There he was beset by both blizzards and altitude sickness, and had to spend several days resting in bed. He made several attempts to reach the col, surviving some nasty falls, being finally defeated by a 40 foot ice wall which even the 1933 expedition had struggled to climb. The Sherpas tried to persuade him to give up, in vain. On 31 May he set off for his last attempt. The final entry in his diary reads: 'Off again, gorgeous day'.

After finding Wilson's remains a year later, Warren and his two companions, Eric Shipton and Edwin Kempson, wrapped his body in a tent and interred it in a crevasse. That night they sat together under an overhanging rock, reading aloud from Wilson's diary. The three men were moved by his account of his struggles. 'A moving and gallant document,' Kempson recalled. Warren called it 'an extraordinary documentary revelation of monomania and determination of purpose,' while Shipton declared: 'We cannot fail to admire his courage.'

Yet questions obtruded. If Wilson had set off for the North Col, how was it that he had died in his camp back on the Rongbuk Glacier? Where was his sleeping-bag, when most of his other equipment, including his notebook, rucksack, stove and Union Jack, was found in the snow beside him? And what of the Sherpas, supposedly camped a few hundred yards away? Had they not seen his hapless efforts to reach the North Col, or realized he was dying close by?

Some speculated that the Sherpas had retreated to wait for Wilson at a more amenable altitude. Perhaps they knew he had died but were so frightened of having lost their sahib that they did not tell the authorities the full story. Perhaps they even took his sleeping-bag for themselves.

Wilson has advocates, however, who believe he reached the North Col, maybe even higher, before being compelled to descend, abandoning his equipment en route. As with Mallory and Irvine, they hope that one day the missing items will be discovered to prove their case.

Mountaineers continue to stumble across Wilson's remains, spewed with macabre regularity from the glacier. His diary has a permanent home at the Alpine Club archives in London. It perhaps reveals the ultimate truth: that Wilson could never have returned from Everest empty-handed, obliged to admit that his faith had been unfounded.

With macabre regularity, Wilson's remains surface periodically from the slopes below the North Col. This photograph was taken in 1989 by Roger Mear.

ONE DAY MOUNT EVEREST WILL BE CLIMBED

by Eric Shipton

One day Mount Everest will be climbed; of that there can be little doubt. It may be achieved at the next attempt; there may be another twenty failures.

The wide interest which the Mount Everest expeditions aroused among the non-climbing public, the great confidence of each successive expedition in its ability to reach the summit and the fact that several parties have been forced to turn back when success was apparently almost within their grasp, have caused a good deal of perplexity and perhaps have made the repeated failures seem rather foolish. To see the matter in its true perspective it is well to remember that in spite of all the attempts that have been made during the last 60 years upon the giants of the Himalayas by climbers of many nations, not a single mountain of 26,000 feet has yet been climbed. Most prominent among these attempts were the repeated, desperate and sometimes disastrous German efforts to climb Kangchenjunga and Nanga Parbat. There were no fewer than five German expeditions to Nanga Parbat in the 1930s. On the first of these, in 1932, the climbers appeared to come so close to their goal that when I discussed the prospects of the second attempt in 1934 with the leader, he appeared to regard its success almost as a foregone conclusion, in much the same way as we had assessed our chances on Everest in 1933. It would seem almost as though there were a cordon drawn round the upper part of these great peaks beyond which no man may go. The truth, of course, lies in the fact that, at altitudes of 25,000 feet and beyond, the effects of low atmospheric pressure upon the human body are so severe that really difficult mountaineering is impossible and the consequences even of a mild storm may be deadly, that nothing but the most perfect conditions of weather and snow offer the slightest chance of success,

Eric Shipton made his prediction that Everest would eventually be climbed in Upon that Mountain, *published in 1942. Seven years earlier a young Sherpa porter named Tenzing (third from left) had queued to sign on for his first Everest expedition.*

and that on the last lap of the climb no party is in a position to choose its day.

In this connection it is not irrelevant to reflect upon the countless attempts to climb the Matterhorn before the summit was finally reached in 1865 – attempts by the best mountaineers, amateur and professional, of the day. Compare the two problems. The Matterhorn could be attempted on any day in each successive summer; attempts upon the summit of Everest have been launched on, at the most, two days of a few arbitrarily chosen years. The upper part of the Matterhorn could be reached in a single day from a comfortable hotel in the valley, so that the same party could set out day after day to attempt their climb, gaining personal knowledge and experience of the problem with each successive effort; no man has yet succeeded in making more than one attempt upon the summit of Everest in any one year – few have tried more than once in a lifetime. Climbing on the Matterhorn is an experience of supreme mental and physical enjoyment; mountaineering on the upper part of Everest is a heavy, lifeless struggle. The actual climbing on the Matterhorn is no more difficult than that on the last 2,000 feet of Everest. Today the Matterhorn is regarded as an easy climb for a competent party in reasonably good conditions. And yet year after year it resisted all the efforts of the pioneers to climb it; many

proclaimed it to be unclimbable. It was certainly not that these men were incompetent. The reason must be sought in that peculiar, intangible difficulty presented by the first ascent of any peak. How much more should we expect this factor to play a part in the defence of the great peaks of the Himalayas!

No, it is not remarkable that Everest did not yield to the first few attempts; indeed, it would have been very surprising and not a little sad if it had,for that is not the way of greatmountains. Perhaps we had become a little arrogant with our fine new techniques of ice-claw and rubber slipper, our age of easy mechanical conquest. We had forgotten that the mountain still holds the master card, that it will grant success only in its own good time. Why else does mountaineering retain its deep fascination?

It is possible, even probable, that in time men will look back with wonder at our feeble efforts, unable to account for our repeated failure, while they themselves are grappling with far more formidable problems. If we are still alive we shall no doubt mumble fiercely in our grey beards in a desperate effort to justify our weakness. But if we are wise we shall reflect with deep gratitude that we seized our mountaineering heritage, and will take pleasure in watching younger men enjoy theirs.

'ED, MY BOY,
THIS IS EVEREST'
1951-1969

A REMARKABLE VIEW

Below: *The new view of Everest: after the successive failures from the north, the post-war expeditions approached from Nepal to the south. The photograph, almost certainly taken by Eric Shipton from 20,000ft/6,096m on Pumori in 1951, showed that the route to Everest via the Khumbu Glacier and Icefall was open. Pages 58–59: a similar perspective, obtained by Galen Rowell at 18,000ft/5,486m from Kala Pattar in 1984. The words quoted were Hillary's encouragement to himself as he hesitated on the Summit Ridge in 1953.*

After the Second World War it appeared that all routes to Everest were closed. In Tibet, which had provided access to the mountain before the war, the Dalai Lama, its religious leader, felt under threat. It was not merely that its giant neighbour, China, was in turmoil as Mao's army marched into Peking, but the Dalai Lama's horoscope had warned him to beware of foreigners. In 1951 the prophecy was fulfilled as Communist forces who had taken power in China occupied Tibet. For western mountaineers, the traditional route to Everest was barred.

The southern route, via Nepal, seemed hardly more propitious. India was emerging from a hideous civil war which had led to the partition with Pakistan and had made Himalayan climbing seem an irrelevance. Nepal, too, had a long tradition of being wary of outsiders, particularly towards the British with their colonialist record in the region. But gradually the politics of the region changed and Nepal saw the wisdom of a shift towards the western powers. In mountaineering circles, interest in Everest quickened once more – and if Tibet was closed, surely Nepal offered a way.

But where was that way? In 1921, from the col between Pumori and Lingtren, Mallory had looked into the long ice-filled valley that appeared to give access to Everest from the south-west and called it the West or Western Cwm. (A combe or coombe is a deep valley; Mallory, who had done most of his British climbing in Snowdonia, preferred the Welsh version.) But Mallory found it 'cold and forbidding', the glacier 'terribly steep and broken', although he also felt that the South-east Ridge provided a reasonable route to the summit. In 1935 the New Zealander L.V. Bryant photographed the cwm from the same place. In 1950 the indomitable Bill Tilman, together with the American Dr Charles Houston, ventured up the Khumbu Glacier and concluded that the manifestly unstable icefall below the cwm was an impossible barrier.

The British remained undaunted. A Himalayan Committee had succeeded the pre-war Everest

Committee and a young London doctor and climber, Michael Ward, proposed a reconnaissance to take a closer look. Ward was encouraged by photographs he had gathered, including Bryant's and Tilman's, and also several shots taken by British RAF pilots during unofficial reconnaissance flights from India at the end of the war. One provided a full-frontal view of the West Face of Lhotse at the head of the Western Cwm, suggesting that if the cwm could be broached, there was a clear traverse line across the face to the South Col. A second; equally promising, photograph showed the entire South-east Ridge, from the South Col to the summit, from which it appeared that there were no insuperable climbing difficulties.

At first the Himalayan Committee was sceptical, but Ward's case was pressed by several allies, including the respected Scottish climber, Bill Murray. And so, within a matter of months, the 1951 reconnaissance expedition set out on foot from the foothill town of Dharan, four weeks' walk from Everest. Murray and Ward were there, together with Tom Bourdillon and the charismatic Eric Shipton, veteran of all four British attempts of the 1930s and considered the finest British mountaineer of his day, who had been appointed expedition leader. They were joined en route by two New Zealanders, Earle Riddiford and Edmund Hillary.

The selection of the New Zealanders was typical

Shipton. The expedition was supposed to be solely British, and the British remained resolute in excluding the Swiss, as they had done between the wars; when the Swiss Alpinist Rene Dittert applied to join the 1951 team, he was smartly turned down. But where New Zealand was concerned, Shipton took a different view. He had been impressed by the performance of the New Zealander Bryant during the 1935 reconnaissance, and had even thought of emigrating there. It was, he conceded, a 'momentary caprice' to invite Hillary and Riddiford to take part – but one which was to have 'far reaching results'.

At first Everest hid itself. From the Thyangboche Monastery, barely 15 miles away, it remains largely obscured by the great Nuptse-Lhotse Ridge. Only when the party headed beyond Thyangboche and along the Rongbuk Glacier did its members obtain the view they had long sought. On 30 September, Shipton and Hillary climbed to a point at 20,000 feet on the peak of Pumori. Revealed before them was the North-west Face of Everest and the whole of the Western Cwm. Shipton was transfixed.

'The whole of the North-west Face was visible,' he wrote. 'With our powerful binoculars we could follow every step of the route by which all attempts to climb the mountain had been made. How strange it seemed to be looking at all those well-remembered features from this new angle, and after so long an interval of time and varied experience; the little platform at 25,700 feet where we had spent so many uncomfortable nights, Norton's Camp VI at the head of the North-east Spur, the Yellow Band and the grim overhanging cliffs of the

The British reconnaissance expedition of 1951 comprised four British climbers and two from New Zealand. The leader, the mercurial Eric Shipton, is standing to the left of the group; next to him, left to right, are Bill Murray, Tom Bourdillon and New Zealander Earle Riddiford. Seated are Mike Ward and the second New Zealander, Ed Hillary, invited, with Riddiford, to take part thanks to Shipton's 'momentary caprice'.

*The 1951 team was
encouraged by unofficial
RAF reconnaissance
photographs taken in
1945. One of the most
significant (right) showed
the South Col, the snowy
ledge in the lower left of
the picture, and above it
the South-east Ridge, with
a clear route to the
summit. But the 1951
team was stopped by the
giant crevasse (far right)
just below the Western
Cwm.*

Black Band, the Second Step and the Great Couloir. They were all deep in powder snow as when I had last seen them in 1938.'

There was more. 'The most remarkable and unexpected aspect of the view,' Shipton went on, was that he and Hillary could see the length of the Western Cwm and beyond, to the West Face of Lhotse, the South Col and the slopes between them. Guessing that the head of the cwm was around 23,000 feet, some 2,000 feet higher than they had predicted, they saw a 'perfectly straightforward route' to 25,000 feet on Lhotse and from there a traverse to the South Col. 'The sudden discovery of a practicable route from the West Cwm to the South Col was most exciting.' There remained the small matter of the Icefall. For the next month, interspersed with trips to neighbouring valleys and peaks, the team probed for a route through.

It was a daunting place, 'a wild labyrinth of ice-walls, chasms and towers', Shipton wrote, with hip-deep snow, rarely a clear view ahead, and constant apprehension that the pinnacles around

them would collapse or that the ice-blocks they walked on would drop away.

On their final foray, at the end of October, they reached the far side of the Icefall and were on the very lip of the Western Cwm, a sanctuary no human had ever visited, leading gently onwards to the heart of the Everest massif. But for the moment it lay beyond reach for a giant crevasse blocked their way. Bill Murray said the crevasse was the biggest he had seen. Splitting the glacier from side to side, it ranged between 100 feet and 300 feet wide, was at least 100 feet deep, and had a sheer ice-wall on the far side. 'We were defeated,' Murray wrote, and the team withdrew.

Shipton himself concluded: 'The fact that we had climbed the Icefall without mishap made the decision all the more difficult. But there was nothing for it but to submit, hoping that we would get another chance in the spring.'

*The southern approach:
with Tibet closed, the map
(right) shows the new
route to Everest through
Nepal found by the 1951
reconnaissance team.
After photographing
Everest from Pumori,
Shipton and his team
found a route through the
Khumbu Glacier and
Icefall to the entrance to
the Western Cwm. (The
dotted line shows the
boundary between Tibet
and Nepal.)*

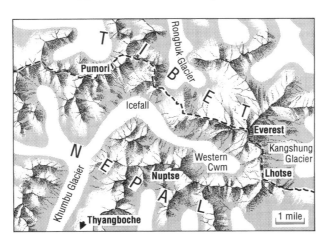

THE MYSTERY OF THE YETI

The 1951 reconnaissance expedition returned home not only with dramatic reports of a potential route to the summit; it also brought news of the yeti.

Otherwise known as the abominable snowman, the yeti had featured in Himalayan folklore for centuries. Stories of a creature, half-human, half-beast, which inhabited the kingdom of the snows were embedded in legends of the mountain kingdoms of Tibet and Nepal. 'Yeti' is a Nepalese word, while its alternative name derives from an imaginative translation of the Tibetan *metohkangmi* – literally 'filthy snowman'. There had been tales of the yeti from Himalayan travellers but most were second-hand and none had any satisfactory evidence.

This time it was different: the 1951 expedition had photographs. The principal picture (below, right) appeared quite convincing. It showed, clearly delineated in the snow, the single footprint of a creature with a large outer toe, three smaller ones alongside, and a well-defined heel. Judged against the head of an ice-axe, it measured 13 inches by 8 inches. There was a second photograph (below, left) showing a line of footprints in the snow. They were published in *The Times* on 6 December 1951 under the dramatic headlines: FOOTPRINTS OF THE 'ABOMINABLE SNOWMAN'.

Of all the purported evidence of the existence of the yeti, the 1951 footprints remain the single most persuasive item. But are they all they seem? When zoologists scrutinized the photographs they found it hard to imagine what kind of creature could have left such tracks. The Natural History Museum suggested they could have been made by a giant monkey; another expert theorised that the creature in question was a cross between an ape and a bear – a species as yet unknown. Other curiosities intruded: from the print in the snow it appeared that the ball of the creature's foot was concave, whereas in all known bipeds, including humans, it is convex.

Those who doubted the authenticity of the prints have focused their attentions on the man who took the photographs, Eric Shipton. Renowned for his part in the attempts of the 1930s, Shipton attracted respect and controversy in equal measure. He led the 1951 reconnaissance and was originally nominated to lead the 1953 bid. But his lack of organisational abilities and his prejudice against large expeditions told against him, and he was replaced by John – later Lord – Hunt.

Shipton was renowned for a mischievous sense of humour and for his liking for travellers' tales. Among his adversaries was the geologist Noel Odell, a colleague on the 1938 expedition. Shipton liked to tell how in 1924 Odell had collected some rock specimens which, befuddled by altitude, he had mistaken for sandwiches: the story, Odell said later, was 'complete nonsense'. Shipton also told of finding a notorious 'sex diary' beside the body of the solo climber Maurice Wilson; that too has proved untrue.

The sceptics suspected, in short, that Shipton fabricated the crucial 1951 print. There *was* a line of prints in the snow that day, made by a conventional animal such as a goat. By the sceptics' theory, Shipton embellished one of these prints, adding the thumb-like big toe, and etching the outline of the heel. He had conceived it as a joke on his colleagues but once the photographs had been published in *The Times* it was too late to admit the truth.

Curiously, no one remarked at first on the fact that the single print was markedly different from the prints in the line of tracks. Shipton himself ignored the difference in his own writings, but when finally challenged claimed that the pictures had been wrongly captioned by *The Times*.

Shipton's contemporaries were divided in their views. Two colleagues from the expedition, Bill Murray and Dr Mike Ward, insisted that he would not have perpetrated such a hoax; others, such as Sir Edmund Hillary, believe he could have done so. Shipton himself supplied a wry and possibly revealing comment in his account of the footprints for *The Times*. He conceded that they had 'aroused a certain amount of public excitement' but added that it was 'interesting, and perhaps a little sad, that the British Museum appears to have taken the matter more seriously than the Society for Psychical Research.'

The picture (left) *shows Mike Ward against a clear line of tracks; but the tracks are markedly different from the close-up of a supposed single footprint, as shown beside an ice-axe* (right).

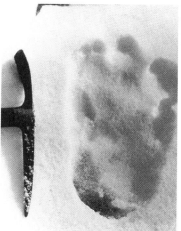

A NEW WORLD

by Raymond Lambert

The first climbers to attempt the Western Cwm approach, identified by the British in 1951, were the Swiss. Intensely frustrated at having been excluded from Tibet through the 1920s and 1930s, the Swiss seized their chance when the Nepalese government gave them permission for an expedition in 1952. After camping by the Khumbu Glacier they pushed a route through the hazardous icefall, overcoming the giant glacier which had blocked the British in 1951 and becoming the first humans to stand in the Western Cwm. They climbed the Lhotse Glacier to reach the next historic landmark, the South Col, where they embarked on their summit bid on 27 May. There were four men in the summit party: Raymond Lambert, an outstanding Alpinist, climbing with Tenzing Norgay, the Sirdar (leader) of the expedition Sherpas, who had been to Everest three times with the British; and the Swiss pairing of René Aubert and Léon Flory.

The Khumbu Icefall, shown in Doug Scott's 1972 photograph (left) was the barrier which stopped the British in 1951. Perpetually shifting, scored by monstrous crevasses, it has presented a perpetual hazard since. After negotiating it safely in 1952, the Swiss prepared for a summit bid headed by Raymond Lambert (left in picture, right) and Tenzing, who had added Norgay – 'the fortunate one' – to his name.

At ten in the morning, after the three Sherpas had vanished beyond the hump above the Col, we set out on two ropes of two men each, Aubert and Flory, Tenzing and myself, carrying one tent and food for one day. As soon as we left the zone of ice and stone, we broke into sheets of crusted snow. We made towards the base of the South-east Ridge, at the foot of a large buttress. The weather was clear, the intensity of the wind had diminished, as if it concentrated its anger upon the col itself.

Having reached the foot of the buttress, we were disillusioned. It was too steep. The rocks that overlooked us were undoubtedly negotiable at 13,000 feet, but not at 26,000 feet. Flory and Aubert pushed on 100 yards to make sure that the Eastern Face offered no way out, and they ran up against a slope of more than 60 degrees, which vanished into the sky.

So we returned in our steps, moving along the base of the large buttress and attacked the couloir which runs down it. The snow was good and the ascent easy. We made steps between the snow and the rock. We constantly relieved each other in the lead, we gained height quickly and the tents on the col already seemed small. Soon we reached the top of the couloir but the dry rocks allowed us to continue by moving over to the right. We waited for Aubert and Flory while taking oxygen like some precious liqueur; then we continued the climb straight up.

Suddenly I emerged on to the ridge above the large buttress and there discovered a new world, the whole Eastern Face of the mountain, plunging for more than 16,000 feet to the Kharta Valley and Tibet. And in the mist, on the far horizon, other chains of mountains broke through. Behind us the summit of Lhotse had fallen away; it was now no more than 300 or 400 feet above us. We were at about 27,500 feet.

It was fine and there was no wind. Both of us were fit. Should we sleep there without a primus and without sleeping-bags? Perhaps the next day . . . ? Tenzing interrupted my reflections.

'Sahib, we ought to stay here tonight!' He indicated the tent he had been carrying since the start. I smiled, for our thoughts had been pursuing the same course.

It took the Swiss five days to find a route through the Icefall. After passing through a couloir menaced by avalanches which they called 'Suicide Passage', they came to the giant crevasse just below the Western Cwm which stopped the British in 1951. They climbed down 60 feet and crossed it via a snow bridge, and then erected a rope bridge (above) which proved precarious but effective. Four weeks later they climbed to 26,300ft/ 8,016m on Lhotse and then, with Everest's South-east Ridge looming before them (picture far right), began the descending traverse to the South Col. After their failure in the spring of 1952, the Swiss returned for a second attempt in the autumn, but storms prevented them from getting little higher than the South Col.

Flory and Aubert joined us. Like us they were in good shape. They too might stay and try their luck the next day. This is doubtless what they desired. But there was only one tent and very little food. We had only set out to make a reconnaissance and to fix the site of Camp VII. In an undertaking like that, the party matters more than the individual; the individual is nothing without the party. In order that the privileged pair should have not only a chance of success but a possibility of returning, it has to be supported at the last camp by a second pair. Though its task might appear to be less brilliant, it needs men who are just as determined and in equally good physical shape – perhaps in better shape, since they should be capable of going to seek and bring back, whatever the risk, those who have taken their lives in their hands.

Between the four of us there was no argument. Aubert, who was one of those who found and saved me in the Combe Maudite in 1938, and Flory, reliable, cautious and determined, agreed to leave us. 'You two stay. We will wait for you at the col.'

We watched them move off, growing smaller and ever smaller down the slope, until they reached the col an hour later. Now we were only two! How many men and how much effort had been necessary to bring us to this farthest point of the expedition!

We pitched our tent with great difficulty. The altitude and the wind made our movements awkward. Our legs would not obey us and our brains scarcely functioned. Our hands were more skilful without gloves, but to take them off would cost us dear. The sun had gone down behind Nuptse and the temperature fell instantly. We took a last look towards Kangchenjunga and Tibet. Tenzing extended an arm westwards, pointing to a

disquieting sea of clouds. The horizon reddened.

In this improvised bivouac there were no sleeping-bags, no equipment, no primus. Only a tent which slapped in the wind like a prayer-flag. It was a glacial night. The whole being curled up as if seeking to create a mattress of air between its skin and itself. Our muscles stiffened and those of the face became fixed as if from an injection of anaesthetic. Slowly the cold penetrated the bones themselves. There was no question of sleep: the wind and the growling avalanches kept us awake. Which was just as well.

We were overtaken by a consuming thirst, which we could not appease. There was nothing to drink. An empty tin gave us an idea: a fragment of ice and the candle-flame produced a little lukewarm water. The gusts of wind made our heads whirl; it seemed to us that we took off with them into space, like those houses one thinks one sees moving when watching clouds in flight. To resist this vertigo, I tried to fix my thoughts on the next day's attack, and I mused on those who at all the stages were thinking of us. Aubert and Flory at the col, Dittert at Camp V, Wyss at the Base Camp. In a state of semi-hallucination the entire expedition seemed to me to be a stretched bow and ourselves the arrow. A poor blunted arrow at that. Could it reach its target?

This was the boundary between waking and sleeping. I dared not sleep, must not sleep. Tenzing shook me and I awoke, and I shook him in my turn. Amicably we beat one another and pressed close together throughout the night. In the sky the stars were so brilliant that they filled me with fear.

The shadows became clearer. The shape of Tenzing, rolled up like a ball, began to stand out from the background of the tent-cloth, which gradually grew lighter. Dawn entered the half-open tent and with it came anxiety. The wind hurled a handful of ice-needles into my face. Nevertheless, we had to open our eyes. The weather was not reassuring, for the sky was very dark to the west and south. The summits of Lhotse and Nuptse were hidden in a mass of dark clouds, and the valley was drowned in fog.

What should we do? We looked at each other, undecided, but once more we understood each other without speaking. I indicated the ridge with a wink and Tenzing answered by nodding his head. We had gone too far to give up. Our preparations were quickly made, for we had worn everything, except the crampons, from fear of frost-bite. They took longer to put on again, for our numbed hands were clumsy and bending over literally took our breath away. Laden with the last three canisters of oxygen, sufficient for six hours, we set off below the ridge on sheets of snow broken by bands of rock. One step, three breaths, one step . . . when we rested for a moment, we slobbered at the inhaler; it could only be used during a halt because the resistance of the valves was too great for our lungs when the effort of moving was added. At about every 20 yards we relieved each other in the lead to economize our strength and in order to inhale while letting the other pass. When the slope steepened we advanced like dogs following a scent, sometimes on all fours.

But the weather grew worse. Waves of mist passed, carried along on the south-west wind. Then the sun reappeared and reassured us. We rose slowly, terribly slowly. Nevertheless, we still rose.

In the clear intervals Lhotse emerged from the storm clouds and it was already below us. The whole landscape and all the summits fell away. The peaks which had seemed monstrous from the lower camps had lost their splendour; they became hills, like the Verte or the Jorasses, seen from Mont Blanc. But the clear intervals did not last; the dense fog, filled with a drift of frozen snow, enveloped us again. All our vital functions were slowed down. There was a confused impression of being on some other planet. Asphyxia destroyed our cells and our whole beings deteriorated.

At about eleven o'clock we came out again, on to the ridge, sinking deeply into the wind-crusted snow. There were no technical difficulties; the slope was rather easy and not too steep. We were rather fearful of the cornices to our right and we instinctively kept our distance.

Our pace became still slower. Three steps, a halt, oxygen. Three steps, a halt. Then came a clearing and we saw that the South Summit was at least 200 metres above us. Three steps, oxygen. I watched Tenzing. He seemed well but at moments he swayed a little, trying to find his balance. I tried to keep a watch on myself and asked myself: 'How do you feel? All right, quite all right.' This was euphoria, the worst of all dangers. I remembered the fifth and last bivouac on the Aiguilles du Diable: there, too, I felt well. How did Mallory and Irvine feel when they dissolved into the rarefied air of the North Ridge? Was this not the reason why they did not return?

Granulated snow struck our left cheeks increasingly hard. The wind became more evil. The South Summit was so close: just this band of rock where we were now engaged, the last; just that snow-crest. But no; it was impossible to go on. This was the end. We had taken five hours to gain 200 metres.

Once more the decision was taken without words. One long look and then the descent. Was it an altitude record? No. Failure. That is what we thought. But did we think? Our bodies were of lead, almost without spirit. There was no trace of automatism, for our muscles no longer obeyed our orders. Pick up your left foot and put it in front; now the other. Our tracks had almost entirely vanished. We stopped as often as on the ascent.

We passed the tent. The wind had begun to do its work; it was torn in two places. Would it last till the others could occupy it?

'Leave it there. Perhaps they will have better luck than us.'

And we went on, kept in motion only by the will to resist the lethargy that was invading us. We crouched as we dragged along, descending the couloir and the slope towards the col.

From the col to the tents there were a dozen yards uphill, an insignificant hummock of snow. We could do no more. Flory and Aubert dragged us into our tents, inert, at the limits of exhaustion. Tenzing sank into a deep sleep and did not move until the hour of departure.

For us the adventure was ended.

IT SEEMED LIKE A LIFETIME

by Sir Edmund Hillary

After the Swiss failure of 1952, the British prepared their 1953 attempt. Eric Shipton, who had headed the 1951 reconnaissance, was replaced as leader by John Hunt, an experienced mountaineer and a superb organiser. After finding a route through the ever-shifting Icefall, the team traversed the South face of Lhotse to reach the South Col, while support climbers and Sherpas ferried equipment, supplies and oxygen. On 26 May, Tom Bourdillon and Charles Evans pushed beyond the Swiss high point to the South Summit at 28,750 feet/8,763 metres. Two days later the second attempt began. George Lowe, Alf Gregory and Ang Nyima carried supplies up the South-east Ridge, followed by the New Zealand bee-keeper Ed Hillary and Tenzing Norgay, by now an Everest veteran. After helping to establish a precarious camp at 27,900 feet/8,500 metres, the support climbers descended, leaving Hillary and Tenzing to await the dawn.

An Everest icon: Charles Evans photographed by Tom Bourdillon at the South Summit of Everest, the first climbers ever to reach it. Less than 300 feet above them, the final summit seemed tantalisingly close, but they were too tired to go on.

At 4 am it was very still. I opened the tent door and looked far out across the dark and sleeping valleys of Nepal. The icy peaks below us were glowing clearly in the early morning light and Tenzing pointed out the Monastery of Thyangboche, faintly visible on its dominant spur 16,000 feet below us. It was an encouraging thought to realize that even at this early hour the Lamas of Thyangboche would be offering up devotions to their Buddhist gods for our safety and well-being.

We started up our cooker and in a determined effort to prevent the weaknesses arising from dehydration we drank large quantities of lemon juice and sugar, and followed this with our last tin of sardines on biscuits. I dragged our oxygen sets into the tent, cleaned the ice off them and then rechecked and tested them. I had removed my boots, which had become a little wet the day before, and they were now frozen solid. Drastic measures were called for, so I cooked them over the fierce flame of the Primus and despite the very strong smell of burning leather managed to soften them up. Over our down clothing we donned our windproofs and on to our hands we pulled three pairs of gloves – silk, woollen and windproof.

At 6.30 am we crawled out of our tent into the snow, hoisted our 30lb of oxygen gear on to our backs, connected up our masks and turned on the valves to bring life-giving oxygen into our lungs. A few good deep breaths and we were ready to go. Still a little worried about my cold feet, I asked Tenzing to move off and he kicked a deep line of steps away from the rock bluff which protected our tent out on to the steep powder snow-slope to the left of the main ridge. The ridge was now all bathed in sunlight and we could see our first objective, the South Summit, far above us. Tenzing, moving purposefully, kicked steps in a long traverse back towards the ridge and we reached its crest just where it forms a great distinctive snow-bump at about 28,000 feet. From here the ridge narrowed to a knife-edge and as my feet were now warm I took over the lead.

We were moving slowly but steadily and had no need to stop in order to regain our breath, and I felt that we had plenty in reserve. The soft unstable snow made a route on top of the ridge both difficult and dangerous, so I moved a little down on the steep left side where the wind had produced a thin crust which sometimes held my weight but more often than not gave way with a sudden knock that was disastrous to both balance and morale. After several hundred feet of this

rather trying ridge, we came to a tiny hollow and found there the two oxygen bottles left on the earlier attempt by Evans and Bourdillon. I scraped the ice off the gauges and was greatly relieved to find that they still contained several hundred litres of oxygen – sufficient to get us down to the South Col if used very sparingly. With the comforting thought of these oxygen bottles behind us, I continued making the trail on up the ridge, which soon steepened and broadened into the very formidable snow face leading up for the last 400 feet to the Southern Summit. The snow conditions on this were, we felt, distinctly dangerous, but as no alternative route seemed available, we persisted in our strenuous and uncomfortable efforts to beat a trail up it. We made frequent changes of lead on this very trying section and on one occasion as I was stamping a trail in the deep snow a section around me gave way and I slipped back through three or four of my steps. I discussed with Tenzing the advisability of going on and he, although admitting that he felt very unhappy about the snow conditions, finished with his familiar phrase 'Just as you wish'. I decided to go on.

It was with some relief that we finally reached some firmer snow higher up and then chipped steps up the last steep slopes and cramponned on to the South Peak. It was now 9 am. We looked with some interest at the virgin ridge ahead. Both Bourdillon and Evans had been depressingly definite about its problems and difficulties and we realized that it could form an almost insuperable barrier. At first glance it was certainly impressive and even rather frightening. On the right, great contorted cornices, overhanging masses of snow and ice, stuck out like twisted fingers over the 10,000 foot drop of the Kangshung Face. Any move on to these cornices could only bring disaster. From the cornices the ridge dropped steeply to the left until the snow merged with the great rock face sweeping up from the Western Cwm. Only one encouraging feature was apparent. The steep snow-slope between the cornices and the rock precipices seemed to be composed of firm, hard snow. If the snow proved soft and unstable, our chances of getting along the ridge were few indeed. If we could cut a trail of steps along this slope, we could make some progress at least.

We cut a seat for ourselves just below the Southern Summit and removed our oxygen. Once again I worked out the mental arithmetic that was

On 28 May came Hillary and Tenzing's turn. Photographed by Alf Gregory high on the South-east Ridge during their attempt, they made a powerful team: the phlegmatic and unassuming Hillary, 33, and Tenzing Norgay, at 39 making his seventh trip to the mountain.

Hillary (right) and Tenzing check each other's equipment on 25 May before embarking on their attempt from Camp IV at 21,000ft/6,401m in the Western Cwm. Using oxygen from the start to conserve their energy, they reached the South Col, 26,000ft/7,925m, the next afternoon, while Bourdillon and Evans were making their attempt. After a day spent waiting out a storm, Hillary and Tenzing left the South Col to begin their ascent in blessedly calm weather at 10 am on 28 May.

one of my main preoccupations on the way up and down the mountain. As our first partly full bottle of oxygen was now exhausted, we had only one full bottle left. Eight hundred litres of oxygen at three litres per minute? How long could we last? I estimated that this should give us four and a half hours of going. Our apparatus was now much lighter, weighing just over 20lb, and as I cut steps down off the Southern Summit I felt a distinct sense of freedom and well-being quite contrary to what I had expected at this great altitude.

As my ice-axe bit into the first steep slope of the ridge, my highest hopes were realized. The snow was crystalline and firm. Two or three rhythmical blows of the ice-axe produced a step large enough even for our oversized high-altitude boots and, the most encouraging feature of all, a firm thrust of the ice-axe would sink it halfway up the shaft, giving a solid and comfortable belay. We moved one at a time. I realized that our margin of safety at this altitude was not great and that we must take every care and precaution. I would cut a 40 foot line of steps, Tenzing belaying me while I worked. Then in turn I would sink my shaft and put a few loops of the rope around it and Tenzing, protected against a breaking step, would move up to me. Then once again as he belayed me I would go on cutting. In a number of places the overhanging ice cornices were very large indeed and in order to escape them I cut a line of steps down to where the snow met the rocks in the west. It was a great thrill to look straight down this enormous rock face and to see, 8,000 feet below us, the tiny tents of Camp IV in the Western Cwm. Scrambling on the rocks and cutting handholds in the snow, we were able to shuffle past these difficult portions.

On one of these occasions I noted that Tenzing, who had been going quite well, had suddenly slowed up considerably and seemed to be breathing with difficulty. From past experience I immediately suspected his oxygen supply. I noticed that hanging from the exhaust tube of his oxygen mask were icicles, and on closer examination found

that this tube, some two inches in diameter, was completely blocked with ice. I was able to clear it out and give him much-needed relief. On checking my own set I found that the same thing was occurring, though it had not reached the stage where it would cause me any discomfort. From then on I kept a much closer check on this problem.

The weather for Everest seemed practically perfect. Insulated as we were in all our down clothing and windproofs, we suffered no discomfort from cold or wind. However, on one occasion I removed my sunglasses to examine more closely a difficult section of the ridge but was very soon blinded by the fine snow driven by the bitter wind and hastily replaced them. I went on cutting steps. To my surprise I was enjoying the climb as much as I had ever enjoyed a fine ridge in my own New Zealand Alps.

After an hour's steady going we reached the foot of the most formidable-looking problem on the ridge – a rock step some 40 feet high. We had known of the existence of this step from aerial photographs and had also seen it through our binoculars from Thyangboche. We realized that at this altitude it might well spell the difference between success and failure. The rock itself, smooth and almost holdless, might have been an interesting Sunday afternoon problem to a group of expert rock climbers in the Lake District, but here it was a barrier beyond our feeble strength to overcome. I could see no way of turning it on the steep rock bluff on the west, but fortunately another possibility of tackling it still remained.

On its east side was another great cornice, and running up the full 40 feet of the step was a narrow crack between the cornice and the rock. Leaving

Photographed by George Lowe at 27,500ft/8,382m on the South-east Ridge, (above left), *Hillary (in the lead) and Tenzing, with Lowe, Gregory and Ang Nyima climbing in support, reached 27,900ft/8,503m before setting up Camp IX. They went for the summit at dawn the next day, 29 May.* Below: *Hillary and Tenzing relax at Camp IV after their triumph.*

The news of the ascent was relayed to London in code by The Times *correspondent James Morris. His dispatch inspired triumphal stories in the British press, published on Coronation Day, 2 June. 'The crowning glory' proclaimed the* News Chronicle; *the* Daily Express *headline was 'All this and Everest too'.*

Tenzing to belay me as best he could, I jammed my way into this crack, then kicking backwards with my crampons I sank their spikes deep into the frozen snow behind me and levered myself off the ground. Taking advantage of every little rock hold and all the force of knee, shoulder and arms I could muster, I literally cramponned backwards up the crack, with a fervent prayer that the cornice would remain attached to the rock. Despite the considerable effort involved, my progress although slow was steady, and as Tenzing paid out the rope I inched my way upwards until I could reach over the top of the rock and drag myself out of the crack on to a wide ledge. For a few moments I lay regaining my breath and for the first time really felt the fierce determination that nothing now could stop us reaching the top. I took a firm stance on the ledge and signalled to Tenzing to come on up. As I heaved hard on the rope Tenzing wriggled his way up the crack and collapsed exhausted at the top like a giant fish when it has just been hauled from the sea after a terrible struggle.

I checked both our oxygen sets and roughly calculated our flow rates. Everything seemed to be going well. Probably owing to the strain imposed on him by the trouble with his oxygen set, Tenzing had been moving rather slowly but he was climbing safely, and this was the major consideration. His only comment on my enquiring of his condition was to smile and wave along the ridge. We were going so well at three litres per minute that I was determined now if necessary to cut down our flow rate to two litres per minute if the extra endurance was required.

The ridge continued as before. Giant cornices on the right, steep rock slopes on the left. I went on cutting steps on the narrow strip of snow. The ridge curved away to the right and we had no idea where the top was. As I cut around the back of one hump, another higher one would swing into view. Time was passing and the ridge seemed never-ending. In one place, where the angle of the ridge had eased off, I tried cramponning without cutting steps, hoping this would save time, but I quickly realized that our margin of safety on these steep slopes at this altitude was too small, so I went on step-cutting. I was beginning to tire a little now. I had been cutting steps continuously for two hours, and Tenzing, too, was moving very slowly. As I chipped steps around still another corner, I wondered rather dully just how long we could keep it up. Our original zest had now quite gone and it was turning more into a grim struggle. I then realized that the ridge ahead, instead of still monotonously rising, now dropped sharply away, and far below I could see the North Col and the Rongbuk Glacier. I looked upwards to see a narrow snow ridge running up to a snowy summit. A few more whacks of the ice-axe in the firm snow and we stood on top.

My initial feelings were of relief – relief that there were no more steps to cut, no more ridges to traverse and no more humps to tantalize us with hopes of success. I looked at Tenzing and in spite of the balaclava, goggles and oxygen mask all encrusted with long icicles that concealed his face, there was no disguising his infectious grin of pure delight as he looked all around him. We shook hands and then Tenzing threw his arm around my shoulders and we thumped each other on the back until we were almost breathless. It was 11.30 am. The ridge had taken us two and a half hours, but it seemed like a lifetime.

THE GREAT MYSTERY

by Tenzing Norgay

I have thought much about what I will say now – of how Hillary and I reached the summit of Everest. Later, when we came down from the mountain, there was much foolish talk about who got there first. Some said it was I, some Hillary. Some that only one of us got there – or neither. Still others, that one of us had to drag the other up. All this was nonsense. And in Kathmandu, to put a stop to such talk, Hillary and I signed a statement in which we said, 'We reached the summit almost together.' We hoped this would be the end of it. But it was not the end. People kept on asking questions and making up stories. They pointed to the 'almost' and said, 'What does that mean?' Mountaineers understand that there is no sense to such a question; that when two men are on the same rope they are together, and that is all there is to it. But other people did not understand. In India and Nepal, I am sorry to say, there has been great pressure on me to say that I reached the summit before Hillary. And all over the world I am asked, 'Who got there first? Who got there first?'

Again I say, 'It is a foolish question. The answer means nothing.' And yet it is a question that has been asked so often – that has caused so much talk and doubt and misunderstanding – that I feel, after long thought, that the answer should be given. As will be clear, it is not for my own sake that I give it. Nor is it for Hillary's. It is for the sake of Everest and the generations after us. 'Why,' they will say, 'should there be a mystery to this thing? Is there something to be ashamed of? To be hidden? Why can we not know the truth?' . . . Very well: now they will know the truth. Everest is too great, too precious, for anything but the truth.

A little below the summit Hillary and I stopped. We looked up. Then we went on. The rope that joined us was 30 feet long, but I held most of it in loops in my hand, so that there was only six feet

The crowning moment: Tenzing Norgay on the summit of Everest, holding aloft his ice-axe bearing the flags of the United Nations, Britain, Nepal and India. This was the second of three summit photographs of Tenzing taken by Hillary – 'hoping that one would come out'. Tenzing wrote afterwards that he had offered to take Hillary's photograph, but Hillary declined. Tenzing eventually revealed the truth about who had reached the summit first in his ghosted autobiography, Tiger of the Snows, *published in 1955. Although usually described as a Nepalese Sherpa, Tenzing was in fact born in Tibet.*

between us. I was not thinking of 'first' and 'second'. I did not say to myself, 'There is a golden apple up there. I will push Hillary aside and run for it.' We went on slowly, steadily. And then we were there. Hillary stepped on top first. And I stepped up after him.

So there it is – the answer to the 'great mystery'. And if, after all the talk and argument, the answer seems quiet and simple I can only say that that is as it should be. Many of my own people, I know, will be disappointed at it. They have given a great and false importance to the idea that it must be I who was 'first'. These people have been good and wonderful to me, and I owe them much. But I owe more to Everest – and to the truth. If it is a discredit to me that I was a step behind Hillary, then I must live with that discredit. But I do not think it was that. Nor do I think that, in the end, it will bring discredit on me that I

tell the story. Over and over again I have asked myself, 'What will future generations think of us if we allow the facts of our achievement to stay shrouded in mystery? Will they not feel ashamed of us – two comrades in life and death – who have something to hide from the world?' And each time I asked it the answer was the same: 'Only the truth is good enough for the future. Only the truth is good enough for Everest.'

Now the truth is told. And I am ready to be judged by it. We stepped up. We were there. The dream had come true . . .

Tenzing was widely feted after his ascent, the Nehru family visiting him at his home in Darjeeling. He became the first Field Director of the Himalayan Mountaineering Institute, holding the post for 22 years. He married for a third time in 1964, and died in 1986. His son Jamling summitted Everest in 1996.

HOW WE CLIMBED CHOMOLUNGMA

by Wang Fu-chou and Chu Yin-hua

In 1960 an enormous Chinese expedition – 214 men and women, one third of them Tibetan – approached Everest from the north. After setting up Base Camp at the Rongbuk Glacier they followed the old pre-war British route, taking five weeks to reach the North Col. Climbing painfully slowly, they spent another six days reaching the Second Step at 28,200 feet/8,595 metres before retreating exhausted. Two weeks later they began restocking their lines of camps and on 24 May a four-man summit party left the top camp at 27,900 feet/8,500 metres to begin a second attempt. The overtly ideological report by two members of the summit party, Wang Fu-chou and Chu Yin-hua, together with the lack of technical detail in any Chinese account, left many western mountaineers sceptical towards their claimed ascent.

The authors of the Chinese account, Wang Fu-chou (left) and Chu Yin-hua (right), were Communist Party members. Aged 25 in 1960, Wang was a geologist from Peking, accorded the status of Master of Sports. Chu, 25, another Master of Sports, was a lumberjack from Szechuan province. According to expedition leader Shih Chan-Chun, Wang and Chu had been climbing for only two years before attempting Everest. Shih attributed their success to 'the leadership of the Communist Party and the unrivalled superiority of the socialist system of our country – without all this, we, the ordinary workers, peasants and soldiers, could never have succeeded.'

In the evening of 23 May, after six days of exhausting march, we 13 members of the Chinese mountaineering expedition, led by deputy leader Hsu Ching, reached the Final Assault Camp at 8,500 metres above sea-level. That night we ate very little food. The decision made at the Party meeting to launch the final assault on the summit was like a bugle call for frontline soldiers to push forward against the enemy. We could not suppress our excitement. The thought that we would make the final assault on Mount Chomolungma the next day kept us awake almost the whole night.

On the morning of the 24th, the sky over Chomolungma was clear and serene. According to the weather forecast, it was an ideal day for the ascent. The four team members assigned for the final assault – Gonpa, Liu Lien-man and the writers – after drinking plenty of water and putting rucksacks on our backs, were all set for the task. However, we were confronted with serious difficulties right away. We discovered that we had not sufficient oxygen left. Furthermore, deputy leader Hsu Ching could not be with us, as he had to stay at the Final Assault Camp to direct the whole operation as well as make all necessary arrangements to call for assistance in case of need. During the acclimatization marches, he had always been in the lead to make reconnaissance or open

up roads, but now he was in a state of exhaustion. He obviously felt sorry that he could not go along with us and tears came down his cheeks. With a warm heart he said encouragingly, 'I'll stay here to welcome your successful return!' With tears in our eyes, we also assured him that we would not fail the Party and the people's expectations and would conquer the highest peak of the world. Then with a deep feeling we set off to climb the last 350 metres of Chomolungma.

Soon, all four of us reached the famous Second Step, which is 8,600 metres above sea level. No wonder the British adventurers were stopped short here, and described it as the last hundredweight blow. The step is a sheer cliff of some 30 metres high, with an average gradient of 60 to 70 degrees.

We cleverly skirted around the slope in a direction parallel to the base. But near the top of the step a three metre high vertical rock slab suddenly stood in our way. Liu Lien-man blazed the trail but failed in all his four attempts to open up a way. After each fall, it took him 10 to 15 minutes to get up again. Now he was completely exhausted. This made Chu Yin-hua impatient. He took off his heavy cramponned boots and thick woollen socks. Gripping the crevice with his hands and stepping on the rock surface with his feet, he tried to climb up. But twice he failed and fell down. Then snow began to swirl in the air, which made the climbing all the more difficult. What was to be done? Turn back like the British climbers had done before? No! Certainly not! The whole Chinese people and the Party were watching us. The moment we thought of the big send-off we got at the Base Camp with the beating gongs and drums and loud cheers, the solemn pledge we had taken before we started out, and the national flag and the plaster bust of Chairman Mao which we took along, we felt all powerful again. After taking some oxygen and a short rest, we were determined to climb to the top. This time, Liu Lien-man made use of his experience as a fireman. The short ladder method was employed. He crouched and let Chu Yin-hua step on his shoulders, and with great effort he stood up. Good! Chu Yin-hua got on the rock slab, and then Gonpa too. All of us were overjoyed at the success. It took us three full hours to get on top of this three metre high rock slab.

After walking about 100 metres on top of the Second Step, Liu Lien-man fell down. With great exertion he managed to stand up and march forward again. But after a few steps, he fell again. He did not utter one word, so the rest of us didn't pay any attention. But when he fell for the third time, we began to realize that this veteran mountaineer was completely exhausted and couldn't go any further. And the oxygen he had brought along seemed to be exhausted too. It was then seven o'clock in the evening, and we had another 180 metres to cover before reaching the summit. The oxygen reserves we brought along were also running low. Liu Lien-man is an experienced and skilful climber and a staunch Party member. Without him our ascent to the summit would be much more difficult. On the other hand, how could we leave him at an altitude of 8,700 metres with such thin air? It was too dangerous! Of course, we could sacrifice our personal interests and leave the little oxygen we had to him. But that would endanger our successful assault on the summit. In this dilemma, we did not know what to do. Then the three Communist Party members,

Liu and the writers, held an emergency meeting on the highest peak of the world. At the meeting, Liu was still full of hope of our success. He said, 'Press on. Be sure to finish the job! I'll be alive here to welcome you back.' It was also decided at the meeting that we should get on top of the peak even without oxygen. Liu was then helped to a safe shelter below a cliff, and we said goodbye to him with tears in our eyes. Though he wasn't with us his noble spirit gave us great strength to score the final victory.

In front of us, at 8,700 metres, there was another ice and snow slope. We laboured forward painstakingly in knee-deep snow. For every few steps we had to halt to catch our breath. In scaling a one-metre rock in our way, all three of us slipped several times. It was almost midnight when we got through this stretch of ice and snow.

It was getting darker and darker and we were getting weaker and weaker for every inch we made forward. Then we were confronted with another sheer icy cliff. We were forced to trudge along the northern slope and circle around the cliff westward towards the ridge in the north-west. We were just about to ascend when we discovered our oxygen reserves were all out! At that moment, we remembered the decision made at the Party meeting and Liu Lien-man's words of encouragement, which filled us with confidence to plant our national flag on the summit. We had already reached 8,830 metres above sea-level and nothing would make us turn back! But our legs refused to carry us any further, so we had to go on all fours. Gonpa took the lead, and we two followed closely behind. Onwards, and onwards! We forgot time and cold. Suddenly we noticed Gonpa had disappeared. With a great surprise we looked upward. We spotted a shadow on top of the towering peak just a few metres away. It was Gonpa himself! We were overjoyed with excitement. Immediately, we forgot our fatigue, and great strength seemed to come back to us. When we went up to the top, we found there was another peak, still a few metres higher than the one we had just surmounted. That was the highest point of Chomolungma. Then we made our final assault with still greater exertion. Breathing became so difficult that each inch forward meant tremendous efforts. The last few metres of ascent took us no less than 40 minutes.

At this time, we saw the star-studded sky above us on the top peak of Chomolungma. To the south of the crest was gleaming white snow, and to the north was nothing but dull grey rocks. We stood on an oval shaped space, the boundary line between snow and the rocks.

We stayed upon the crest for about 15 minutes.

When the Chinese made their second ascent of Everest in 1975, they took pains to erect a red-painted metal tripod on the summit as evidence of their success. After doubts had been expressed in the west about the new Chinese claim, climbers from Chris Bonington's South-west Face Expedition found the tripod when they reached the summit four months later. The Chinese scored a further point over the mountain's name. In 1960, their use of Chomolungma appeared as another overtly ideological act, a rejection of the allegedly colonialist Everest in favour of the original Tibetan appellation. But Chomolungma – 'Goddess mother of the world' – became increasingly used by westerners alive to local sensibilities (the name Sagarmatha, asserted by the government of Nepal, also found favour).

The Chinese described their 1975 ascent as extravagantly as in 1960. The summit party (above) 'demonstrate the heroism of the Chinese people, for whom there are no unscalable heights or unvanquishable fortresses'. There is no mention in the Chinese account of placing a ladder against the corner that forms the highest section of the Second Step, which has been used by every climber ascending the step since.

We placed the Chinese national flag and a plaster bust of Chairman Mao Tse-tung separately on a great rock to the north-west of the summit and covered them with small stones. Then in accordance with international usage, we pencilled a note with our signatures and placed it under a heap of rocks. We were speechless, but our hearts were filled with joy and excitement. We had successfully completed the task the Party and Chairman Mao Tse-tung had entrusted to us.

After a short stay on the summit, we started to descend. The great excitement overshadowed our extreme fatigue. We were worried about our comrade Liu Lien-man. The day was breaking when we came down from the snow-covered slope. In the distance we could see Liu Lien-man still there alive. We learned that after we had departed,

Liu found out that he still had some oxygen left, but he didn't take any for himself. He thought of his comrades battling towards the summit of Chomolungma, and wrote in his diary that the oxygen was reserved specially for them. Finally he fell into a state of semi-consciousness. As soon as we found out what he had done, and as he offered us his breathing apparatus and a piece of candy which he had saved for a long time, we were all moved to tears by his noble character and embraced him and kissed him.

Soon the red sun rose slowly from the east behind the mountains, and shed its shining rays upon us. Ah, it was the shining light of our motherland! It was the shining light of the Party and Chairman Mao Tse-tung who gave us boundless strength and wisdom.

RIDICULOUSLY FAR-FETCHED?

The Chinese portrayed their ascent of Everest in 1960 as a triumph not merely of the human spirit but also of a political system. 'Summing up our conquest of Everest,' wrote expedition leader Shih Chan-Chun, 'we must in the first place attribute our victory to the leadership of the Communist Party and the unrivalled superiority of the socialist system of our country.'

It was in part assertions like these – even more ideological in content than the account by the summiteers, Wang Fu-chou and Chu Yin-hua – that brought unrestrained scepticism among western mountaineers over whether the Chinese had reached the summit at all. 'Propaganda is always suspect,' snorted the *Alpine Journal*.

The Chinese accounts were deficient in other respects valued by mountaineers. It seemed unlikely that a series of high-altitude party meetings could compensate for the inexperience of the climbers. It also seemed improbable that the Chinese party should have managed to climb through the night to reach the summit. Whether or not the propaganda was to blame, all the accounts were short on technical details. Nor was there a summit photograph – although that was a self-fulfilling corollary of the Chinese claim to have finished their ascent in the dark. A further commentary in the *Alpine Journal* concluded that 'the Chinese claim, though not impossible, must be considered as non-proven.'

Over the years the mountaineering world has softened in its view. There had been doubts over a photograph which the Chinese claimed to have taken soon after dawn at 8,700 metres during their descent; on closer analysis, their claim looked credible. The Chinese account of reaching the summit in semi-darkness without oxygen became less risible when western climbers accomplished the same feats. Then there was Chu Yin-hua's heroic tale of removing his boots and socks to climb the Second Step: surely not even the

The Chinese looking at the remains of Camp 5 used by the British expedition in 1933

Everest climbers of 1933 say Chinese claim unsure

NO DETAILS OF CRITICAL STEPS

BY OUR OWN REPORTER

Three British veterans of the North face of Mount Everest agreed last night that the film the Chinese claim records a successful assault on the mountain does not, in fact, substantiate that claim. On the evidence of the film alone, the verdict must remain "not proven."

Sir Percy Wyn-Harris, former Governor of Gambia, Professor Lawrence Wager, of the chair of geology at Oxford, and Mr Jack Longland, director of education for Derbyshire, saw the film at a special showing arranged by the "Guardian" in London last night.

To refresh their memories of their own climb in 1933 (Sir Percy alone of the three returned to Everest in 1936) they also saw film taken during that attempt.

The two sets of film tallied right up to the point where the fifth camp of the 1933 expedition was reached by the Chinese. Their film showed the ruins of the camp, which the earlier film showed the British mountaineers repitching.

The Guardian's front-page story reflected scepticism over the 1960 ascent. But most experts later accepted the Chinese claim, and the summit climbers appear in official lists of ascents.

most determined Party member would take self-sacrifice to such lengths. That, too, became plausible when he showed visiting American climbers his toe-less feet. Finally, Chris Bonington went to Peking and talked at length with the 1960 leader, Shih Chan-Chun, returning to declare that he had 'no shadow of a doubt' about the Chinese ascent.

Some western authorities remained cynical, even when the Chinese claimed a second ascent in 1975. *Mountain* magazine described this as 'ridiculously far-fetched' but the last word was with the Chinese. Four months later the British South-west Face expedition reached the summit to find a six-foot tripod defiantly anchored there as evidence of the Chinese success.

PROMISES TO KEEP

by Tom Hornbein

In 1963 came the Americans' turn. Led by Norman Dyhrenfurth, their expedition had two aims: to reach the summit by the British South Col route; and to forge a new route up Everest's West Ridge, with the further objective of descending via the South Col and thus making the first traverse of the mountain. The twin objectives caused conflict in the expedition, with most of its resources being pledged to the South Col teams. Two men clung to the vision of climbing the West Ridge: US anaesthesiologist Dr Tom Hornbein and philosopher and mountain guide Willi Unsoeld. After Jim Whittaker and Nawang Gombu had reached the summit via the South Col on 1 May, Hornbein and Unsoeld battled through storms on the West Ridge to reach a tenuous bivouac site at 27,250 feet/8,305 metres on 21 May, poised for their summit bid.

Everest's West Ridge (left) soars 5,000 feet from the West Shoulder, with Tom Hornbein and Willi Unsoeld shown in the foreground of Barry Bishop's photograph. After climbing 1,000 feet up the ridge, the team struck out on to the North Face and followed the deep cleft now known as the Hornbein Couloir. Hornbein (above) took the title of his account from a poem by Robert Frost: '. . . And I have promises to keep/And miles to go before I sleep.'

At four the oxygen ran out, a most effective alarm clock. Two well-incubated butane stoves were fished from inside our sleeping-bags and soon bouillon was brewing in the kitchen. Climbing into boots was a breathless challenge to balance in our close quarters. Then overboots, and crampons.

'Crampons, in the tent?'

'Sure,' I replied, 'It's a hell of a lot colder out there.'

'But our air mattresses!'

'Just be careful. We may not be back here again, anyway. I hope.'

We were clothed in multilayer warmth. The fishnet underwear next to our skin provided tiny air pockets to hold our body heat. It also kept the outer layers at a distance which, considering our weeks without a bath, was respectful. Next came Duofold underwear, a wool shirt, down underwear tops and bottoms, wool climbing pants, and a lightweight wind parka. In spite of the cold, our down parkas would be too bulky for difficult climbing, so we used them to insulate two quarts of hot lemonade, hoping they might remain unfrozen long enough to drink during the climb. Inside the felt inner liners of our reindeer-hair boots were innersoles and two pairs of heavy wool socks. Down shells covered a pair of wool mittens. Over our oxygen helmets we wore wool balaclavas and our parka hoods. The down parka lemonade-muff was stuffed into our packs as padding between two oxygen bottles. With camera, radio, flashlight, and sundry mementoes (including pages from Emerson's diary), our loads came close to 40lb. For all the prior evening's planning it was more than two hours before we emerged.

I snugged a bowline about my waist, feeling satisfaction at the ease with which the knot fell together beneath heavily mittened hands. This was part of the ritual, experienced innumerable times before. With it came a feeling of security, not from the protection provided by the rope joining Willi and me, but from my being able to relegate these cold grey brooding forbidding walls, so high in such an unknown world, to common reality – to all those times I had ever tied into a rope before: with warm hands while I stood at the base of sun-baked granite walls in the Tetons, with cold hands on a winter night while I prepared to tackle my first steep ice on Longs Peak. This knot tied me to the past, to experiences known, to difficulties faced and overcome. To tie it here in this lonely morning on Everest brought my venture into contact with the known, with that which man might do. To weave the knot so smoothly with clumsily mittened hands was to assert my confidence, to assert some competence in the face of the waiting rock, to accept the challenge.

Hooking our masks in place we bade a slightly regretful goodbye to our tent, sleeping-bags, and the extra supply of food we hadn't been able to eat. Willi was at the edge of the ledge looking up the narrow gully when I joined him.

'My oxygen's hissing, Tom, even with the regulator turned off.'

For the next 20 minutes we screwed and

Of its twin targets, the 1963 US expedition completed a South Col ascent first. Above, *the South Col team traverses the Lhotse Face, with the Geneva Spur immediately ahead, the South Col and South-east Ridge beyond. The first South Col pair, James Whittaker and Nawang Gombu, reached the summit on 1 May. A second South Col pair, Barry Bishop and Lute Jerstad, made their bid on 22 May, the day when Hornbein and Unsoeld went for the summit from the West Ridge.*

Pages 80/81: *Sherpas photographed by Al Auten as they skirt a series of crevasses in the Western Cwm, with the plunging buttresses of Nuptse in the background.*

unscrewed regulators, checked valves for ice, to no avail. The hiss continued. We guessed it must be in the valve, and thought of going back to the tent for the spare bottle, but the impatient feeling that time was more important kept us from retracing those 40 feet.

'It doesn't sound too bad,' I said. 'Let's just keep an eye on the pressure. Besides if you run out we can hook up the sleeping T and extra tubing and both climb on one bottle.' Willi envisioned the two of us climbing Everest in lockstep, wed by six feet of rubber hose.

We turned to the climb. It was ten minutes to seven. Willi led off. Three years before in a tent high on Masherbrum he had expounded on the importance of knee-to-toe distance for step-kicking up steep snow. Now his anatomical advantage determined the order of things as he put his theory to the test. Right away we found it was going to be difficult. The couloir, as it cut through the Yellow Band, narrowed to 10 or 15 feet and steepened to 50 degrees. The snow was hard, too hard to kick steps in, but not hard enough to hold crampons; they slid disconcertingly down through this wind-sheltered, granular stuff. There was nothing for it but to cut steps, zigzagging back and forth across the gully, occasionally finding a bit of rock along the side up which we could scramble. We were forced to climb one at a time with psychological belays from axes thrust a few inches into the snow. Our regulators were set to deliver two litres of oxygen per minute, half the optimal flow for this altitude. We turned them off when we were belaying to conserve the precious gas, though we knew that the belayer should always be at peak alertness in case of a fall.

We crept along. My God, I thought, we'll never get there at this rate. But that's as far as the thought ever got. Willi's leads were meticulous, painstakingly slow and steady. He plugged tirelessly on, deluging me with showers of ice as his axe carved each step. When he ran out the 100 feet of rope he jammed his axe into the snow to belay me. I turned my oxygen on to '2' and moved up as fast as I could, hoping to save a few moments of critical time. By the time I joined him I was completely winded, gasping for air and sorely puzzled about why. Only late in the afternoon, when my first oxygen bottle was still going strong, did I realize what a low flow of gas my regulator was actually delivering.

Up the tongue of snow we climbed, squeezing through a passage where the walls of the Yellow Band closed in, narrowing the couloir to shoulder-width.

In four hours we had climbed only 400 feet. It was 11 am. A rotten bit of vertical wall forced us to the right on to the open face. To regain the couloir it would be necessary to climb this 60 foot cliff, composed of two pitches split by a broken snow-covered step.

'You like to lead this one?' Willi asked.

With my oxygen off I failed to think before I replied, 'Sure, I'll try it.'

The rock sloped malevolently outward like shingles on a roof – rotten shingles. The covering of snow was no better than the rock. It would pretend to hold for a moment, then suddenly shatter and peel, cascading down on Willi. He sank a piton into the base of the step to anchor his belay.

I started up around the corner to the left, crampon points grating on rusty limestone. Then it became a snowploughing procedure as I searched for some sort of purchase beneath. The pick of my axe found a crack. Using the shaft for gentle leverage, I moved carefully on to the broken strata of the step. I went left again, loose debris rolling under my crampons, to the base of the final vertical rise, about eight feet high. For all its steepness, this bit was a singularly poor plastering job, nothing but wobbly rubble. I searched about for a crack, unclipped a big angle piton from my sling, and whomped it in with the hammer. It sank smoothly, as if penetrating soft butter. A gentle lift easily extracted it.

'Hmmm. Not so good,' I mumbled through my mask. On the fourth try the piton gripped a bit more solidly. Deciding not to loosen it by testing, I turned to the final wall. Its steepness threw my weight out from the rock, and my pack became a downright hindrance. There was an unlimited selection of handholds, mostly portable. I shed my mittens. For a few seconds the rock felt comfortably reassuring but cold. Then not cold any more. My eyes tried to direct sensationless fingers. Flakes peeled out beneath my crampons. I leaned out from the rock to move upward, panting like a steam engine. Damn it, it'll go; I know it will, T, I thought. But my grip was gone. I hadn't thought to turn my oxygen up.

'No soap,' I called down. 'Can't make it now. Too pooped.'

'Come on down. There may be a way to the right.'

I descended, half rappeling from the piton, which held. I had spent the better part of an hour up there. A hundred feet out we looked back. Clearly we had been on the right route, for above that last little step the gully opened out. A hundred feet higher the Yellow Band met the grey of the summit limestone. It had to get easier.

'You'd better take it, Willi. I've wasted enough time already.'

'Hell, if you couldn't make it, I'm not going to be able to do any better.'

'Yes you will. It's really not that hard. I was just worn out from putting that piton in. Turn your regulator clear open, though.'

Willi headed up around the corner, moving well. In ten minutes his rope was snapped through the high piton. Discarding a few unsavoury holds, he gripped the rotten edge with his unmittened hands. He leaned out for the final move. His pack pulled. Crampons scraped, loosing a shower of rock from beneath his feet. He was over. He leaned against the rock, fighting for breath.

'Man, that's work. But it looks better above.'

Belayed, I followed, retrieved the first piton, moved up, and went to work on the second. It wouldn't come. 'Guess it's better than I thought,' I shouted. 'I'm going to leave it.' I turned my oxygen to four litres, leaned out from the wall, and scrambled up. The extra oxygen helped, but it was surprising how breathless such a brief effort left me.

'Good lead,' I panted. 'That wasn't easy.'

'Thanks. Let's roll.'

Another rope-length and we stopped. After six hours of hiss Willi's first bottle was empty. There was still a long way to go, but at least he could travel ten pounds lighter without the extra cylinder. Our altimeter read 27,900. We called base on the walkie-talkie.

Willi: West Ridge to Base. West Ridge to Base. Over.

Base (Jim Whittaker, excitedly): This is Base here, Willi. How are you? How are things going? What's the word up there? Over.

Willi: Man, this is a real bearcat! We are nearing the top of the Yellow Band and it's mighty tough. It's too damned tough to try to go back. It would be too dangerous.

Base (Jim): I'm sure you're considering your exits. Why don't you leave yourself an opening? If it's not going to pan out, you can always start working your way down. I think there is always a way to come back.

Willi: Roger, Jim. We're counting on a further consultation in about 200 or 300 feet. It should ease up by then! Goddammit, if we can't start moving together we'll have to move back down. But it should be easier once the Yellow Band is passed. Over.

Base (Jim): Don't work yourself up into a bottleneck, Willi. How about rappeling? Is that possible or don't you have any reepschnur or anything? Over.

From their Camp IV at 25,100ft/7,651m, the West Ridge team struck out leftwards on the North Face, following the line of the Diagonal Ditch (above) which led to the foot of the Hornbein Couloir. Willi Unsoeld's photograph, taken on 21 May, shows five Sherpas carrying loads and following the tracks made by Al Auten and Jim Corbet.

The Hornbein Couloir proved the key to the ascent. Here, Willi Unsoeld leads a group to Camp V West at 27,250ft/8,305m. Hornbein had identified the gully as a possible ascent route from an Indian Air Force photograph.

cracks only added to our desire to go on. Too much labour, too many sleepless nights, and too many dreams had been invested to bring us this far. We couldn't come back for another try next weekend. To go down now, even if we could have, would be descending to a future marked by one huge question: what might have been? It would not be a matter of living with our fellow man, but simply living with ourselves, with the knowledge that we had had more to give.

I listened, only mildly absorbed in Willi's conversation with Base, and looked past him at the convexity of rock cutting off our view of the gully we had ascended. Above – a snowfield, grey walls, then blue-black sky. We were committed. An invisible barrier sliced through the mountain beneath our feet, cutting us off from the world below. Though we could see through, all we saw was infinitely remote. The ethereal link provided by our radio only intensified our separation. My wife and children seemed suddenly close. Yet home, life itself, lay only over the top of Everest and down the other side. Suppose we fail? The thought brought no remorse, no fear. Once entertained, it hardly seemed even interesting. What now mattered most was right here: Willi and I, tied together on a rope, and the mountain, its summit not inaccessibly far above. The reason we had come was within our grasp. We belonged to the mountain and it to us. There was anxiety, to be sure, but it was all but lost in a feeling of calm, of pleasure at the joy of climbing. That we couldn't go down only made easier that which we really wanted to do. That we might not get there was scarcely conceivable.

Willi was still talking.

Willi: Any news of Barry and Lute? Over.

Jim: I haven't heard a word from them. Over.

Willi: How about Dingman?

Jim: No word from Dingman. We've heard nothing at all.

Willi: Well listen, if you do get hold of Dingman, tell him to put a light in the window because we're headed for the summit, Jim. We can't possibly get back to our camp now. Over.

I stuffed the radio back in Willi's pack. It was 1 pm. From here we could both climb at the same time, moving across the last of the yellow slabs. Another 100 feet and the Yellow Band was below us. A steep tongue of snow flared wide, penetrating the grey strata that capped the mountain. The snow was hard, almost ice-hard in places. We had only to bend our ankles, firmly plant all 12 crampon points, and walk uphill. At last, we were moving, though it would have appeared painfully slow to a distant bystander.

Willi: There are no rappel points, Jim, absolutely no rappel points. There's nothing to secure a rope to. So it's up and over for us today . . .

While the import of his words settled upon those listening 10,000 feet below, Willi went right on:

Willi (continuing): . . . and we'll probably be getting in pretty late, maybe as late as seven or eight o'clock tonight.

As Willi talked, I looked at the mountain above. The slopes looked reasonable, as far as I could see, which wasn't very far. We sat at the base of a big, wide-open amphitheatre. It looked like summits all over the place. I looked down. Descent was totally unappetizing. The rotten rock, the softening snow, the absence of even tolerable piton

As we climbed out of the couloir the pieces of the puzzle fell into place. That snow rib ahead on the left skyline should lead us to the Summit Snowfield, a patch of perpetual white clinging to the North Face at the base of Everest's final pyramid. By 3 pm we were on the snowfield. We had been climbing for eight hours and knew we needed to take time to refuel. At a shaly outcrop of rock we stopped for lunch. There was a decision to be made. We could either cut straight to the North-east Ridge and follow it west to the summit, or we could traverse the face and regain the West Ridge. From where we sat, the West Ridge looked easier. Besides, it was the route we'd intended in the first place.

We split a quart of lemonade that was slushy with ice. In spite of its down parka wrapping, the other bottle was already frozen solid, as were the kippered snacks. They were almost tasteless but we downed them more with dutiful thoughts of calories than with pleasure.

To save time we moved together, diagonalling upward across down-sloping slabs of rotten shale. There were no possible stances from which to belay each other. Then snow again, and Willi kicked steps, fastidiously picking a route between the outcropping rocks. Though still carting my full load of oxygen bottles, I was beginning to feel quite strong. With this excess of energy came impatience, and an unconscious anxiety over the high stakes for which we were playing and the lateness of the day. Why the hell is Willi going so damned slow? I thought. And a little later: he should cut over to the ridge now; it'll be a lot easier.

I shouted into the wind, 'Hold up, Willi!' He pretended not to hear me as he started up the rock. It seemed terribly important to tell him to go to the right. I tugged on the rope. 'Damn it, wait up, Willi!' Stopped by a taut rope and an unyielding Hornbein, he turned, and with some irritation anchored his axe while I hastened to join him. He was perched, through no choice of his own, in rather cramped, precarious quarters. I sheepishly apologized.

We were on rock now. One rope-length, crampons scraping, brought us to the crest of the West Ridge for the first time since we'd left Camp 4 West yesterday morning. The South Face fell 8,000 feet to the tiny tents of Advance Base. Lhotse, straight across the face, was below us now. And near at hand 150 feet higher, the South Summit of Everest shone in the afternoon sun. We were within 400 feet of the top! The wind whipped across the ridge from the north at nearly 60 miles an hour. Far below, peak shadows reached long

across the cloud-filled valleys. Above, the ridge rose, a twisting, rocky spine.

We shed crampons and overboots to tackle this next rocky bit with the comforting grip of cleated rubber soles. Here I unloaded my first oxygen bottle though it was not quite empty. It had lasted ten hours, which obviously meant I was getting a lower flow than indicated on my regulator. Resisting Willi's suggestion to drop the cylinder off the South Face, I left it for some unknown posterity. When I resaddled ten pounds lighter, I felt I could float to the top.

The rock was firm, at least in comparison with our fare thus far. Climbing one at a time, we experienced the joy of delicate moves on tiny holds. The going was a wonderful pleasure, almost like a day in the Rockies. With the sheer drop to the cwm beneath us, we measured off another four rope-lengths. Solid rock gave way to crud, then snow. A thin, firm, knife-edge of white pointed gently towards the sky.

Buffeted by the wind, we laced our crampons on, racing each other with rapidly numbing fingers. It took nearly 20 minutes. Then we were off again, squandering oxygen at three litres per minute, since time seemed the shorter commodity at the moment. We moved together, Willi in front. It seemed almost as if we were cheating, using oxygen; we could nearly run this final bit.

Ahead the North and South Ridges converged to a point. Surely the summit wasn't that near? It must be off behind. Willi stopped. What's he waiting for, I wondered as I moved to join him. With a feeling of disbelief I looked up. Forty feet ahead, tattered and whipped by the wind, was the flag Jim had left three weeks before. It was 6.15. The sun's rays sheered horizontally across the summit. We hugged each other as tears welled up, ran down across our oxygen masks, and turned to ice.

Another icon: Lute Jerstad of the South Col team, photographed by Barry Bishop, approaches the summit. The US flag was planted by the first South Col team three weeks before. Jerstad and Bishop summitted at 3.15 pm on 22 May, three hours before Unsoeld and Hornbein. The four bivouacked at 28,000ft/8,534m during the descent, the highest Everest bivouac yet. Unsoeld and Bishop suffered frost-bite. In the morning support climbers Dave Dingman and Girme Dorje helped them down.

Frost-bite victims Bishop and Unsoeld wait to be flown from Base Camp to Kathmandu. Bishop lost several finger tips and all his toes; Unsoeld nine toes.

I WAS IN HEAVEN

by Sonam Gyatso and Sonam Wangyal

The Indians made two strong bids to climb Everest in 1960 and 1962, coming within 500 feet/150 metres of the summit. They succeeded in 1965, when Captain A.S. Cheema and Nawang Gombu (the first man to make two ascents) reached the summit on 20 May via the South Col. Two days later, Sonam Gyatso and Sonam Wangyal made their attempt.

Sonam Gyatso (top) and Sonam Wangyal (below) were two of nine members of the Indian expedition who reached the summit. Gyatso wrote: 'I asked my family to pray for me. Their prayers were answered.' For Wangyal, 'the dreams of my father had come true.'

Sonam Wangyal

May 22: 5 am. This was 'D-Day'. The winds were blowing furiously; their speed I estimated at 140 kilometres per hour. The tent walls were flapping and the whole tent was shivering and trembling. Come what may, we were determined to go ahead; never did we think of abandoning our attempt. Both Gyatso and I prayed fervently. We had, somehow, confidence that we would succeed; our faith in God could not be shaken. Gyatso had a small statue of Karmapa and a few prayer-flags which had been given to him by Rimpoche of Lachung. The prayer-flags had been given specially to ward off the evils of weather and protect us from the wrath of the elements.

Slowly and laboriously, but not reluctantly, we started getting ready. By 5.30 am the sun had come out. Lo and behold, the winds were dying down! We tried to contact the Advance Base Camp but did not succeed. We put on our crampons at 6.40 am and left the camp for the most cherished goal of all mountaineers. Could we make it? The question loomed large in our minds. It kept on recurring all the time. But we never lost hope.

Immediately we were out of the tent, we were on the sharp ridge known as 'the Razor's Edge'. Each step had to be cut carefully lest one was dashed down. One could not help seeing Makalu sparkling in the distance. It stood out in its splendid isolation and its snow-encrusted majestic wall was quite awe-inspiring.

Gyatso was leading but he found it difficult as the pain in his waist was cutting deep into his flesh. I asked him, 'Would you rather that we went back?' He gave a very emphatic, 'No'. He had an unshakeable feeling that he would succeed. He had been told by Karmapa and Rimpoche that he would do so. They could not be wrong.

Gyatso's determination gave me hope and increased my confidence. I took the lead on the rope. Slowly we went up as the moaning of the winds died down to a whine and then to a whisper. Two hours after we had left the last camp we reached the point where Cheema and Gombu had left their second oxygen bottle. We too dumped our half-used oxygen bottles there. We were now carrying only one full oxygen bottle each. Thank God, 13lbs of weight had been removed and we could increase our pace a little.

We kept advancing steadily and cautiously, getting nearer and nearer the South Summit. Occasionally a step had to be whacked out of the snow but mainly we chose to stay on the rocks on the left side of the ridge. Two hours later, we were on top of the ridge. From there we could see the final Summit Ridge which was not as difficult as the one which we had just surmounted. But we could not see the main summit. It was still a long way I thought. We had to continue with our effort, muster all our strength and go on and on till we reached our goal. At last there was no wind. The sun was sparkling over the snow and the glare was at times blinding.

We rested for five minutes. We had now to descend about 30 feet and it was a fairly steep slope. The cornices down below looked like ice flowers and looked so real that one had an irresistible desire to go down and pluck them. Gyatso belayed me, and gingerly I walked down the ridge on rock and snow. We were on the main Summit Ridge.

The ridge was not much corniced on its lower portion but we chose to walk on rocks. The Advance Base could be clearly seen from here. I was sure that I could even make out some of my colleagues moving about in the camp. They looked like tiny pebbles.

Our progress was slow. Gyatso was in severe pain

but he would not give up. We reached the rock chimney, called 'Hillary's Chimney'. On one side of it was rock, on the other was snow and a frightening crevasse below. Climbing the chimney was not difficult. After a short rest we were off again. There was a lot of ice and snow ahead of us. Then we came to a hump; we crossed it and saw another hump. This too was surmounted, and . . .

Joy of joys! We saw the summit hump and the Indian Tricolour fluttering from the American flag-pole. Both of us were excited beyond words. Gyatso forgot his pain. The last few steps to the peak of Everest, we walked side by side. It was 11.30 am when after six hours of trudging, climbing, heaving, belaying, kicking and whacking we reached the top. So this was it. We were on top of the world. When I was selected for the expedition I had asked my family to pray for me. Their prayers had been answered.

Both Gyatso and I fell down on our knees and prayed. We embraced each other, thumped each other on the back and shook hands. I must confess, I was a little frightened. I was new to Everest, the mountain overwhelmed me. The fear of getting back safely was suddenly uppermost in my mind. It was the same fear I had felt when I went first to the Icefall. Gradually that fear had dissolved, but now it came back.

I took out a flag-pole from my rucksack. It was a folding type. I buried it deep in the snow and hoisted the Indian national flag on it. Then I planted a yellow prayer-flag which had been given to me by my father. My father had given seven such flags and six of them had already been planted on other parts of Everest. A ring which my sister had given, I buried in the snow and stones of the summit.

The sun was bright and a gentle wind was streaming by gracefully. I bowed before the prayer-flag and prayed. Gyatso did the same. We got up and took in the view. There were clouds far far below us. The Thyangboche Monastery was glittering in the sun like a diamond in a setting of emeralds. The other peaks, lower down, looked like heaps of flour. Far away in the horizon, on the other side, we could see the verdant patches of the high plains of Tibet.

We stayed on the top for 50 minutes, hoisting various flags given to us by our friends and taking a number of photographs. I collected a few stones and a little snow from the summit as sacred mementoes. The snow I kept in a thermos flask. For a good 20 minutes, while we were on the summit, we did not use oxygen but when breathlessness was overpowering us, we resumed the breathing of oxygen from our oxygen bottles. We firmly put on our oxygen masks as we prepared to leave the summit.

Sonam Gyatso

The dream of 20 years of my father, Mr Rinzing Ngo Dup, had come true. I looked towards Rongbuk Monastery and saw clouds in the lower valleys. I saw the Rongbuk Glacier and the beautiful green patches. There were plenty of small peaks jutting out of the clouds all around us like thick needle-points. I felt very humble and offered a few Cadbury chocolates and sweets; I offered all I had to Chomolungma.

My approach to the mountains is religious. I revere them and hold the holy peaks in respect. I approach the mountains with humility. I love nature and have a passion for flowers, plants, rocks and snow.

Everest has always been sacred to me. In 1957, when I went to Nanda Devi, I had done so without informing my wife. In fact I had told her that I was going on some official duty. When she saw the report of the expedition in the newspapers and read about me, she was hurt and angry. She wrote a long letter of complaint. She was frightened of mountains and did not want any evil to come to me. On my return I had to assure her that mountains were the abode of gods and gods would not be cruel to me. I promised her that whenever I went on an expedition, I would each time collect some holy snow and stones of the mountain for her. So she had looked forward to my climb on Everest and I knew that she was waiting for the *parsad* [a sacred offering]. I took some sacred snow and holy rocks from the top of Everest for my wife. On the Everest peak I felt as if I was in heaven. There was nothing higher than us anywhere.

A scarf given to me by my wife was placed on the summit. Two idols, one of Lord Buddha and the other of Lord Krishna, given to me by my friends were planted there. Kohli had given me two pairs of rosaries, one belonged to Hari Dang, a member of the 1962 Indian Everest expedition, and the other had been given to Kohli by his father. These, too, were placed on the summit. A large Indian national flag on a strong flag-pole was planted permanently on the top of Everest by the side of the American flag-pole of 1963.

Guru Rimpoche had given me a small statue which too I placed on the summit but before leaving I picked it up and brought it back with me for my safety. Later when Guru Rimpoche asked me why I had brought back the icon, I said that I was frightened and needed its protection for the return journey. The Guru smiled and asked me to keep the idol always with me.

The leader of the Indian expedition was Mohan Kohli (above), *a navy officer who had taken part in the two previous Indian attempts. In 1965 there were four successful teams: the fourth consisted of Hari Ahluwalia and Sherpa Phu Dorji* (pictured below), *together with Harish Rawat.*

'ALL THE WORLD
LAY BEFORE US'

1970-1979

SORRY, HARSH, YOU'VE HAD IT

by Murray Sayle

The 1971 International Expedition was launched in the idealistic belief that a team of men and women from a dozen different nations could unite to meet a common challenge. Led by Norman Dyhrenfurth, it had two routes as its goals: one, the unclimbed South-west Face; the other, a direct version of the American West Ridge route of 1963. Sadly, the expedition soon fragmented, riven by personal and national rivalries. The highest point achieved, by the British Don Whillans and Dougal Haston, was around 27,400 feet/8,352 metres on the South-west Face. The most tragic incident came when the popular Indian Army officer Harsh Bahuguna, who had almost reached the summit in 1965, attempted to retreat from the West Ridge during a blizzard on 18 April. Sayle reported the episode for the London Sunday Times.

Companions Wolfgang Axt (left) from Austria and Harsh Bahuguna from India take a breather in the Khumbu Icefall. A few days later Bahuguna was fighting for his life.
Pages 88/89: *Doug Scott's transcendental summit shot of Dougal Haston at dusk on 24 September 1975. The comment is Scott's.*

Since we set off on this expedition, I considered Harsh Bahuguna one of my closest friends among the climbers. We often walked together on the march in, and talked about all sorts of things: his wife and two small daughters, his obsession with Mount Everest, and his career in the Indian Army.

Harsh – which in Sanskrit means 'happiness' – came from an Indian tribal group, the Garhwali, who are famous as soldiers and hill climbers (they are first cousins of the Gurkhas of Nepal). His uncle, Major Nandu Jayal, died in 1958 while attempting another Himalayan giant, Cho Oyu.

Harsh himself came within 800 feet of the summit of Everest as a member of the successful Indian Army expedition of 1965. His own attempt was delayed to the last of the Indian groups because of stomach trouble, and then a sudden break in the weather robbed him of his chance of the summit.

I was not alone in thinking that Harsh was a special friend – after his death, I found that at least two-thirds of the climbers were sure they were particularly close to him. But, if he had a special companion on the expedition, it was undoubtedly the Austrian Wolfgang Axt. They ate together, shared a tent on the march in and another at Base Camp, shared much of the dangerous work of forcing a passage up the Icefall (where they were outstanding) and they spent the last five days of Harsh's life together in a tiny tent perched high on the West Ridge of Everest.

They made odd, but clearly close friends. Axt is 6 feet 3 inches, beautifully built, and his approach to people, to life itself, is in terms of physical strength and endurance. He is married to the former Austrian women's 60 metre sprint champion; and no one has ever heard him discuss any other subjects but health diets, fitness, climbing mountains and related topics. He often told us how much he enjoyed climbing with Harsh.

The sequence of events which ended with Bahuguna's death and the subsequent dissensions began on the evening of 17 April, when a deputation called on Norman Dyhrenfurth, our Swiss-American joint leader, in his tent at the Advance Base Camp in the Western Cwm (Camp II, 21,700 feet), and presented something like an ultimatum. The visitors were Carlo Mauri, the Italian mountaineer and adventurer (he was a member of the Ra voyage), Pierre Mazeaud, the member of the French National Assembly who hopes one day to be Minister for Youth and Sport, and other members of the ridge team.

They said what everyone knew: that, largely because of the weather, the face route was looking hopeful and the ridge route, for which the deputation had opted, was lagging behind. Unless more Sherpa porters were switched to ferrying supplies to the ridge they said, then the whole ridge group should turn their efforts to the classical, 'easy' route – up the South Col.

Dyhrenfurth is a genial man who prefers discussion and consensus to giving orders. He was severely hampered by a bad case of high-altitude laryngitis, which he was trying to treat by inhaling steam from a pan of melted snow; but he did his best to explain that both he and the British joint leader, Colonel Jimmy Roberts (directing the Sherpa lift of supplies up the Icefall from Base Camp), were also disturbed about the supply situation. The Icefall, much trickier than usual, was absorbing a lot of Sherpa labour, and a log-jam of supplies was building up at Camp I, perched on an ice-cliff at the top of the fall. The answer, said Dyhrenfurth tactfully, was for the sahibs themselves to start carrying up some supplies.

The deputation had touched on a sore spot which, sooner or later, was bound to disturb an expedition like ours. No one enjoys the dull work of carrying supplies in support – climbing thousands of feet with a reel of rope, a couple of oxygen cylinders and a box of food, then dumping it and climbing down again. And at those altitudes, everyone seems to have a definite stock of energy, no more and no less, although the amount varies with individuals. Ambitious people who conserve their energies for the glamorous summit push are being no more than human.

Still, a story going around the expedition is that one eminent climber by mistake picked up the rucksack of another during a 'support' climb and found he could easily lift it with his little finger.

Base Camp for the 1971 International Expedition was this collection of tents amidst the jumbled moraine of the Khumbu Glacier, photographed by John Cleare under a dusting of snow. Later a five-day storm hit the expedition, compounding the problems with which it was beset.

The Khumbu Icefall was in particularly bad condition in 1971. It was raked by an avalanche at an early stage and the expedition took two weeks to find a safe route. Here three climbers are tackling the final crevasse before reaching Camp I at the entrance to the Western Cwm.

And, when our chapter of calamities began, there were only two oxygen bottles in the high camps on the face, only one on the ridge.

Not that all work on the two routes up Everest had ceased for lack of supplies. The same day as the deputation, Odd Eliassen of Norway and Michel Vaucher of Switzerland (Yvette's husband) completed a fixed-rope traverse across a steep ice-slope near the foot of the ridge, cutting out an unnecessary 300 foot descent before the final crossing of the glacier to Advance Base Camp. And, far up the ridge, Bahuguna and Axt had spent four days together moving Camp III, the first on the ridge, 1,000 feet nearer the summit.

That night the All-India Radio forecast bad weather for the Everest area. As we supply some of the data for this forecast, we assumed that the Indian broadcast was telling us about the unsettled weather we already had. In fact, the forecast well understated what was coming.

Next morning, 18 April, Norman Dyhrenfurth, reasoning that one good example is worth any amount of ordering or exhortation, set off alone to walk down the Western Cwm from Camp II to Camp I and collect a symbolic load of two cylinders of oxygen, and walk back.

I enter the story, very peripherally, at this point. About the same time, I set out from Base Camp to ascend the Icefall and examine the supply situation in the Western Cwm for myself. We were three on a rope: our Sirdar (boss) of the Sherpas, Sonam Girme, obligingly guiding two duffers, Dr Harka Gurung, the eminent Nepalese geographer, determined to do a bit of field work on his subject, and my clumsy self.

It started to snow as we strapped on our crampons. By halfway up, at a piece of ice we call 'The Dump', it was snowing hard, and by good luck I declined a suggestion that I should stay there overnight without food, fuel or a sleeping-bag.

We passed the final maze of ladders, ropes and log bridges in a freshening blizzard. The racing clouds descended until we could no longer see the tops of the ice-cliffs we were climbing; once, an avalanche of stones as big as barrels crashed out of the clouds 100 yards to our right. Snow smothered the trail a foot deep in an hour; towards the end, even our Sirdar started to lose his way. I got one leg up to the hip in a crevasse; the other two pulled me out.

After a six-hour ascent we arrived, not a moment too soon, in the middle of a ring of red tents – Camp I (20,500 feet), set on a thousand-ton ice-block entirely surrounded by crevasses 50 feet deep. As it happened we were the last people through the Icefall for more than a week. We found the two Americans, doctors David Isles and Dave Peterson, in charge of the camp, and they treated my frost-nipped toes. We were told that Norman Dyhrenfurth had just left for Camp II with his two symbolic bottles of oxygen.

We sat down in our madly flapping tents, powdery snow driving in through every crack, to wait out the blizzard. Only later did we learn something of the tragic events taking place a mile and a half up the cwm.

Dyhrenfurth's route took him close under the 5,000 foot face of Nuptse on his right, and already the mountain was beginning to growl with incipient avalanches as the blizzard plastered thick snow on the face. A small avalanche clipped his heels as he hurried towards Advance Base (Camp II), the snow obliterating the trail before his eyes (there are small but nasty crevasses all the way up the cwm). Then, away on his left, he heard a man shouting. The wind whipped the words away, but to Dyhrenfurth it sounded like a cry for help. He redoubled speed to Advance Base.

About the same time, Wolfgang Axt plodded exhausted and alone into Advance Base. His blond hair and beard were stiff with ice. The first person he met was Antony Thomas, a BBC director who is making a documentary on the climb. Axt's first words were 'Harsh is in difficulties up there.'

A concerned knot quickly gathered – Odd Eliassen of Norway, Michel Vaucher of Switzerland, Carlo Mauri of Italy, Pierre Mazeaud of France, Don Whillans and Dr Peter Steele of Britain. While Axt related, as well as his tired condition permitted, what had happened, they began preparations for a rescue attempt. Through the swirling snow, they could occasionally hear the same muffled shouts Dyhrenfurth had heard.

Both men were very tired, Bahuguna especially, said Axt, so at about 3.30 pm when the weather began to deteriorate seriously, they had decided to come down to Advance Base from Camp III.

All had gone well with the descent, Axt leading, until they reached the horizontal fixed rope traverse. Neither of them had seen it before, as Vaucher and Eliassen had installed it only the previous day.

These rope traverses are common in the Alps, where Axt has done most of his climbing, but less so in the Himalayas, where Bahuguna had gained most of his experience. A rope, slung horizontally between a series of ice pitons, enables a climber to cross an ice-wall, going sideways. The climber clips a carabiner (a sort of snap link) over the rope; this is in turn fastened to a harness round his body. He then propels himself along by using his hands on the rope, and digging the front points of his crampons into the ice at his feet.

The tricky part is where the rope, which is not completely taut, passes a piton: the last bit of rope is uphill and the climber must unclip, pass the piton without support, and clip on again.

Axt said that he had gone first along the rope traverse and round a corner where his companion was out of sight, then across an easier second section of the rope. At the end of the traverse he waited about 20 minutes; but then, feeling his feet beginning to freeze and the storm getting worse, he returned to Advance Base to get help.

As this was being told, Dr Steele called for a Sherpa volunteer to come with him and bring his resuscitation gear, and Ang Parba at once stepped forward, while Don Whillans collected as many ski sticks as he could lay hands on to mark a new path over the glacier moraine. The forlorn rescue effort set out through the blizzard at 5.15 pm, Michel Vaucher and Odd Eliassen in the lead, Whillans, Dr Steele, Ang Parba, Carlo Mauri and Pierre Mazeaud close behind.

Vaucher and Eliassen found the dying man still clipped to the traverse rope, at a point where he should have unclipped to pass a piton. He had lost a glove, his hands were frozen, his face was coated with ice and his protective clothing had been pulled up by his harness to expose his mid-section to the driving storm.

Asked by Eliassen, 'Are you okay?' he appeared to mumble an affirmative. The Swiss and the Norwegian were unable to move Bahuguna sideways, so they tried to lower him on a 130 foot rope which Eliassen had brought for the purpose. Meanwhile, at the foot of the ice-slope, Dr Steele, Mazeaud and the Sherpa were trying to find a level and sheltered spot for a resuscitation attempt. But the rope was 35 feet too short, as near as they could judge in the snow and darkness.

Whillans, who had been following the unsuccessful lowering operation, decided to try a last forlorn hope. Without an ice-axe or a protective rope, he clawed his way on the front points of his crampons across the steep ice-slope to where Bahuguna hung upside down by his harness from the end of the rescuers' rope. Whillans managed to right him. His face was blue; he was unconscious, with wide staring eyes. He was barely alive, and could not have lasted more than half an hour.

Whillans, clinging by his crampon points to the ice-cliff, had no way of getting the dying man up or down, and in a blizzard at night at 22,000 feet, had only one decision to make – although he said later it was probably the hardest of his life.

'Sorry, Harsh old son, you've had it,' he muttered, in a north-countryman's gruff farewell, and scrambled back over the ice.

Next morning, the climbers struggled through the storm to a breakfast of sorts in the 'Indian' tent – ironically, an Indian Army bell tent very like the ones used on the Everest expeditions in the 1920s. Major Bahuguna had borrowed it for our expedition. Rations were short and everyone deeply depressed. Axt came in, refreshed from his sleep. 'How is Harsh?' he asked cheerily. 'Ist tod,' someone said in German – 'He is dead.' Axt was thunder-struck, a pitiable spectacle. Grimfaced, Dyhrenfurth announced there would be an inquiry in the Indian tent, and directed Bill Kurban of the BBC to tape-record the brief proceedings.

Those concerned related what they knew in their own languages, except Odd Eliassen, who spoke English. Axt, normally bursting with self-reliance, had difficulty in enunciating his statement. Dyhrenfurth asked Axt only two questions, both in a hoarse whisper, difficult to hear against the raging storm.

'Why were you not roped together?'

'We had run out of rope in establishing the way to Camp III.'

'Why did you not go back along the traverse to look for Harsh after you had waited 20 minutes for him?'

'I was getting cold, I thought I had better fetch help.'

The blizzard raged a full week after that, and by the time it ended it was apparent to most of us that even the South Col route was no longer possible. If the supply lines can be re-established, if the weather holds, if morale can be restored then there is just a chance that something can be saved from the disasters we have faced.

After the tragedy, climbers and Sherpas attempted to drag Bahuguna's body back down the Western Cwm. But they were defeated by the still-raging storm and it was ten days before they could get through. Bahuguna's death soured the expedition further and some members went home. British climbers Don Whillans and Dougal Haston reached 27,400ft/8,352m before the expedition withdrew.

ALL THE WINDS OF ASIA

by Peter Boardman

In 1975 the British, led by Chris Bonington, made a fresh attempt on the South-west Face, following failures by at least six teams including the ill-fated international expedition of 1971. The key lay in overcoming the Rock Band, the formidable black cliff starting at 26,000 feet/7,925 metres. After Nick Estcourt and Tut Braithwaite found a route via a series of ramps and gullies, Doug Scott and Dougal Haston went to the summit on 24 September – the first British climbers to do so. They were rewarded with stupendous views and survived the highest Everest bivouac yet, at 28,750 feet/8,763 metres. Two days later Peter Boardman and Pertemba followed them to the top. As they started down, they were astonished to see the climber and cameraman Mick Burke making a solo attempt. Burke decided to press on, arranging to meet Boardman and Pertemba at the South Summit on his descent. Boardman's account of their anguished wait is one of the most affecting passages in mountaineering literature.

Peter Boardman (above) was 23 when Bonington asked him to join the 1975 team. Then working as a climbing instructor in Scotland, he had made several bold Himalayan ascents, and had impressed Bonington with his 'quiet maturity'. The climber in the background is Dave Clarke.
Right: *The South-west Face plastered with monsoon snow and ice. The British overcame the great Rock Band by following the gully to its left.*

All the winds of Asia seemed to be trying to blow us from the ridge. A decision was needed. It was four in the afternoon and the skies were already darkening around the South Summit of Everest. I threw my iced and useless snow-goggles away into the whiteness and tried, clumsily mitted, to clear the ice from my eyelashes. I bowed my head into the spindrift and tried to peer along the ridge. Mick should have met us at least three-quarters of an hour before, unless something had happened to him. We had been waiting for nearly one and a half hours. There was no sign of Doug and Dougal's bivouac site. The sky and cornices and whirling snow merged together, visibility was reduced to ten feet and all tracks were obliterated. Pertemba and I huddled next to the rock of the South Summit where Mick had asked us to wait for him. Pertemba said he could not feel his toes or fingers and mine too were nailed with cold. I thought of Mick wearing his glasses and blinded by spindrift, negotiating the fixed rope on the Hillary Step, the fragile one foot windslab on the Nepal side, and the cornices on the Tibetan side of the ridge. I thought of our own predicament, with the 800 feet of the South Summit Gully – guarded by a 60 foot rock step halfway – to descend, and then half of the great 2,000 foot traverse above the Rock Band to cross before reaching the end of the fixed ropes that extended across from Camp VI. It had taken Doug and Dougal three hours in the dawn sunshine after their bivouac to reach Camp VI – but we now had

only an hour of light left. At 28,700 feet the boundary between a controlled and an uncontrolled situation is narrow and we had crossed that boundary within minutes – a strong wind and sun shining through clouds had turned into a violent blizzard of driving snow, the early afternoon had drifted into approaching night and our success was turning into tragedy.

A mountaineer when he is climbing is doing, seeing and feeling and yet on his return home from the hill he often baulks at recollection in public of these experiences because he treasures the privacy and intensity of his memories. And yet, as Hornbein remarked after being asked to write about his ascent of the West Ridge:

'I soon learned, Everest was not a private affair. It belonged to many men.'

The stories of man's adventures on Everest have almost reached the stature of myth in the popular imagination of the 20th century. The full record of our expedition will eventually appear to add to these stories. I do not aspire here to document the planning and events of the expedition, nor to presume to evaluate its achievements, nor to predict the future of climbing on Everest. I fear that at such a cold touch the pains and charms that are my memories of Everest will fly.

My memories are of a keen apprehension that turned into a living nightmare. Even on the leech infested walk-in we dreamt about the climb to

come – one morning Tut and Doug confessed, with gallows humour, 'I keep getting stranded above the Rock Band' and, 'Dougal got severe frost-bite last night'. Whilst Nick and Tut were tackling the Rock Band I wrote:

'Everyone is very optimistic that we'll crack it soon, but it's still early days. We've been lucky with the weather and there could easily be a storm at any time to curtail or even set back all movement.'

'Think upwards' seems to be a good dictum for success in climbing and the Everest summit was in my mind night and day all the time I was moving up the face into position for the second attempt. Aside from the physical effort and practical judgement and worry there is a dreamlike quality in the climbing on Everest. At Camp V I wrote:

'The face is a strange unreal world. All dressed up in one piece oversuits and six layers on the feet, oxygen mask and goggles one seems distanced from where one is and what one is doing, like a sort of moonwalk.'

This half-glimpsed quality was preserved far back in my mind. As a child I used to daydream over a painting in a big picture book, *Adventure of the World*, which depicted the tiny bold figures of Hillary and Tenzing on the top of a summit that thrust out of a sea of clouds.

As Pertemba and I crossed the traverse above the Rock Band in the early dawn of our summit day it felt as if we were on that highest peak above the clouds, as if the sight of the endless cloud sea was joining hands with the dreamland of the past. The weather was changing and the cloud layer was up to 27,000 feet, covering Nuptse and everything beyond it. Only the top of Lhotse peeped out below us, whereas above us the sun sparkled through the snow smoking over the Summit Ridge. For three days I had been jumaring up fixed ropes, counting steps and trying to keep in front of some Sherpas coming up to Camp IV, gasping up to Camp V, and then following Nick and Tut's intricate route through the Rock Band. But now I felt free and untrammelled, and exhilarated as if I had just become committed on the start of a climb in the Alps. Pertemba and I moved, unroped, steadily away from the end of the fixed line and kicked away the spindrift from the tracks that Doug and Dougal had made two days before. Everest, the myth, with its magic and history, seemed to make me feel strong, thinking upwards. Invincible together.

The snow was only a few feet deep on top of the rocks and the route wavered around spurs and over rock steps. The South Summit gully was steep but there was a fixed line hanging over the rock step half way up it. As I reached the South Summit, Pertemba dropped behind and I waited for him. His oxygen mask had stopped working. One and a half hours and several cold fingers later we had slit open the tube and cleared the two inches of ice that were blocking the airway, and patched the mask back into working order. We changed to fresh oxygen cylinders and moved, roped now, along the ridge towards the summit of Everest. Its red ribbons were fading in the strong light and fluttering prayers from the other side of the mountain. The Chinese tripod was catching drifting snow and leaning defiantly in the wind. Its presence was strangely reassuring. Pertemba attached a Nepalese flag to it and I hung a Deadman snow anchor from it. We ate some chocolate and mint cake and I burbled into a tape-recorder. We started down.

We were amazed to see him through the mist. Mick was sitting on the snow only a few hundred yards down an easy angled snow-slope from the summit. He congratulated us and said he wanted to film us on a bump on the ridge and pretend it was the summit, but I told him about the Chinese maypole. Then he asked us to go back to the summit with him. I agreed reluctantly and he, sensing my reluctance, changed his mind and said he'd go up and film it and then come straight down

Tension at Base Camp (left): while Haston and Scott go for the summit on 24 September, their colleagues keep watch from Advance Base in the Western Cwm. Expedition doctor Charlie Clarke has the binoculars; Nick Estcourt, who helped forge the route through the Rock Band, is on the telephoto lens. Right: Haston, photographed by Scott, crampons up a 60 degree snow slope as he heads for the South Summit Gully, visible just above his rucksack.

Three more of Scott's shots from summit day. Above: *Haston moves up unconsolidated snow above a rock step in the South Summit Gully or Couloir.* Right: *Haston on the ridge between the South Summit and the Hillary Step – to Scott's relief, the snow was more stable here.* Far right: *when Scott and Haston reached the Hillary Step, normally a rock pitch, they found it banked with 40 feet of loose, granular snow. The experienced Haston, photographed nearing the top, with the shadows lengthening as night approached, took a full half hour to climb the step.*

'We were amazed to see him through the mist.' Boardman and Pertemba met Burke a short distance from the summit. Burke wanted his colleagues to go back to the summit with him so that he could film them there, but Boardman was reluctant so Burke said he would go on alone. Before parting, Boardman took the last photograph of Burke (above). *The previous day* (right) *Haston and Scott had gone to the summit in clear conditions. In Scott's photograph, the South Summit is just behind Haston; the main summit is less than 250 feet above them. Lhotse is the peak below and to the left.*

after us. He borrowed Pertemba's camera to take some stills on the top and we walked back 50 feet and then walked past him whilst he filmed us. I took a couple of pictures of him. He had the Blue Peter flag and an auto-load camera with him. He asked us to wait for him by the big rock on the South Summit where Pertemba and I had dumped our first oxygen cylinders and some rope and film on the way up. I told him that Pertemba was wanting to move roped with me – so he should catch us up fairly quickly. I said, 'See you soon' and we moved back down the ridge to the South Summit. Shortly after we had left him the weather began to deteriorate.

A decision was needed. I pointed at my watch and said, 'We'll wait ten more minutes.' Pertemba agreed. That helped us – it gave some responsibility to the watch. I fumbled in my sack and pulled out our stove to leave behind. The time was up. At first we went the wrong way – too far towards the South Col. About 150 feet down we girdled back until we found what we thought was the South Summit Gully. There was a momentary lessening in the blizzard, and I looked up to see the rock of the South Summit. There was still no sign of Mick and it was now about half past four. The decision had been made and now we had to fight for our own lives and think downwards.

Pertemba is not a technical climber, not used to moving away from fixed ropes or in bad conditions. At first he was slow. For three pitches I kicked down furiously, placed a Deadman and virtually pulled him down in the sliding, blowing powder snow. But Pertemba was strong and adaptable – he began to move faster and soon we were able to move together. Were we in the gully? I felt panic surge inside. Then I saw twin rocks in the snow that I recognized from the morning. We descended diagonally from there and in the dusk saw Dougal's oxygen cylinder that marked the top of the fixed rope over the rock step.

We abseiled down to the end of the rope and tied a spare rope we had to the end and descended the other 150 feet. From there we descended down and across for 1,000 feet towards the end of the fixed ropes. During our traverse we were covered by two powder snow avalanches from the summit slopes. Fortunately our oxygen cylinders were still functioning and we could breathe. It was a miracle that we found the end of the fixed ropes in the dark, marked by two oxygen cylinders sticking out of the snow. On the fixed rope Pertemba slowed down again and I pulled him mercilessly until he shouted that one of his crampons had fallen off. The rope between us snagged and in flicking it free I tumbled over a 15 foot rock step to be held

Boardman's photograph of Pertemba was taken from the same place as Scott's picture on pages 101–102 . In 24 hours the weather had decisively changed for the worse, bringing peril to all three climbers then on the Summit Ridge. Boardman and Pertemba survived; Burke disappeared. Burke's colleagues are certain he reached the summit. Then, in the storm which hit the ridge, he is believed to have walked through a cornice and fallen down the Kangshung Face.

on the fixed rope. At one point a section of the fixed rope had been swept away. At half past seven we stumbled into the 'summit boxes' at Camp VI. Martin was there and I burst into tears.

The storm pinned the three of us to Camp VI at 27,600 feet for 36 hours. Pertemba and I shared one of the two boxes and were completely dependent on Martin. Pertemba was snow-blinded and I was worried about my feet. Martin had a good supply of gas and he kept us supplied with tea and oxygen cylinders. Our box was becoming buried in snow every four hours and Martin kept on dragging himself out to clear them, damaging his fingers from frost-bite. It was miserable inside the box, the snow was pressing the walls and it felt like that medieval dungeon cell known as 'the little ease' – maddeningly too short to stretch out, too low to sit up. Pertemba lay back, his eyes closed and lips moving in silent incantation. I felt isolated from my friends lower down the mountain by a decision and an experience I could not share.

During the second night the wind and snow ceased but their noise was replaced by the roar of avalanches sweeping past either side of the snowy crest on which we were perched and plunging over the edge of the Rock Band. Dawn came – clear and cold, sad and silvery. We looked across the traverse and up the gully to the South Summit but there

was no sign of Mick. We turned and began the long repetitive ritual of clipping and unclipping the piton brake and safety loop and abseiling, rope-length after rope-length, 6,000 feet down to the Western Cwm.

As we emerged from the foot of the gully through the Rock Band we could see tiny figures outside the three boxes of Camp V, 1,000 feet below us. It took a long time to reach them, for many of the anchors on the fixed ropes had been swept away. Ronnie, Nick, Tut and Ang Phurba were waiting for us and helped us down into the living air and warmth of the Western Cwm and the reassuring faces of Camp II.

Peter Boardman was acclaimed as one of the finest writers of his generation. After he disappeared on Everest in 1982 (see page 125), together with Joe Tasker, another superb writer, a prize was instigated in their joint names. It is administered by a board including members of both their families. The Boardman Tasker prize is now the foremost literature award in the mountaineering world. There is one Everest summiter among the list of winners: Stephen Venables (*Painted Mountains*, 1986) who climbed Everest in 1988 (see page 167). Maintaining the Everest theme, the 2000 prize was awarded to Peter and Leni Gillman for their biography of George Mallory, *The Wildest Dream*.

A BREATH OF FRESH AIR

by Doug Scott

We took off our masks and I could see Dougal's face lit up in the setting sun and filled with happiness. This usually reticent man became expansive, and we thumped each other's backs and congratulated each other. The wind had dropped to nothing as we stood up there in wonder at the scene before us. It was everything and more than we had dared to hope for. Beyond the Rongbuk Glacier silver threads meandered out north and west across the brown land of Tibet. Peak after peak in all directions. We tried to name them, and also spent time looking down the north side, picking out features from the history books.

The sun filtered down behind layers of cloud, occasionally breaking through in an explosion of light. We watched this happen several times – one sunset after another – until we had only about half an hour left before it got dark. We gathered up the rope and prepared to move back down our tracks. We left nothing on top, because we had nothing to leave – except the tripod [left by the Chinese four months before] and flag already there.

We moved down rapidly, hoping to follow our tracks down to Camp VI. We abseiled down the Hillary Step from a deadman and left a 40 foot piece of rope hanging there, as it jammed when we tried to pull it down. As we blundered on, lightning flickered through the sky, all the way from Kangchenjunga to Ama Dablam. It was pitch dark when we reached the South Summit. Dougal searched for the tracks going down the Nepal side, but they were blown over with snow, so we set about bivouacking at the South Summit Col at 28,700 feet. Dougal heated some more water while I enlarged my previous hole into a cave.

We soon had a home, and the primitive fear of a night in the open was assuaged. We would survive, but it was the quality of the survival that mattered.

With so many other mountains and crags to climb, we were determined not to lose any fingers and toes on Everest, so we set to work massaging. I now regretted leaving my down clothing, as I had only the gear I climbed in to keep me warm.

The oxygen ran out at 8.30 pm and the stove was finished at midnight. To keep warm, I hacked away at the cave with my axe until it was so large that it could have housed five people. It was essential to stay awake and concentrate on survival. I carefully took off my socks and stuffed them under my armpits, while I rubbed my toes and tried to ensure that snow did not get on my rucksack – which was my seat. Mostly I shivered and cursed, telling Dougal how desperately cold it was, as if he didn't know.

Once, when I was massaging my feet, I left a sock out in the open and found it frozen stiff when I came to put it on again. Dougal must have thought me a right softy when I accepted a place for my feet inside his down clothing, one foot at his crutch, the other under his armpit. But still the cold seeped into our backs, into our kidneys, and seemingly into our very bones. We

began to wander in our thoughts: Dougal had conversations with Dave Clarke, our Equipment Manager, perhaps hoping that he would arrive with our sleeping-bags. I kept on chattering away to my presence and to my feet. It was a long nine hours.

At 5.30 am we crawled out of our hole and went over the ridge into Nepal, for we had spent an illicit night out in China. The wind grew stronger, and clouds were gathering all around, as we plunged down rapidly, hoping to gain more oxygen and warmth. We reached the tent and safety at 9 am, got into our sleeping-bags, put a brew on, and lay back breathing oxygen; then we radioed Chris with the news. We knew that we weren't going to lose any digits as the warmth seeped back into our bodies and out to our extremities.

I came down with ambition fulfilled, and an empty space for noble thoughts and feelings; but I knew that space would soon be swamped back in the city – it had happened before. We had taken a big breath of fresh air, and now it was back to the valley and people, to breathe it out ready for the next breath, perhaps in Alaska, the Andes, or even back here again in the Himalayas.

After reaching the summit, Scott and Haston faced the alarming prospect of spending the night on the mountain without protective equipment. They sheltered in a hastily-excavated snow-hole at the South Summit, thus surviving the highest bivouac ever made. In Scott's photograph, Haston is making a brew at the South Summit during their ascent.

WOMEN ON TOP

The first woman to the summit: right, 35-year-old Junko Tabei from Japan, the 39th person and first woman to succeed. She is celebrating at Base Camp on the shoulders of Ang Tsering, the Sherpa who guided her to the summit via the South Col route on 16 May 1975. She was followed 11 days later by Phantog, aged 37 (below), a Tibetan member of the expedition making the second Chinese ascent of Everest by the North Col and North-east Ridge. Wanda Rutkiewicz (below, bottom) was the third woman and first European to succeed. From Poland, renowned as the world's best female mountaineer, she died on Kangchenjunga in 1992.

The first western woman to approach Everest was the redoubtable American Elizabeth Cowles, who accompanied the crusty Bill Tilman and the two Houstons, father and son, when they made their unofficial reconnaissance to the South Side in 1950, a year ahead of the British. Until then, Everest had been regarded as a strictly male preserve, apart from the occasional woman among the Tibetan porters enlisted by the pre-war British. Cowles, who had climbed extensively in North America and the Alps, was the expedition photographer, and so far impressed Tilman with her cooking that he observed: 'Hitherto I had not regarded a woman as an indispensable part of the equipment of a Himalayan journey but one lives and learns.'

The first women to be accredited expedition climbers were those referred to in the official account of the 1960 Chinese expedition which reached the summit from the north. The team was said to comprise '214 men and women', though no women were in the summit team. In 1970 the Japanese Setuko Watanabe reached the South Col with a mainly male expedition, and in 1971 the Swiss Yvette Vaucher was the only woman on the ill-starred International Expedition.

In 1975, Junko Tabei became the 39th climber and first woman to succeed. Aged 35, from Japan, she had taken up climbing while a student of English and American literature in Tokyo, having become enthralled with the mountains during a school trip to a volcano at the age of ten. Small and slight, with an air of fragility to belie her stamina and determination, she was soon accomplishing the hardest routes with the best male climbers of her day. Working as a science magazine editor, and resolving to steer clear of any emotional entanglements to provide as much free time as possible for her sport, she found her greatest personal challenge climbing with other women.

In 1970 Junko made her first Himalayan climb when going to the summit on an all-women expedition to Annapurna III, and the following year she was invited to be climbing leader of a women's expedition to Everest in 1975. Since she was now married, this meant breaking the social taboo that Japanese women were not expected to leave their husbands. But her husband gave his blessing, on condition that they had a child first. Junko told him she wanted a family too, but having children was not like laying an egg. All the same, by the time the expedition set off she was the mother of a two-year-old girl.

The expedition set up Base Camp on 16 March. By 3 May it had established Camp V on the South Col before bad weather forced a retreat. The next day an avalanche swept over Camp II. Junko was among seven Japanese injured, together with six Sherpas. Even so she and the expedition sirdar, Ang Tsering, reached the summit 12 days later.

If there was a race to become the first woman to stand on the summit, it was a close run thing. Just 11 days later, Junko was followed by Phantog, a Tibetan member of the 1975 Sino-Tibetan expedition which climbed Everest by the North-east Ridge. Aged 37, the mother of three, she had, according to official expedition reports, an all-too-typical background as the 'daughter of a serf' who had been subjected to brutal oppression since childhood. Duly 'liberated' by the Chinese takeover of Tibet in 1959, she was sent to work on a state farm near Lhasa and while there was selected for training as a mountaineer. Following the first ascent of Everest in 1953, the Chinese undoubtedly saw mountaineering as a way to achieve national prestige.

Phantog took part in the second ascents of Mustagh Ata and Kongur Tiubie and was then chosen as deputy leader of the Everest expedition. Like her comrades, she climbed using only minimal 'inhalings' of oxygen. She said that above 7,000 metres she was moving in a trance, knowing only that she must keep on upwards. She lost three toes to frost-bite but her achievement, according to the Chinese, demonstrated how the revolutionary courage of women steeled in the Great Proletarian Cultural Revolution enabled them to storm the most formidable fortresses and expose the reactionary fallacy of male supremacy inherent in the teachings of Lin Piao and Confucius.

While Phantog had proven for the Party that women could do an equal share with men – altogether 14 women on the expedition went above 7,800 metres – there is little doubt it was something she enjoyed. She went to live in Wuxi, south China, where she became a director of sport and physical culture, but admitted she had never accustomed herself to the sweet local diet and frequently felt homesick for her native mountains.

The first European woman to climb Everest was Wanda Rutkiewicz of Poland, a member of a large-scale international expedition which put 16 climbers on the summit via the South Col in 1978. Rutkiewicz, who won a reputation as the world's most accomplished woman mountaineer, resolved to become the first woman to reach all 14 of the 8,000 metre summits but died while attempting Kangchenjunga, her ninth, in 1992.

Rutkiewicz was followed on Everest the following year by the German, Hannelore Schmatz, on a South Col expedition led by her husband, Dr Gerhard Schmatz. It was a striking success, as eight climbers plus five Sherpas reached the summit, but Schmatz did not live to enjoy her triumph. She and her partner, the American Ray Genet, were forced to bivouac above the South Col during their descent and died of exposure.

A five-year gap ensued before the fifth woman, Bachendri Pal, reached the summit as one of seven women on an Indian expedition whose clear intention was to put an Indian woman on top. In 1986 the Canadian Sharon Wood became the first woman to do so by a new route, her expedition making the first ascent of the West Ridge from Tibet. An accomplished climber and mountain guide, Wood had previously made a major first ascent on Huascaran Sur in the Andes with the American Carlos Buhler.

In autumn 1988 came the first two ascents by US women, Stacy Allison, from Colorado, and Peggy Luce, from Seattle, both via the South Col route. A few days later came a controversial ascent by New Zealander Lydia Bradey, climbing alone and without oxygen from the South Col. Her summit account was confused and the climbing world was sceptical, but eventually accepted her claim.

Other notable firsts have followed. In 1990, Marija Stremfelj and her husband Andrej, from Slovenia, became the first married couple to succeed together; followed on the same day by the American Cathy Gibson and her Russian husband, Aleksei Krasnokutsky. In 1993, journalist Rebecca Stephens, making a gutsy ascent in poor weather from the South Col, became the first British woman to succeed. A second British climber, Ginette Harrison, made an ascent via the South Col in the post-monsoon season. (Harrison was killed in an avalanche on Dhaulagiri in 1999.)

In 1995, Alison Hargreaves, a British climber with two young children, made a bold solo ascent, without oxygen, via the North-east Ridge. Hargreaves died when she and five other climbers were blown off the summit ridge while descending K2 later that year. In 1999 South African Cathy O'Dowd became the first woman to make ascents by two different routes when she reached the summit via the North-east Ridge, adding to her South Col ascent in 1996. By the end of 2000, there had been 62 ascents by 59 different women – around 5 per cent of all ascents, and 6.5 per cent of total summiters. Four women died during their descents – a death rate of 6.6 per cent, just over twice that of men who reached the summit.

Woman number seven, and the first from the US, was Stacy Allison (above, top). South African Cathy O'Dowd (above) was the first woman to make two ascents by different routes.

Left: Alison Hargreaves summited via the North-east Ridge, solo and without oxygen, on 13 May 1995, but three months later died in a storm while descending from the summit of K2.

THE LONELIEST PEOPLE IN THE WORLD

by Peter Habeler
Translation: David Heald

The question of whether to use supplementary oxygen on Everest provoked controversy from the start. The pioneers of the 1920s were divided, some regarding it as akin to cheating, others as a logical benefit of the era's new technology. Their oxygen sets were cumbersome and unreliable, and may have provided no more energy than was required to carry the equipment itself. But by the time of the early ascents of the 1950s and 1960s it was regarded as a prerequisite of success. In the 1970s a new generation of climbers revived the old arguments, contending that only pure, unaided ascents were truly valid. Foremost among them were the Tyrolese pair of Reinhold Messner and Peter Habeler, who began climbing other 8,000 metre peaks without oxygen equipment. In May 1978 they embarked on their attempt on Everest, leaving their South Col camp at 5.30 am on 8 May, with Habeler, for one, convinced they could die.

In the first phase of the ascent, Reinhold gained a small lead. We wanted to go up to the South Summit without a rope. Reinhold was carrying a 15 metre long rope connection on his rucksack which we would use at the very top. I had my camera equipment with me, reserve clothing, goggles, as well as a small amount of food.

Shortly before beginning the steep ascent which leads up to the South-east Ridge, I saw Reinhold. He was sitting on a rock plateau and was looking towards me. From this point on, we made a track together and took the lead alternately. The flank in which we found ourselves was filled with such large snowdrifts that we sank into them up to our hips. Then extremely thick fog came up and we were afraid that we would lose sight of each other. We were now at exactly the same height as Mallory and Irvine had been before they disappeared for ever from the view of their comrades in the fog. This thought shot through my mind as we rested. On thinking back, I have the impression that I spoke to Reinhold about this, but that isn't true. We never exchanged a single word, mainly because we were far too short of breath. Nevertheless, the memory of a conversation between us is very vivid indeed. I believe that we were then as close to each

other spiritually as two people possibly can be. Perhaps this was due to the fact that, during these hours, we must have been the loneliest people in the whole world.

Much has been written about the fact that at extreme altitudes, like those of Everest, the veil which hides the great beyond is particularly thin, so thin that even completely normal people have supernatural experiences of which they otherwise only read in ghost stories. There is a saying that whoever is killed up on the mountain wanders forever after his death and guides the living mountaineers during their last metres to the summit.

I don't believe in ghosts or fables, and I am fully convinced that most of these stories can be explained by a strained and overwrought imagination. In the lonely environment, which is so hostile to life, the imagination conjures up all manner of strange desires or horrifying apparitions.

But not everything can simply be rationally explained away. For example, not the feeling that you are talking to a human being who, in reality, is not saying a word, but who is nevertheless simultaneously reacting to unspoken thoughts. I mention this now because I can remember most clearly our own situation at that time. Nothing surprised me then at all. Everything seemed to be totally normal; I had completely lost the feeling of being in the Himalayas and of climbing Everest. I could just as well have been on the Mösele or the Ahornspitze at home. The fog cloaked everything, and made us forget both the vastness and the greatness of our surroundings. We were merely traversing a steep snowfield which had to be tracked step by step. Occasionally I stopped, rammed the ice-pick into the snow and leant on it for a quarter or half a minute, gasping for breath and trying to recover. Then, somehow, I would gain a new strength and could go on for ten or 20 more steps. Strangely, after I had put behind me a few hundred metres of altitude, I no longer felt so lethargic. On the contrary, everything seemed to go more easily. Perhaps this was due to the fact that we were getting better accustomed to this unimaginable altitude.

Naturally, wading through deep snow did represent an enormous drain on our strength. Where possible, we made a detour on to ice-covered rock where the wind had blown away the layer of snow. Although, technically, it is much more difficult to climb over rock which is iced up than it is to find a track through deep snow, it seemed to us to be easier. We had to concentrate so hard on every foothold and handhold that there was no time left to think about our exhaustion.

After four hours, towards half past nine, we stood in front of the tents of Camp V at an altitude of 8,500 metres. Mallory and Irvine, too, had managed to get this far. From now on we would be entering completely new territory. We were left totally to our own resources. If anything happened to us now, no rescue team would be able to come up to help us, no helicopter – nothing. The smallest accident would mean certain death.

Reinhold and I had often spoken together about the fact that, in this last phase, it would be impossible to help each other should anything untoward occur. Although we were incredibly close to each other, and formed an indivisible unit, we were agreed on one thing. If one of us should get into difficulty, the other would have to try at all costs to find safety for himself alone. The small amount of strength which remained to each of us was hardly enough for one; any attempt to rescue, or even to recover the other, would be doomed to failure.

I sat in front of the small tent which was half covered by snow, while inside Reinhold tried desperately to get a cooker going to brew up tea. I snuggled up to the side of the tent in order to rest in the lee side, and stared out into the fog. Occasionally the wall of fog would lift for a moment, and I could see deep below me the Valley

Messner (left) and Habeler in Base Camp, shared with an Austrian expedition, before their attempt. They already had an impressive list of successes to their name, including the fastest ascent of the notorious North Face of the Eiger, halving the previous record; and an ascent of Gasherbrum, 11th highest mountain in the world, without oxygen. Messner took a romantic view of attempting Everest without oxygen: 'Mountains are so elemental that humans do not have the right to subdue them with technology.' The more pragmatic Habeler wrote of 'the fearful certainty that there would be no possibility of rescue if anything went wrong'.

of Silence. I could see Lhotse, and again and again I looked up to the South Summit where an enormous trail of snow signified that up there a far more violent storm was raging than down here in Camp V. The weather would undoubtedly worsen. The fine weather period was over.

Perhaps our attempt on the summit was finally over too, our Everest expedition wrecked once and for all. Of one thing I was convinced: I would never come up here a second time. Already the desire to turn back was almost overpowering. To bivouac here in Camp V, and perhaps to wait for the weather to improve, was also completely out of the question. We would probably never have got out of the tent at all again, and in no event would we have had the physical or mental strength to climb any further. Our energy would have lasted at the most for the descent and no more. Yet climbing on was, under these circumstances, also a 'way of no return'.

In 1956, two Japanese had mastered the route from the South Col to the summit in one go. This had taken them a whole day, and having therefore reached the main summit late in the afternoon, they were forced to bivouac on the way back. Consequently, in spite of carrying oxygen, they had suffered terrible injuries through frost-bite. But neither Reinhold nor I had time to think of these dangers. The will to push on blotted out

The goal almost in sight, Habeler, battered by the wind, drags himself up the final section of the Summit Ridge. 'I was physically finished,' he wrote. 'I seemed to step outside myself, and had the illusion that another person was walking in my place.'

everything else, even the wish to turn back or at least to sleep. We wanted in any case to go on up, even if we could only reach the South Summit which is 8,760 metres high. After all, to conquer even the South Summit without oxygen would have been a tremendous success. It would have proved that one day it would be possible to reach the main summit by human strength alone.

It took exactly half an hour for Reinhold to prepare the tea. My deliberations were also shared by him; we exchanged them wordlessly. We were completely united in our determination to continue the assault on the summit.

Once again we set off. The tracks of our predecessors, which could still be seen in the snow, served as an excellent orientation guide. The clouds were moving over from the south-west, from the bad weather corner of the Himalayas. We had to push ourselves even more because that promised bad news. We found ourselves in the lower area of the jet stream, those raging winds of speeds up to 200 kilometres per hour, upon which the enormous passenger planes are carried from continent to continent. We had traversed the troposphere and were approaching the frontier of the stratosphere. Here cosmic radiation was already noticeable and the intensity of the ultra-violet radiation had multiplied. Only a few minutes without our snow-goggles sufficed, even in the fog, to diminish our powers of vision. In a very short space of time direct insolation would lead to snow-blindness and painful conjunctivitis.

Reinhold and I photographed and filmed as often as we had the opportunity. To do this, we had to take off our snow-goggles and we also had to

remove our overgloves. Each time it became more difficult for us to put the gloves back on again. But losing them would have led to the very rapid paralysis and frost-bite of our hands.

Since it was no longer possible to go on in this deep snow, we had made a detour towards the South-east Ridge. Here the wall dropped 2,000 metres down to the south-west. One false step and we would have plunged down into the Valley of Silence. The exposed and airy climb on brittle rock without any rope demanded extreme concentration. Reinhold was right behind me. I took the lead to the South Summit. Completely without warning, we suddenly found we had passed through the clouds and now stood on the last stage before our goal.

At this point the storm attacked us with all its might. However, in spite of the storm and the fatigue, my fear of the mountain had dissipated with the clouds. I was quite sure of myself. Over there lay the main summit, almost near enough to touch, and at this precise moment I was sure we were going to do it. Reinhold, too, told me later: 'This was the moment in which I was convinced of the success of our adventure.'

A sort of joyful intoxication overcame the two of us. We looked at each other – and shrank back. From Reinhold's appearance I could only conclude that my own was very similar. His face was contorted in a grimace, his mouth wide open while he gasped panting for air. Icicles hung in his beard. His face was almost without human traits. Our physical reserves were exhausted. We were so utterly spent that we scarcely had the strength to go ten paces in one go. Again and again we had to stop, but nothing in the world could have held us back now.

We had roped ourselves together because the Summit Ridge, as Hillary has already described it, was densely covered in cornices. It is true, however, that in an emergency a rope would not have helped us.

We crawled forwards at a snail's pace, trusting to instinct alone. The sun glistened on the snow, and the sky above the summit was of such an intense blue that it seemed almost black. We were very close to the sky, and it was with our own strength alone that we had arrived up here at the seat of the gods. Reinhold signified to me with a movement of his hand that he wanted to go on ahead. He wanted to film me climbing up over the ridge, with the bubbling sea of clouds below.

To do this he had to take off his snow-goggles in order to focus the camera better. It occurred to me that his eyes looked inflamed, but I thought nothing more of it, no more than he did. Our altitude was now 8,700 metres, and we had obviously reached a point in which normal brain functions had broken down, or at least were severely limited. Our attentiveness and concentration declined; our instinct no longer reacted as reliably as before; the capacity for clear logical thinking had also apparently been lost. I only thought in sensations and loose associations, and slowly I was overcome by the feeling that this threatening fearful mountain could be a friend.

Today I am certain that it is in these positive and friendly sensations that the real danger on Everest lies. When one approaches the summit, one no longer perceives the hostile, the absolutely deadly atmosphere. I have probably never been so close to death as I was during that last hour before reaching the summit. The urgent compulsion to descend again, to give in to fatigue, which had overcome me already in Camp V, had disappeared. I was now feeling the complete opposite. I had been seized by a sense of euphoria. I felt somehow light and relaxed, and believed that nothing could happen to me. At this altitude the boundaries between life and death are fluid. I wandered along this narrow ridge and perhaps for a few seconds I had gone beyond the frontier which divides life from death. By a piece of good fortune I was allowed to return. I would not risk it a second time, my reason forbids me to gamble with my life in such a way again.

In spite of all my euphoria, I was physically completely finished. I was no longer walking of my own free will, but mechanically, like an automaton. I seemed to step outside myself, and had the illusion that another person was walking in my

place. This other person arrived at the Hillary Step, that perilous 25 metre high ridge gradient, and then climbed and pulled himself up in the footsteps of his predecessors. He had one foot in Tibet and the other in Nepal. On the left side there was a 2,000 metre descent to Nepal; on the right the wall dropped 4,000 metres down towards China. We were alone, this other person and myself. Although he was connected to me by the short piece of rope, Reinhold no longer existed.

This feeling of being outside myself was interrupted for only a few moments. Cramp in my right hand bent my fingers together, and tore me violently back to reality. I was attacked by a suffocating fear of death. 'Now I've had it.' This thought went through my head, 'Now the lack of oxygen is beginning its deadly work.' I massaged my right forearm and bent my fingers back, and then the cramp eased.

From then on I prayed, 'Lord God, let me go up right to the top. Give me the power to remain alive, don't let me die up here.' I crawled on my elbows and knees and prayed more fervently than I have ever done in my life before. It was like a dialogue with a higher being. Again I saw myself crawling up, below me, beside me, higher and higher. I was being pushed up to the heights, and then suddenly I was up again on my own two feet: I was standing on the summit. It was 1.15 on the afternoon of the 8th May 1978.

And then suddenly Reinhold was with me too, still carrying his camera and the three-legged Chinese surveying instrument. We had arrived. We embraced each other. We sobbed and stammered and could not keep calm. The tears poured from under my goggles into my beard, frozen on my cheeks. We embraced each other again and again. We pressed each other close. We stepped back at arm's length and again fell round each other's necks, laughing and crying at the same time. We were redeemed and liberated, freed at last from the inhuman compulsion to climb on.

After the crying and the sense of redemption, came the emptiness and sadness, the disappointment. Something had been taken from me; something that had been very important to me. Something which had suffused my whole being had evaporated, and I now felt exhausted and hollow. There was no feeling of triumph or victory. I saw the surrounding summits, Lhotse, Cho Oyu. The view towards Tibet was obscured by clouds. I knew that I was standing now on the highest point in the whole world. But, somehow, it was all a matter of indifference to me. I just wanted to get home now, back to that world from which I had come, and as fast as possible.

The goal attained: Messner, photographed by Habeler, squats on the summit. Habeler set another record by descending to the South Col in an hour. Although Messner suffered temporary snow blindness after removing his goggles to film, both men were otherwise unscathed.

NO SACRIFICE COULD BE BIG ENOUGH

by Nejc Zaplotnik
Translation: Stanko Klinar

As interest in new routes on Everest grew, one of the most enticing challenges was the 'West Ridge Direct', following the ridge to the summit instead of veering into the North-west Face on the line taken by the Americans in 1963. A French attempt in 1974 ended in disaster but in 1979 a Yugoslav expedition made a new bid. At the end of April it had established a camp on the ridge at the point where the Americans had traversed on to the face. Having been pinned down by hurricane-force winds for five days, it pushed on up the ridge, encountering some of the highest Grade V rock climbing yet attempted. After two summit bids had stalled, the Stremfelj brothers – Andrej and Marko – and Nejc Zaplotnik reached Camp V at 26,640 feet/8,120 metres on 12 May. Following a night of ferocious winds and temperatures of minus 35°C, the climbers set off for the summit at dawn.

Nejc Zaplotnik made his attempt with the Stremfelj brothers, Andrej and Marko. During the previous three days two bids had already failed through bitter cold, faulty oxygen equipment and difficulties in finding the route.

We had spent the night at Camp V. After our gulp of tea we put on the oxygen masks with the valves set at half a litre per minute. Thus we waited until dawn, warding off one of the coldest nights on the mountain. In nights like that the stars seem to touch the earth while shooting stars soundlessly cross the dark carpet of the sky. The wind tugged at the strings of the tent. The anticipation of a great day filled our hearts. I had lived for this moment and now I was ready. It was clear to me that it was going to be a matter of life and death. Long ago I had decided that Everest was worth my toes. Fingers and hands, I had thought, should be spared. But now I was suddenly convinced that no sacrifice could be big enough.

The oxygen had thinned my blood, making it spread pleasant warmth throughout my body, and I fell asleep again. It was two o'clock and Andrej was busy clattering with the dishes. I knew it was my turn to do the cooking, but I was reluctant to abandon the cosiness of my sleeping-bag.

We forced ourselves to drink, but not with much success. We tied our laces and prepared two oxygen cylinders each. The flags for the summit had long been put in the rucksack, along with the

best wishes – our own and those of friends in lower camps. Two pairs of gloves were put on and we were ready. It was five o'clock. We crawled out of the tent and shouldered our gear. The highest summits all around were just becoming tinged with the early sunshine. Apart from Cho Oyu they were all below us, far below!

The lower part of the route was somewhat familiar to us, as it had been described well by our companions. Easy rock interspersed with snow extends towards a gully coming down from the ridge. I was fairly high up when Marko called to me saying that his oxygen valve had gone. He had already replaced it once and did not have another spare. Oh, damn it! I felt tears of wrath rise to my eyes. Marko could do nothing more than wave his hand in farewell. Angrily I dashed with my ice-axe against the rock. I would have damned well like to have smashed them all – axe and rock and valve and everything else. But no! My task was to climb. I turned my thoughts to the rocks ahead. Exposed traverses brought us into the gully. We were making quick progress, with Andrej following close after me. But then suddenly I heard an ominous 'p-shshshshsh . . . ' Andrej's valve had gone too. 'Oh, cursed be all the devils and every cloven-footed creature in the world!' But I knew that the situation was critical and I forced myself to calm down. I gave him my spare valve. And then crack and p-shshshsh again! I unscrewed the bad valve and hurled it down the precipice. I would have liked to have hurled the oxygen bottles after it, too. And what now?

'Andrej, take my valves and bottles. You will lead the ascent, as you will have the oxygen, and I will follow you without.'

But Andrej did not agree. He knew very well that climbing without oxygen in that awful cold and severe terrain, at a temperature of minus 40°C and a wind of 120 kilometres per hour would cripple me for life. I fastened Andrej's rotten valve back to his bottle and, by spitting on it, tried to find out how badly damaged it was. To my great joy the hissing lessened. The frozen saliva had stopped the little hole in the security valve. I fell to licking that damned cold metal like one obsessed until the hissing was stopped completely. A patch of the skin of my tongue got torn off and remained glued to it, too, but it held right up to the top!

On we went. The gully is blocked by a vertical smooth chimney. Over the slabs on the left was dangling a white rope, which had been fastened there by Marjon and Viki. My jumar bit into the frozen rope, my crampons scratched on the smooth granite slabs. I had set the valve at four litres per minute, and yet I gasped for breath while working up the rope with my heavy gear on my back. Andrej was standing below shooting pictures. All right, we would need documents. How often had we said that truly nice things were only to come later, when back at home we would be sitting at table and looking at the Himalayas on the screen. No cold any more, just an inexhaustible tea-pot on the table. No ferocious wind, but just the familiar swirling of the cigarette smoke rising towards the ceiling. A room full of friends, all married to the mountains for good like ourselves, and the screen full of the Himalayas, sweet and kind and homely. There would be slippers on our feet instead of crampons, the wine would loosen our tongues and make the hearts swell with memories and alluring new plans.

I often slipped on the rope but was careful not to be left hanging. The harness would then have choked me. Even so I could hardly breathe. When after hard labour I had reached the top of the rope I waited for Andrej. I took off my set and switched off my oxygen.

The gully is split into two branches. The previous day Romi and Dule had chosen the one to the right and missed the route. They had landed on a gendarme, from where further progress along the ridge seemed extremely problematic, so they had come back to try the left couloir. But they had lost too much time. At 3 pm they had only reached the ridge, and retreat was inevitable. By following their route we came up to a steep rock step just below the ridge. The edge of the step was smooth and verglassed, offering no holds at all. Should we take the rope and belay? No! Speed was the only security. Fortunately we were both used to soloing, as we had done no end of solo climbs in the Alps, and trusted each other completely.

I rammed the spike of the axe into a smooth granite crack, pulled myself over the edge and landed on the ridge, face to face with a wind that almost swept me away into Tibet. Andrej joined me, but it was only with our four limbs dug deep in the snow that we could resist the onslaught of the huge current of air dashing against us. The rocks around us droned like a big organ. Far below we could see the big river of ice winding its way through the Western Cwm and over the debris of the Icefall. Nuptse and its slanting ridge did not obstruct the view to the southern horizon any more. I gazed to the east where Makalu should have been but Lhotse still blocked the view.

The wind caused our goggles to become constantly coated with ice. We cleaned them every minute, but it helped little. Whenever we dived back into shadow, we simply took them off, even at the risk of incurring snow-blindness. We hoped it wouldn't affect us before we reached a camp. Afterwards we would cope with it somehow. The ridge was sharp and snowy, interspersed with rock steps, which allowed no breather. Then we reached the Yellow Band. Actually, we found ourselves in the middle of it. Layers of yellow granite slope down from under the top of Everest and enliven the dark flanks of Changtse, finally to be drowned in dry, brown Tibet.

Now I forget so many things. All less remarkable details on our way to the summit have escaped my memory. When after a few days at Base Camp Andrej and I tried to recall the exact route and make a diagram, we found that it was beyond us to explain how we had passed from the Yellow Band on to the Grey Step. All we could remember was that the passage was not so hard as the band below and the step above, that there were snowfields interspersed with smooth wind-blown slabs and now and then a steep wall. We did remember, however, that the Grey Step had been looming large above us, virtually overhanging, and that the wind did its best to blow us off the ridge. And that it was all like a nightmare. We had been so bent on reaching the summit that anything less important was drowned in oblivion for good.

Andrej Stremfelj (above) continued in the attempt with Zaplotnik after his brother, Marko, had been compelled to turn back because of a defective oxygen set.

Expedition leader Tone Skarja conducted a reconnaissance of the route in 1978. A Frenchman and five Sherpas had been killed by an avalanche below the Lho La during an attempt on the route in 1974, but Skarja selected a line clear of the avalanche fall-line.

We reached the foot of the Grey Step. A hundred metres of repulsive, vertical and over-hanging rock. I was about to go straight ahead, just a few metres to the left of the ridge, where a system of cracks offered a possibility. I was taking off my gloves as part of the preparation for taking off my crampons when Andrej turned right, round an edge, on to the South Face. The initial pitch on that side is harder than these cracks, but the wall eases off sooner. We took the South Face — one single drop of 2,500 metres down into the Western Cwm. A tiny brittle ledge took us into the magnif-icent exposure above the precipice. Entranced we climbed up, climbed as we do at home, in the Alps! I dug out a little stance in the snow and drove a weak peg into the brittle rock. I finally took off my gloves and roped myself up, with Andrej belaying, while I tackled an overhanging crack. The cold of the rock bit immediately and ruthlessly into my bare fingers. After a few more moves and touching more rock they became frozen hard and totally numb. I had set the oxygen valve to the maximum supply, but there was nothing that could help ward off the cold. The 15 kilogram burden on my back threatened to pull me down. There was no time to test the holds, or the frozen fingers would have let go. Suddenly, with a broken-off piece of rock in my hands, I landed in the snow below, held by the rope thanks to Andrej's presence of mind. Knee-deep in the snow I waved my hands to make blood come back to my fingers. The blood obeyed, but, oh, how it hurt! I would have howled with pain if I had had any breath left. Andrej was silent. His faith in me was not shaken. So I tackled the overhang again. A bit higher a foothold broke off. I remained hanging on my fingers for a while, but having lost all support for my feet I slipped again. Bloody hell! What is the time, Andrej? A quarter to twelve. We are damned late! Shouldn't we go back? Andrej asked. No answer. We would talk it over on top of the Grey Step.

I tackled the overhang now slightly more to the left. It was even more arduous there, the rocks hanging even farther out beyond the vertical, but the strain would be limited to a shorter section. I made a loop on the rope, then climbed as high as I could and passed the loop round a hump of rock. But when I stepped into the loop I found that the hump was too small to hold the rope and I started slipping down again. My fingers were fast losing strength, and yet I kept pulling myself up. Somehow I managed to catch a tiny hold with one of my feet, but at the same time I pressed the little tube for the oxygen supply against the rock with my knee and pulled it out of my mask. Oh, God help me! I'll choke! I rallied the last of my will power and dragged myself on to a snow-covered miniature ledge. The tube was pushed back in its place and I paused to take some oxygen. The fingers had long stopped hurting, they were totally numb again. But Andrej, we will win! We will win the battle! Not the battle against the mountain, but against ourselves and our shortcomings. You can't fight against the mountain. There you can only survive or die. There are no more alternatives, and the choice is yours. We two will survive, we two must survive . . .

I followed a narrow ledge leading as far as the crack on my right-hand side which I had attempted before. It was easier there now, but still impossible with gloves on. At the end of the pitch I hammered in a piton. The crack was shallow, two centimetres only, but I had no choice. I switched off the oxygen. The first bottle was empty. Cloud suddenly descended upon us. But it did not matter. I did not think of Makalu any longer, I did not long to see it any more. I only wished we would escape from this hell safe and sound. While Andrej was climbing, the piton was bending under his weight. We both were literally hanging on it. Would it break off? I did not feel any fear but trusted in my good fortune. Andrej was swinging in mid-air on one jumar, half-choked by the rope and harness. He thought he would never do it.

Finally he touched the rocks and found some support for his feet. Memories of previous hard training in domestic hills crossed my mind. How often had we been running, as if for life, in heat and rain, in snow and mud, with tongues dangling down to our knees, day after day, every day. Now we reaped what we had sown. I was glad that we were together on the hill. Friendship means more than the greatest success.

By now we had used up one bottle of oxygen each. We let the empty shells slip into the abyss. Andrej took over the lead in the following pitch. It was decidedly easier. Belayed by the rope from above I advanced quickly. We were now on top of the Grey Step. The wind had grown into a hurricane. The rope, however, was put back into the rucksack, and only then did we remember to switch on the radio. What impatient moments they must have gone through in the camps below, and we never bothered so much as to come on the air.

'Hello, Tone, come in, please.'
'I'm on the air.'
'We've just managed to climb the Grey Step. It looks easy ahead of us. Three more hours and we reach the top.'
'Bravo, boys!'

'Tone, what's the time? We're late, aren't we?'
'Not at all. It's only twelve. Over and out for now. We'll be continually on the air.'

How was that? At a quarter to twelve we had been at the foot of the Grey Step, it had taken us three hours to climb it, and now it was twelve. Andrej dug out his watch from under his gloves and down jacket – it was truly no more than twelve o'clock. How was that possible? It must have been nine before, but Andrej, upset by my falls, must have mixed up the hands and read it as a quarter to twelve. So we were not late – we would manage without a bivouac. Then I realized that my hands were still numb. The fingers were as white as wax, and I did not feel them at all. I panicked. I had been so preoccupied with climbing that I'd had no eye for anything but hard passages we had had to negotiate. Now I fell to rubbing my fingers, but I could not bring any life back to them. I swung my arms at their full length like a windmill. Finally there was the first trace of pain, the herald of the more severe pain to come. With the blood streaming again through the cramped veins, I calmed down. The skin remained white, though. But that was harmless.

The cloud settled down, totally obstructing our view. Gentle snow-slopes gradually narrowed up into a gully, which rose steeper and steeper towards the final step below the summit. We were now 8,600 metres high. The ridge soared steeply again, vanishing somewhere in the cloud. We did not have to take our gloves off any more. We helped each other now and then on awkward spots, which saved us the trouble of taking out the rope. The ridge assumed the form of a knife-edge, but the rock was firm. I held on to the crest of the ridge with my hands and let the crampons scratch along a vertical slab on the South Face side. Oh, the passion of rock-climbing! We forgot where we were. We strove to reach a goal just a few metres ahead, and once that was reached we fixed a new one a few metres higher. We had to take off the ice-coated goggles, as we could not see the little footholds on the smooth rock any more. And then we surmounted the very last steep step. What followed was a gentle slope with black gravel where the wind had swept off all the snow. Then a sharp crest of snow, and then we made out the aluminium tripod. The Chinese pyramid! I waited for Andrej and let him go first. A matter of friendship, nothing else. At that moment I felt tears rising to my eyes. On Gasherbrum I had been in front, and now it was Andrej's turn. At first he did not want to accept, but then he did and was the first to make the final step . . .

The Yugoslavs accomplished some of the most testing climbing yet undertaken on Everest – Tone Skarja called the West Ridge 'the highest grade V in the world'. In Zaplotnik's picture (left), Stremfelj crosses steep ground on the Yellow Band, 1,600ft/488m below the summit. Two days after Stremfelj and Zaplotnik reached the summit, three more climbers – Stane Belak, Stipe Bozic and Ang Phu Sherpa – repeated the route, but Ang Phu died in a fall while the group was descending by the Hornbein Couloir.

THE SUMMIT AT 40° BELOW

by Andrzej Zawada

Translation: Ingeborga Doubrawa-Cochlin and Peter Cochlin

As successive new routes on Everest were climbed, one alluring objective remained: a winter ascent. The challenge was taken up by the Poles, who already had a formidable reputation for winter climbing in the Himalayas. The expedition leader, Andrzej Zawada, argued that it was time to 'open up new horizons' by making a winter attempt on Everest. The expedition faced difficulties from the start. Unable to afford more than five Sherpas, the climbers had to do all their own portering and faced plunging temperatures and recurring storms which wrecked their camps. Finally, in mid-January 1980, they set up a camp on the Lhotse Face, with just four weeks left before their Nepalese climbing permit expired.

The Polish winter expedition of 1979, pictured here in their Base Camp on the Khumbu Glacier (Zawada is second left, front row), faced temperatures of minus 45°C and winds above 100mph. Illness and exhaustion took a constant toll and at times the expedition seemed doomed to fail.

Pages 114–115: The Kangshung or East Face offered a new vision of Everest for the 1980s. In Ed Webster's photograph, Robert Anderson (left) and two porters from the 1988 Kangshung expedition approach the face as they prospect for a camp site. The 'dreamlike sense of disbelief' was noted by Venables, upon completing a new route on the face.

On 15 January Camp III was erected on the wall of Lhotse by the group from Zakopane. Everyone was delighted with our progress – only 11 days of climbing and already three camps established. Then, over the radio we received the team's first impression of conditions ahead: the wall of Lhotse was one large ice mountain! There was no pack snow in which it is so easy to hack out steps. The huge bergschrund below the ice-wall which drops down from the Geneva Spur was virtually impossible to climb. Now we would have to go up the right-hand side between the seracs. On this route there are two overhanging barriers of ice and we would have to use fixed ropes. Our elation at having set up Camp III so swiftly turned to depression.

From Camp III to the saddle of the South Col was a distance of 850 metres. Just 850 metres! At this height and in those wintry conditions, to climb these 850 metres was only just about in the realms of human possibility. We lost nearly one month trying to climb them, and during the many attempts half our team was out of action.

The first attempt was undertaken by Cichy, Heinrich, Holnicki and Wielicki on 23 January. They made a very brave attempt, using fixed ropes which had been left by other expeditions in the autumn and fixing new ones themselves. Wielicki reached the highest point, but even he, after depositing some gear, had to return to Camp III. Two days later another attempt was made by Zurek and Pawlikowski, but hurricane-force winds made climbing impossible. During their retreat, Zurek was blown over by the wind and fell about 20 metres to the nearest piton. Although he was very badly bruised, he managed to reach Camp III unaided, and then, with the help of colleagues, made his way to Base Camp. On his way down he twice fell into crevasses. Unfortunately his injuries did not allow him to take any further part in the expedition and he had to go back to Poland.

All the time the bitter, raging winds made any movement arduous. Even getting to Camp III was a major problem. Several times Dmoch, Heinrich and Olech started out, but even with their great determination, they were unable to win the battle against the icy hurricanes. Week after nervous week went by. On 10 February we tried once more; but once again the weather defeated the indefatigable Heinrich, while his partner, Lwow, returned with frost-bite in his hands. More and more people were unable to take part in the climbs above Camp III, and our doctor, Robert Janik, had more and more work to do in Base Camp attending to the sick and injured.

During this phase of the expedition – the first ten days of February – only four members of the team were able to survive in these appalling conditions and to adjust to the high altitudes. They were Cichy, Fiut, Heinrich and Wielicki, and my plans and hopes were very much bound up with them. Which of them would reach the South Col? I was convinced it was only a psychological barrier preventing us from reaching it. If a person could climb to Camp III at 7,150 metres twice, three and even four times, I felt he could also climb to 8,000 metres, without any doubt. In my mind, I was nervously arranging the right combination of strengths and weaknesses to create the ideal partnership for the final assault. However, it turned out to be unnecessary, because at the critical moment the climbers with necessary qualities of mental and physical endurance were there. But before we could make the final assault, we still had to reach the South Col.

On 11 February, Cichy, Fiut, Holnicki and Wielicki set out. Each climbed at his own pace. A large sheet of solid, glassy ice made the climb very exacting. They reached the Yellow Rocks and climbed towards the Geneva Spur. From this point upwards there was the beginning of an exposed traverse in the rocks, slanting to the left of the ridge. In the middle of this, Holnicki retreated. The other three reached the South Col at 4 pm. There was a whirlwind raging and Cichy, who had helped to carry up some of the equipment, quickly withdrew to Camp III. Fiut and Wielicki tried unsuccessfully to erect a rather complicated American tent in these ferocious conditions, but gave up and took shelter in a small, one-pole bivouac tent. It saved their lives, but they had no chance to rest since they had to struggle all night to hold their small tent down in the savage storm. The oxygen they used revived their strength and warmed their bodies but they were not even able to make tea. Inside the tent the thermometer showed minus 40°C! Our earlier plan of placing the tent in a snow hole was unrealistic.

The constant winds driving through the saddle of the South Col had blown away all the snow, laying bare one gigantic rubbish tip containing multicoloured bottles of oxygen, butane canisters, and various assorted things. All night long we were in radio contact with the two climbers on the South Col. The appalling conditions terrified all of us below. There was a great deal of discussion between camps, and when Cichy suggested that the two climbers on the South Col should go on and try and conquer Everest there were howls of protest. The whole success of the expedition was at a critical stage. If it was almost impossible to survive one night on the South Col, how could we even consider attempting the next 850 metres? There was no choice but to retreat.

I was now convinced that the future of the expedition was out of my hands. How powerless is any leader at moments like these? How convenient is it, when an expedition breaks down in these circumstances, to blame the weather conditions? If I wanted to save the expedition there was only one thing to do, and that was to attempt the climb myself. My partner Szafirski agreed that this was the best way to get us out of the impasse. I was very worried as to how well I would be able to climb 1,500 metres in one attempt. I was in Camp III for the first time, yet I had to climb immediately to the South Col. We were climbing with oxygen, the weather was exceptionally mild, but despite this the climb took us the whole day. Shortly before sunset I reached the vast saddle of the South Col, just behind Szafirski. The dome of the summit of Everest was burning with an incredible purple glow. After removing our oxygen masks we were barely able to recognize one another, so bloated and livid were our distorted faces. Our movements in this thin atmosphere reminded us of scenes from the landing on the moon. We began to erect the Omnipotent Gore-Tex tent to establish Camp IV. We succeeded in bending only two of the fibreglass supports, which proved sufficient to form the barrel-like shape of this new type of tent. We lit two butane heaters and immediately it became very warm inside.

Every evening we discussed our plans for the next day. That evening Cichy and Wielicki informed me that they would like to return to Camp III to attempt an assault on the summit. This was a pleasant surprise for me, particularly since Wielicki had suffered serious frost-bite in his toes and had not had much rest after climbing to the South Col. At the same time Heinrich informed us that he was going to climb from Camp III to Camp IV.

The following morning Szafirski started to climb, taking an extra oxygen bottle to leave as a reserve for the final assault team. He reached 8,100 metres but I was unable to climb with him since I had not acclimatized enough. Instead, I started to check the pressure in the oxygen bottles which had been discarded all over the South Col, and found six with a pressure higher than 230. After midday, Heinrich and Pasang reached Camp IV. They had climbed without any oxygen and were in excellent shape. We convinced Heinrich that he should go for the summit the following morning, provided the weather conditions were satisfactory. We left them our oxygen masks, and at about 4 pm started to go down.

I felt the lack of oxygen very much. Szafirski was in front of me – he was in a hurry to get down.

After sunset, darkness came very quickly as usual. I was on a narrow ledge just before the Yellow Rocks, and could not find the piton with the next fixed rope. Szafirski had already descended through the rock band. I switched on my torch but still could not find the place. I decided to traverse out on the icy wall, hoping to reach the fixed ropes. I managed to chip out two tiny footholds in the ice and stood on them tentatively with only the front spikes of my crampons. Below was a sheer drop of 1,000 metres of icy slab which ended in the open crevasse. Finally common sense prevailed and I made my way back to the rocks. The only thing to do was to wait for the dawn. I cut out a small platform and built a small wall of ice-blocks on the windward side. I took out all the clothes I had in my rucksack and put them on. Trembling with cold, I began the long wait. I was at 7,600 metres and it seemed as if the unusually bright stars were just above my head. Suddenly, down below, I saw lights moving in the vicinity of Camp III. It was Cichy and Wielicki. At great personal risk they were climbing up to come to my rescue. At about 2 am they reached me. They gave me some hot soup and rubbed me until I felt warm again. In the morning, I was back in Camp III.

The permission for this expedition was valid from 1 December till the end of February. The Nepalese Ministry, however, had asked me to agree that attempts to reach the summit would not continue after 15 February when we should start to raze our camps and withdraw to Base Camp. I asked if they would release us from these restrictions but by 14 February I had received no reply. On 15 February we sat by our radio telephones and waited with great anxiety for news from Heinrich on the South Col. If the reply was in the negative then his attempt on the summit of Everest would be our last chance. Climbing without oxygen, Heinrich and Pasang managed to reach 8,350 metres before returning. Meanwhile, the Ministry kept us waiting right up until the last moment, for it was 5 pm before they informed us that they had granted us two further days of climbing – our last two days! Now everything depended on the weather and strong nerves. On the morning of 16 February I said goodbye to Cichy and Wielicki as they left for the South Col.

They climbed with oxygen and reached the South Col after five hours whilst I made my own way down to Camp II where Wielicki, Heinrich and Pawlikowski were waiting. The rest of the expedition was at Base Camp. That evening we kept looking at the sky to see if the weather was going to change. During the night we listened to the winds howling on the ridges above; but in the

Western Cwm it was calm. The two climbers on the South Col told us they were in very good shape. They read the temperature outside their tent – it was minus 42°C.

On the morning of 17 February they reported to us over the radio at 6.30 am that they were about to start their climb, each taking one bottle of oxygen. From that moment it was impossible to sit still. The tension was unbearable. Hope and despair followed one another at each passing moment. As the hours passed and there was still no word over the radio, our anxiety was overwhelming. As a safety precaution Wielicki and Pawlikowski climbed up to Camp III. Then finally, at 2.25 pm the voice of Leszek Cichy resounded over the radio: 'Guess where we are!'

We were out of our minds with happiness. It was the most wonderful moment of our lives. Then we had to concern ourselves with their safe return from the summit. Wielicki had frost-bite in his toes, and they were both exhausted since their oxygen had run out on the South Summit. We spent another very tense night when Cichy reported his arrival at Camp IV but did not say Wielicki was with him; but everything turned out happily and on 19 February the whole team sat down to a celebration supper at Base Camp. We were the first to conquer Everest in winter! Each one of us had the right to feel the victor, including the absent Krzysztof Zurek, because each of us contributed to success and shared the common ideal.

Mountains only take on any meaning when humans are present among them. Humans experience the feelings of victories and defeats, and take with them something of these experiences when they return to the valley. Already our winter expedition of 1980 was behind us.

When the climbers reached the Lhotse Face (shown foreshortened above) they found it consisted almost entirely of sheer ice. Storms continued to drain the expedition's resources and with only four fit climbers it took a month to climb the face and reach the South Col. The British magazine Mountain *said that the climbers were 'treading the borderline between willpower and insanity'.*

A Partner in Myself

by Nena Holguin

Despite his success without oxygen equipment in 1978, Reinhold Messner remained convinced that the ultimate ascent had yet to be achieved. In 1978, he and Peter Habeler had been aided by an Austrian expedition climbing via the South Col; in 1980, Messner resolved to climb Everest without supplementary oxygen and entirely alone. He and his partner Nena Holguin, together with a Chinese liaison officer, set up Base Camp at the Rongbuk Glacier. At first the monsoon snowfall made climbing impossible but in mid-August the weather cleared. Messner began his attempt on 18 August, carrying a 44lb rucksack which included a tiny tent, sleeping-bag and mattress, a stove, food and a camera. His account is related by Nena, who waited for him beneath the North Col.

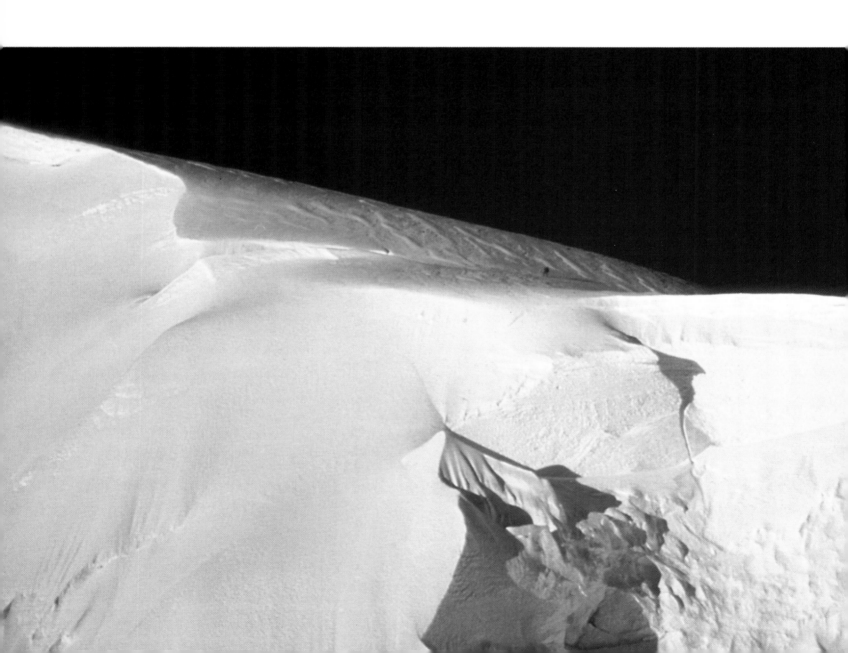

Being alone on a mountain does not guarantee you an experience of utter loneliness. Just in the same way that mingling in a crowd can never deprive you of solitude. It's merely that in one situation there's an accentuation of your fears and problems, while in the other you can easily become distracted or even encouraged to look away from them.

Well, there's nothing to distract me from my fears now. I'm 50 metres below the North Col and I've fallen down, down, down. It felt like eternity in slow motion, rebounding back and forth off the walls of ice, although it was in reality only eight metres deep.

And so I'm standing on a narrow platform. Is it thick or thin? I look up. I look down. It's all the same. It's black – everywhere. My headlamp's died. I see a twinkle from a lone star through a small hole somewhere up above.

All I can say is that despite all those fears I overcame on Nanga Parbat in '78 some new ones have been born. I fumble with the lamp. Ah ha! It

works. I try to make some sense of my situation. I know I shouldn't be down here. 'If I can climb out of here I'm going straight back down this crevasse-ridden snowfield and we're packing up and heading home.' 'But will I die down here instead?' 'Nena's not really so far away; there are only a few hundred metres between us. Down there at our camp along the glacier she's tucked away safely in a warm sleeping-bag.' 'There's a rope down there. Perhaps she could climb up this high alone and help me? But will she ever know where I am?' All the while these thoughts are racing through my mind, somehow I still don't feel all that uncomfortable. I'm actually quite relaxed, feeling peaceful and calm within.

Concentrating now on my next moves I find a small ramp leading diagonally across the ice, leaning inward but none the less taking me upward and out of this hole. I'm able to rationalize quickly once I step out into the crisp clear air. I must have been a little careless before, I tell myself. So, with great care, I span my body across the crevasse and using my ski sticks as an anchor step forward, arriving safely on the uphill side.

My natural instincts take over. It's not difficult now. As I reach the North Col the ridge extends above me up over gentle rolls, rising with only a gradually steepening gradient. The sun takes its time: centimetre by centimetre gold light floods the vastness beyond and the peaks reveal their summits one at a time according to their majestic height. I move on, my boots gripping the hard surface.

To say that the climbing goes on without incident can only mean that there's no particular interruption to one's smooth rhythm; there is always the sense of fascinating incidents going on inside. My whole being is taking part, witnessing this beautiful perfect day, perfect simply because I'm part of it, wide awake and aware with all my senses.

It's going quite well and I'm satisfied with myself. I'm in no rush. Time is mine to waste away. Time to think. Reflecting on my first solo attempts on a Himalayan giant, I'm able to realize a lot of things about myself and my approach to solo climbing. This time I'm here much more for the fun of it. In 1973 when I first headed off to solo Nanga Parbat my ideas were more vague, without direction. I was out to prove to the world, to prove to myself, that I could climb an 8,000-er alone. At the start I was determined but in the end I was heading nowhere. Perhaps then I was even stronger physically than I am now but psychologically I was unprepared.

In 1978 when I again set off for Nanga alone

Left: *Almost lost in the white landscape, Messner – just entering the shaded section – starts up the North Ridge from the North Col, covered in heavy monsoon snow. Nena watched and photographed from their Advance Base on the East Rongbuk Glacier. Messner camped below the North-east Shoulder that night but the next day was no longer visible from below.*

Messner's bivouac tent, purpose-built for the attempt, consisted of a Gore-Tex cover stretched between two semi-circular aluminium poles. He photographed himself with a delayed-action camera mounted on his ice-axe.

things had changed. I was much more in tune with my own body. I had not set off with the object of conquering a peak nor indeed of returning home a hero. What I wanted was to come to know and understand the fears of the world, my own fears. I wanted to feel new again. But it was a long struggle even then to accept myself completely. And for this reason it was perhaps my most important climb. There were still things I had to prove to myself – my self-sufficiency without dependence. During that climb my human side was awakened. It was a battle against my own body in which the will had to take control. It is difficult to say which stress is greater in such a situation, the physical or the psychological.

Here I am once more driving myself onward. I want to live out this dream, this feat of climbing Everest alone which before my solo ascent of Nanga seemed so far away, so impossible. Now for some reason it seems even easier than Nanga. There was no difficulty for me to leave the base at 6,500 metres and head on up here today.

I don't feel so far away from everything as I arrive at my first bivouac spot. There's a good flat surface on a snow-covered rock platform at 7,800 metres. Every preparation goes slowly and smoothly and I find it totally enjoyable to empty my rucksack and erect my small Gore-Tex home. The bright sun reflecting off the snow offers a great deal of warmth and comfort as I chew dried meat and sip this salty brew of Tibetan tea leaves. I don't feel alone. I instead sense a companionship. There's always that someone to keep me company when I reach these altitudes on my own. Perhaps it's that partner within myself.

I couldn't have asked for better circumstances. The daylight fades away leaving the glacier below

in deep black shadow and this world of mountains surrounding me illuminated by spectacular orange then red rays. Darkness falls and I'm at home inside.

I have to make the choice now of going on with less food and gas or going on painfully slower bogged down by the security of those extra rations. I lighten my load and with the tent rolled up loosely and fastened to my rucksack prepare to carry on. The night has been rewarding. My strength and energy levels are replenished after my sleep has been disturbed only by the powerful gusts of wind rather than by the ill effects of high altitude.

At 9 am the first sunlight gives a refreshing start. I'm feeling positive. But then as I begin to wade through snow over my knees my whole manner of thinking changes from this steady harmonious rhythm. What to do? I shall never get anywhere at this rate. I scan the slope of the North Face as it stretches across the Norton Couloir. It certainly is a Great and Grand Couloir, I realize, as I think about its other names. It is impressive to think of the tons of snow that must through the years have thundered down that deep scar in the mountainside.

Obviously several avalanches have swept the face recently and it becomes apparent that my only chance of success lies in picking my way gingerly over a beaten-down snow surface to the couloir from where, with hopes of hard snow in the gully, I will be able to advance. So with a slow and cautious pace I move out across its wide dimension.

It is definitely not steep yet still it leaves me with an air of uncertainty. Anything falling from above will without a doubt sweep me from my feet. But then I allow these thoughts to become distracted occasionally as I look directly above my head and study the First and Second Steps, remembering the 1924 epic of Mallory and Irvine. How impossible it would have been for two climbers within that age of climbing technology and theory to surmount and overcome that great rock barrier, the protruding Second Step, not to mention at some unbelievable speed.

It seems too late in the afternoon as I arrive exhausted at an altitude of 8,200 metres. I'm not feeling as encouraged as yesterday. I've climbed the whole day but I'm only 400 metres higher.

On a mushroom of rock, ice and snow I feel safe enough to bivouac. It sits like a perch out above the entirety of all that's living – mountains, land and people. I haven't excluded myself from them. I'm in fact much more with them from here. I retire stretched out but the altitude is trying to take over. I'm no longer comfortable. Eating and drinking are an effort. 'It's too cramped in here.' 'There is simply not enough room.' 'Will I ever sleep?'

Already I'm feeling my power drifting away as I look out in the early morning at the puffy grey monsoon clouds swirling in all directions and rising quickly from the east. But I'm determined to go on. One litre of water takes too long to bring out of its icy cold nature to a warm satisfying temperature. So I drink the water lukewarm, take the camera around my neck and, wearing my crampons, grasp hold of my ice-axe and begin. I'm lightweight so perhaps there's a chance.

As I lose my orientation success is far from my mind. I'm thinking for the moment. The psychological burden of searching a way through the rock, clouds and ice up to the couloir, then a steep snow flank leading on to the rocky buttress extending down from the Summit Pyramid, weighs heavily on my spirit. Can I carry it?

Somehow and for some reason I go on. I'm nowhere in particular. I'm just climbing automati-

cally, instinctively. I don't expect it but suddenly it's there – the tripod, the blessing of proof, the curse of destruction upon this perfect place of solitude.

While sitting on top of Nanga in '78 I felt as though I was born again, a witness to the whole creation. Now I've brought another dream into reality but there are no words to express this new feeling. The physical stress has reached its limit and the mind can't even react during that instant. I'm simply there.

At times I've searched out a face-to-face encounter with loneliness, searched for understanding and felt a loneliness that was no longer a handicap but a strength. But in no way could I ever claim to have found aloneness. I've merely opened a few doors, to have some slam behind and others lead to more.

Slowly and carefully, step by step, I've learned to know something of myself, to love myself. Sometimes I took chances, I dared, and other times I held back too long. But along my way there's no turning back. I'm delighted on my voyage inward for there is always room to grow.

Messner's photograph shows his first camp at 25,590ft/7,800m. On the second day of his ascent, Messner found the North Ridge covered with thigh-deep snow and decided to traverse the North Face to the Norton Couloir. After a second night at 26,900ft/8,200m he left his tent and most of his equipment to make a light-weight dash for the summit. His ascent was soon regarded as one of the supreme achievements of mountaineering.

TO SPEND ETERNITY

by Maria Coffey

By the 1980s mountaineers were focusing on the 'last great problems' posed by Everest. One was the full ascent of the North-east Ridge, starting from the East Rongbuk Glacier and overcoming the three pinnacles which rise from the ridge between 26,000 and 27,500 feet (around 7,900 to 8,350 metres). In 1982, Chris Bonington led an attempt by a compact, lightweight team determined to climb without oxygen. It ended in disaster. Peter Boardman and Joe Tasker, two of the most respected climbers – and finest writers – of their generation, embarked for the pinnacles on 15 May. They were last glimpsed at dusk on 17 May, but failed to respond to any radio calls. Three days later, in circumstances chillingly reminiscent of the disappearance of Mallory and Irvine, Bonington concluded that his team-mates had died. That autumn Boardman's wife Hilary and Tasker's partner Maria Coffey travelled to Everest. By mid-September they had reached the Rongbuk Valley and were a short walk from the Langma La, within sight of the Kangshung Face.

The expedition's first attempt reached the top of the First Pinnacle but had to turn back when Dick Renshaw suffered a mild stroke. Chris Bonington's photograph (left), taken from Camp II on 5 May, shows Tasker, Boardman and Renshaw at around 27,000ft/8,230m on the First Pinnacle. Above: Maria Coffey, whose extract is taken from her book, Fragile Edge.

The rain fell relentlessly through the night and into the morning, turning to snow as we crested the valley and moved into a landscape of rock and sparse vegetation. I walked alone, locked into private thoughts and listening to the sounds of my own body moving through the silent surroundings.

Hilary's footprints were ahead of me in the snow, and I found her waiting in a small cave on the edge of a lake of the clearest blue which reflected the rocky slopes above it. A thermos flask and food stood ready: her sense of when my energy was about to flag was uncannily accurate, and she would always be there with supplies. Our trekking team was spread out as we moved along at individual paces, each reacting differently to the altitude. Hilary and I had been the first away that morning, carrying packs in case we reached the next camp site long before everyone else and wanted to put up our tents. The track was easy to follow, and Dong, our interpreter, had given Hilary careful instructions. It was good to feel so independent, and to realize that we had gained the trust of our Chinese guides.

We set off again after our snack and I hung back until Hilary was out of sight, reassured by her tracks but wanting to feel the solitude and remoteness of the place keenly around me once more. My pace settled into a regular plod and I moved slowly and easily, feeling warm and comfortable despite the low temperature. Wet snow fell around me, flakes landed on my face and immediately dissolved. The protective clothing was a cocoon, my breathing was amplified inside the jacket hood. A sense of peace settled over me. Suddenly, and totally unexpectedly, I felt Joe's presence. I have no explanation for this; my rejection of Catholicism in teenage years left me suspicious of the spiritual side of life. What happened on those high slopes in Tibet may have been generated by my own mind or may have been a manifestation of some form of energy from Joe. I really do not know, but I had experienced this awareness of him before. Shortly after hearing of his disappearance, I had asked my friend Sarah Richard to drive me to his house in Derbyshire where we had lived before he left for Everest. I wanted badly to be in the house and among all his things, yet it was a dreadful journey, knowing that I would not find him at home, not then or ever again. I sat in the car, distraught, unable to speak to Sarah, feeling sucked towards a horrible finality. And then, as we left the outskirts of Manchester and headed towards open country, I felt him there, all around me, comforting and reassuring. We reached Sarah's cabin first. She got out and I slid over into the driver's seat. I wanted to go to the house alone.

'Are you sure you're all right?'

She bent down to look through the open window. Her face was concerned.

Tasker (left) and Boardman rested for a week before making a new attempt on the Pinnacles, returning to Advance Base on 13 May. Before departing, Tasker wrote to Maria: 'There is a big job for Pete and me to do but hopefully it will go well.' Boardman told his wife Hilary: 'All is on our shoulders. It is a great committing adventure.'

'Yes, I'm fine now. It's not far. I'll see you in a while.'

I drove along a back lane, and experienced the same heightened awareness as when Dick Renshaw first told me Joe had disappeared. The afternoon was vibrant, trees reached out their branches towards the car and the leaves on them shimmered. Joe's presence was still there when I arrived and unlocked the house. I had been too preoccupied with work on my own place to visit it while he was away. It felt like minutes since the day we had left, even though it was three months before. I wandered around inside, soaking in the familiarity. On the bed I wrapped myself in the duvet, my nostrils filled with his smell, and I felt him about me then most powerfully. I cried, talked aloud like a child, and finally slept. A deep, dreamless, peaceful sleep. When I awoke the sun was still streaming through the window. Leaving the house was difficult. My impulse was to stay there, and wait. Only when I parked the car at the bottom of the track leading up to Sarah's cabin did the feeling of Joe gradually fade.

She was standing in the garden among long grasses, shading her eyes against the sun to watch my approach. The scene was uncannily still, as if she were a figure in a painting. I began to tell her.

'I know,' she said. 'He was in the car when I was driving. I felt him. It was really strong. I wasn't going to say anything in case it upset you.'

It has happened several times, only infrequently, but always intensely and without warning. And so, in Tibet, heading towards the Langma La Pass from where I hoped to glimpse the Kangshung Face, I did not try to block the feeling but allowed it to flow. Without knowing how or why, I felt infused by Joe as I plodded along. I listened to him

talking to me, encouraging me. He was all around. I felt the gentle pressure of his hand on the back of my neck. This was utter contentment, a sense of rightness as I headed up the wintry slopes.

Joe, or whatever the sensation had been, ebbed away, leaving me relaxed and smiling and still walking at a measured pace. The track became very narrow, cutting through a steep scree slope along a valley side. Far below me lay a long, densely grey lake with no reflection. Snow fell lightly, the air was damp and the cloud cover so low that mist swirled around me from time to time. My boots crunching on the loose rock broke the silence. In the distance, where the track curved and was swallowed by mist, some shapes took form. Several scrawny cattle swayed along the track until I had to scramble up the slope and make way for them. Behind the animals, carrying staffs and walking slowly and steadily, were an old man and a young boy. The man was slight, his face narrow, wrinkled and serene, and from his chin a long white beard fell in two strands. Their grey woollen blankets and felt boots seemed insubstantial against the snow and rocks. They stopped and regarded me seriously.

'Chomolungma?'

The old man pointed to where he had come from, towards the Langma La Pass. I nodded, and waited. All morning I had felt a stillness within me, a tenuous but undeniable link to a dimension outside the well-known and understood parameters of my world. Being high in the Himalayas, sensing the solidity, force and sheer permanence of the environment, was opening up my mind and allowing in a chink of awareness of the full scope and mystery of existence. This man and boy seemed creatures wholly connected to the mountain they stood upon. The child gazed up at me, unsmiling, with an air of wisdom and experience far beyond his years. His companion shook his head gravely. 'Chomolungma, Chomolungma,' he repeated, and taking my hands in his he intoned a prayer, perhaps a blessing. I welcomed this: I wanted to draw from this knowledge of ages that he surely possessed. He raised his hand in farewell and moved past me with the boy, towards their cattle. I watched until they went out of sight and imagined how we must have looked from high above, three tiny figures passing through a vast and unmoving landscape.

Beyond the prayer-flags of the Langma La Pass a bank of thick cloud lay over the Kangshung Face. Hilary sat very still, gazing towards it. I put my hand on her shoulder.

'The man and boy – did you meet them? Did he bless you?'

She nodded. We waited together, silently willing the mountain to reveal itself, until the three Swiss trekkers who made up our team arrived.

Jacques was in bad shape. We were now at 17,400 feet, he had pains in his chest and his pallor was a worrying grey. We divided up the contents of his small day-pack and his friend Denny stayed close and kept a watchful eye on him. Coming down the steep path from the pass, into the Kharma Valley, a yak driver and one of the porters prayed loudly at a high, sheer rock face and left offerings, small piles of food, on a ledge. At the head of this valley was Chomolungma, a sacred mountain, and they were showing respect.

On the valley floor the waters of a lake, startlingly blue from the copper salt, reflected our progress as we filed along its shores – heavily-laden yaks and porters, tired trekkers. A crowd of beaming girls appeared and crowded round as the tents were erected. When they left I discovered that one of my gaiters and two stuff-sacks had gone with them, articles that had belonged to Joe. My fury was unreasonable, but I couldn't help feeling that they had taken away a tiny part of him. I drifted into a disgruntled sleep, woken near dawn

by Hilary shaking snow from the tent roof and lighting candles to dry out the interior.

Chomolungma kept her Eastern Face shrouded for the next two days as we moved closer to the mountain across dramatically changing terrain. Moonlike landscapes on the high plains transmuted to muddy trails through lush vegetation in the valleys. We pressed on, crossing and recrossing rivers by rickety bridges or by precariously hopping from stone to stone, trudging through mud, willing the clouds to life. I remember Charlie Clarke and Chris Bonington predicting that there would be little chance of good weather on the east side of the mountain, but I was still convinced we would be lucky. The feeling of drawing so close was intense. Hilary was voluble in her grief: she talked and cried openly. I became increasingly withdrawn, conscious of tension building inside me. If Chris was right, if Joe and Pete had fallen down the Kangshung Face, then they were not far away, they were somewhere in the crevasses at the foot of Chomolungma. I immersed myself in an awareness of Joe's proximity, allowing it to override my loneliness and the reality of the loss. Asleep and awake I dreamed of somehow getting

On 15 May, Boardman (ahead) and Tasker set off for the foot of the North-east Ridge. They stayed at Camp II that night and the following day reached Camp III, a snow cave at 25,750ft/7,850m, just below the foot of the First Pinnacle.

to his body, wrapping myself around his frozen form and breathing warmth and life back into him. It was an illusion born out of hopeless desperation.

Drying out round the stove at the end of the fourth day of trekking, we made a group decision to turn back. Going further towards the face meant crossing a glacial moraine that could be unstable after so much rain, and there was no indication of the weather clearing. Early the next morning Hilary and I walked up to a rocky knoll to make our private goodbyes. The Kangshung Face was ahead of us, hidden by the heavy mist that clung to it so resolutely, but I could feel its presence. Joe could be nearby, held somewhere within its folds. Perhaps this was as close to him as I would ever be again. With that thought the illusion snapped. There were no miracles to be had, the relationship was over, except for what I could cling to in memory. Chomolungma could not give him back to life. I sat down and began to weep, heaving sobs which bent me double as in the early days of grief. Hilary held me until I quietened and then I leaned on her and tried, brokenly, to express my thoughts. She looked over my head.

'Zhiang is coming.'

Our liaison officer walked slowly by, placed something on the cairn at the very top of the knoll, and then stood and looked towards the cloud-covered mountain. When he returned his face was set tight as if holding in feelings, and he did not glance in our direction. We went up to the cairn. Two cans of beer were set there, and a small posy of flowers lay between them. An offering to the mountain and a sign of respect to Joe and Pete.

We retraced our steps, back through the dense vegetation, up the muddy slopes and on to the windy plain. As night fell the mist rolled in around the camp site. In the big wigwam I chopped vegetables, drank whisky and tried to socialize, but I couldn't concentrate on conversation. My mind was outside, out in the mist and heading towards the mountain. After dinner I walked through the fog until I was out of earshot of the camp and away from its light. Squatting on my haunches, I felt the cloud close in and I imagined Joe walking towards me with his relaxed, loping stride, dressed in his usual garb of jeans, boots and sweater which varied little with the seasons. Had his ghost emerged from the mist I would hardly have been surprised, but nothing moved, there was no sound. I remembered an American girl I had met years before, in Patagonia. I had just arrived at Fitzroy National Park and she and her team of Italian climbers were preparing to leave. Her boyfriend had died on a nearby mountain the previous year, and she had travelled to South America to find his body and bury it. One of the climbers was a priest. They had reached the point on the glacier where her boyfriend and his companion had landed after the falls, said Mass and lowered the bodies into crevasses. She was young, in her twenties. As we talked she was using an ice-axe to hammer nails into the wall of the wooden hut that was at the 'road head' of the park.

'This was his,' she said, waving the axe.

'You mean . . . '

'We found it beside him. I may as well use it. These nails will be good for hanging stuff on. And who knows, I might come back some time.'

'Are you glad you came?'

'Sure I am. Now I can believe he's really dead. Now I have a picture of him. Now . . . ' She stopped for a second, her voice caught. 'It was good to at least be able to say goodbye.'

That girl . . . I couldn't remember her name, or what part of America she was from, or why she was with Italian climbers. But the feeling I had on that day came back clearly, my admiration of her composure and my wonder at her strength. I could never have foreseen it back then, but now I was envious of her, for her chance to say goodbye.

My legs had begun to cramp, and I was cold and damp. I stirred, stretched and returned to our tent, which was aglow with the light of several candles.

Crawling in, I discovered Hilary in the middle of a full-scale nosebleed. Her red thermal underwear was matched by the mounds of bloody tissues scattered around the sleeping-bags, and she was distraught with a mixture of grief and frustration at not being able to stop the flow of blood. I calmed her and the bleeding ceased, but her confusion carried through to her sleep. During the night her anguished cries woke me.

'No! No! Pete! *Pete!*'

She sat bolt upright, suddenly awake. In the dream she had relived the avalanche she had survived in Switzerland earlier that year, but I and her two nieces were with her and Pete was trying to dig us all out. For a while, then, we lay awake and she talked about the real avalanche, which had happened when Pete and Joe were on Everest, six weeks before they disappeared. She wrote to Pete about it and he replied: 'What is important is that you are alive and so am I.'

The sharp frost of the morning gave us hope that the mountain would appear. The clouds were playing a teasing game, allowing a glimpse of a peak and then covering it up again. Makalu appeared for a time and there was confusion over whether or not it was Chomolungma. We ran up a slope for a better view, our lungs heaving and

burning in the thin, cold air. The face we saw was massive, spectacular and terrifying, but it was not the Kangshung.

Jacques was weak and despondent, so we took turns at walking with him and giving him encouragement. As I plodded up snow-covered slopes behind a yak, past tiny blue lakes, with the sun breaking through and snow peaks appearing, the loveliness would send a shiver through me and I would be glad to be alive and to be there. Hilary and I hung back at the Langma La Pass, watching the clouds around Chomolungma, willing the curtain to open and show us the awesome vista behind. Three times the mists rolled back to reveal the summit, but the face stayed shrouded. Zhiang was hovering anxiously, wanting us to leave and follow the others, but we needed the steadying of those minutes, letting our thoughts settle before heading down from the mountain. It occurred to me that perhaps it was no coincidence that the Kangshung Face was not being revealed to us. Perhaps it was, after all, easier for us this way. I

blew a kiss towards the east side of Everest and turned away.

Verdant hillsides pungent with juniper, and the gentle colours of irrigated fields and villages: after the landscapes of the high passes I felt I was seeing the lower Kharta Valley with new eyes. And as we began the drive to the northern side of Chomolungma I was calm, almost happy. Two eagles hovered high above us on the air currents. Joe and Pete, I thought, watching us leave. It was a fine place to spend eternity.

In May 1992, climbers from Kazakhstan found Boardman's body in a sitting position close to the Second Pinnacle, a short distance from where he and Tasker had last been seen ten years before. There was no sign of Tasker. It seemed likely that Tasker had fallen from the ridge and that Boardman had died, probably of exhaustion and the effects of altitude, while attempting to descend through the pinnacles alone. The climber who found Boardman's body said that he was in a position of repose, 'looking like he was asleep'.

Chris Bonington took this long-distance photograph of the Pinnacles from the Advance Camp on the evening of 17 May. One of the pair – Boardman or Tasker – was just visible as a tiny dot on the snow slope approaching the Second Pinnacle. At 9 pm the two climbers disappeared behind the Second Pinnacle and were never seen alive again. Bonington and support climber Adrian Gordon waited for them in vain at the North Col the next day. After four anguished days Bonington and his colleagues gave up all hope for the missing men.

A New Star to Follow

by Eduard Myslovski
Translation: Michael Nicholson

The first Soviet team to attempt Everest - and the first Soviet expedition to the Himalayas - arrived in March 1982. Instead of the easy option of a South Col ascent, its goal was a new route, the Central Pillar, which abuts the South-west Face to join the West Ridge at 27,230 feet/8,300 metres. The difficult technical climbing, some of the hardest accomplished on Everest, exhausted many of the climbers, but on 30 April two Russians, Eduard Myslovski and Volodya Balyberdin, together with Sherpa Nawang, were ready to begin their attempt from Camp III at 25,750 feet/7,850 metres.

Eduard Myslovski, 44, from what was then Soviet Russia, led the first summit bid. Early in the expedition he appeared to be suffering from altitude sickness and was warned by doctors not to go above 6,000 metres. He ignored their advice and proved one of the fittest climbers in the team. But his attempt was at a high price, as shown by his bandaged hands.

We did not have a good start. The night had not left us as rested as we ought to have been. Stripping our packs down to essentials, we set off once again, but after two rope-lengths I noticed that the gap between Nawang and Volodya was widening rapidly.

I climbed up to where the Sherpa stood. At first we used sign language, then we took off our oxygen masks and communicated in English. There were tears in Nawang's eyes. He was distraught. He told me that he couldn't climb any further or help us any more, as his sight was too bad. I offered to swap goggles with him. We went another few yards, then stopped again. Nawang apologized for not being able to help. We went down to a little plateau under an overhang and there we decided that he would go back down to Camp III. Still asking our forgiveness, he bowed, placed his hands to his forehead, said goodbye and left. I sorted through the load he had been carrying and added a rope and another two cylinders of oxygen to my own rucksack.

While Nawang and I were settling matters, Volodya had pressed on up the mountain, and the gap between us had increased to an hour and a half or even two hours. We climbed up a steep rocky couloir and a small rock face. The going got harder and harder. Volodya stopped and shouted down: 'Let's lighten our load, or we'll never make it to Camp IV today.'

I left the two cylinders of oxygen behind, as well as a gas burner and two gas cylinders, but my rucksack didn't feel any lighter for it. Volodya left some of his oxygen too. Evening was coming on. Then a light fluffy snow started falling. If I'd been living near Moscow, I would have been delighted to see snow like that, but here I cursed it. The rock face turns slippery. Your movements become uncertain. You can't put a foot down without first cleaning the foothold. Your hands start freezing, and the snow clings to your goggles.

It started getting dark. Volodya rounded a turn in the cliff wall. I felt crushed by loneliness and fatigue. Before me was an almost vertical section with the ropes winding away up it. Of course it is possible to follow fixed ropes, even at night, but would I be in a fit state to climb tomorrow? I decided to leave my rucksack and get up to Camp IV travelling light. That way I could be in before base made contact and started worrying. By the time I made it to the tent, everywhere was in complete darkness. We decided that in the morning Volodya would go on ahead and fix the ropes, while I retrieved my rucksack.

The next day was May Day and we congratulated each other on the holiday. Base Camp sent its greetings too, and we set to work. While Volodya went ahead, I went back down for my rucksack. After I had collected it, I was approaching the camp, with some two and a half pitches left to climb. Ahead lay a difficult section of vertical rock face with very small footholds. Volodya had given

me his jumar clamp as he did not need it today and I decided I would use it to help me up this face. The rope across the face was extremely slack. I had only taken two steps when I was hurled back against a smooth section of the face like a pendulum. I lost my footing and hung almost horizontal, pulled down by my rucksack. The weight of it wrenched at my shoulders, stopping me from taking breath and gathering my strength. It became harder and harder to breathe, and I realized that my oxygen had run out. It wouldn't be long before I lost consciousness, and then it would be all over: I'd be left hanging from the rope until I froze to death, like Harsh Bahuguna in 1971. It wasn't exactly a cheerful prospect.

My last hope was to free myself as quickly as possible from the weight of the rucksack. I took off my gloves and, after a great deal of effort, managed to unfasten the strap. By now my hands were seizing up with cold. There was just one thought running through my head: 'Get a move on, you're running out of time!' It was useless to shout for help: I had my mask on, and anyway Volodya was round a fold in the face. Somehow I managed to struggle out of my rucksack, catching it in the

crook of my left arm. Again and again I tried to fasten it to the rope with my other hand, but to no avail. Gasping for breath beneath my mask, and snarling with impotent rage, I let my left hand drop and the rucksack plummeted down, ripping through my oxygen line and taking with it my spare gloves, cameras, ropes, karabiners, crampons, oxygen . . .

I pulled off my mask, taking the air in in deep gulps, and hauled myself up on the ledge. It was then that I noticed that my fingers had turned white. I warmed my hands and struggled up to the tent at Camp IV, but the effort and tension had so exhausted me that I could hardly stand on my feet.

Meanwhile, Volodya had put in a good day's work, fixing the ropes above the camp. We totted up how much equipment we had left and decided to carry on with the job next day. White blisters were forming on my fingers. Some of them burst, and Volodya helped me bind them with plaster. That night my hands hurt, but I could put up with it.

The next morning Volodya made me a crude rucksack out of a tent-sack and we headed up the mountain. There were steep rocky pinnacles with

The Soviet expedition set up Base Camp in the customary site below the Khumbu Glacier. It put a second camp about the Khumbu Icefall and a third in the Western Cwm close to the foot of the Central Pillar on the South-west Face. At the end of March the higher camps were hit by a storm, forcing a retreat to base.

snowy caps and sharp ridges, dropping away on either side for thousands of feet, but still it was easier than the section of cliff face just before Camp IV.

Ahead of us lay a serious obstacle, a rocky pinnacle which we decided to skirt round to the left. Volodya was working his way underneath an overhanging section, hammering in pitons and fastening loops to them. He had hardly any distance to go to the top when a piton tore loose, sending him slithering three or four yards down the face. He got his breath back, then went up again, inching his way even more carefully than before. At last we had the wall behind us, and the ropes were securely fastened.

Meanwhile Seryozha Bershov had been climbing up behind us bringing more oxygen. It was marvellous to see him, and we quizzed him about how things were going on further down the mountain. He negotiated the difficult stretch and left three cylinders of oxygen, before hurrying back down. He was due to spend the night in Camp III. What a terrific fellow he is. After all, he didn't have to climb this far: he could have left the oxygen at Camp IV as we had agreed.

We pressed on. The West Ridge was still not in sight, but we could sense that it was near at hand. I worked my way along a sharp snowy ridge, then Volodya came out into a steep icy couloir. I crossed the ice up to the rock face, which was as brittle as rotten wood. We climbed for another two ropes, showering each other with stones to our mutual annoyance: the altitude and our growing fatigue were taking their toll. We decided not to climb any further, left our remaining gear there and went back down to Camp IV for the night.

In the evening we were very moved to hear over the radio the voices of our friends and loved ones, wishing us luck, together with songs by Grieg:

they were playing taped messages, recorded by our families at home in Moscow. This was a very special present for us. It brought tears to my eyes to hear my favourite songs and ballads sung by those dearest to me - my wife and daughters.

In the morning we set off to establish Camp V. We did not use oxygen to work our way along the ropes we had fixed the previous day. We climbed another 40 metres along the ridge beyond our high point, then set about the difficult task of hacking out a level patch in the ridge for the tent. I went on another rope higher, and from there I could see the route along the West Ridge to the summit. It was still quite a distance to go even though the difference in altitude couldn't have been more than 350 metres.

We crawled into the tent and contacted Base Camp. They wished us good luck for the ascent. It had been a hard day. I was so exhausted I couldn't be bothered to take off my boots, especially since I would have to put them back on in the morning – no small task up here. This would be our last night's rest before the summit. It was cold . . .

The strain of the past few days and the proximity of the summit made it impossible to get off to sleep, and we passed the night half dozing. Volodya had forgotten to put his boots inside his sleeping bag. By morning they were stiff and had to be warmed up over the primus. We drank some tea and went out to start the ascent. We climbed in silence, Volodya in front. We had set our rate of oxygen consumption at the minimum to make it go further. From time to time we would stop to pick out our route and, at last, came out on to the West Ridge, leading up to the summit of Everest.

We met a shallow, rocky rise, then a crest of snow, then a short rock face where we had to do some climbing. And so we gained altitude. Below us on a snowy slope near some rocks we could see an orange tent left by one of the previous expeditions. This section had already been done by other climbers, and that was somehow comforting: others had made it and so would we. We sheltered from the wind in a hollow to make contact with Base Camp. We were feeling good, and better still when the sun came out from behind the mountain.

We trudged on towards the summit. Ahead lay the famous belt of reddish cliffs, the last but one obstacle before the summit. A thin fixed rope, frayed by the wind, wound up the cliffs like Ariadne's thread, helping us to pick our route. It was hung here by Yugoslav climbers in 1979. On this section our progress was hindered because, to lighten our load, we had brought only a 20 metre rope and there were few convenient places where we could organize a reliable belay.

Above the cliff, however, it was like going up a staircase. The rocks rose in smooth steps, like tiles, leading us on to the next hurdle – a 20 metre wall. This was probably the last obstacle in our path. Volodya left some of our hardware behind – we wouldn't need it higher up. Now there was no ambiguity about the route, and in any case it was marked here and there by an empty yellow oxygen cylinder, a lost ice-pick or parts of a broken radio.

We walked on and on, but the summit seems never to come. A snowy incline rises ahead of us in a series of steep slopes, alternating here and there with shattered grey cliffs. Now we're already level with the South Summit. That means we're nearly there. And then, at last - the moment we've been waiting for for so long! Volodya stands on the summit and gets out his movie-camera. I walk past him and sink down on to the snow.

That's it. From here there's nowhere higher to go.

I glanced round. What an extraordinary feeling of space! The dark blue dome of the sky, the Himalayas with their flocks of fleecy white clouds, the rolling landscape of the Tibetan foothills. I looked at the surrounding peaks and recognized the summits of Makalu, Cho Oyu and, right next to us, Lhotse.

Afterwards I would often be asked what I felt at that moment.

Happiness? Hardly.

Exhilaration? No.

Relief? Yes, to some extent.

Exhaustion? Maybe. I can't remember.

There was just a feeling of having got the job done: at last our climbers had set foot on this part of the planet too. It was a triumph for Soviet mountaineering. But if the triumph was not to be marred we still had to make our way down.

When I finally stepped on to level ground once more at Camp I, I stopped, sat down on a rock facing the mountain, and all at once it struck me: that's that! The dream I had lived with for many years. The mountain – the highest in the world – which I had never been on. The mystery. The guiding star. The goal. They had all been part of me, but now they were gone

Now I had to find a new star to follow.

Myslovski's loss of his rucksack, which included his outer gloves, exacted a heavy toll. Because he had been reduced to wearing only a pair of thin woollen gloves, he suffered serious frostbite and had parts of his fingers amputated on his return to Moscow.

The Soviet expedition put no fewer than 11 climbers on the summit. In this group, photographed at Camp I after their success, Balyberdin is on the left-hand end, Myslovski at the right: the first summit pair, both were from Russia. Centre left is Mikhail Turkevich, from the Ukraine, one of the second pair who reached the summit later that day, 4 May. Centre right is Sergei Yefimov, another Russian, who went to the summit on 5 May.

A FINE DAY FOR ME

by Carlos Buhler

The Kangshung Face of Everest was long considered unclimbable. In 1921, George Mallory dismissed it as impossible and the shared wisdom was that the avalanches which swept down it made it an unthinkable proposition. But in the early 1980s mountaineers began to reassess the risks. In 1981, a US expedition which included Ed Hillary and Kurt Diemberger climbed a giant buttress in the centre of the face before being stopped by the avalanche threat. The Americans returned in 1983, bringing a rocket launcher and motor winch to fix an aerial ropeway for load-hauling. There were tensions over tactics and the composition of the summit party often changed due to illness but the expedition built on the previous efforts. In extracts from his diary, Carlos Buhler, at 28 an experienced international mountaineer, describes the swings of mood and fortune as the team prepares for its summit push.

26 September

Camping at Pinsetter. Up and down and up and down. The radio's been going all morning! The people at Snow Camp told me not to come down - there were of course no loads to bring up. Then they told me to go up. Then to stay put. Then the whole day's carry was aborted - snowing too hard! So here I sit at Pinsetter, waiting to see what the weather will do. We're going to have to wait for October sun to settle those slopes. But I'm uncannily easy about time today. One month in base and it doesn't worry me a bit. Hey, I hope we don't lose anyone on that upper route by avalanche. Could be dicey up there. This is the strangest mountaineering venture I have ever been on. This is so far from what alpine climbing is all about that I sometimes wonder what I am doing here.

27 September

I can't believe what just happened. I mentioned that I thought we should be sensitive to Geoff Tabin since he was feeling kind of left out and had a rough first experience on the mountain. One of the guys said I had no business saying such things and that it wasn't good for the team's chances if people worried about one member - natural selection was the thing. I just about felt like leaving there and then. Tears came to my eyes and I was embarrassed that someone might notice. But I don't really care. This whole episode reaffirms my thinking about going on a large trip like this.

Anyway, Lou and I came jugging up to the Helmet Camp. I made the mistake of getting ahead and felt pushed all the way – next time I'll plod along behind. The whole thing could be over in ten days. Depends on the weather of course. I'd be glad to

The 1983 US Kangshung Face expedition took on Everest's most awesome challenge - a 3,500 foot rock and ice buttress rising from the Kangshung Glacier, demanding the full range of modern climbing techniques. The expedition named it the Lowe Buttress, after their climber George Lowe, but it is also known as the American Buttress. Left: Jay Cassell is shrouded by spindrift as he sets off up the final ice-slope at the top of the buttress. Above came a 7,700 foot climb up avalanche-prone snow slopes. Right: The ice formations of the East Face were wrought into fantastical shapes, particularly in the claustrophobic gully named the Bowling Alley between Snow and Pinsetter Camps on the lower part of the buttress. The climber is Dave Coombs.

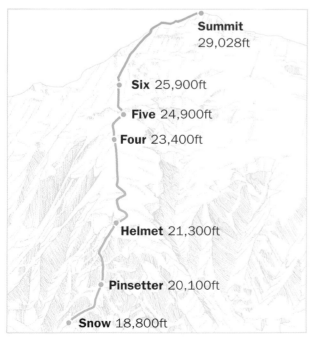

Summit 29,028ft

Six 25,900ft

Five 24,900ft

Four 23,400ft

Helmet 21,300ft

Pinsetter 20,100ft

Snow 18,800ft

It took the expedition 28 days to overcome the American Buttress. In Buhler's photograph, which shows an 800 foot section of the buttress, between 19,500 and 20,300 feet, a climber at the foot of the Mushroom Ridge appears dwarfed by the task. Diagonally upwards to his right can be seen the entrance to the Bowling Alley. The diagram (left) shows the three camps on the buttress – Snow, Pinsetter and Helmet – followed by the line of camps on the snow face above.

have it over in ten days. Ranking the strongest guys, I probably won't make the first four. But so what. I'm really not too excited about this type of climbing anyway.

28 September

I'm pretty tired out today. Lou and I broke trail to 23,500 feet. I gave it what I could as it was my first opportunity to be out in front. We'll be carrying tomorrow to the site of Camp IV. I was very glad to be able to make the sort of contribution I did today. There's something special about the insignificant act of forging ahead where no one has been before. I think today was my happiest day so far. The summit was not really close but the jumping-off point for the top didn't seem too far away. The South Col loomed over there to the left of us. Looked relatively close, yes it did. Well, ten days and someone will be on top. Everybody's expounding on how strong the team is since all eight people made it up to our Camp III at 23,500 feet. I can only say that it ain't easy. Spirits are high though, and I'm sure that there'll be plenty of summiters.

29 September

The gang's all here, or almost. I will probably fall into my inferiority complex as we argue over where to put camps etc. I took a day off, really. Only hauled up a winch load of tents. A light load which I hope will let me recover from yesterday's trail break to 23,500. Anyway I'm not sure I can recover at 21,300. We'll just have to see. If the weather stays good we'll have a summit attempt in one week or thereabouts. Suits me fine. With 13 people up here, I'll be more than ready to get the hell off the peak. I don't do too well with 12 other people. It'll be interesting to see how I do up high. I should push my altitude record on this trip, if nothing else. As I jugged up with my winch load, I really felt that the route was a unique and extraordinary one – very technical, unbelievably so for a big mountain route.

Later: I feel recovered somewhat. That's valuable knowledge. I'm glad that I can get a little back in a semi day off. I did a carry too, up from the winch, which is a good sign. Boy oh boy, what is this next two weeks going to bring? If winds come in ten days, only the first team will make it. Summit, summit, summit. Who cares?

1 October

Today was a fine day for me. We slept in Camp IV and broke the route to Camp V, at what we all hope is over 25,000 feet. The wonderful thing was that my body responded to my will with such success. I actually was able to get into a rhythm that felt comfortable even at 25,000 feet. I am so astounded, really, that my body has responded so well these last four days at altitude.

The crux of the situation is becoming clear to me as I lie here in bed . . . I have been chosen to be part of the first summit team! This is absolutely unbelievable for me, the boy who grew up in Harrison, New York, pudgy and unathletic as I was. So I'm honoured today – knowing that I'm not the strongest member or the most experienced – but that still I am considered a decent bet for the first attempt. Whether we make it depends on a lot of things. But being given that vote of confidence is really nice. If we four stand on the summit within five days, that will be time to reflect on an awful lot that's occurred in my life. Dream? Why not? How often does one get the chance to dream about making the summit of Everest by a new route?

2 October

Snowing out down here on the Helmet. We lie around resting, eating, drinking. I feel pretty damn good. Ready to try for the top, beginning tomorrow to Camp IV. Will it really happen?

3 October

Once again, all has been changed. Group A had to be pared down to three and it was obvious who that one person taken out should be. So when Jim put me in the second three-man team, with Kim and Lou, I was completely ready for it. As a matter of fact, I feel really good about going with those two guys. We have so much experience packed into those first six climbers that I don't see how we could be a stronger team. So, after a bad weather day such as we had yesterday and today, tomorrow looks beautiful. I feel so good about this six-man team and so honoured to be part of it, it's difficult to describe. Now we wait again, and watch for the weather. And pray that in five days my dream comes true. I will stand on the summit of this Chomolungma, Sagarmartha or Mt Everest. Yes. Dream it shall be yours!

5 October

All's quiet in Camp IV. The A team is off to Camp V. Lou and Kim are behind them, destined for carrying and establishing Camp VI. I'm carrying to Camp V also, but I'm drinking a brew first. Windy out, and thick clouds below don't give confidence of good summiting weather. If all goes well, it'll be over in four days. Be nice to stand on top of this beast. Very nice. And get down in one piece, happy and healthy.

6 October

Dave has suspected pulmonary oedema. Suddenly we're thrown into the position of first summit

A crenellated knife-edge ridge – the Horizontal Ridge – no more than three feet wide provided an airy route to Pinsetter Camp at 20,100ft/ 6,126m, with the Kangshung Glacier below. The expedition spent days carrying 30lb loads across this section.

attempt team. Me, the weak link in this team. I feel so sorry for the A team. I cried as George and Kop sat here and spoke with Jim on the radio. I'm in no way as strong as Lou and Kim. But no one else is either. I would just not be fair to myself not to take my rightful turn and try for the top. So here we sit, the three B team folks, brewing up and sitting around. I've never felt so much pressure to make a summit because of not giving up my place to George. But I'm not going to let that get to me. I'm just here to do my very goddamned best.

7 October

Today we go up. Lou is packing up. Summit weather is all around. Perfectly clear. A hard night at 25,200 in Camp V. Kim is a gem up here, singing.

10 October

Well, George climbed Mount Everest yesterday. So did Dan and Jay. Lou, Kim and I did it the day before. Everest. Six on top. A dream comes true. First summit team. Kim, Lou and myself open the Kangshung Face to Everest's summit.

It's hard to keep a clear head through it all. Our move up to Camp VI on the 7th was uneventful. I moved up slowly and didn't race with Lou or Kim. That night we brewed up for four or five hours and then again at 1 am when we got up to go for the summit. Until 4 am we drank and drank. What followed was ten and three-quarter hours of gruelling trail breaking. It took us six hours to do the first 1,300 feet to 27,500 on the 'normal' ridge. Terrible, absolutely *terrible* snow conditions left us pretty wiped out. We ran into the seven Japanese trying to climb Everest without oxygen there and continued on.

I was amazed at the slope leading up to the South Summit – treacherous as hell. There was wind slab after we came up the Hillary Step and the thought of Mick Burke disappearing here in 1975 made me extremely wary. I tried to stay low on the left side of the ridge to avoid the huge cornices dropping over the East Face. I led it all with apprehension, but contentedly knowing that it was the final push to victory for the entire expedition. Kop had warned me that a few false summits would appear to be the top but when the true apex came it would be unmistakably clear. It was a good tip. When the top did come into view I waited for Kim and Lou to come up with me. The day was fantastic and the sun beat warmly on us even on those last few metres. Together the three of us cramponned up to the crest. It was all kind of a dream.

The air around us was very calm and it seemed as though we could have lit a candle on the

Some of the climbing on the buttress was the steepest and most testing achieved on Everest. In the photograph (left) Dave Cheesmond is using the technique known as jumaring or jugging to climb a rope on the overhanging section of the black wall above Mushroom Ridge. (The rope had been fixed in place by the lead climber.)

Right: *Pinsetter Camp, located on an exposed ledge halfway up the buttress. It was named Pinsetter because it lay directly above Bowling Alley Gully.*

Above: *To ease the task of carrying their equipment up the buttress, the expedition used winches to ferry loads. The first, powered by a 5hp engine and designed by expedition member John Boyle, could lift an 80lb pack almost 1,000 feet up the buttress; here, Kim Momb is poised to land a new load. A second winch, using a counterweight of snow packed into a canvas bag, took the loads a further 700 feet. The expedition carried half a ton of equipment in this way.*

Right: *The open slopes at last: after spending four weeks on the buttress, the expedition finally reached the snow slopes above. In Buhler's photograph, Dan Reid and Lou Reichardt are carrying loads to Camp IV; Kim Momb is behind them, and another party of four can be seen below them, to the left. The Kangshung Glacier is 5,000 feet below; the summit 6,000 feet above.*

summit. My small Olympus camera conveyed the truth of the temperature. It was hopelessly frozen. Kim took out a walkie-talkie and radioed down to Advance Base Camp. We could hear some Tibetan chanting – the local Yak herders who had stayed at Base Camp had begun to chant prayers for us at 5 am that morning and hadn't stopped all day long. I was pretty moved by their voices.

We took out a bunch of flags that needed to be photographed. As we'd removed our oxygen equipment, things went a bit slow. I was particularly interested in the way the Rongbuk Glacier led out north to Tibet. Then came the gear photos - there was not much time to enjoy the view. I felt like we were a long way out on a fragile limb and the desire to start the descent burdened me. A strong sense of quiet satisfaction began to creep into my mind. In my oxygen-starved state, the dreamy realization that our goal was in our grasp began to take form. All we had to do was descend without an accident. I couldn't help thinking over and over of Mick Burke. I felt we had a long way to go that day.

We started down at 3.25 pm. I stopped to pick up a few stones and then Lou and Kim were out of view. It took a moment to realize I was alone at the top of the world – my moment to be the highest soul standing on earth. The descent was not so good. At the Hillary Step we bottlenecked with the five Japanese still going for the summit. Lou was moving like an old man – I only found out later he had stopped using oxygen because it was fogging up his glasses. I watched him go down the step ever so slowly, and when he and I reached the South Summit Kim was already far ahead. I could see him far down on the South-east Ridge. He must have been nervous about getting caught out

after dark and was pouring on the speed. It was about 4.30, the sun was already low in the sky, and I too was feeling very pressed for time. Then we met a climber just coming up to the South Summit. I presumed he was another of the Japanese team we had met earlier in the day. Like them, he was climbing without an oxygen bottle.

'How much time to summit?' he asked me in broken English. I didn't know what to say. It was so late now and with darkness coming the temperature would drop maybe 40 degrees. My throat was like dry ice and I could hardly speak. I pointed to my mask and said, 'With oxygen, maybe one hour. Without oxygen?' and just shrugged my shoulders.

'No time! No time!' he verbalized his thoughts as he looked up towards the Hillary Step where one of the Japanese was still working his way up the fixed ropes. He was absolutely right about the time. But someone trying Everest without oxygen is a motivated man and it was up to him to make his own decision, I thought. He told me he wasn't a Japanese climber but a Sherpa. He wanted to go down. It seemed the sensible thing to do, but again, I'd already made the top.

I took out a spare insulated mitten from my pack and my second water bottle which was inside it. I knew I wouldn't need it if we could get to the tent that night and set it down in the snow where I hoped the Japanese would find it. I carried on down the slope from the South Summit. It was hard packed snow and a fall would have been nearly impossible to arrest. I noticed that like me Lou was facing out as he descended. I was 40 or 50 feet ahead when I heard Lou's dry, raspy cry for help. I wheeled round and saw him splayed out on his back on the 35 degree slope with his head downhill. It didn't make sense! I sprinted up the slope on my front points and threw my body against his. The exertion made it feel that my air supply had been cut and I choked and gasped for air. For a few seconds we were a tangled mass of limbs and ice-axes. Lou had stepped into a small 10 or 12 inch crevasse, probably caused by the creep of the snow cover on the slope. He had his leg wedged in up to his knee and it was holding him in place on the slope as it curled over the lip of the crevasse.

After righting himself, Lou faced in for the remaining several hundred feet of steep slope. I wanted to catch Kim up before he dropped down on to the East Face and have him wait in case we had any more trouble getting down. I could see the Sherpa I had spoken to was also coming down. I descended as quickly as I could to Kim. By now he must have been quite cold and was insistent on going on. I felt there was nothing for me to do but wait for Lou to catch up.

After a few minutes I again heard Lou shout. When he reached me, Lou explained what he had seen. A body had gone sliding by him on the slope and tumbled off the ridge on to the South-east Face and disappeared. It was the Sherpa I'd spoken to on the South Summit who had decided to turn back. We considered climbing into the South Col to tell the two Japanese who had stayed there, but then we met another Sherpa who was the first man's colleague. He seemed strangely impassive when we told him what had happened. With heavy hearts we started down on to the East Face. It was late and the sun dropped below the horizon before long. Kim was out of sight. We slid and plunged down the deep trough we had made on the way up. About 8 pm we reached the single tent of Camp VI.

Inside we found George, Kop, Jay and Dan. Kim had passed them and continued down to the next camp to make room for Lou and me. He was indeed incredibly fit. We six spent a terrible night in the three-man VE24 tent.

The next day Kop decided not to try for the summit after hearing about the Sherpa who had died. George reached the top ahead of Jay and Dan on 9 October. On his way up George crossed paths with the Japanese climber, Mr Endo, as he staggered down the mountain after a debilitating bivouac near the South Summit. Jay and Dan reached the top together several hours later in a whiteout. The weather was rapidly changing. As it turned out, only three of the five Japanese we had passed on the Hillary Step made it off the mountain alive. George brought down the ice-axe of one of the Japanese that he found stuck in the snow above the Hillary Step and sent it to his family in Japan.

11 October

I'm pretty wasted still today. Don't understand it really. But I'm going down after breakfast. Truly time to go home. I'm not getting stronger. I just lay in my bed all yesterday during a ten inch snow storm. This has foiled the attempt by the third summit team. We're clearing the mountain now. Everyone's coming off and when Dan and Jay are down the whole team will be safe. I'm just shocked at how wiped I still am.

13 October

These past days I have begun to realize that we actually opened a new route on Everest. That I was on top of that mighty peak and given the honour of breaking the way to the summit. I could never

The crowning moments: on 8 October, 38 days after starting the climb, Carlos Buhler, Kim Momb and Lou Reichardt went to the summit. They were followed by George Lowe, Daniel Reid and Jay Cassell on the next day. Lou Reichardt's photograph (far left) *shows Buhler on the final stretch – very icy, Buhler found, and 'treacherous as hell'. It was from near here that three members of a Japanese expedition slipped to their deaths while the Americans were making their ascents. Left:* Carlos Buhler, photographed by Reichardt, celebrates on the summit. In his diary Buhler wrote: 'It was all a kind of a dream.'

have imagined it. It is still sinking in. Mr Wong Fu Chou (our Liaison Officer, and the first Chinese on the summit of Everest, in 1960), lays heavy praise on us all. It seems all too much to believe.

14 October

For a long time I don't think I'll want to participate in another large expedition. But if I had to choose one major expedition over the last ten years from the USA to be a member of, this is the one. The folks have all returned healthy, successful and, amazingly enough, good friends. It doesn't mean there weren't differences. But on the whole everyone is on pretty damn good terms. That puts something very special into this trip.

18 October

My last view of Everest's East Face on this spectacular sunny day. Makalu, Chomo Lonzo, Lhotse and Everest. All in the most majestic of proportions. I still can't see myself on top. But knowing I was there makes me proud to have pushed myself to such a goal. Amazing activity, this mountain climbing. Right from the start I knew it was for me.

SWEET AND SOUR

by Andy Henderson

The first Australian bid came in 1984. It was a bravura attempt, by five young men who had never tackled an 8,000 metre peak before. They selected a new route, up the monumental snow-slopes of the North Face and into the Great (or Norton) Couloir, a giant, claustrophobic gully which had first deterred the British in the 1920s. After establishing a line of camps on the face, they prepared to enter the couloir. Andy Henderson's account describes two days during the expedition: 3 September, the day after an avalanche hit their route; and 3 October, when the team made its bid from Camp VI, some 2,300 feet/700 metres below the summit. There were four in the summit group: Henderson, Tim Macartney-Snape, Greg Mortimer and Lincoln Hall, who turned back after climbing 650 feet/200 metres.

Andy Henderson photographed in the snow cave at 22,640ft/6,900m which comprised Camp II. Although the cave was hit by an avalanche, the climbers considered it 'bomb-proof'.

September 3

With promptings from a lump of flesh at the base of my brain, chemicals begin flooding my system.

Increase heart rate.

Increase breathing.

Increase audio acuity.

'Andy dai, chia linos.' Loud, insistent but bearable.

Okay. Let's try a vision hookup. Eyes open and . . . nothing. Increase visual acuity . . . yes! There's a nose, about four inches away, framed by a beard and balaclava, sleeping-bag hood (his) and sleeping-bag hood (mine). Jim wallows slowly, like a harpooned whale on a gentle swell, his eyes firmly closed against the light which streams through the tent door. So far, so good. Let's try for a movement. More chemicals, boost tactile response, boost motor responses, boost vision, boost hearing, try and jack the level of consciousness up sufficiently to handle a search. My arm snakes out of my pit, towards the light, my hand loaded with info about a mug, possibly filled with tea. Such is my level of consciousness that 'I' know little or nothing of this.

My hand succeeds in its mission, and commences to close around the plastic mug of tea. Fractionally earlier, temperature sensors in my fingers have sent their messages to the brain. As my fingers make first contact, the temperature data hits my brain like a bombshell. The air temperature is low. Very low. Life threateningly low. *PANIC!* More chemicals. Clamp down on peripheral blood supply, boost consciousness, boost

EVERYTHING. DO SOMETHING. Confusion reigns, my arm jerks, and tea courses down my face and sleeping-bag to the tent bilges where it joins the other frozen foulness.

I have now attained a sufficiently high level of consciousness to attempt the intricate task of speech.

'Shit,' I mumble. Not bad for a first attempt, but the lips were not quite in the right position, the tongue was a bit slow off the mark, and there was a general lacklustre air about the whole effort. Again.

'Shit.' Better, much better. Tenzing, squatting in the darkness outside, chuckled quietly.

'Ako chia. Andy dai?'

'Uhn . . .' and I shove the mug out of the door again. It's 4 am and the stars are burning in a Guinness black sky. At this time of the day (night?) under the clear skies of Tibet it's mind bogglingly cold, and I'm forced to wipe a thin rime of ice off my glasses with a foetid pit liner. Jim was also fully awake now, propped up on one elbow and careful of his precariously balanced tea mug, as he rummaged through a chaos of medical equipment for his headtorch. If I have learned anything over the years it is that you should always know where your headtorch is when you hit the pit at night. Also your glasses, and piss-bottle. Especially your piss-bottle.

I was already dressed as I wriggled free of my pit. All I had to do was pull on my duvet booties, collect my mug and head for the mess tent. Around me the night was punctured by glowing-

domes and tunnels, the stillness by the quiet feral sounds of partner plotting with partner, by people worshipping the equipment they hope will keep them alive, by friend exhorting friend. As I shamble towards the four-person dome that serves as a mess tent for 12, my booties first crunch glacial ice and rubble, and then, briefly, biscuit pieces and other food detritus. Between the small stores tent and the mess and cooking tents the glacier is littered with the evidence of my careless-ness. When we had retreated from Camp I several days before, in the face of continuing snow falls, I had been the last to leave, and so was responsible for securing the camp against storms and scav-engers. The pikas [rodents] and goraks [crows] had outwitted me, and had eaten, or rendered inedible, an extraordinary quantity of freeze-dried chocolate and cheese. I could only hope the freeze-dried macaroni cheese would have the same effect on the little bastards as it had on humans, in which

case they would have a short and constipated life.

In the cooking annexe of the mess tent candles flickered as Naryan and Tenzing laboured over the gas and shellite stoves to produce breakfast. It was their unenviable job to get the climbers and film crew out of bed in the morning, feed them, and then try to organize the shambles left in their wake. As well as these duties, they acted as managers for Advance Base Camp and Camp I. By comparison, Naryan and Tenzing regarded their stints carrying on the avalanche prone lower slopes of the face as light relief.

In the mess tent Jim and Colin wolfed down their porridge, knowing that, as members of the film crew, they would have to leave well before the climbers to get their several hundredweight of junk into position on time. Geof Bartram, Greg and myself were able to proceed at a more relaxed pace, slowly consuming our porridge before leisurely wandering through a plethora of vitamin

Everest's monumental North Face, rising 9,000 feet from the Rongbuk Glacier. The Great or Norton couloir, which the Australians followed, is to the left of the protruding ridge descending diagonally leftwards down the face from the summit. The anvil-shaped shadow below the foot of the ridge is an ice wall which the climbers bypassed to the right, taking them on to the great snowfield which they called White Limbo. Above that is the rock wall shown on pages 148–149.

Looking down from Camp II, with the Rongbuk Glacier 4,000 feet below. In Lincoln Hall's photograph, Greg Mortimer is approaching the camp over the snow slope to the bottom right.

pills, ginseng pills, pills for stress and pills for work. It was still dark when, full of pills, we rattled towards our dump of ski equipment, and arriving, called down curses of great potency upon those who had nicked our gear. Stocks in particular often went missing, and these soon became jealously guarded talismans, to be labelled, bound and stored near your tent for personal use only.

On the firm snows of pre-dawn it would take about two hours to reach our gear dump opposite the North Face. With the sun still below the

North Col, the Northern Cwm was in shadow, although the upper section of the face was stippled with light. One of the reasons I had taken to high altitude climbing was to avoid Alpine starts. I was yet to succeed, but it was hard to feel bitter in the pre-dawn stillness. Skis buzzed gently on the crusty snow, biting sweetly to climb. To the west, peaks blazed with the light of a new day. It would be a good one.

After the heavy snow, Geof, Greg and I were anxious to get back on the hill, whilst Tim and

of the Great Couloir, at an altitude of about 22,000 feet, and had dumped gear there for Camp II. Now a long tongue of debris stretched from the bottom of the route across the névé towards us. We continued exploring, and were soon forced to contact Advance Base Camp again.

'We've found the tent and one of the stoves we left behind,' I radioed. 'Camp II seems to have been relocated all over the glacier.' Greg repeated the conversation for the benefit of Geof's movie camera, and everyone was grateful that the avalanche hadn't wiped out an established, occupied camp.

'How's the gear dump?' asked Tim, referring to the stash of personal gear left in a 'schrund at the bottom of the face.

'OK, we think. We'll go up and check.'

Wimps like myself had left harnesses, crampons, etc at this site. The good skiers like Tim had also left their climbing boots, having changed into cross-country ski boots for the trip from the 'schrund to Camp I. For Tim it was three hours up, 20 minutes down.

The dump had been obliterated by the same avalanche that had taken out the Camp II site.

Two days later the gear still hadn't been recovered. Tim and Lincoln had come up from Advance Base Camp and at 21,000 feet the team had constructed a hole which seemed about the size of an Olympic pool, probed with avalanche probes, and had generally given the area a thorough going over. One of my most enduring memories of the expedition is of Tim solemnly tramping around on this vast cone of avalanche debris 'dousing' for gear with two pack stays lashed together. He had a few problems getting volunteers to work on his random pits, and soon even he

Tim Macartney-Snape approaching Camp II. He has just climbed the gully (diagonally below to his left) which was the hardest technical pitch of the route.

Lincoln had judged it to be still too dangerous. It was one of those minor disagreements which often arise during expeditions - you have to respect the other person's judgement - so Tim and Lincoln were back at Advance Base Camp.

Two and a half hours later Greg broke the silence.

'There seems to have been an avo down our route.'

Before the heavy snows we had fixed rope up the face to the mid-point of a rib on the western side

had given up. Almost all those who had lost boots were able to replace them, either from camera crew gear, or in the case of the more obsessive, from their own stocks. Only Tim, with his huge feet, had no spares.

3 October

'Andy . . . '

'Uhn . . . '

'Not coming . . . too cold . . . too slow . . . '

'Uhn . . . OK.' On the day of the summit attempt Lincoln was dropping out.

The huddled figure in the shadows of the Great Couloir, bent double with the effort of conversation, looked small and very alone from my position high on the Yellow Band. Lincoln means many things to me, but I'm not used to thinking of him as either small, or alone - it was unsettling. I had had similar feelings two days before, as Geof, after giving me his share of the communal gear, disappeared down the fixed rope. Geof's decision to retreat in the face of overwhelming altitude problems was unavoidable, and had to be made before leaving the fixed ropes, which ended at about 25,000 feet, but I knew he would be bitterly disappointed. Never a peak bagger, Geof delighted in getting high just to see what he could see, and would have loved to have made it to 8,000 metres. I could feel his distress through the thin air.

I had my own problems now and was not able to give Lincoln the sympathy he deserved, and perhaps needed. The gentlest of people, he has a flair for disorganization which could make others weep with frustration. It never ceased to amaze me, then, how good he was at getting expeditions financed, and then to the bottom of their chosen mountain. Once there he generally contrived to reach the top somehow.

I concentrated on steadying my breathing for a few seconds then shouted down. 'Can you . . . see Tim?'

'Uhn . . . above you . . . on snow.'

More deep breaths, then 'Need a rope . . . crampon broken.'

'Too far . . . '

Christ! All thoughts of Lincoln fled from my mind, and I found myself panting furiously. I was too terrified to try to downclimb the shattered limestone of the rock band, and the ground appeared to ease off ahead, so onwards and upwards. But first the crampon. By wedging the pick of my axe between two rocks I was able to tremble down on one leg and take the bloody thing off. The binding post had broken, but the damage would be reparable once I was in a less intimidating position. With the crampon off I

148

whole arrangement was gently tilted at an angle of about 20 degrees.

Some distance above I could see two figures moving up and towards an obvious ramp between the couloir and the Rock Band. Moving over to a dry patch of flat pebbles I collapsed, and tried to figure out how to repair my broken crampon. Tim had the only rope, 50 metres of 9 millimetre, and there was no way I was going to let myself be separated from it any further than was absolutely necessary. I worked as fast as possible, my hands stripped to a single layer of inner gloves for the job.

Tim, long and gangly on first inspection is, in fact, a nuclear powered magician. Greg is, superficially, a much more human creature - at least he drinks - but is a real fiend when it comes to technical climbing and past experience showed that he had a fair working relationship with the local mountain gods. The two of them were moving pretty nicely, given the altitude, and in the 20 minutes it took me to fix my gear and pull my gloves on again they had disappeared.

Above the Black Band I found Greg's pack in a pile of rocks, and dumped my own next to it. Tim had taken no pack, preferring to store everything he needed in the pockets of his windsuit. The two were in sight again, and I took off in hopeless pursuit across another hanging plain, steeper this time, to some desperate moves on a few metres of mixed ground, and then diagonally right towards the West Ridge. When I reached it the others had disappeared – again.

I stood on the ridge, huddling against the thin, lazy wind, and saw the long shadow of Gyachung Kang, to the west, reaching out across the glaciers and lesser peaks towards me. I felt lonely, and out of my depth.

It would be dark in a few minutes, and I would be left like an idiot, standing 50 metres below the peak of the highest mountain on earth, blind in my prescription glacier glasses, blind without. My regular glasses were in the top of my pack, somewhere below, and I was separated from them by several hundred metres of steep slab, and at least one tricky section of mixed ground.

I turned immediately, and started retracing my steps, hoping to make it across the mixed ground before it became too dark, hoping that I wouldn't have to wait too long at the packs for the others.

As it was, Greg nearly cramponned my hand as I removed it from the last of the rock - I doubt I would have felt it. I was unbelievably pleased to see the pair again, but neither appeared to be in significantly better shape than myself. Silently we descended to our packs, our only rope, our only headtorch. I don't think I even asked if they had

The view from the tent: Camp IV at 26,750ft/ 8,150m. The cramponned feet belong to Lincoln Hall, who had returned after climbing 650 feet on the summit day because he realised that the group was climbing too slowly to reach the top and descend before nightfall. His three colleagues in fact returned at 3 am, blessed by the good weather shown in Hall's photograph.

Pages 148–149: In the middle of White Limbo, the great snowfield that rises almost 2,000 feet, Mortimer (foreground) and Macartney-Snape toil towards the rock wall that appears to block the route. The climbers passed it to the left, entering the couloir that led to the summit 4,400 feet above.

struggled up to the brow of the rock band, scaring myself badly several times in the process. Suddenly Greg and Tim appeared above me, half hidden by a change in angle of the slope.

'Broke a crampon . . . need a rope.'

'Too far . . . keep going.'

'Come down . . . ?'

'No . . . keep going . . . nearly there.'

Tim hadn't lied, and soon I had scrambled to the top of the rock. Above me stretched a steep snow-slope, and then, where I had last seen the others, the ground kicked back. A few minutes later I understood Tim's reluctance to move on to this steep slope again. The snow was rubbishy beyond belief, and I wondered what held it in place, especially as it now had a deep diagonal trench slicing through it.

I held my breath and tottered out across the nauseating junk until I was in striking distance of the top. By lashing out with my axe, and scrabbling wildly with my feet, I was able to flop over on the easier ground, and into a new and wonderful world.

I lay, like a beached jellyfish, on the edge of a vast, blazing white shelf. At first this plane of wind-smooth snow appeared to hang suspended in mid-air, but looking behind me I saw the eastern edge of the slope was bounded by the upper extension of the Great Couloir, and the upper edge by a high band of black rock. The right-hand end and lower edges ended abruptly in space. The

summitted – which they had.

At the packs, my hands which had happily clutched the head of my axe now refused to grasp the zippers on the top of my pack. I was puzzled by this, and spent a few moments staring at them whilst my brain attempted communication. They continued to be wilful and disobedient.

'Tim . . . can't manage the zippers . . . give me a hand with my glasses?'

Wordlessly he changed my glasses, but by this time the only things visible were what Tim's torch washed over.

Greg and Tim must have talked over the descent route previously, because the only discussion during the following few hours concerned bivvying. The idea was quickly dismissed. Descent by the way we had come up was out of the question as we didn't have enough rope to make it down the Yellow Band in one go, and didn't even have any snow anchors, much less rock gear. The logical route was to descend the Great Couloir, and hope that when we reached rock the rope would be long enough.

Hundreds of metres of downclimbing soon thrashed shattered muscles to numbness. The ground was steep enough to warrant facing the slope, and the sight of the headtorch bobbing around below and between my feet, combined with the measured, rhythmic movements of my body to paralyse the mind. Tim would be weaving his spells, Greg would be in survival mode, haggling with the mountain over the whys and wherefores of life and death, and I was comfortably numb, and cruising.

Several lifetimes dragged past.

Eventually voices started below, and the light danced about in an unaccustomed pattern. An abseil was being rigged - later I discovered we had abbed off Greg's pack buried in the last margins of snow - and Greg disappeared with the headtorch. Finally a muffled shout drifted up and it was time to move. By the time I reached the end of the rope, which seemed to terminate a distressing distance above anything that might have been called easy ground, my crampon had come off again. Tim appeared mysteriously from somewhere, worked his magic and I was soon doing climber impersonations again. It was only 100 metres or so to our Super Diamond tent, and the eastern side of the couloir was bathed in an elegant silver light from the moon, but now I was in the grip of a powerful lethargy, and it irked me to have to move at all. Tim and Greg had vanished in the moonlight, and it was a long and lonely journey to the tent.

I collapsed through the tent door, where Lincoln packed me into a pit and fed me hot drinks. Greg was slumped unconscious on one side of the tent. Tim fought impotently with the laces of his ski boots, I dribbled tea over frozen claws and sleeping-bags with equal dispassion, and Lincoln was on the radio discussing our condition with Jim, and arranging for Geof to move back up to the snow cave (Camp II).

It was sometime past 3 in the morning, 16 hours after we had first left Camp IV. We were in a small tent, on an even smaller ledge, at 27,000 feet and I couldn't understand why Lincoln looked so worried . . .

Of the four who went for the summit, Henderson paid the largest price. After the team set off from Camp IV at 26,700ft/ 8,150m early on 3 October, one of Henderson's crampons broke. He had to remove his outer gloves to repair it and his hands froze. The first picture was taken in a hospital in Lhasa, the second a year later in New Zealand, six months after the injured parts of Henderson's fingers had been amputated.

Back on the Rongbuk Glacier after the climb, Lincoln Hall (left) swaps stories with Tim Macartney-Snape. Hall turned back at 27,400ft/ 8,350m; Macartney-Snape and Greg Mortimer reached the summit. Andy Henderson failed by just 150 feet. None of the climbers used supplementary oxygen.

AVALANCHE!

by Brummie Stokes

In 1984 the British mountaineer Brummie Stokes was joint leader of an attempt on the North Face. Stokes, a member of the British special services regiment, the SAS, had climbed Everest by the South Col route with a British army expedition in 1976, though losing several toes to frost-bite. The 1984 team, composed entirely of SAS members who aimed to reach the summit via the Hornbein Couloir, set up Advance Base Camp on the Central Rongbuk Glacier on 24 March. By 3 April, the camp was well established and the expedition had reached 23,000ft/7,010m on the North Face. 'It was so peaceful as we made our way to our sleeping bags,' Stokes wrote. 'No one could have had any inkling of what was to happen.'

During the night the wind started to blow up, but sheltered as we were in our tents in the lee of the hill, we knew little about it as we snuggled deep in our bags and slept off the effects of our little yellow sleeping pills.

Pulling on my boots inside my tent at 6.15 the next morning, I heard Merv scream a warning, but it came too late. A chunk of ice whistled through the tent in front of my face and the whole world went crazy. The tent, with me inside, was picked up and thrown down the mountainside by what I took at the time to be a big wind. I felt myself being lifted from the ground and rolled around inside the small blue capsule as it was flung down the hill, all my kit tossing and tangling around me as we went. I was screaming with panic, convinced I was going to die without seeing anyone ever again. My mind was racing: I had to do something.

Bouncing off the snow, I felt my shoulder jar as it hit something. I then noticed that a small hole had been made by the ice when it flew through the tent earlier. Pushing my hand into the hole, I ripped a large tear down the side of the bubble I was in, deflated it quickly and was half outside as tons of snow began piling in on top of me. I blacked out.

When I came to, I was swimming for the surface through the suffocating snow. I fought my way clear, knelt up and opened my eyes. What I saw horrified and scared me. Snow and ice blocks were piled up everywhere, bodies lay crumpled and half-buried in the snow, and there were such strong winds blowing, it was almost impossible to scramble to my feet. A loud rumbling noise echoed in my ears together with a high-pitched whine of the wind as it tore savagely at my clothing. I stood up but was immediately bowled over again.

'Oh no!' I thought. 'It's starting again!' Any minute now I expected to be blown away once more, and cried out in anguish, 'God! No! No! Please don't make it now! Please, please don't make it now!'

I was shouting at the wind to stop, like a crazy man. I couldn't understand what was going on, what had happened. Later I learned that Merv, who had screamed the warning, had been standing outside his tent and had seen a 400 foot frontage of serac high on the mountain start to tumble towards us. The crash that followed - after it had fallen free for a thousand feet - shook the whole amphitheatre and triggered off avalanches of powdered snow from both Everest and Changtse. The whole lot poured on to us, completely devastating our camp and sweeping it away.

Still numb with fear and shock, I looked up the hill to where Merv was waving and yelling over the wind, 'I'm all right!' But he continued to wave, obviously trying to tell me something. I made out the words: 'Help me! Help me! Bring an axe!'

Dazed, I looked round at the tatters of my tent: no axe, no anything. It had all gone, all been buried. I turned to look down the slope and felt a hot iron on my head.

'Ohhh! My neck, my neck! It's broken!' It hurt so much, I couldn't move it, and I fell back to my knees clutching at my head, which seemed to be lying on my left shoulder. I had never felt such pain, but something in my mind insisted I get up and help Merv.

Staggering towards where he was bending over something, I felt the snow give way beneath me and fell into a shallow crevasse. Once more, panic rose almost uncontrollably. I hung on: a burst of adrenalin gave me the strength to drag myself out and over to Merv.

'An axe, an axe, we need an axe,' he was saying, but I had not understood why until I saw for myself that Tony had been killed and Andy's head was buried under an ice block. There were no tools anywhere with which to dig him free, and in desperation I pulled a plastic spoon from my pocket and scraped away at the snow covering the ice block that trapped Andy's head. He was conscious, but very dazed and did not really understand what was happening. We kept reassuring him as Merv and I scrabbled away at the solid ice until, with a crackling sound, the ice block moved and we had him free.

Learning from Merv that Graham was alive, although badly bruised and shocked, I wandered off to look for some oxygen and the remnants of a tent with which to protect Andy from the icy wind.

Miraculously, the radio, my oxygen masking and one cylinder were located from the area where my tent had come to rest, and I quickly fitted the mask on to Andy's face and switched the control valve to maximum. There was instant reaction in Andy's eyes as the oxygen brought his body warmth.

'How's Tony?' His first words were for his friend and climbing partner. Choking back tears, I had to tell him that Tony was dead.

Merv appeared the least injured of us all. He pulled out a torn length of tent fabric from the rubble and wrapped it around Andy, doing his best to console him. I made my way over to Graham.

Just after 7 o'clock I made radio contact with Bronco at Base Camp. In what must have been an almost hysterical voice, I told him what had happened and begged him to get a rescue party up as soon as possible with tents and sleeping-bags.

Archie and John, I learned, had left Base Camp already and so were on their way to us unaware of what had happened. They heard the roar of a large avalanche, but thought no more about it. Two miles below our camp, they came upon the first signs that all was not well. A blue sleeping-bag lay flapping in the wind on the glacier, not far from our boulderstone. The higher they got, the more debris they encountered. Bits of tents, hats, and, as Archie was to comment later, 'There were lumps of ice the size of Minis scattered everywhere'; the camp had been pushed half a mile from where it had stood.

Knowing by now that they had to expect tragedy, it must have been a harrowing experience for them to come up and find out what had happened: John later told me that they half-thought to find us all dead. Even so, we could read the extent of the damage by the expression in his face: Tony dead, Andy with broken ribs and shoulder, me with a damaged neck, Graham with frost-bite on his fingers, Merv bruised, and all of us in a state of shock. Nothing had escaped the avalanche. Our kit lay scattered over a square mile. All we could do was gather up what clothing we could find and keep warm in, and get ourselves down to Base Camp as quickly as possible.

An hour and a half later, we spotted the others making their way slowly up the glacier towards us and, leaving Andy in the care of Archie and John, the rest of us limped down to meet them. I tried to ignore the burning pain in my neck at each jarring step, and to put from my mind for a moment the horror of what had just happened. But it would not go away. The whole thing had been so harsh, so brutal, and had happened so fast. So many things now needed to be done. Until now I had been reacting instinctively, had kept going solely on the adrenalin. Now, away from any immediate danger, a wave of emotion swept over me and I felt absolutely drained. Dropping to the ground on the cold snow, I wept bitterly. Why, why, why had this happened? Just when all was going so well for us?

The elemental power of an avalanche is captured by Ed Webster's photograph taken below the East or Kangshung Face in April 1988, with climber Stephen Venables in the foreground. The avalanche swept five miles across the Kangshung Glacier. The avalanche which hit the British team below the North Face on 4 April 1984 killed Tony Swierzy and injured three other climbers including Brummie Stokes, who suffered a fractured neck. Stokes later returned to Everest for two attempts on the North-east Ridge.

ABSENT FRIENDS

by Chris Bonington

In 1985 Chris Bonington, Britain's best-known contemporary mountaineer, made his fourth visit to Everest. Until then, his role had been that of the expedition leader, watching the chosen summit teams make their bids. That year he joined a Norwegian expedition making an attempt using supplementary oxygen via the now-standard South Col route. It was a poignant return for Bonington to the mountain where his friends had died: Mick Burke, Pete Boardman, Joe Tasker. The expedition made steady progress, moving up to the South Col on 20 April, where Bonington shared a tent with Pertemba - Boardman's summit partner of ten years before. If Bonington succeeded, he would set a new landmark: at almost 51, he would be the oldest person to stand on the summit.

Sir Chris Bonington, knighted in 1996, has been described as the ambassador of British mountaineering. His 1985 Everest attempt came after three decades of climbing major new routes and leading expeditions throughout the world. Despite using supplementary oxygen, Bonington (climbing behind Pertemba, right) found the South-east Ridge below the South Summit exhausting work. 'Ever steepening, sometimes rock, mostly snow, it was much harder than I had imagined.'

The South Col was far more extensive than I had imagined, a flattish expanse the size of a football pitch and littered with the debris of previous expeditions: discarded oxygen bottles, skeletons of tents, clusters of old food boxes - unsightly memorials to the ambitions of our predecessors. On the far side rose the final slopes of Everest, and although they are called the South-east Ridge they were less of a ridge than a face of snow and broken rocks that looked steep and inhospitable.

I was pleased to be sharing a tent with Pertemba, who had already climbed Everest twice before. I could feel his friendship and at the same time was spoilt, for he insisted on doing the cooking. It was essential to drink as much as possible through the afternoon, to guard against the dangers of dehydration, and we also ate tsampa, the traditional Sherpa dish of roast barley flour, boiled into a thick porridge and spiced with chilli sauce. It was a great improvement on the dried high-altitude rations we had been consuming.

I didn't sleep very much - I doubt whether any of us did - although I was excited rather than apprehensive. There was none of the stabbing fear that had preceded climbs like the North Wall of the Eiger or the Central Tower of Paine in Patagonia so many years before. I drifted into sleep, to wake to the purr of the gas stove. Pertemba had started to heat the water he had melted the previous evening and stored in a thermos.

Two hours later we were ready to start; boots, kept warm in our sleeping-bags, forced on to our feet; outer windproofs and down jackets turning us into Michelin men as we wriggled out into the bitter cold of the night. It was minus 30ºC and the wind gusted around the tents. A struggle with oxygen equipment, last-minute fitting of the Sherpas' face masks, and we were ready.

There were six of us: the two Norwegians, Odd Eliassen and Bjorn Myrer-Lund; the three Sherpas, Pertemba, Ang Lhakpa and Dawa Nuru; and myself. The South Col is at just under 8,000 metres, so we had some 850 metres left to climb. It was 1.30 am when we set out across the flatness of the col, crampons slipping and catching on the stones underfoot, then on to a bulge of hard smooth ice that slowly increased in angle as we approached the ridge. Each of us followed the pool of light cast by our headtorch. Pertemba was out in front - he had been here before. I was bringing up the rear and it wasn't long before the gap between me and the person in front increased. We were now on a snow-slope, a tongue reaching up into the broken rocks that guarded the base of the ridge. At the top of the snow was rock, crumbling steps, easy scrambling but unnerving in the dark with all the impedimenta of high-altitude gear.

I was tired already; not out of breath but listless, finding it progressively harder to force one foot in front of the other. Three hundred metres, an hour and a half went by. God, I was tired. I had dropped behind, the lights of the others becoming ever distant glimmers, weakening all the time. They stopped for a rest, but as I caught up, started once again. I slumped in the snow and muttered, almost cried, 'I'll never make it.'

Odd heard me. 'You'll do it, Chris. Just get on

your feet. I'll stay behind you.'

And on it went – broken rock, hard snow, then soft snow which Pertemba ploughed through, allowing me to keep up as I followed the well-formed steps made so laboriously by the people in front. The stars were beginning to vanish in the grey of the dawn and the mountains, most of them below us now, assumed dark silhouettes. The crest of the ridge, still above us, lightened and then the soaring peak of the South Summit was touched with gold from the east as the sun crept over the horizon.

By the time we reached the crest, the site of Hillary and Tenzing's top camp in 1953, all the peaks around us were lit by the sun's low-flung rays. The Kangshung Glacier, still in shadow, stretched far beneath us. The Kangshung Face itself was a great sweep of snow, set at what seemed an easy angle. Just below us some fixed rope protruded, a relic of the American expedition that climbed the face in the autumn of 1983. Across the face was the serrated crest of the North-east Ridge. I could pick out the shoulder where we had excavated our third snow cave in 1982 and, above it, the snow-plastered teeth of the Pinnacles where we had last seen Pete Boardman and Joe Tasker.

It was 5 in the morning. We were at 8,300 metres and it was time to change our cylinders. We set out again, plodding up the crest of the ridge, our shadows cast far into Nepal. Ever steepening, sometimes rock, mostly snow, it was much harder than I had imagined. It seemed to go on for ever. Glancing behind me, the black rocky summit of Lhotse, fourth highest mountain in the world, still appeared higher than us. A last swell of snow, with the wind gusting hard and threatening to blow us from our perch, and we were on the South Summit. We gathered on the corniced col just beneath it, the very place where Doug Scott and Dougal Haston had bivouacked on their way back in 1975.

There was a pause. Pertemba had broken trail all the way so far but the ridge between the South Summit and the final steepening of the Hillary Step looked formidable, a knife-edge of snow clinging to the rocky crest, with an intimidating drop on either side. Odd was worried about our oxygen supply. It had been three hours since we had changed bottles and he questioned whether we had enough to get back. The others had been climbing with a flow rate of three litres per minute, but I had found that this had not been enough. I had been turning mine on to four and so would have even less. But at this stage I was prepared to risk anything to get to the top.

Pertemba said decisively: 'We go on.'

Bjorn took the initiative and pushed to the front. Ang Lhakpa got out the rope, 20 metres between the six of us, and Bjorn tied one end round his waist so that it trailed behind him, more of a token than anything else, as we followed. The going to the foot of the Hillary Step was more spectacular than difficult, but the step itself was dauntingly steep.

Odd took a belay and Bjorn started up, wallowing in the unconsolidated snow, getting an occasional foothold on the rock wall to the left. Pertemba followed, digging out an old fixed rope abandoned by a previous expedition. The step was about 20 metres high and Bjorn anchored the rope around a rock bollard near its top. The others followed, using the rope as a handrail.

I was last, but Dawa Nuru waved me past. I gathered he had run out of oxygen - he and Ang Lhakpa had been climbing on just one bottle while carrying our spare bottles to the crest of the ridge. As I struggled up the step, panting, breathless, apprehensive, I felt what was almost the physical presence of Doug Scott beside me. It was as if I could see his long straggly hair and wire-rimmed glasses and could sense his reassurance and encouragement, pushing me on. Then Les, my father-in-law, appeared too. A man of quiet wisdom and great passion, he had thrown the I Ching just before I left home and predicted my success. This was something that had given me renewed confidence whenever I doubted my ability to make it.

Doug and Les got me to the top of the Hillary Step and disappeared. I seemed to have the mountain to myself, for the others had vanished round the corner ahead. I felt as if I had to squeeze out my last bit of will power to join them. Push one foot in front of the other, pant hard to capture what little air and oxygen was flowing into my mask, and then take another careful step along the corniced ridge that led to the summit.

A break in the cornice and there, framed below me to the right, was the North-east Ridge, with its crazy ice towers and snow flutings, seeming to go on and on. I thought again of Pete and Joe - perhaps their bodies were still down there. Another step, and the ridge was hidden by a curl of snow. Now I was at the spot where Pete Boardman had last seen Mick Burke in 1975. Pete and Pertemba had been on their way back down; Mick - that cocky, aggressive, very funny figure I remembered so well - was going for the summit on his own. He never came back. Thoughts of other lost friends from Everest came flooding in: Nick Estcourt who forced the route through the Rock Band in 1975 and died on K2; and Dougal Haston,

'Everything was dropping away on all sides – I had reached the summit at last.' Bonington took this shot of his five colleagues as they prepared to depart. Pertemba (right) is replacing in his rucksack Pete Boardman's T-shirt which he had taken to the summit in Boardman's honour. Bjorn Myrer-Lund (left) is answering a call of nature – 'it could be a record for the highest on earth,' Bonington suggested.

who died skiing in Switzerland the year after going to the summit with Doug Scott.

Suddenly I was nearly there. Odd, Bjorn and Pertemba were beckoning to me, shouting, their voices muffled by their masks. I crouched in a foetal position and cried and cried in great gasping sobs - tears of exhaustion, tears of sorrow for so many friends, and yet tears of fulfilment for something I had so much needed to do and had done with people who had come to mean a great deal to me. Everything was dropping away from me on all sides - I had at last reached the summit of Everest. I hugged Pertemba, who crouched beside me. Odd and Bjorn, who were raising and photographing the Norwegian flag, came over and embraced me.

It was time to look around. The summit is the size of a pool table, but we could move about on it without fear of being pushed over the edge. To the west lay the Tibetan plateau, a rolling ocean of brown hills with the occasional white cap. In the east rose Kangchenjunga, a huge snowy mass, and in the west the great chain of the Himalayas, with Shisha Pangma, China's 8,000 metre peak, dominating the horizon. Immediately below us, across the Western Cwm, was Nuptse, looking stunted now. To the south was a white carpet of cloud covering the foothills and plains of India. We were indeed on top of the world.

Another figure appeared, moving slowly and painfully. It was Dawa Nuru, coming to the summit without oxygen. I still felt numbed, took pictures automatically, without really being aware of what I was taking. There was no sign of the Chinese maypole Doug and Dougal had found in 1975. There were, however, some paper prayer flags embedded in the snow which must have been left there the previous autumn.

Pertemba had brought with him the T-shirt that Pete Boardman had worn to the summit in 1975. It was a hand-painted one that Pete's local club, the Mynedd, had presented to him. Hilary, Pete's widow, had given it to Pertemba when he had visited her in Switzerland, and now he had brought it to the top of Everest once more in honour of his friend.

We lingered for another 20 minutes before starting the descent. I was first away, pausing to collect a few pebbles of shattered rock. The limestone had been formed many millions of years ago at the bottom of the ocean from living organisms and had been thrust up here, to the highest point of earth, by the drift together of the two tectonic plates of India and Asia. The thrust continues. The Himalaya, the youngest of the earth's great mountain ranges, is still being pushed up. Each year Everest is a few centimetres higher.

Bonington's record for the oldest ascent lasted just nine days. On 30 May he was supplanted by the American Dick Bass, who at 55 years 130 days was more than four years older. Bass's record lasted until 7 October 1993, when he was surpassed by Roman Blanco from Spain, who was 60 years, 160 days. On 12 May 1999 Blanco was overtaken by Lev Sarkisov, from Georgia, who was just one day older; on 19 May 2000 Sarkisov gave way to Toshio Yamamoto, from Japan, who was an impressive 63 years, 311 days.

A DANGEROUS DAY

by Mal Duff, leader of a British attempt on the North-east Ridge in 1985

We were numb. Not cold numb, although that was there at times, just battered numb; numb from eight weeks of strain; from scything wind cutting at the flesh; from pirouetting columns of spindrift driving and dancing around us; from weighty effort and load carrying; from eating, drinking and living high on the North-east Ridge of Everest.

I plodded on lost in a world of spindrift, casually watching as Tony was again hurled to his knees, everything on automatic, both sides of my brain arguing, bullying and reasoning.

'I'm hurting.' - 'But who wouldn't. After all I am carrying an enormous load. At this sort of altitude I deserve to hurt. Anyway I'm managing 50 paces between rests even though the wind's blowing out Tony's tracks and the bastard snow is falling as it has been for weeks.' - 'I'm over 8,000 metres and stunningly tired.' - 'It's bound to hurt. What a wimp, just ignore it and keep going.' - 'God this is hard.' - 'Yes, but the oxygen should help, that's what it's for and anyway 25 kilograms is tiring at sea-level so no wonder this is bad. We're higher than the South Col but on a longer and harder route and still miles from the summit, so we have to carry. So that's that! Okay?' - 'Well I really am okay but my lungs are heaving and my thighs burning.' - 'What the hell. *This is Everest* and life is tough.'

Tony was crouched on a rock 40 metres away, a small spark of life where none should exist. The spindrift swirled and battered without respite, skirling over the ridge, pluming 100 metres before hurling itself upon us intent on extermination. Reaching the lee of the rock, a haven in the storm, and contacting Tony, another human in this madness, became all important. Fifty steps, then 60, then 70 . . . A shattering pain erupted low in my chest. As usual in the mountains problems arise with devastating swiftness. A muscle rip in my diaphragm choked the

ability to inflate lungs. A moment of panic subdued by years of training. 'No matter what, I must try to live, to descend, or even to die but I must try. Do something. Try, think, work and rationalize because this is the big one, the master problem, that perhaps you've been seeking for years unwittingly.' I couldn't help thinking of Pete Thexton on Broad Peak with a collapsed diaphragm; of him going blind and dying. I buzzed with panic. Zipping strokes of worry contested. A mental battle fought - the first, I knew, of many before the day or I expired.

We needed the oxygen regulator and mask for those coming up so we spent what seemed like hours unscrewing it from a thread caked in ice. The hose and valve were totally frozen. Realization dawned that I had been dragging this load and not getting any oxygen. I had been sucking atmosphere through the mask so it was not surprising that I had suffered, and now I was miles from anywhere with lungs like wet sponges, no power, maybe going blind and definitely slowly dying.

We dumped our loads, marked the spot and turned downhill. Now on this ridge some of it is flat, some up, and the majority down, but it is still an effort. It was nearly 1,000 metres before I could reach the top of the fixed ropes and slide. I could only manage two or three steps at a time. It all seemed too much. Tony went to Camp IV to pack his gear and packed mine too. I put on my rucksack and kept descending and monitoring progress. No sign of going blind which would have been worrying, but a definite fuzziness, which wasn't surprising, as I was probably only absorbing the same amount of oxygen as at 9,000 metres. I could manage three steps downhill or one uphill, with rasping pants between.

At the nasty snow step above the second buttress I was mighty pleased that Allen Fyffe had fixed a rope the

previous day. This place was hard and dangerous, and it was really nice to clip in and slide down a little. A few hundred metres further brought the mixed ground leading to the fixed line down the second buttress. Tony had clipped on and gone on into the spindrift. I was confused. I missed a wand and ended up too low, got extremely angry and scrambled up in a panic. This was easy stuff to fall from, my balance was all wrong and what a bloody awful waste of energy, energy that I'd been harbouring for lower down.

At 7,600 metres between the two buttresses I met Rick coming up and going well and Jon sitting down and looking tired. Both looked at me sort of sideways and asked if I needed help getting down. But I was still upright so I declined and they went on. Tony was waiting at the top of the first buttress. We had a chat and he went on ahead to Camp III to put on a brew.

Between Camp III and Camp II we met Bob and Chris on their way up. At Camp II we reached the end of the fixed ropes. Tony went first in an effort to break steps because the snow had filled all the tracks. I clipped on to the rope and stumbled and slid, triggering avalanches which thundered down the couloirs. I tried not to sag on to the ropes - just in case . . . Energy dredged from the flesh of my body, until finally I reached the four huge abseils down to the bergschrund. Below, tied to Tony, I staggered across the glacier, resting endlessly, to reach Advance Base late in the evening.

I was over one stone lighter.

Mal Duff died of a heart attack in his sleep at Everest base camp in April 1997.

Storm on the West Ridge: Ed Webster's photograph shows climbers fighting up fixed ropes at 22,000ft/6,700m on the West Shoulder in 1985, the same year as the North-east Ridge attempt described by Mal Duff.

'YA GOTTA WANT IT!'

by Sharon Wood

By 1986 five women - compared to 182 men - had reached the summit. None were from North America, and none had done so by a new route. In April an 18-strong Canadian expedition began an attempt on the West Ridge, aiming to become the first team to reach the ridge by the North Spur of the West Shoulder and continue from there to the summit. Sharon Wood was a mountain guide from Alberta with big-mountain experience in the Andes. By mid-May exhaustion and stress had reduced the team to half a dozen active climbers. With time running out, Wood and her climbing partner Dwayne Congdon were selected to make the summit bid.

19 May, morning, Camp V, 25,000 feet

I wriggled my body through the snow tunnel entrance until my head came up level with the platform and I could look inside. My first sight was disappointing: Barry Blanchard and Kevin Doyle huddled together looking tired and beaten. No one had slept well that night. We were all spent from running the race for the last two months against the encroaching monsoon. At best we had another week before the bad weather shut us down; at worst it had already arrived.

Some time ago we had entered a second race, our wasting bodies against time. Here we breathed a quarter of oxygen that one breathes at sea-level. For our bodies to continue to get fuel in this atmosphere our muscle is metabolized for energy. We looked like we had spent the last year in a refugee camp. The deterioration rate works faster the higher we get. It is this element that makes Everest most unattainable to the mountaineer.

We had a hard day ahead of us, the hardest yet, but this felt like our last chance. If we succeeded in getting this camp in place today two of us would push on for the summit tomorrow. We had made the decision to start using supplementary oxygen. Each tank weighed 20lbs; by the time we strapped on two bottles each, on top of the supplies for Camp VI, our packs came to 70lbs per person. The oxygen we had thought would help instead hindered us. At the oxygen flow-rate we set, it was just enough to compensate for the weight difference.

We followed the last stretches of rope out across the face. Six hours of maintaining a painfully slow pace against the ever increasing winds got us approximately a kilometre across on to the face. At 26,500 feet we came to the end of the ropes. This is where the climbing begins by entering a gash that splits the formidable North Face right to the summit, a snow-and-ice gully of 40 to 60 degrees in angle, sometimes narrowing to shoulder-width and broken by the occasional steep rocky step. Only 2,500 feet to go but over the most difficult terrain and without the aid of ropes. The ropes were our umbilical cord to home, to safety, the last connection to security. We would soon leave them behind. I was the first to arrive. I scratched out a perch on the 45 degree slope and busied myself with untangling and dividing up a 600 foot section of small diameter rope that we planned to use on the difficult sections higher up. Barry arrived and settled in to wait for the others. I gratefully continued to occupy all thought and energy in my struggle with the rope.

Barry let out a muffled cry from under his mask, pointed upwards and dove for the anchor at my feet. Helpless, trapped in my sluggishness, I looked up to see a cascade of rocks ricocheting off the walls of the gully, crashing and bouncing straight for us. There was no time for me to do anything but watch in fear.

By some miracle the rocks missed us. In those few moments of terror, it seemed like hours of heart-beats and thoughts had rushed by, precious, irretrievable energy lost. Barry and I went no further than to exchange glances. It was just last year on another climb that I had been torn off my feet and had my shoulder broken when I was

struck by a much smaller rock. Now this message from the mountain: commit or go home, but do not hesitate.

Minutes later Dwayne and Kevin arrived. Unaware of the previous excitement, Dwayne asked, 'What are we waiting for?'

The departure from the ropes was an experience I had anticipated for years. It was time to enter that icy gauntlet. I looked up and strained my eyes to focus on some trailings of old rope dangling high on the walls, left there from past attempts. They had been beaten by the wind, and were now barely recognizable, just ghostly tattered shreds. The relentless wind, our constant adversary, tore rocks and snow from the face thousands of feet above and funnelled it into the narrow chasm we were climbing. We hugged the walls, hoping the larger debris would miss us. If the person leading faltered, someone else would step in front to keep us moving.

Climbing up through that gauntlet was like crossing thin ice; the only things supporting me were my hopes. All the words of advice and support given to me by friends came pouring back as clearly as the day they were said.

Just a few days ago our leader, Jim Elzinga, pulled Dwayne and me aside. He said, 'Just treat that place up there like any other mountain. Don't die for it. No mountain is worth that cost.' Later the four of us were fighting our way back up the mountain through a bad part of a storm. I repeated Jim's argument to Kevin. 'The hell it is,' he replied. 'It's a one-shot deal. We can't come back tomorrow!' He promptly turned and continued with his teeth to the wind.

That day and the next we rode mostly on Kevin's and Barry's resolve. Their commitment became a great source of inspiration and drive. They clearly made it their goal to get Dwayne and me to that high point, Camp VI, in spite of the difficult and

The Canadians' route took them from the Rongbuk Glacier on the Tibetan side of Everest up the 5000 foot North Spur on to Everest's West Shoulder. From there a one-and-a-half-mile climb took them to the foot of the West Ridge proper. Above: Two climbers at 22,000ft/6,706m on the rising series of snow crests on the North Spur. The steepest sections of the spur reach an angle of 60 degrees.

dangerous conditions, and in spite of the fact that they would climb no higher unless Dwayne or I fell sick. This concept of 'treat it like any other mountain' has its place, but if the truth be known, one's bearing on limits - the margin one leaves - is altered significantly in a place like this. Mount Everest is the grand arena. Here performance takes precedence over all else. It was this element in combination with people like Kevin Doyle who possessed an overpowering, infectious sense of commitment that drove me on.

20 May, mid-morning, above Camp VI, 27,000 feet

Summit day - Dwayne and I cowered against the wind-ravaged cliffs. We had been climbing for hours but making little progress. Jim Elzinga's raspy voice crackled over the radio: 'Ya gotta want it!' They could see us. Those words echoed down the caverns of my memory, taking me back one year to a dismal day in Toronto. I was attempting to follow Jim through his regular training regime of running up the 1,000 feet of stairs of the CN Tower - not once but three times in the same go. No one else possesses the power to motivate and inspire me to such a masochistic act. I could hear his feet pattering up the metal stairs many flights above me. The same words had echoed down the grey cold stairwell, down through the depths of my fatigue: 'Ya gotta want it!' Simple but highly effective.

Dwayne and I began to solo up through the Rock Band trailing out a rope and securing it to use later as a handrail to find our way back down. We knew it would be dark the next time we groped for it. Each step higher involved more and more concentration until we reached a level where the involvement was so intense it prevailed over all else and the fears and doubts faded. It was this state of ultimate commitment and performance which proved to be the most exhilarating experience of the trip.

Sharon Wood photographed on the summit by Dwayne Congdon; after Wood unfurled her flag the wind tore it from her grip.

20 May, evening, 30 feet below the summit

At 29,000 feet, in slow motion, at times reduced to all fours, we made the last few steps. I regretted leaving my ice-axe two hours ago. Back there, I had assumed we were only 20 feet from the summit. I had perched myself on a rock, unzipped four layers of zippers and dug into the depths of my clothing to where the radio had been warmly nestled all day. I knew that in just a few feet we would step on to the wind-exposed ridge where the temperature would drop drastically.

I had kept the radio on and turned up to full volume all day, but we had only spoken into it once. To talk we had to bare our fingers and at those temperatures we would risk frost-bite in seconds. When I pressed the transmit button I surprised myself with the sound of my own voice. I then realized how little Dwayne and I had spoken that day. We were so well synchronized in thought, determination and decision that we had not found it necessary to exchange many words.

When I finally spoke over the radio I sounded as though we were out for a day hike; I think I wanted to alleviate all the concern I sensed from our

In the picture (left) *Sharon Wood is crossing easy-angled snow between Camps IV and V at around 24,000 feet. The expedition fixed ropes on these sections as a protection against the intense wind. Once at the foot of the West Ridge, she and Congdon followed the American 1963 route.*

anxious onlookers and team-mates. After all, it was 8 pm in the evening, darkness would surely intercept before we got down, forcing a night on the mountain without shelter.

I explained that we were doing well and just 20 feet from the top. Cheers of joy and congratulations crackled through the receiver, then came the news that for some reason they could no longer spot us. The reason was to become clear just around the corner. Dwayne came up and led through towards the top. But what we thought would take us minutes took us another hour as we surmounted one false summit after another. Finally there was no more up. We came together for the final steps to the highest point on earth.

At 9 in the evening on top of Mount Everest the sun can be seen setting over an awesome curving horizon. I am sure it was beautiful but to us it meant something very different. We took our masks off and kneeled down, succumbing to the wind, our relief and our fatigue. We were aware we had made it, but there was nothing more. The radio was silent, long forgotten; there was nothing anyone could do for us now.

One nagging concern dominated: here we were on the highest point on earth and the sun was setting; when it set we would be left behind. Encumbered in our multiple layers of insulation and our oxygen apparatus, we managed an awkward embrace.

We stole a brief and knowing glance down upon a peak, 1,200 feet below and just 30 miles away: Makalu, the fifth highest mountain in the world, a mountain we had failed on two years before. We had come so close. To have that experience behind us was comforting. We had learned some valuable lessons there; we had paid our dues. We belonged here.

There was no time to entertain any philosophical revelations; we simply had a job to finish. Dwayne got out his camera; I got out the flags and we began clicking off the frames one by one. Just as I had unfurled a huge yellow flag, the wind tore it from my grip.

I followed its chaotic course down across the knife-edge ridge and out over the giants of the Himalayas until it finally disappeared. I felt so small. It could have been a dream.

PLAUDITS AND BRICKBATS

The Japanese have an impressive record on Everest, with the third highest number of ascents. They have specialised in large-scale media-sponsored expeditions, sometimes arousing controversy through their tactics and figuring sadly high in the fatality statistics. They have also provided examples of individual courage and daring to rank with any in the Everest story.

The Japanese were prominent in early attempts on the South-west Face. In autumn 1969 Naomi Uemura, their foremost Himalayan mountaineer, led a group which reached around 26,500 feet. In 1970 they made a dual attempt on the South-west Face and the South-east Ridge. Like the Americans in 1963, they were uncertain which route to make their priority and in the end concentrated on the South Col. Uemura and Teruo Matsuura became the first Japanese to reach the summit on 11 May, followed by a second pair the next day. Uemura was a member of the ill-starred International Expedition which reached 27,400 feet on the South-west Face the following year. The Japanese fared no better during a post-monsoon attempt on the face in 1973, but Yasuo Kato and Hisahi Ishiguro scored a notable double by going to the summit from the South Col. No climber had succeeded in the post-monsoon period before and none had done so without an intermediary camp on the South-east Ridge.

Following the British ascent of the South-west Face in 1975 – and Junko Tabei's feat in becoming the first woman to reach the summit, via the South Col – the Japanese switched their attention to the North Face and North Ridge. After a reconnaissance in 1979, they achieved multiple success in 1980. Yasuo Kato went to the summit via the North Col and North-east Ridge route previously climbed only by the Chinese, becoming the first non-Sherpa climber to make a second ascent. A week later Tsuneoh Shigehiro and Takashi Ozaki made the first full ascent of the North Face, climbing direct from the Rongbuk Glacier into the Hornbein Couloir, despite running out of oxygen several hundred feet from the summit.

Kato returned to Everest in 1982, aiming to make the second winter ascent. This time his luck ran out. He reached the summit from the South Col on 27 December, while his partner, Toshiaki

Above, top: *Naomi Uemura, the foremost Japanese mountaineer of his generation and a member of the first Japanese team to climb Everest, in 1970.* Bottom: *Yasuo Kato, who achieved three notable ascents in ten years, including the first in the post-monsoon season; the photograph is a self-portrait after he reached the summit alone via the North-east Ridge in 1980. Kato disappeared on Everest after a winter ascent the following year.* Right: *photo opportunity at the North Face Base Camp during the Asian Friendship Expedition – comprising climbers from Japan, China and Nepal – in 1988.*

Kobayashi, gave up 200 feet below the top. They were hit by a storm while bivouacking at the South Summit and were never seen again, almost certainly having been blown off the mountain.

In 1983 came a multiple tragedy which brought strong international criticism. Five Japanese climbers reached the summit from the South Col on 8 October, arriving shortly after the US Kangshung team. Two slid to their deaths during the descent and a Sherpa, Pasang Temba, fell after retreating from the South Summit. *The American Alpine Journal* accused the Japanese of 'inexcusable tactics' by climbing individually and not accepting responsibility for their colleagues. That criticism could not be levelled at Kazunari Murakami when two of his colleagues were forced to bivouac after a South Col ascent in October 1985, one snowblind, the other with severe frost bite. Murakami carried oxygen to them from the South Col the next morning, saving their lives.

In 1988 the Japanese took part in the Asian Friendship Expedition, with no fewer than 254 members from China, Nepal and Japan, including 36 from Japanese television. Nine climbers and a three-man TV crew reached the summit via the North and South Col routes on 5 May, the pictures being beamed to 300 million viewers.

The 1990s brought several notable ascents. In December 1993, a ten-man team made the first winter ascent of the South-west Face, mostly following the British 1975 route. Despite savage winds and a temperature of minus 23°C they placed six climbers on the summit in a five-day period, doing so just three weeks after setting out through the Khumbu Icefall. In spring 1994, three climbers from Aichi Gakuin university, together with seven Sherpas, made the third ascent of the Polish South Pillar route. And in spring 1996, reverting to the more traditional Japanese siege tactics, a large party from Nihon University made the first integral ascent of the North-east Ridge. A British-Australian pair had been the first climbers to climb through the Pinnacles in 1988, descending to the North Col. The Japanese first climbed the Pinnacles and then two climbers and four Sherpas made the complete ascent from the East Rongbuk Glacier to the summit (see pages 183–185).

GET DOWN OR DIE

by Stephen Venables

One of the most challenging ascents was made by the British mountaineer Stephen Venables in 1988. He and three Americans, climbing without porters or supplementary oxygen, put up a new route on the Kangshung Face, following a buttress south of the line taken by the US expedition of 1983. After superb technical climbing followed by a struggle through heavy snow, the team reached the South Col on 10 May – the first climbers to do so from Tibet. Two days later, Venables and the Americans Robert Anderson and Ed Webster made their attempt. With his colleagues falling behind from exhaustion, only Venables reached the top. He was in an appalling predicament, hours behind schedule, with bad weather brewing and darkness imminent, facing the perilous solo descent to the South Col. At 3.50 pm, having spent just ten minutes on the summit, Venables started down.

The clouds were closing in fast and in three hours it would be dark. I stood up, took the ice-axe in my mittened hand, had one last look down Mallory's ridge, then hurried away back south. After descending a short way I stopped for my final summit task. Just below the top there was an exposed outcrop of shattered rock, where I knelt down to collect some pieces of limestone and stuff them in a pocket.

The wind was mounting now, starting to blow spindrift in my face. I hurried on, using gravity to speed myself back towards the Hillary Step. As I came over the last hump the clouds enveloped me completely. Suddenly I realized that I was heading too far to the right, down towards the South-west Face. I headed back up to the left, peering through my iced-up sunglasses at the swirling greyness. I was utterly alone in the cloud and there was no sign of the South Summit. I felt disorientated and frightened, remembering the tragedy of 1975 when Mick Burke, the last person to complete the South-west Face, went alone to the summit and never came back. Somewhere up here, in conditions like this, blinded behind iced glasses, even more myopic than me, he had made an unlucky mistake, probably falling through one of those fragile cornices overhanging the Kangshung Face. I suddenly noticed the dim outline of one of those bulbous overhangs just in front of me and veered back right. For God's sake don't do a Mick Burke. Just concentrate. You've gone too far left now. Head for that rock - must be solid ground there. Now I could pick out some tracks - my tracks almost filled with spindrift already, but tracks

nonetheless. This is right. But it's so difficult. Must have a rest. I sank down and sat in the snow. Then I continued wearily, too slowly, legs sagging, head bowed. I stopped after only a few paces but forced myself not to sit down, leaning instead on my ice-axe. I took a few steps again, willing my legs not to sag and crumple.

It was snowing now, stinging my face and encrusting my glasses. I had to wipe them with a clumsy mitten, clearing a hole to peer through, searching for landmarks. I recognised clumps of rock and followed them to the pinnacle above the Hillary Step. Then came the hard part, taking off mittens, pulling up some slack in the fixed rope and clipping it into my waist belt karabiner with an Italian hitch. I pulled my mittens back on and started to abseil down the cliff. Even though I was moving downhill it was exhausting. Possibly the waist belt was pulling up and constricting my diaphragm, for I had to stop and rest during the 20 metre abseil, gasping for breath. I continued in a frantic blind struggle to the bottom of the step where I fell over and collapsed on the side of the ridge, hyperventilating furiously.

It had never happened before and I was terrified. This was quite new - this ultra-rapid panting, like a fish out of water incapable of getting oxygen into its gills. I panted harder and harder, clutching at the air, frantic to refill my lungs. But nothing seemed to get beyond my throat and for a ghastly moment I thought that I was going to suffocate. Then the air started to get through, and I gasped great sobs of relief as my breathing slowed to normal again.

Venables, clothing askew and plastered with snow following his open bivouac at 27,900ft/8,500m, was photographed by Webster when he and Anderson met Venables above the South Col on the morning after his ascent. 'I remember vividly Ed and Robert's relief at seeing me alive,' Venables wrote.

Left: *Tibetan villagers from Kharta act as porters on the last day of the team's trek to its base on the Kangshung Glacier. The leading figure is Paul Teare.*

The 1988 team, like their US predecessors in 1983, had to undertake demanding technical climbing on a 3,000 foot buttress on the lower half of the face. In the picture (above), taken several weeks before their summit push, Paul Teare is ascending a fixed rope on an ice pitch, first climbed by Ed Webster, which leads to the crest of Cauliflower Ridge at the top of the buttress.

I had to move. Get off that rope and continue. Take mittens off and unclip from the rope. Now, quickly get those mittens back on again. The first one is always easy but the second one won't go. I can't grip it - can't make those useless numb fingers work. It's all too difficult. I'll never get it on and my fingers will freeze solid. No more piano playing. But I must get that mitten on or I'll never get down. Concentrate. That's it, ease it up the wrist.

I slumped over again, gasping with exhaustion. The wind was flinging snow at me and I was starting to shiver. I was completely blind and tore at my sunglasses, letting them hang down round my neck by their safety leash. At least I could see a little now, only blurred shapes, but better than nothing. There's a bit of a clearing. That's the South Summit up there on the far side of the bridge. No sign of Robert or Ed. They must have gone down by now. Crazy to continue to the top in these conditions and no reason to wait for me. There's no one to help me. Either I get myself down or I die. It would be so easy to die – just lie down here and rest and soon the wind would kill me. It would be the easiest thing in the world but I'd look so bloody silly. No use to anyone climbing Everest then lying down to die. No, pull yourself together and move. It's not possible to get out the other pair of glasses without taking off mittens

again, so we'll just have to move very carefully on half vision.

My invisible companion, the old man, had reappeared and together we moved forward, determined not to die. We stumbled half-blind along the ridge, crouched over the ice-axe, peering anxiously through the driving snow, almost on all fours, laboriously dragging ourselves across the rocks, clinging carefully to avoid the death slide down the South-west Face. Fear and instinct kept me moving over the rocks. Then I recognized the dry hollow by the overhanging rock where Boardman and Pertemba had waited in vain for Mick Burke to return. I wondered briefly whether I should bivouac there, but decided to continue, determined to get right back across the bridge to the South Summit. That was the critical point beyond which I was confident that I could survive.

The visibility was still atrocious and I strayed too close to the crest on the left. Suddenly my left leg shot down into a hole and I collapsed in another fit of hyperventilation. I may have trodden on the cornice fracture line, but I think it was just a deep snowdrift. Whatever it was, the jolt almost suffocated me, but I regained my breath and forced myself on up the 15 metre climb to the South Summit. I collapsed again and this time, as I regained my breath in great anguished gasps, I was filled with pity for the poor old man who was finding it all a bit too much.

We floundered eventually up to the crest of the South Summit where my mind must have gone almost blank, for I can only recall blurred images of snow and cloud and the gloom of dusk. I can remember nothing of the descent of the knife-edge ridge, I only have the vaguest recollection of slithering back over the bergschrund and then I was back on the big snow-slope, sitting down to slide, because it is easier to sit than to stand.

We were racing the darkness, using gravity to hurry down towards the safety of the South Col. But even sliding is hard work, because you have to brace your legs and brake with your ice-axe. It was somewhere down here that Peter Habeler, during his phenomenal one-hour descent from the summit to the South Col, spurred on by his fear of permanent brain damage, almost flew out of control down the Kangshung Face. I was anxious about the big slope below me and kept stopping to walk further right towards the ridge. Then on one slide the old man became very frightened. We were gathering speed in a blinding flurry of powder snow. The surface underneath felt hollow and unstable and seemed to be breaking off in avalanches. We were sliding faster and faster down to the east and the old man was hating it. He had suddenly become a musician. Musicians hate this. The composer is sliding on his cello, riding the avalanche to his death. Please stop! Now!

I dug my heels in and leant over hard on my ice-axe, dragging the ferrule deep into the snow, and came to a halt. We were about to collapse and had to rest as soon as possible, but we could not sit down here. Too steep and insecure. Quick, cut a ledge. Ice-axe and burrowing hand - that's it. Quick. Just enough of a hollow to sit down. Must rest. Must have a pee. The old man says do it in your pants – it'll keep you warm.

I could wait no longer and with one last frantic effort I plunged the ice-axe deep into the snow and used it to heave myself up on to the ledge. Then my strength gave out and I collapsed, wetting myself and suffocating in another fit of hyperventilation.

Poor old man . . . that's better now, he's breathing again. He just needs to rest. What was all that business about music – cello music? What has that got to do with avalanches? Who is this composer? Dvorak wrote a cello concerto. Kate plays the cello - but she's a woman. It's all too confusing. Better to concentrate on reality – on me sitting here on this precarious ledge in the snow. And why did I believe that nonsense about peeing in my pants? All wet now. It must have been the shock.

I was getting chronically exhausted and it was now virtually dark, so I decided to stay where I was. I sat there for about an hour, shivering as the cold pressed through the snow. Then I decided that my precarious perch was too dangerous and that I should try to continue down to the South Col where Ed and Robert would be waiting in the tents. I lowered myself to my feet, faced into the slope and started kicking steps carefully across the snow, back towards the crest of the ridge. There I tried to orientate myself, climbing backwards and forwards over the rocks, trying to recognize individual outcrops from the morning. But it was dark, there was no moon and, although the afternoon storm had blown over, there were still drifting

Looking down from the buttress, Ed Webster's photograph shows Camp I, with the American Buttress (1983 route) to the left, the Kangshung Glacier below. The tiny figures beside the tent are Paul Teare (left) and Robert Anderson.

clouds to confuse my vision. Even after putting on glasses and switching on my headtorch, I found it very difficult to judge shapes and distances. I started to worry that perhaps my glissade had taken me lower than I thought and that I was now below the point where I had to turn right into the couloir.

After about half an hour of wandering about, the old man suggested that we should stop here for the night and wait for daylight to re-orientate ourselves. I decided that he would be warmest sitting on a rock and soon I found a ledge on the ridge where we could sit down. But it was precarious and sloping and we both longed to lean back properly, so we traversed back out on to the snow and dug a horizontal ledge where we could lie down properly. At about 9 pm we settled down for the night.

The emergency bivouac had many precedents. During the American traverse of Everest in 1963 Willi Unsoeld and Tom Hornbein completed the first ascent of the West Ridge, reaching the summit just before dark at 6.15 pm. Two companions had reached the summit by the normal route the same afternoon and were waiting near the South Summit when Unsoeld and Hornbein started to descend the South-east Ridge. When they met, Hornbein tried to persuade the other three to continue down to the top camp but they soon became lost in the dark and had to resign themselves to a night out in the open at about 8,500 metres. They survived the intense cold and descended safely the next day, but afterwards Unsoeld had to have nine frost-bitten toes amputated and one of the South-east Ridge duo, Barry Bishop, lost all his toes.

In 1976 two British soldiers, Bronco Lane and Brummie Stokes, were also forced to bivouac on the same slope just below the South Summit, descending in bad weather. Twelve years later in Kathmandu, Stokes was to show me his mutilated toeless feet. Lane had to have fingers as well as toes amputated, but at least both of them were alive, unlike the German climber, Hannelore Schmatz, who in 1979 insisted on stopping to bivouac before dark, even though her Sherpas were urging her to carry on down to the safety of their top camp. She died sitting in the snow and for several years her frozen body was a grisly landmark on the South-east Ridge, until it was recently buried or swept away by an avalanche. I also knew about the Bulgarian climber who had died whilst descending the difficult West Ridge in 1984. Meena Agrawal, who had been a doctor to another Everest expedition that year, had later told me how she had talked to the Bulgarian on the radio, trying to comfort

him and persuade him to live through the night; but eventually the man had been unable to hold up the receiver any longer and had presumably died soon afterwards.

I had no intention of dying that night. I was alone just above 8,500 metres (about 28,000 feet) but the wind which had frightened me so much at the Hillary Step had now died away and the air temperature was probably not much lower than minus 20°C. I was lucky with the conditions and I knew that I could survive in the excellent clothes I wore, but I had to resign myself to the probable loss of toes. Six months earlier, caught out high on Shisha Pangma, Luke and I had dug a snow hole and crawled inside to take off boots and warm each other's toes. But now I was nearly 1,000 metres higher, I was alone and I barely had the strength to cut a ledge, let alone a proper cave where I could safely take off boots. I had climbed with the specific intention of not bivouacking, so I had no stove to melt snow. Only a trickle of half-frozen juice remained in my water bottle and in the last 24 hours I had drunk less than a litre. Dehydration was thickening my blood, already viscous with the concentration of red blood cells necessary to survive at altitude, and circulation was sluggish to the remote outposts of the vascular system, particularly my toes.

If the weather had been worse, I would probably have found new reserves of strength, either to dig a snow hole or to search harder for the correct descent route. But as the air was calm I lay inert, huddled up in the snow with my spare mittens providing meagre insulation under my hips and my ice-axe plunged into the slope in front of me, like a retaining fence post.

I was not really alone. The old man was still with me and now there were other people as well, crowding my tiny ledge. Sometimes they offered to look after parts of my body. At one stage during the long night the old man became rather patronizing towards a girl who was keeping one of my hands warm. Perhaps it was then that Eric Shipton, the distinguished explorer so closely involved with the history of Everest, took over warming my hands. At the end of the ledge my feet kept nearly falling off where I had failed to dig a thorough hollow in the snow. I was aware of several people crowding out the feet, but also trying to look after them. They were being organized by Mike Scott.

I had never met Mike Scott but I knew his father Doug, who had bivouacked even higher than this, right up on the South Summit in 1975. He and Dougal Haston had been half-prepared for an emergency bivouac, carrying a tent-sack and a

Pages 170–171: *Ed Webster's breath-taking photograph shows the moment, at 4pm on 10 May 1988, when the four-man team became the first climbers to reach the South Col from Tibet. Battling against the ferocious wind, with Lhotse in the background, are Venables followed by Teare, with Anderson appearing over the lip of the col. Shortly afterwards they found a site for their tents but the wind was still raging the next morning, delaying their attempt by 24 hours.*

stove. When they emerged from the South-west Face late in the day, they had started digging a cave and had made a hot brew before climbing the final ridge to the summit. After photographing the magical sunset from the summit they returned to the snow cave where their oxygen ran out and they settled down for the highest bivouac ever. Scott had no down gear, yet on that bitterly cold autumn night he had the strength not only to survive but to concentrate on 'the quality of survival', warming and talking to his feet throughout the night. When he and Haston descended to the haven of Camp VI the next day, neither had frost-bite.

I drifted in and out of reality, occasionally reminding myself that I was actually alone, before returning to my confused hallucinations. Towards dawn, as I started to long for warmth, my companions teased me by announcing that there were some yak herders camping just round the corner with tents and food and hot fires. They left me alone with the old man and went to investigate. It was good to be left in peace for a while and I reminded myself that yak herders could not possibly be living up here at 8,500 metres; but later the people returned to tell me that while the insidious cold of the snow had been creeping through my body they had been enjoying hot baths and food. Now I longed even more desperately to be warm.

At some stage during the night I stood up to enlarge my ledge. After that I felt slightly more comfortable and less precarious. Eventually I think that I must have slept, for I remember an actual awakening and sudden realization that the long night was finally over.

I sat up shivering. There was pastel light in the sky and only a soft blanket of grey cloud remained in the valley far below. All the people, even the old man, had gone but I had survived my night out. My body was stiff and my feet were dead, but my fingers were still alive inside their down mittens. The hairs on my eyebrows, moustache and beard were stuck together with great lumps of ice and a frozen film encased my wooden nose. My iced sunglasses still hung useless round my neck, but my other glasses were clear, so that I could see the route down.

I could not believe that it had all seemed so strange in the dark, now that I could see the shoulder just below me, with the little dip where one had to turn right into the couloir. If only I had seen better in the dark I could perhaps have descended to Camp III and saved myself all that shivering!

The sun was rising over Kangchenjunga as I stood up shakily, picked up my ice-axe and set off

wobbling and sliding down the slope. Soon I was back in the couloir, daring myself to sit down and slide wherever possible. Once I went too fast and gave myself another alarming attack of hyperventilating, but after that I stayed in control. The world was sparkling in morning sunlight and life was wonderful. I was alive and warm again, I had climbed Everest and soon I would be back in the valley.

Suddenly I saw two people in the couloir, down by the Dunlop tent. It took a while for my dulled mind to realize that they must be Ed and Robert, who had also failed to reach the South Col in the dark and had taken shelter in the Asians' abandoned tent. They turned round and saw me sliding towards them and a few minutes later we were reunited. I cannot remember what we said. Only a few words were spoken and they were probably banal; but I remember vividly Ed and Robert's relief at seeing me alive and a deep warmth of friendship as the three of us roped together for the final descent to the South Col.

After meeting Venables on the South-east Ridge in the morning following his ascent, Anderson (right, supporting Venables) and Webster helped him back to the South Col. The three men still faced a long and hazardous descent to safety.

After reaching the South Col, the three climbers, suffering from their prolonged period at high altitude, survived a perilous descent to Base Camp. Venables lost three toes from frost-bite, Webster lost the tops of all his fingers.

'A BLEND OF FASCINATION AND HORROR'
1990-2000

OUR LAST CHANCE

by Rebecca Stephens

By 1993, no British woman had yet climbed Everest. Several contenders were hoping to claim the prize, among them Rebecca Stephens, a journalist who had reported a British-American attempt on the Pinnacle Route in 1989. After reaching 23,500 feet/7,163 metres she had succumbed to Everest's lure and four years later, having gained experience in other ranges, she was back. Her attempt met several setbacks and she watched in frustration during spells of good weather as other teams went to the summit. Finally, on 17 May, her opportunity arrived.

Rebecca Stephens prepared for her Everest attempt by climbing Mt McKinley, but had still never previously been above 23,500 feet. At first the idea of climbing Everest was a 'childlike dream' – then it became 'an addiction'.

Pages 174–175: Disaster day, 1996. Doug Hansen nears the summit on 10 May. It is past 3 pm, perilously late, and Neal Beidleman's photo shows the storm building from below. Hansen died on his descent; Beidleman survived, as did Mike Groom, descending in photo. The quote is Jon Krakauer's, from his epochal account, Into Thin Air.

It was our last chance for the summit. The season was drawing to a close, the monsoon was encroaching, and the talk was of cold beers in Namche Bazaar. This was it, our last moment – and the Sherpas thought it was too dangerous to climb.

'Guys, don't give up on me now. Please not now.' These were my thoughts as Sherpas Ang Passang and Kami Tchering lay huddled in a small, domed tent on the South Col. Tcheri Zhambu and I were in another, positioned for a summit bid. 'There's black cloud in the valley. Not good weather. We're young,' they cried.

'Well,' I mused, 'the perfect excuse.' A large part of me thought: 'I can go back to bed, put my head down, forget the whole bloody thing.' But another part of me wanted that summit. Why was making a decision always so impossibly hard? To go or not to go. It had seemed that way for as long as I could remember. Choice is a terrible thing. Until Everest I had thought climbing easy – not physically easy, necessarily, but simple. There was only one aim: to climb to the top. No buses to catch, timetables to meet; no finances to juggle, bathrooms to clean, taxmen or editors to appease. No clutter.

Everest put an end to that. By virtue of its sheer size, Everest makes complicated all things that should be simple. Camps need to be established: tents, sleeping bags, stoves, billies, food and drinks put in place. Oxygen – for those who use it – needs to be positioned. And teams are large: nine round-eyes in our case, and seven Sherpas. A lot of people. A lot of variables – before counting the biggest variable of all: the weather.

I was tired of decision-making. Twice in the past week I had thought we should make a bid for the summit, but circumstances dictated otherwise. Twice I had watched other teams ascend hopefully and descend triumphant. Now one more chance – just one, a slim one – had presented itself.

We had already been to Camp IV on the South Col once before. Only yesterday, back at Camp II at 22,500 feet at the foot of the Lhotse Face, John Barry, the expedition leader, said: 'It'll be a monumental test of will.' He was referring to the task of retracing our steps to Camp IV; and he was right – almost. The hard bit for me was not the climb itself but simply summoning the energy to pack my rucksack, put on my climbing harness, my boots and crampons and set off, again. The weather forecast was poor, too, and I convinced myself that I would be walking into failure. I would climb to the Col – that ghastly, inhospitable, frightening place – only to have to retreat once more. My chance of success, I thought, was no more than one in a hundred. 'You're a realist,' said Sandy Scott, our doctor. 'I'd have said three to four per cent.'

I was scared, too. I would be alone on the South Col. Originally I had assumed that John would be climbing with me. But he had stayed a third night on the South Col to look after another climber, Harry Taylor, snow blind after making an oxygen-less ascent. Now John was exhausted, and unable to join me in my attempt, and I would be making all the decisions. The South Col is at 26,000 feet – too high to expect to feel good. Too high, in fact, to sustain life, without oxygen, for more than a couple of days. 'But you won't be on your own,' Sandy said. 'You'll be with Tcheri Zhambu, Kami Tchering and Ang Passang.'

When Stephens first reached the Western Cwm (left) *she found the heat intense as it was reflected off the ice and snow. She had planned to climb with the expedition leader, John Barry, but he exhausted himself while rescuing Harry Taylor, who had returned snow blind from a solo summit ascent.*

The Sherpas were twice as strong and twice as fast on the hill as any man I had met, and always smiling. But I had never climbed with them before. 'They know this mountain better than anyone,' said Sandy. Ang Passang and Kami Tchering had both been to the South Summit several times. 'And they're cautious,' he said. I felt ashamed. Sandy was right. The Sherpas would look after me.

The four of us set off from Camp II at 5 am. Dawn was just breaking. Once on our way we travelled quickly, across the head of the Khumbu glacier in the Western Cwm and up the steep Lhotse Face. I had a huge advantage over our previous attempt. Then, we had used oxygen from Camp III, at around 24,000 feet, a little over halfway up the face. The oxygen bottles were British, solid and strong to meet British standards, which was great except that each bottle weighed a hefty 6.5kg, and that was without the brass attachments, regulator and mask.

For the second attempt we handed over an astronomical sum of money to the New Zealanders for their spare titanium bottles, made in Russia. They were the best: small, simple to use, and most important, light. I had plenty of them. I plugged in at Camp II and shot up the fixed ropes to Camp III in under four hours. Previously, my best time, without oxygen, had been 5 1/2 hours. We stopped for a quick brew in our tent at Camp III, perched on the tiniest snow shelf between seracs, and then went on our way, across the Lhotse Face – just a

walk, really – and up and over the Geneva Spur to the South Col.

Tcheri Zhambu and I were on the Col by 1 pm. Ang Passang and Kami Tchering had raced ahead and were already ensconced in their tent, brewing us tea. I loved watching them. They were so dextrous. They were small – Tcheri Zhambu was tiny, about 5ft 2in, but the efficiency of their movements amazed me. The tent I shared with Tcheri Zhambu was full of snow, littered with food wrappings and sort of crescent-shaped. It had been domed the last time I was in it but the poles had buckled in the wind and the canvas collapsed. It was chaos and yet Tcheri Zhambu managed to sort the oxygen, dry his feet, manage the radio and collect snow for a brew, all without knocking over the noodle soup warming on the stove in the corner. I did nothing. I wasn't allowed to.

At 7 pm we were due to rest before setting out. But first I had to call Camp II. They had bad news: the forecast was still gloomy, winds up to 45 knots, thundery showers. All we could do was to continue to rest as planned.

We put our heads down, just for a couple of hours. Didn't sleep, just rested.

'Tcheri Zhambu,' I whispered after some time had passed.

He stirred.

'Tcheri Zhambu, there's no wind.' I could hardly believe it: the forecast was as wrong as it could be. Tcheri Zhambu sat bolt upright – it was 10 pm, we planned to leave at 11 pm – and immediately lit the stove for a brew. It takes a while, all this brewing, collecting and melting snow, but an hour passed and it was now that I had the distinct impression something was up. The Sherpas – Ang Passang and Kami Tchering in the other tent, and Tcheri Zhambu in mine – were talking among themselves in Nepali.

'What's going on?' I asked Tcheri Zhambu.

'Weather not good.'

'But there's no wind,' I retorted. I stuck my head out of the tent: the mountain was clear, the sky full of stars.

'Ang Passang says black cloud in valley. Too dangerous.' After shaking off my sudden feeling of relief that I would not have to make an attempt after all, there was only one thing for it. I put on my boots, tripped out of my tent and into theirs.

'Ang Passang?'

'Black cloud dangerous,' he said. 'We're young.' What to do?

'Ang Passang, pass the radio please.'

John and Sandy were sleeping by the radio that night so that I could call them at any time. The boys at base camp were doing the same. I was touched.

I explained. 'John, Ang Passang says we may not find our way. And there's lightning. You have a view on that?'

'I don't know, Becs.' This was desperate. 'The weather's going to get worse, not necessarily in the next two hours, but it's going to build up. Whether it will hold off long enough I wouldn't like to say.' The discussion went round in circles: Camp IV to Camp II, Camp II to base camp, back to Camp IV. 'Talk it over very gently with Ang Passang and let him make the decision,' said John. 'It's his life too.'

We waited an hour. The wind didn't pick up and stars still crowded the sky. Then I saw three lights making their way up the hill from the Col. I don't know how the decision was finally made, but one thing was for sure: if those three people thought there might even be the slightest chance of making the summit, I could not go back to bed.

At 12.30 am we were ready to go: water-bottles, chocolate, gloves, glasses, radio, crampons on, ice-axe in hand, oxygen on back, mask on face. 'Get on those fixed ropes,' said John. 'Get on to the South Summit. Reassess the situation there. And good luck. I think you're going to be OK. Over.' I heard him talking to base camp: 'The beauty of fixed ropes,' he told them, 'is that you can't get lost. If the worst comes to the worst they can turn round and rattle down the ropes, back to the tent.'

I wonder if he would have been happy to let us go if he had known what we were to discover. There were no fixed ropes. They must have been buried in the snow.

Soon after setting off, there were just three of us. Tcheri Zhambu had a cough, and was forced to turn back only a couple of hundred yards from the

Stephens made her attempt with Sherpas Ang Passang and Kami Tschering (a third, Tcheri Zhambu, turned back shortly after setting off from the South Col). In the picture (below) Stephens and the two Sherpas return to the South Col after a five-hour descent from the summit.

Col. It was dark, very dark. To add to the fun I had let my head torch batteries run flat, as had Ang Passang. Kami Tchering led, turning his head every few paces so we could follow. It was much steeper than I had imagined: icy in patches, in other places rock camouflaged under the thinnest powdering of snow. Crampons scraped and slipped. I wondered how the hell we were going to get down again.

But for the moment we were heading up, and, I thought, rather well. The two Sherpas, apparently, felt otherwise. It was about 4 am, still dark. They sat in the snow and refused to budge.

'What's the matter, guys?'

They were chatting away on the radio in Nepali. I spoke to John: 'Nawang says you've got two cold, scared Sherpas,' John told me. (Nawang was the cook at Camp II.) Well, perhaps: thin cloud now engulfed us and there were no longer stars visible in the sky. 'Maybe if you can persuade them to keep going until dawn, that might do the trick.'

Maybe. 'Look, Ang Passang, let's just keep climbing until we catch up with the three ahead. We can discuss it with them.' I tried everything. 'Take my jacket.' (I had a spare one.) 'If you get to the top? Of course you can come to London.'

There was a reluctance, but they – we – moved on. We never did discuss the matter with the three climbers ahead. We caught up with them, said our hellos and climbed on past (they had no oxygen). It was hard work, and harder for the Sherpas than for me. I was on three litres of oxygen per minute, they were on one. We would take seven paces, maybe eight, and rest for a minute, another six paces, and rest again. When the snow deepened, we took it in turns kicking steps.

Up and up. The dawn broke and light snow blew in our faces from the east. The whole of Tibet was one ominous snow cloud, and I worried that it might envelop us. The nagging doubt that afflicts all mountaineers – should we turn back? – haunted me every step, until somewhere along the South-east Ridge leading to the South Summit the Sherpas' attitude changed. They wanted that summit too.

It took an age to climb that ridge, and I didn't know when it would come to an end. The snow was deeper, the air thinner, and it was impossible to take more than one or two steps without bending over double to recover breath. Then we were on the South Summit. I had read hundreds of books and talked to countless people, and thought I knew what to expect. Yet the view along the final ridge staggered me. Everything we had climbed thus far was snow or ice. This was rock, mostly: angular lumps falling away sharply left and right.

'You can go first, Kami Tchering,' I said.

'No, you can go.'

'No, you go.'

Kami Tchering led. It wasn't difficult by Alpine standards; perhaps *peu difficile*. But it was exposed. Best not look down. This was Hillary Step territory. I could see it ahead, a large rhomboid boulder standing on its head. But first we had to inch our way along the ridge. There were fixed ropes, in parts, but where there were not, one slip and it would all be over. When we reached the step a knotted bunch of tatty old ropes hung from some unseen anchor. I grabbed it and jostled and heaved myself on to a sloping mantel, the top of the rhomboid, I supposed, two-thirds of the way up. From here it was relatively simple. I planted my axe into a snowy shelf and scrambled up.

I was happy when I left the rockier part of the ridge behind. Ahead, cornices swept in vast, frozen waves to the right, overlooking Tibet, and steep rocky slopes fell away to the left, into Nepal. The ridge was broader, more gentle, a little kinder. It undulated on, as ridges do, one bump and then another. And then we were there. I knew it was the summit: it had lots of flags on top. It wasn't very dramatic. But the joy on the Sherpas' faces made my heart near burst. They grabbed the radio: 'Summit, summit, summit. We make summit.'

I suppose it is fear that forbids one to bask in such moments for too long. The cloud cleared for a moment to reveal a view across the Tibetan plateau that stretched for miles: to China and Mongolia, no doubt. But I only glanced for a second. It was cold, and the wind had picked up.

Going down was exhausting; I knew it would be. And dangerous, too. The five people who had died this season died here, descending from the summit to the Col. I concentrated so hard; and the Sherpas were wonderful: 'Slowly, slowly,' they said. Kami Tchering led, while Ang Passang paced himself just behind me. It took about five hours to get down, and for an hour of that time the snow cloud that had filled Tibet invaded our path and masked our vision almost completely. But I felt calm, and when it cleared, there, far below, was a small, red figure on the Col, excitedly waving his arms. It was Tcheri Zhambu. A half hour later and he was unstrapping my crampons and rubbing my hands warm because, casually, I had remarked that I was chilly. He boiled some noodle soup, but I wasn't hungry. Gently, he insisted I should crawl into my sleeping bag and rest, but I couldn't sleep.

It didn't matter, though; nothing mattered that night. We'd climbed our mountain and we were safe, and I felt deeply content in a way that I had never felt before.

Stephens celebrates after the ascent: 'I felt deeply content in a way that I had never felt before.'

THE RUSSIANS ARE CRAZY

by Nikolai Zakharov

Translation by Flura and Bill Sumner

The 1990s brought two new routes on Everest. In May 1995, a large-scale Japanese expedition made the first complete ascent of the North-east Ridge (see pages 183–185). In May 1996, a Russian team climbed the daunting 3,000 foot couloir to the left of the North Ridge. Having done so, they pressed on for the summit in rapidly-deteriorating conditions, then found themselves descending in a blizzard, without oxygen, after dark. The expedition leader, a trainer at a sports club in the city of Krasnodar, tells the story.

Nikolai Zakharov – known as Kolya – came to Everest with a formidable record, with three major new routes in the Pamirs and another on the East Ridge of Cho Oyu. He and his team also brought the Russians' reputation for stoicism, fortitude – and for pressing on in the most daunting conditions.

Right: *Zakharov marked the expedition's four camp sites on his photograph of the North-north-east Couloir – now also known as Zakharov's Couloir.*

The idea of climbing Everest by a new route occurred to me in 1994 when my mountain climbing friends in our Siberian city of Krasnoyarsk and I began to think about this mountain. My first idea was the North-east Ridge, but in spring 1995 the entire ridge was climbed by a Japanese expedition with Sherpas. So that fall several of us went to Tibet to choose a new route.

As we approached Everest on the East Rongbuk Glacier, the North-east Wall came into view and I saw a very beautiful couloir on the right part of the wall. I immediately said to Alexander Kuznetzov: 'That is our route!' to which he replied, 'You are crazy! Find something simpler.'

Alexander and I ascended the North Col to 7,000 metres and looked carefully at the face. The route we studied began at the top of the glacier at a bergshrund below a very steep 500 metre ice wall. Above the ice wall, 400 metres of rock led to a great snow and ice couloir of almost 1000 metres. It led to the North Ridge at about 8,250 metres and above there the route exited to the North-east Ridge and thence to the summit.

Our impression was that this route could be very dangerous because of snow avalanches and rockfall and would have technical difficulties. But we noticed a small rock ridge that paralleled the couloir that might provide an alternative way. The angle varied from about 45 degrees to more than 60. I liked the route more and more and had the feeling of excitement that comes in the moments immediately before big competitions.

From information received from Elizabeth Hawley in Kathmandu there had been three unsuccessful attempts on the wall. Russell Brice, who earlier had attempted the couloir, answered my questions with something like: 'It was very cold and always there was a frightening wind like

in a wind tunnel. We climbed to 7,800 metres and gave up.'

We began to plan how to climb this wall. The work appeared to be large, especially since we wanted to climb with a strong group from only one city and not use high-altitude Sherpas. Throughout 1995 I carefully prepared our team of strong Krasnoyarsk alpinists for Everest. Our team consisted of Sergei Antipin, Valerii Kohanov, Evgenii Bakaleinikov, Grigorii Semikolenov, Igor Ilin, Nikolai Smetanin, Alexander Kuznetzov, Peter Kuznetzov, Constantin Kolesnikov, Alexander Bekasov, and Evgenii Kozyrenko. Our doctor was Sergei Maiorov and our photographer Alexander Abramovich. Sergei Bayakin was our expedition leader and I was climbing leader and trainer. We did seven special training climbs in the Pamirs, Tien Shan, Caucasus, and Sayan. We trained through the Siberian winter, often climbing in minus 30 degree temperatures on rock near Krasnoyarsk.

Our expedition established base camp on 5 April 1996 on the Rongbuk Glacier at 5,200 metres. At Advanced Base Camp at 6,300 metres we divided into three separate groups of four climbers each. According to our plan, each group would work in rotation to establish the route, fix ropes and establish camps. By 6 May we had established Camp I at 7,020 metres at the top of the ice wall and Camp II at 7,500 metres, the first place in the couloir where we could chop out a ledge to pitch a tent. Then we fixed ropes to 7,900 metres and hauled our necessary equipment to Camp II.

The route so far had been physically difficult, with heavy snow often slowing our ascent. There was always strong wind. It came from different directions and sometimes swirled around us like a washing machine filled with small chips of ice. Often it was hard to balance or even stand at all. The technical climbing in the couloir was difficult to protect while leading. We couldn't find rock anchor points and only occasionally found ice screw placements. We did not have problems with snow avalanches, but we did experience rockfall, especially when the weather was warm. Several times we had to repair tents that had been split open, luckily when they were unoccupied.

By 10 May we were ready to make our attempt. There was only time for one and so we decided to go from Camp II in alpine style, carrying every-thing on our shoulders. We selected our six strongest and most acclimatized climbers for this final push. After a spell of rest at Base Camp, we set off on 15 May. We reached Camp I that night and the next day we climbed the rocks to Camp II. On 17 May we took all our gear, food, and oxygen

and climbed to 7,950 metres where we spent the night on a platform about a metre wide, with our legs hanging over the edge. The next day was very difficult. The upper part of the couloir was steep and filled with deep snow; our packs weighed more than 22kg, and a strong wind blew directly in our faces. We began to use our bottled oxygen even though we knew we had barely enough for our summit bid, and none at all for sleeping.

We reached the North Ridge in the dark. Peter Kuznetzov and Alexander Bekasov traversed to a height of 8,300 metres and spent the night on the ridge. The remaining four of us spent the night immediately below the ridge at 8,250 metres. On 19 May we joined up in the camp at 8,300 metres. While we had climbed the wall and felt a measure of satisfaction, we were exhausted from the heavy work of many days hauling loads, difficult technical climbing, and carrying extremely heavy rucksacks. There was no celebration – that could

Climbers in the foot of the couloir at 22,280ft/ 7,400m. The angle of the couloir varied between 45 and 60 degrees. Protection was poor and there was intermittent stonefall when the sun reached the route.

come later. Our focus remained on the days ahead.

What was left, it seemed to us, was the very simple classical ridge. But everything turned out to be far more difficult.

There was a very strong wind the night of 19 May and we could not leave for the summit until the wind subsided around 8 am. Soon after we left camp, Alexander's feet felt very cold and he returned to the tents, not wanting to risk frostbite. The rest of us continued climbing. When we were at 8,500 metres the sky filled with clouds and it began to snow. After we climbed the First Step, the visibility was about 30 metres and after the Second it was no more than 10 metres. Ahead were Peter Kuznetzov, followed by Valerii Kozanov and Grigorii Semikolenov. I was next, but kept looking back and waiting to keep Evgenii Bakaleinikov in view. Evgenii had poor eyesight and the driving snow quickly covered our tracks.

The rock slabs above the Second Step were covered with thick, flaky, unreliable snow and we moved very slowly. All the same, we did not stop. I passed the bodies of two climbers at about 8,600 metres and 8,750 metres. We left the snow for a rock slope and the summit ridge. A full blizzard set in. The summit was somewhere very close to where I was, no more than 15 or 20 minutes away, but visibility was zero. Peter came down from the summit and we decided to wait for Valerii and Grigorii to return from the summit and for Evgenii to reach us. I gave up my own summit attempt. Once we were all together we had to regroup and begin our descent immediately, staying very close to each other. It was 6 pm and the blizzard raged.

One by one our oxygen bottles were soon empty. We shared our masks until the last bottle was gone. By 7 pm it was dark. The most difficult part of the descent was not the Second Step, where we had fixed a rope next to the Chinese ladder, but finding the exit from the North-east Ridge to our camp in the blizzard. We reached our tents at Camp III, where Alexander was waiting for us, at 10 pm.

The next day at the North Col we heard someone say: 'Crazy Russians!' Somehow we weren't offended – in fact the words seemed pleasant. Soon the celebrations began.

When I look back on the climb four years later, I am left with some strong feelings. It is true that the climb was 'crazy'. I would never do it again. But I write this from the position of having done the climb. If I were to be confronted with the same choices and had the same dreams, but did not know the harrowing experiences to come, I would go to the North-east Wall of Everest again.

At the same time I am very proud of the way we trained and climbed as a team. I was 15 minutes away from the summit of Everest and I turned back. It was a simple choice. We were a team and to have gone on could have killed all of us. As it was we all came back home. I am also proud that we did the new route on Everest that we had dreamed of and summitted on the precise day we had anticipated in our plan. And when I went back to Everest in 2000, I was pleased to hear people asking: 'And where is that Zakharov Couloir?'

Ecstasy on the summit: the normally restrained Russians express their joy and relief on reaching the top in a blizzard. Pictured is Valerii Kohanov, one of three to succeed, along with Grigorii Semikolenov and Peter Kuznetzov, who took the photograph. Zakharov turned back barely 15 minutes from the top but returned to Everest in 2000, going to the summit via the North-east Ridge.

THE NORTH-EAST RIDGE COMPLETE

By 1995, the first complete ascent of the North-east Ridge – from the East Rongbuk Glacier to the summit – remained an unclaimed prize. In 1988 the Australian Russell Brice and British Harry Taylor at last climbed through the three daunting pinnacles which rise from the ridge below its junction with the North Ridge, but were forced by bad weather and poor snow conditions to descend to the North Col.

In March, 1995, a formidable Japanese team arrived. From Nihon University, it included 13 climbers, six research scientists, two Chinese liaison officers, an interpreter and 31 Sherpas, and had 20 tons of supplies. On 9 April, after establishing Advance Base on the East Rongbuk Glacier, it embarked on its attempt.

Headed by Kiyoshi Furuno, the leading group of climbers took nine days, fixing ropes for much of the route, to reach the foot of the First Pinnacle at 7,850 metres, where they set up Camp V. Switching teams, they embarked on the three pinnacles on April 25. A 60-degree gully followed by a narrow snow crest led to the top of the First Pinnacle

(8,170 metres). Then came a knife-edge snow arete and an 80-degree snow wall to the top of the Second Pinnacle (8,250 metres). Finally, on April 29, they climbed an angled gully to a snowy peak just beyond the Third Pinnacle (8,400 metres) and pitched Camp VI on the ridge beyond, a short distance before the junction with the North Ridge.

While the climbing team retreated to Base Camp, Sherpas and support climbers restocked the camps with supplies. Other Sherpas established two camps along the North-east Ridge. On 9 May Furuno, Shigeki Imoto and ten Sherpas, equipped with oxygen, reclimbed the Pinnacles. They camped beyond the Pinnacles that night and reached the base of the Second Step the next day, where they found that the Chinese ladder had collapsed. Although

they were carrying an extendable aluminium ladder, they reinstated the Chinese ladder that night.

Starting at 4 am, Furuno and Imoto, plus four Sherpas, went for the summit on 11 May. They climbed the Second Step without difficulty and reached the summit at 7.15 am. 'After an hour on the summit,' recites the official expedition account, 'the group started down, raced back through the pinnacles, and descended all the way to Advance Base that day, arriving at 6.15 pm, just before the sun set.'

Above: *A Sherpa, using oxygen, contours on exposed ground beyond the Third Pinnacle on 9 May, the first day of the full ascent.* Left: *The steep snow wall, reaching 80 degrees in places, leading to the top of the Second Pinnacle. One climber is nearing the top of the snow. A second is a short way behind, while a third is waiting at mid-height. The Japanese spent three weeks climbing and preparing the Pinnacles, then went for the summit in a three-day push.*

Four more photographs from the Japanese ascent. Left, above: *Kiyoshi Furuno's stunning shot of climbers approaching the First Pinnacle. They 'faithfully followed the crest of the ridge'.* Left, below: *climbers at 27,230ft/ 8,300m on the Second Pinnacle.* Right, above: *a climber on rock to the right of the prominent buttress near the top of the Third Pinnacle.* Right, below: *the Pinnacles (centre right on crest of North-east Ridge) as seen from advance base on the East Rongbuk Glacier. The team also had to climb the buttresses to the left of the Pinnacles.*

The day began so well. In Klev Schoening's photograph, taken mid-morning at 28,200ft/8,600m on the upper South-east Ridge, the climbers are making good progress in seemingly perfect weather. The four leading figures (left to right) are Anatoli Boukreev, the strong and experienced Kazakh climber who was guiding for Scott Fischer's commercial group, Mountain Madness; Mike Groom, an Australian guide with Rob Hall's commercial group, Adventure Consultants; American Jon Krakauer, a climber and writer in the Adventure Consultants team; and Andy Harris, a New Zealander guiding for Adventure Consultants. But the string of climbers below contained one element of the impending disaster, as the bottlenecks were about to begin. The highest peak in the background is Makalu.

THE LONGEST NIGHT

by Charlotte Fox

In spring 1996 came the most prolonged and most public Everest disaster. Ten teams were making attempts via the South Col, including five of the new 'commercial' expeditions, whose members paid up to $65,000 to be guided to the summit. Early on 10 May, 33 climbers, guides and Sherpas embarked from the South Col. Twenty-four reached the top, but during their descent the South-east Ridge was hit by a ferocious storm. Five climbers died and a sixth was horribly maimed by frostbite. In the first of three accounts, Charlotte Fox takes up the story from the point during the ascent when she and her companions headed up from the South Summit.

Charlotte Fox, a member of the Mountain Madness group, was one of the most experienced clients on the mountain. From Aspen, Colorado, she spent the winters working as a professional ski patroller. She had climbed throughout North and South America, in Antarctica and in the Himalayas, where she was the first American woman to climb the 8,000 metre peak Gasherbrum II. When the storm hit the mountain, her experience and fitness proved invaluable.

After more waiting, the rest of us slowly moved off the South Summit. The snow on the ridge was funky and, when I pulled out my axe, I found I had punched a view through to Tibet. At last we huffed and puffed one by one through the strenuous, but not difficult, Hillary Step, and emerged onto the broad, slanting summit ridge. I remember Lopsang passing me. Further on, beneath the summit, he assisted Sandy Hill, who lay bewildered-looking in the snow not far from the top. In front of me, Mike Groom, a Hall guide, kept stopping and looking behind, keeping an eye on the slow-motion client Yasuko Namba, whom I had to pass on the narrow ridge before the Step. Martin Adams, another of my team, came by me on his way down and stuck his hand up with five fingers splayed. 'Five minutes, Charlotte, just five more minutes!' With this, I grinned behind my oxygen mask and inwardly rejoiced. We had taken nearly 14 hours to go 2,800 feet!

Then the never-ending ridge ended; there was a group of people on a small crest of snow . . . and nothing else. Though a stiff wind was blowing, the sky was a deep blue, and there was a 100-mile view all around. I felt more relief than elation that I had arrived . . . and a deep fear that this was not a place meant for humans. We were hanging it *waaaaay* out. I checked my watch: 2.15 pm – close enough to the 2 pm turn-around time I remember being agreed upon in camp.

When Tim arrived behind a slow pack, I told Neal I was going down. There wasn't much time for an extended celebration. But Neal wanted to keep our group together. Minutes ticked by as we waited for the last of our team to arrive, have their photographs taken, and shake hands all around. I didn't look at my watch again when we finally did leave and, because of the timeless feeling that accompanies high-altitude climbing, I have no idea how long we were on the summit.

It was on the way down that I first noticed clouds blowing up from below. We had seen this phenomenon often enough in the last month – the clouds rose in the afternoon from the humid lowlands of Nepal and rolled up the Khumbu Icefall toward the Lhotse Face. These clouds looked a little more black and menacing, but at least we were headed down. One by one, we climbed back down the Hillary Step, tiptoed across the narrowest part of the climb to the South Summit, and just when I thought we could really make some time to the Balcony, Sandy, just behind me, went from tired and slow to stop. She told me to leave her. I encouraged her to find the strength to keep going, the best reason being her son, Bo. She struggled, but collapsed again, clinging to a thin piece of line. 'Charlotte, get out the hypodermic.'

Wow! I had forgotten that Ingrid Hunt, our expedition doctor, had given us all a shot of dex-

Lopsang: Lopsang Jangbu Sherpa, sirdar (leader) of Mountain Madness Sherpas
Hall: Rob Hall, leader of Adventure Consultants
Neal: Neal Beidleman, Mountain Madness guide
Sandy: Sandy Hill Pittman, client
Scott: Scott Fischer, Mountain Madness leader
Martin: Martin Adams, client

Traffic jam on Everest: in Scott Fischer's photograph, three climbers are above the Hillary Step, and one climber is climbing the step while the others wait their turn. It is already 1 pm, and perilously late.

amethasone, a steroid effective in reducing cerebral edema and a last-ditch chance for survival in situations such as this. Sandy rolled over. I unzipped the rainbow zipper on her down suit, and though I'd never given a shot before, jammed that baby in right through her pile into the big muscle just over her buttocks as Ingrid taught us to do in Base Camp. Sandy didn't even flinch.

In five minutes or so Sandy recovered enough to

be assisted down by Neal, who had by then caught up to us with most of the rest of our group. Only Scott remained behind with Lopsang. We passed Scott a few minutes below the summit while he was still on his way up and exchanged weak high fives. None of us knew he was hurting. All he said to Neal in passing was that he was 'so tired.' Weren't we all! And at this point he was still moving – all that counts. Our little group continued its way down to the balcony, where I caught up to Klev Schoening, who was just leaving to follow Martin down the mountain.

'Neal may need help with Sandy. Can you wait a few minutes?' I said to Klev. Behind Sandy and the rest of our friends we could see Scott, still stumbling along in the company of Lopsang. At this point I checked my watch and took the opportunity to change my headlamp battery. It was 6 pm – one hour until dark. We all plunged off the Balcony together into a surprising six to eight inches of new snow. The storm had been more serious than we realized. Suddenly, there was an alarming crack and flash – thunder and lightning, above 8,000 metres. Terrifying.

At last we made our way to the final fixed line. Camp IV could be seen not far below us. But, as we were nearing the end of the rope, everyone in our group became backed up as Mike Groom attempted to assist Yasuko and teammate Beck Weathers. They were sitting in the snow, immobile. Neal proceeded to help Yasuko, while Mike took Beck. At this moment the storm closed in on us and sealed in the darkness of night.

I took one last look at the tents – so close – and then kept moving with the others. We spent an interminable time descending carefully in the darkness and increasing wind, spreading out individually in our search for camp. The ground flattened out; we were walking among oxygen bottles, but still no tents. Neal had the presence of mind to gather the dispersing people before anyone was lost.

Suddenly I felt myself close to an empty void. The ice dropped away into blackness and swirling snow. Neal sensed it too, and screamed to everyone to back off and huddle down right where we were. We would try to outlast the storm in the hopes that it would break up early in the evening as it had in the previous nights and we could find our way back to the tents.

Then began the longest night. It is estimated that the temperature dropped to around –40°F and the winds funneling over the South Col between Lhotse and Everest increased to a fierce 70 miles per hour. We had had little sleep and not much to eat or drink for two days, we were out of oxygen, and we had just summitted the highest mountain in the world. We were fried. How would we survive?

Klev and Tim, as well as Neal, had been keeping track of our group of 11 in the search for the tents. Now they got everyone together on the hard ice to conserve warmth and maintain a basic energy level with continued movement. The two began a cheerleading routine that kept many going through the long wait. 'Charlotte, beat on Sandy's back!' Tim would yell at me. 'Are you beating on Sandy's back? Answer me!'

At this point, my energy level began to wane. I was good to the tents from the summit, but could I make it through a night in this weather in my depleted state? I thought not. The effects of the dexamethasone were apparently wearing off Sandy; her efforts to keep moving were slowing, as were mine. Finally, we just lay together in a heap and waited, I hoped, for that warm, fuzzy feeling that comes with hypothermia, and death.

Hours passed. Miraculously, the storm abated. Stars emerged from the spindrift and the hulks of Lhotse and Everest became evident. Klev shouted that he recognized where we were and where the tents should be. Half-frozen, we staggered to our feet and made an attempt to shuffle off. My knees kept buckling and I couldn't seem to make headway. If only I'd not given up hope and tried to keep my body warm and moving! I sank slowly into a heap again, telling Tim to go to the tents. His reply was that he was feeling pretty good and would stay with me. The group moved off without us; they promised to send back help. Soon after, we heard Sandy calling out in the darkness. She wasn't doing well, and had to crawl back to Tim and me. Also present, and now ambulatory, were Yasuko and Beck.

Tim turned his attention to the four of us. With the hope that we were going to get out of this thing alive, Sandy and I took to slapping each other and working our arms and legs as never before. We had to be able to walk. My hood was still tightly drawn around my face as protection against the intensely blowing wind, so I was only dimly aware of Beck and Yasuko beside Sandy, Tim and me.

It must have been a couple of hours more of shaking, slapping and screaming into the wind from the pain of the cold that Anatoli [Boukreev] suddenly appeared in my headlamp beam. He dropped a bottle of oxygen in front of Sandy and said, 'Come with me.' He happened to grab me first and I struggled to my feet, willing my legs to work this time. They did. My arm in his, I stumbled along beside him through the moonscape of the South Col until we were suddenly at the tents of Camp IV. I had the weird sensation of my eyes freezing inside my head; we were walking directly into the biting wind. Anatoli did not want me to stop to adjust my goggles. We weren't going to stop for anything. He returned to lead in Sandy, with Tim following behind.

Anatoli had made one foray out before he found us, and, after getting better directions from Neal back at the tents, had been successful thereafter. After three trips out to, as it turned out, the edge of the Kangshung Face, he left it to the other members of Rob Hall's team to help Beck and Yasuko back to the tents of Camp IV. He had done as much as he could, and, in the end, much more than anyone else. Tim told me that, while Anatoli's efforts to bring us in were truly heroic, he had figured out how to get us in himself. Anatoli beat him to it. I won't split hairs.

It was not until the next morning that I asked about Scott. Because of darkness and blowing ice, I hadn't been able to discern who was in our huddle. I was shocked to learn that Scott was still not far above us on the mountain, and that Beck and Yasuko lay near death at our bivy site.

Knowing that the fresher Sherpas were attempting to rescue Scott, it was all the rest of us could do to prepare ourselves to go down. The torpor was incredible; finding and putting on a boot took half an hour. Finally, supplied with new bottles of Os, we emerged from our cocoon into the face of that bitter wind and began our descent. It was a long day to Camp II, where more news came to us of the others still on the mountain and how rescues were going. The wind blew plumes of snow off the upper mountain. Things didn't look good.

The crowded summit: a throng of climbers atop Everest in the early afternoon. Storm clouds were already building from below.

LIKE A MIRAGE

by Anatoli Boukreev and Weston DeWalt

During a lull in the hurricane that savaged the South Col on the night of 10–11 May, six climbers stumbled back to their tents. That left five climbers, Charlotte Fox included, marooned on the col. It was then, in a supreme act of mountaineering heroism, that Anatoli Boukreev, the Kazakh climber who was guiding for Scott Fischer's Mountain Madness expedition, went out into the storm to rescue Fox and her colleagues Sandy Hill Pittman and Tim Madsen. Meanwhile, Fischer had collapsed on a ledge 1,200 feet above the col. Although Sherpas reported that Fischer was beyond help, Boukreev – who related his account to the writer Weston DeWalt – resolved to make a final bid to save his life.

Boukreev (above) had climbed Everest – without oxygen – twice before. Fischer (below) was leading his first Everest commercial expedition.

I slept like two hours and after seven-thirty that morning Pemba came with tea. And I heard some Sherpas pass by our tent, and I ask Pemba, 'What is the situation now? Somebody go to Scott or no?' And he gave some tea and he was just quiet. No answer. I said, 'Scott needs help. Please send some Sherpas up.' So, he went to the Sherpas' tent and he began to talk. And now I have no power. It would be for me a stupid idea to go again. I needed some recovery time.

At probably eight-thirty I took a look at our climbing route from yesterday, and I can see the storm has lost power. I see some Sherpas going up, and he says, 'Okay, father of Lopsang started together with Tshi Sherpa,' and I ask, 'They carry oxygen?' and he tells me, 'Yes.'

And then I speak with Neal. 'Okay, this is my position. I would like to stay here,' and he says okay and he worked for the clients and took them down.

A strong wind had come up, and I kept myself inside the tent, but around one or two I went out, and I spoke with Todd Burleson and Pete Athans with Alpine Ascents (another commercial expedition) who had come to Camp IV to help with getting climbers down from the trouble we had had. I asked them, 'Do you know what is happening?' and they said some Sherpas had returned with Makalu Gau, so I went to the Taiwanese tents.

When I went into the tent, I saw this Makalu Gau, his face and hands all frostbitten, but he was talking a little bit, and I asked him, 'Did you see Scott?' and he says, 'Yes, we were together last night.' And I had hopes that Scott could survive,

but with this news I thought, 'Scott is finished, dead already,' and I got upset about this, but this news is only from the Taiwanese, so I want to talk with our Sherpas who went up.

I go inside the Sherpas' tent, and the father of Lopsang is crying with great sadness, and he says, 'We cannot help.' And he speak very small, very little bit of English. I don't understand. 'What is happening?' And they said to me, 'He died.' And then I said, 'Was he still breathing?' and they told me, 'Yes, he's still breathing, but no more signs of life.'

I asked, 'Did you give him oxygen?' and they said, 'Yes, we give oxygen,' and I asked, 'Did you give him some medicine?' and they said, 'No.' And now I understood, so I went outside the tent and talked with Todd Burleson and Pete Athans, and I asked, 'Can you help me go up to help with Scott? People say he is still alive, like 8,350 metres.'

Pete Athans, who spoke Nepali, understood the situation, and he said to me, 'Actually I spoke with the Sherpas, and they said it's impossible to help Scott.' And I said, 'Why? Maybe we will try.' He says, 'But it is bad weather coming. Storm didn't finish. And people try to give him oxygen, but oxygen didn't help him.' Todd Burleson was quiet, but Pete Athans talked with me. And he said, 'Scott was, yes, able to breathe, but he wasn't able to drink tea, just people put his tea inside of his mouth, but he couldn't swallow.'

And Pete Athans said, 'Impossible. For this situation, impossible for him.' I said, 'But maybe, maybe some breathing, if he has some breathing, maybe oxygen will improve, and I go out again.'

I went inside the tent again with Lopsang's

father and asked him, 'Can you say little more information? Did you give him no medicine? When you gave him new oxygen?' He said, 'Oh, we gave him one bottle oxygen, put mask, and open oxygen.'

And I said okay and got a radio from the Sherpas and radioed to Base Camp, and I spoke with Dr Caroline Mackenzie of Rob Hall's expedition and asked her, 'This is the situation, what do you advise?' And she is upset also and says to me, 'Anatoli, try to help everything that is possible for you; please try to find some possibility.' I said, Okay, I will try everything that is possible, but what is your advice?' She said, 'Okay, about medicine, do you have this small packet with the injections?' And I told her, 'Yes, I have the injection.' And she said for me to try it with Scott, and I promised her I would try everything.

Then, I go to the Sherpas' tent, and see that Lopsang is using oxygen and some other Sherpas are using oxygen. And I said, 'Okay, I need some oxygen. I need three bottles of oxygen and a thermal bottle of tea. Can you make it for me?' And people said, 'Why you need?' I said, 'I will go up.' People say, 'It is stupid idea.'

So, I left the tent and then Lopsang's father came and began to speak with Pete Athans in Nepali, and Pete Athans came and said, 'Anatoli, what do you want to do?' I said, 'I will go up; I need oxygen; I need thermal bottles of tea.' And Pete Athans tried to explain to me that it was a bad idea. He said, 'Now the storm has gone down a little bit, and if you go now, you will get this storm again.' I said to him, 'This is what I need to do.'

I knew from my experience; I explained to him my position. This situation with Scott was a slow process; maybe Scott, if he had oxygen, would possibly revive. Scott is just before the Balcony, and he has enough oxygen maybe until seven o'clock. I need some oxygen.

Pete is like the Sherpas, and I understand he thinks it is a stupid idea, but I get some oxygen. I ask for three, but get only two. I think maybe it came from David Breashear's expedition, but I don't know for sure. I began to hurry; I began to prepare myself, but as I prepared, the wind began to come higher. It is just around four o'clock, maybe four-fifteen.

I took my pack and was leaving, and I saw Pete Athans outside of the tent, and I asked Pete Athans, 'Maybe you will go up?' He said just, 'No.' And I said, 'How many will try to help?' And just – he got sad, he just cried a little bit. He thinks there is no chance.

I just started from the tents and maybe 150 metres ahead, I saw a small moving point,

Fischer's photograph, taken late in the afternoon of 10 May, shows climbers descending the summit ridge below the Hillary Step, as the storm clouds close around them. The first five climbers, all in the Mountain Madness group, are (left to right): Lene Gammelgaard, Tim Madsen, Charlotte Fox, Neal Beidleman (guide) and Sandy Pittman. All five survived the hurricane on the South Col; Fischer collapsed, probably from altitude sickness, 1,200 feet above the col.

It was Boukreev who led up the Hillary Step shortly after midday on 10 May. In Neal Beidleman's photograph, the wind is whipping Boukreev's rope out over the Kangshung Face.

somebody coming down to me, and I was very wondered. I thought it was like a phantom, a miracle, and I began to hurry. And in a short time I came upon this man, who was carrying his hands without gloves up in front of his body like a surrendering soldier. And I did not know then who this was, but now I understand it was Beck Weathers. [Boukreev had not been told that Weathers, who had been left for dead on the South Col during the storm of 10–11 May, had been

found alive the following afternoon.]

I said, 'Who are you?' He didn't speak or answer, and I asked him, 'Did you see Scott?' And he said to me, 'No one I saw. No one I saw. It is my last time in the mountains. I don't want to come back to these mountains. Never, never . . . ' It was like crazy talk.

Just I think my head is broken, and I am thinking, 'Anatoli, you need to be able to think if you go up again.' And I yell back, 'Burleson! Pete!

Please help me!' And I asked them, 'Can you help with this man? I will go. I will keep my time.' And they tell me, 'Don't worry, we will take care of him.'

Everyone said it was stupid to go for Scott, but I saw this man survived, and this was a push for me. And I took a mask, everything, and I began to move with oxygen, without resting, and I climbed steadily, but darkness started to come, nightfall just began. And also a strong wind began with a

blizzard and a difficult time.

And just around seven o'clock, five minutes past probably, I found Scott. Dark also, with a serious storm, and I saw him through the snow, again like a mirage. I saw the zipper of his down suit open, one hand without a mitten, frozen. I opened his face mask, and around the mask face it is frozen, but a different temperature, and under the mask it is like a blue colour, like a big bruise. It is like not life in the face. I saw no breathing, just a clenched jaw.

I lose my last hope. I can do nothing. I can do nothing. I cannot stay with him.

It began to storm again, seven o'clock. Oxygen – I lose my last hope, because I thought when I started, 'Oxygen will improve his life.' If by now oxygen does not improve, no signs of life, no pulse or breathing . . .

Very strong wind began, I am without power, without power. And for me, just what do I need to do? Actually, I understood this. If I found him like Beck Weathers, it would be possible to help him. He was revived. Like Beck Weathers revived, he would need help and possibly giving him this help, like oxygen, everything would be possible. It would be possible to help Scott. I understand there is no way for me. No way for him. What do I need to do?

And I saw his pack and I roped it around his face to keep away the birds. And with maybe four or five empty oxygen bottles around, I put them on his body to help cover. And just maybe seven-fifteen I started to go down fast. And I understand I lose power, I lose emotion. I can't say how it was. I was very sad.

Storm began, very strong, new blow of fresh snow with strong wind. And I began to use the ropes, and when I finish at like 8,200 metres, visibility is gone. Began just darkness, probably seven-forty, impossible to see. And I found again Kangshung Face, same place, I think, near Yasuko Namba probably. I can see just two metres, but I understood. And then I go some more in a changed direction, and the snow on the ground is finished and I began to see some oxygen bottles. I turn back a little and go up a little, and I saw some tents.

I know these are not our tents, but next will be ours. When I found this place, I began to hear some voices. And I go without visibility, by the noise. And I come to the noise in a tent. I open. I see this man just alone by himself. I saw Beck Weathers, and I don't understand why he is alone, but I lose power, go for my tent, because I cannot help. Some sleeping bag I have. Just I crawl inside of my tent and go to sleep.

IN THE NICK OF TIME

by Jon Krakauer

Among the survivors of the hurricane was Jon Krakauer, a climber and writer whose book about the disaster, Into Thin Air, *became an immediate best-seller. Its compelling tale of blunders and chaos, heroism and fortitude touched a nerve in America's psyche, as well as bringing awareness of Everest to a wider public. In this extract, with its chilling undertones of a tragedy foretold, Krakauer describes his descent from the summit in rapidly worsening conditions.*

Krakauer, pictured answering reporters' questions in Kathmandu, was already a committed mountaineer and accomplished writer when he agreed to cover the 1996 attempts for Outside *magazine, joining Rob Hall's Adventure Consultants team. After his 18,000-word article was published, he expanded it into a book. By 2001,* Into Thin Air *had sold nearly four million copies in the US alone and was already regarded as a touchstone work, bringing a remarkable surge of interest in mountaineering.*

From the Balcony I descended a few hundred feet down a broad, gentle snow gully without incident, but then things began to get sketchy. The route meandered through outcroppings of broken shale blanketed with six inches of fresh snow. Negotiating the puzzling, infirm terrain demanded unceasing concentration, an all-but-impossible feat in my punch-drunk state.

Because the wind had erased the tracks of the climbers who'd gone down before me, I had difficulty determining the correct route. In 1993, Mike Groom's partner – Lopsang Tshering Bhutia, a skilled Himalayan climber who was a nephew of Tenzing Norgay's – had taken a wrong turn in this area and fallen to his death. Fighting to maintain a grip on reality, I started talking to myself out loud. 'Keep it together, keep it together, keep it together,' I chanted over and over, mantra-like. 'You can't afford to fuck things up here. This is way serious. Keep it together.'

I sat down to rest on a broad, sloping ledge, but after a few minutes a deafening BOOM! frightened me back to my feet. Enough new snow had accumulated that I feared a massive slab avalanche had released on the slopes above, but when I spun around to look I saw nothing. Then there was another BOOM!, accompanied by a flash that momentarily lit up the sky, and I realized I was hearing the crash of thunder.

In the morning, on the way up, I'd made a point of continually studying the route on this part of the mountain, frequently looking down to pick out landmarks that would be helpful on the descent, compulsively memorizing the terrain: 'Remember to turn left at the buttress that looks like a ship's prow. Then follow that skinny line of snow until it curves sharply to the right.' This was something I'd trained myself to do many years earlier, a drill I forced myself to go through every time I climbed, and on Everest it may have saved my life. By 6 pm, as the storm escalated into a full-scale blizzard with driving snow and winds gusting in excess of 60 knots, I came upon the rope that had been fixed by the Montenegrins on the snow slope 600 feet above the Col. Sobered by the force of the rising tempest, I realized that I'd gotten down the trickiest ground just in the nick of time.

Wrapping the fixed line around my arms to rappel, I continued down through the blizzard. Some minutes later I was overwhelmed by a disturbingly familiar feeling of suffocation, and I realized that my oxygen had once again run out. Three hours earlier when I'd attached my regulator to my third and last oxygen canister, I'd noticed that the gauge indicated that the bottle was only half full. I'd figured that would be enough to get me most of the way down, though, so I hadn't bothered exchanging it for a full one. And now the gas was gone. I pulled the mask from my face, left it hanging around my neck, and pressed onward, surprisingly unconcerned. However, without supplemental oxygen, I moved more slowly, and I had to stop and rest more often.

The literature of Everest is rife with accounts of hallucinatory experiences attributable to hypoxia and fatigue. In 1933, the noted English climber Frank Smythe observed 'two curious looking objects floating in the sky' directly above him at 27,000 feet: '[One] possessed what appeared to be squat underdeveloped wings, and the other a protuberance suggestive of a beak. They hovered motionless but seemed slowly to pulsate.' In 1980, during his solo ascent, Reinhold Messner imagined that an invisible companion was climbing beside him. Gradually, I became aware that my mind had gone haywire in a similar fashion, and I observed my own slide from reality with a blend of fascination and horror.

I was so far beyond ordinary exhaustion that I experienced a queer detachment from my body, as if I were observing my descent from a few feet overhead. I imagined that I was dressed in a green cardigan and wingtips. And although the gale was generating a wind-chill in excess of seventy below zero Fahrenheit, I felt strangely, disturbingly warm.

At 6.30, as the last of the daylight seeped from the sky, I'd descended to within 200 vertical feet of Camp IV. Only one obstacle now stood between me and safety: a bulging incline of hard, glassy ice that I would have to descend without a rope. Snow pellets borne by 70-knot gusts stung my face; any exposed flesh was instantly frozen. The tents, no more than 650 horizontal feet away, were only intermittently visible through the whiteout. There was no margin for error. Worried about making a critical blunder, I sat down to marshal my energy before descending further.

Once I was off my feet, inertia took hold. It was so much easier to remain at rest than to summon the initiative to tackle the dangerous ice slope; so I just sat there as the storm roared around me, letting my mind drift, doing nothing for perhaps forty-five minutes.

I'd tightened the drawstrings on my hood until only a tiny opening remained around the eyes, and I was removing the useless, frozen oxygen mask from beneath my chin when Andy Harris suddenly appeared out of the gloom beside me. Shining my headlamp in his direction, I reflexively recoiled when I saw the appalling condition of his face. His cheeks were coated with an armor of frost, one eye was frozen shut, and he was slurring his words badly. He looked in serious trouble. 'Which way to the tents?' Andy blurted, frantic to reach shelter.

I pointed in the direction of Camp IV, then warned him about the ice just below us. 'It's steeper than it looks!' I yelled, straining to make myself heard over the tempest. 'Maybe I should go down first and get a rope from camp–' As I was in midsentence, Andy abruptly turned away and moved over the lip of the ice slope, leaving me sitting there dumbfounded.

Scooting on his butt, he started down the steepest part of the incline. 'Andy,' I shouted after him, 'it's crazy to try it like that! You're going to blow it for sure!' He yelled something back, but his words were carried off by the screaming wind. A second later he lost his purchase, flipped ass over teakettle, and was suddenly rocketing headfirst down the ice.

Two hundred feet below, I could just make out Andy's motionless form slumped at the foot of the incline. I was sure he'd broken at least a leg, maybe his neck. But then, incredibly, he stood up, waved that he was OK, and started lurching toward Camp IV, which, at the moment was in plain sight, 500 feet beyond.

I could see the shadowy forms of three or four people standing outside the tents; their headlamps flickered through curtains of blowing snow. I watched Harris walk toward them across the flats, a distance he covered in less than ten minutes. When the clouds closed in a moment later, cutting off my view, he was within sixty feet of the tents, maybe closer. I didn't see him again after that, but I was certain that he'd reached the security of camp, where Chuldum and Arita would doubtless be waiting with hot tea. Sitting out in the storm, with the ice bulge still standing between me and the tents, I felt a pang of envy. I was angry that my guide hadn't waited for me.

My backpack held little more than three empty oxygen canisters and a pint of frozen lemonade; it probably weighed no more than sixteen or eighteen pounds. But I was tired, and worried about getting down the incline without breaking a leg, so I tossed the pack over the edge and hoped it would come to rest where I could retrieve it. I stood up and started down the ice, which was as smooth and hard as the surface of a bowling ball.

Fifteen minutes of dicey, fatiguing crampon work brought me safely to the bottom of the incline, where I easily located my pack, and another ten minutes after that I was in camp myself. I lunged into my tent with my crampons still on, zipped the door tight, and sprawled across the frost-covered floor too tired to even sit upright. For the first time I had a sense of how wasted I really was: I was more exhausted than I'd ever been in my life. But I was safe. Andy was safe. The others would be coming into camp soon. We'd fucking done it. We'd climbed Everest. It had been a little sketchy there for a while, but in the end everything had turned out great.

It would be many hours before I learned that everything had not in fact turned out great – that nineteen men and women were stranded up on the mountain by the storm, caught in a desperate struggle for their lives.

The most remarkable survival story of all: Beck Weathers, an American plastic surgeon, was left for dead on the South Col during the storm of 10–11 May. Late in the afternoon of 11 May Weathers stumbled into the South Col camp, almost totally blind, hideously frostbitten, one arm stretched in front of him like a frozen salute. Weathers, photographed here after treatment in Kathmandu, eventually recovered, although losing both his hands.

The next day Krakauer was told that, far from reaching safety, the man he believed to be the guide Andy Harris had fallen to his death from the South Col. Only much later did he learn that the man he had met was in fact climber Martin Adams, who had survived – while Harris had died higher up the mountain. Krakauer's mistaken identification above the South Col was the result of utter exhaustion.

THE FINAL PICTURE

by Peter Gillman

Two weeks after the slaughter on the South-east Ridge, a South African expedition returned to the fray. The first expedition of the post-apartheid era, it set off for the summit on 24 May. There were six in the summit team, among them British photographer Bruce Herrod. But Herrod fell behind and reached the top, alone, at 5 pm. After making a radio call, he was never heard from again. In April 1997, his body and camera were found at the Hillary Step. This is the story of the two frames the camera contained and what they revealed about the day he died.

Herrod, an accomplished professional photographer, had long nurtured the dream of climbing Everest. When he reached the summit, adorned with climbers' equipment and mementoes, he placed there a vial of water which he and his partner, Sue Thompson, had collected together in Tibet two years before. Then, using the delayed-action shutter of his Canon camera, he framed this meticulous self-portrait.

It was to be the shot of his life. Bruce Herrod had just climbed to the summit of Everest, achieving his supreme ambition as photographer and mountaineer. He composed his picture with meticulous care: the brown Tibetan plateau, 15,000 feet below, falling away to the left; the summit, adorned with its bizarre collection of climbers' mementoes, in the centre; Herrod himself, who had removed his oxygen mask and snow-goggles to ensure that he would be recognisable, stooping into the frame from the right.

As Herrod's delayed-action shutter clicked, his jubilation was clear. Yet it was also a moment of utmost peril. It was already past 5 pm. Herrod, who had been climbing for 17 hours, had arrived desperately late, thereby breaking his promise to his partner, Sue Thompson, that he would turn back if he knew he could not reach the summit by 1 pm.

He was close to exhaustion and utterly alone. Within two hours, darkness would shroud the mountain, making it impossible to reach the sanctuary of the South Col 3,000 feet below, where his colleagues from the South African Everest expedition were camped and waiting for him. He would have to spend the night on the mountainside, enduring temperatures plummeting to minus 30C, his ordeal worsened through acute dehydration and the difficulty of breathing in the thin air.

Herrod seemed composed. In a radio call from the summit to Thompson, who was at their home in West London, he told her he had placed a photograph of her on the summit, as well as a vial of water they had collected together from Lake Manasarowar in Tibet two years before. He also assured her he intended to get down safely. But Thompson was filled with trepidation. She told him he had to start his descent, and assured him: 'I'll be with you every step of the way.' At the same time, she knew Herrod was in 'a dire situation'.

An hour later, Rebecca Stephens – the first British woman to climb Everest – happened to telephone Thompson. Stephens told her that if Herrod could reach the South Summit, thereby overcoming the most hazardous part of the descent, he stood every chance. There were fresh oxygen cylinders at the South Summit, which would help sustain him through the night, and he was due to make his next radio call from there.

There was no call. Somewhere along Everest's icy summit ridge, with drops of more than a mile plunging on either side, Herrod disappeared. After spending most of the night waiting for news, Thompson knew that he must have died. 'By then it had all taken on a very unreal air,' she says. 'It all became a great big blank.'

Herrod had first been to Everest five years before, taking this premonitory self-portrait looking up the Khumbu Valley and Glacier, with the black summit of Everest visible beyond.

For a time she nurtured the fantastical hope that one day he would ring up to say he had descended by a different route and had ended up in Tibet by mistake, before finally accepting that he would not come back. Thompson spent the next year endlessly wondering how Herrod had died. 'It was so hard to imagine what had happened. Almost the worst of it was not knowing.' And had he taken any photographs? That had been his overriding goal, and to know he had achieved it would bring Thompson some relief.

Since Herrod had not mentioned his summit pictures during his final radio call, Thompson had no idea. She also came to feel bitter about what Herrod had done: for taking the risk of going for the summit; for losing the gamble; for dying, for leaving her alone. 'You do feel angry when somebody does what is after all a supremely selfish act. The whole year I said to myself, I just do not believe any mountain could possibly be worth it.'

At the end of April, the first climbers of the year to attempt Everest came upon Herrod's body high on the mountain. Three weeks later, by a miracle Thompson had scarcely dared hope for, other climbers found his camera. Having endured winds of 100mph or more and winter temperatures of minus 60C, it was brought down the mountain and returned to Thompson.

But would these finds resolve the puzzles? Why had he taken so long to reach the summit, and what would his pictures show? And would they bring Thompson a measure of peace?

Herrod's photograph of the Khumbu Icefall, long regarded as one of the most hazardous parts of the approach to the South Face, although deaths there dwindled in the 1980s and 1990s. Three climbers are visible a short distance below the centre top of the frame.

It was the mountains which brought them together. In 1990, Thompson joined a trekking expedition to climb Stok Kangri, a 6,000 metre Himalayan peak in Ladakh. Then 33, a Japanese specialist, Thompson had just quit a highly successful career as an investment analyst in London and Tokyo, intending to spend a year visiting places she had long dreamed of seeing.

Herrod, then 31, was the trek leader, having spent seven years as a geophysicist with the British Antarctic Survey. He was already a keen photographer, and had taken some memorable shots in daunting conditions on the polar ice cap. Like Thompson, he had impressive academic qualifications to his name, including a doctorate from Cambridge for his research into the geophysics of the Ronne Ice Shelf in Antarctica.

Herrod had eyes for Thompson from the start, even fixing the airline tickets at Gatwick so that they sat next to each other on the outward flight. Thompson did not take long to respond. They duly reached the summit of Stok Kangri, and were photographed together in their triumph.

Thompson found Herrod 'considerate, thoughtful and charming, with a wicked sense of humour' – which ran to slipping rocks into trekkers'

rucksacks without their knowing. He was also 'dogged and stubborn but cautious too'; when facing a tough decision 'he thought things through in almost tedious detail'.

Two years later, they set up home in Kensington. They embarked on a new career together, aiming to establish themselves as a travel and adventure writing team. They travelled widely, particularly to the mountain regions of Asia and South America. At first it barely provided a living, although they had savings to help them through. Gradually their earnings increased and Herrod produced a well-received photographic book about Snowdonia, where his love of the mountains shone through. He was especially proud of being accepted as a member of the British Outdoor Writers Guild (which takes photographers too). Colleagues in the Guild found him professional and dedicated, while still diffident at times and eager to learn.

Meanwhile Herrod was nurturing his dream of Everest. Looking back, Thompson is convinced it was there even before they met. As she reads through his letters and postcards, the mentions keep cropping up – 'It's clear he always wanted to climb it one day.' Herrod made several trips to Everest base camp in Nepal, once as location supervisor for a television documentary.

The opportunity he craved arose when he attended a travel-trade exhibition in London in 1994 and met the proprietor of a South African trekking company, Ian Woodall. When Woodall said he was hoping to organise the first South African attempt on Everest, and was looking for a photographer, Herrod did not need asking twice.

Herrod relished the chance to join an expedition with powerful historical resonances – one with black and white members, the first of the post-apartheid era. It was given the blessing of Nelson Mandela, and aimed to raise money for the Nelson Mandela Children's Fund. (In keeping with the aims of the expedition, Thompson is donating fees from Herrod's final photograph to the fund.)

In November 1995, Herrod travelled to South Africa to ask the sponsors what pictures they needed. 'He was always very conscientious in that way,' Thompson says. 'He took his job very seriously.' She also knew that Herrod viewed the expedition as the supreme opportunity of his career, above all as photographer. 'It really was his lifelong goal.' Whereas previously they had considered their career options several years ahead, this time 'we never discussed life beyond Everest at all. It was as if the world had to stop turning until he had climbed it.'

In February 1996, Herrod returned to Johannesburg to join the team. 'He was very geared up, very positive, very focused,' says Thompson, who had gone with him this time. On departure day, Herrod seemed very subdued. 'He was going to be away for three months, the longest we'd even been apart. It was a very difficult day.' Just as they had met at Gatwick, they now said goodbye at Jan Smuts airport. Thompson had a 'rising sense of panic' when for a moment she feared he had disappeared before giving a final wave.

The team reached Everest base camp in Nepal in April. Herrod, who was in touch with Thompson by fax and phone, seemed as committed as ever. But sadly the expedition was already winning the wrong kind of headlines. Some members were unhappy with Woodall's leadership style, and the team fragmented into cliques. There were bitter rows, including a dramatic clash between Woodall and the editor of the *Sunday Times*, which promptly withdrew its backing.

To Thompson, hearing of these events from over 3,000 miles away proved deeply troubling. 'It was awful reading about all this stuff and being unable to do anything.'

Herrod meanwhile was doing his best to keep clear of controversy. Thompson believes his time in Antarctica had taught him the need to suppress disagreement for the sake of group cohesion. She also suspects that Herrod knew that his best chance of making the summit lay in remaining in Woodall's camp. If so, it was a shrewd judgement, for Herrod's prospects were boosted when the top three climbers all quit, and Herrod became the expedition's deputy leader.

As the time for the expedition's summit attempt neared, Thompson found herself becoming more and more anxious. 'I felt terribly apprehensive, but I couldn't really work out why.' She felt more settled after talking to Herrod: 'He was clearly raring to go.' On 9 May, the summit team – Woodall, Herrod, and 27-year-old Cathy O'Dowd, backed by three Sherpas – moved up to the South Col, the barren, wind-scoured plateau at 26,000 feet that serves as the final staging post for the summit 3,000 feet above.

By what proved a stroke of good fortune, the six climbers were not ready to leave at midnight, as planned. For over the next 24 hours a series of disasters unfolded on the mountain. Half a dozen expeditions had been camped at the South Col, waiting for their chance. As they pushed for the summit, a fatal bottleneck developed at the most difficult part of the summit ridge, and many of the climbers who were delayed were hit by a storm during their descent: the wind was blasting at 70mph, taking the chill factor to minus 70C. A number of climbers were marooned without shelter and five died, while another was maimed by frostbite.

Back in Kensington, Thompson had woken on 10 May in a state of high tension. She had mixed feelings when she heard that the South African team had postponed its attempt, followed by immense relief when she heard it had survived the disasters. But Herrod, she says, was appalled by what had occurred. When they talked over what had happened – Herrod was by then back at base camp, a two-day descent from the South Col – 'he was clearly shaken and upset.'

Later Herrod asked for news of the American climber Beck Weathers, with whom he had sheltered on the South Col on the night of 9 May, and who had been helicoptered to Kathmandu after suffering acute frostbite to his face and hands. When Thompson reported that Weathers looked like losing both hands, 'Bruce was very distressed and crying.'

Thompson herself was distressed in turn. After the disasters of 10 May, she had assumed that Herrod would be giving up, and was already planning to meet him in Kathmandu. But Herrod told her by fax that they intended to make a second attempt. She was particularly upset that he had made his decision without consulting her. Previously, 'we would discuss everything in life'. This time, he had simply made the 'bald statement' that he was going for the top. 'I cried all day.'

In a fax, she told Herrod she was 'bitterly disappointed and upset' and 'totally exhausted at the idea of having to gear up again mentally' for the second summit bid. Even so, she concluded, 'I'm still with you all the way – go for it with all the common sense and judgement you have shown so far.' They largely reconciled their differences during a 45-minute phone call on 18 May (the cost on Thompson's phone bill, she ruefully reveals, was £126). 'By the time he went up again I didn't feel nearly as upset and agitated as when they went up on that first attempt,' she says.

Herrod, together with Woodall, O'Dowd and three Sherpas returned to the South Col on 24 May. It is now that the mysteries begin. The US climber David Breashears later reported that Herrod had seemed the fittest of the three westerners in the team. Yet when the six set off around midnight, Herrod was lagging behind – O'Dowd later reported that he was adjusting his overboots – and he never caught up. The attempt was blessed with clear weather, and Woodall reached the summit first at 9.52 am, followed by O'Dowd and the three Sherpas.

Herrod was by now so far behind that supporters in base camp believed he must have turned back. Herrod had not. In a radio call he reported he had 'had a bad morning', without specifying what he meant. Although there has been speculation that he was having problems with his oxygen equipment, Thompson believes that after his previous efforts at high altitude, he had simply met the limit of his physical reserves. But he pressed on, and at around 12.30 pm met Woodall and O'Dowd descending from the summit.

Herrod congratulated O'Dowd with a hug, then said that although the expedition had achieved its objective, he wanted to try for the summit himself. Here too there is controversy. Herrod was climbing so slowly that he had no chance of reaching the summit and returning before nightfall, and some climbers believe that Woodall should have stopped him from going on.

Woodall has said both that he did his best to persuade Herrod to turn back, and that he left it to Herrod to decide. Despite her animosity for Woodall, Thompson takes the view that whatever passed between them, responsibility for the decision was Herrod's alone. What intrigues her most are the contradictions with Herrod's own character that his decision implies.

'A lot of his friends ask me, how could the sanest, most rational human being on earth do such a thing? When we climbed together he was always insistent on safety procedures and thinking ahead about every action and its implications. If it had been me who had gone on, I'd never have heard the end of it.' In truth, she says, 'I think he had simply set his heart on climbing that mountain.'

Thompson was following the day's events by telephoning base camp and by using her computer to read the reports the expedition was posting on the Internet. When she heard that Woodall, O'Dowd and the Sherpas had succeeded, her first reaction was disappointment that Herrod had not made it. She too assumed that he must have turned back, and would soon be back at the safety of the South Col.

At 12.29 pm British time – 5.14 pm on Everest – she called base camp again. It was at that precise moment that Herrod had just radioed base camp to report that he had reached the summit. Thompson's first reaction was to look at her watch to calculate the remaining hours of daylight on the mountain. Among her regrets, when the base camp linked her with Herrod, is her failure to congratulate him on reaching the top. 'It shows how horrified I must have been in my mind – all I could think of was that he should get down. I feel awful in retrospect.'

She also regrets not having asked him why he had been so slow – yet his predicament seemed so extreme, she says, 'I wasn't going to waste time asking what with hindsight would have been very useful questions.'

Indeed, it was Thompson who ended their last conversation. Having told her about the personal mementoes he had left on the summit – placing her photograph and the vial of water from Tibet among the prayer scarves and items of climbing equipment – Herrod seemed to want to carry on talking. But Thompson told him it was time to start his descent.

'I was obsessed with the idea that he had to get moving. I'm sure he sensed the concern in my voice.' After she had assured him she would be with him 'every step', almost his final words were: 'Don't worry, I've got too much to look forward to.'

Thompson's first intimation that Herrod's body had been found came at the end of April, when the Kazakh climber, Anatoli Boukreev, reported coming upon it at the Hillary Step. Boukreev's report was second-hand, leading Thompson to hope that Herrod had reached the bottom of the Step before sitting down in the snow and succumbing to exhaustion and hypothermia.

But what of Herrod's camera? For a year, Thompson had lived with the hope, however remote, that it might be found and retrieved – a hope she had shared with Herrod's mother, who lives in Warwickshire. 'I had always felt that if Bruce had taken a summit shot, it would mean more to me and his family than anything else,' Thompson says.

There was a vital coda to her hopes, for Ian Woodall had the photographs Herrod had shot before his final summit attempt. Thompson was particularly aggrieved about an expedition calendar in which none of the pictures were credited to Herrod, even though she is certain that he took several of them.

Then, on 24 May, Thompson learned that Herrod's camera had been found inside his rucksack, which had been with his body. Together with his ice-axe, the camera was brought down by the US climber Pete Athans, who had just made his fifth ascent. The camera was relayed to London by the British climber Jon Tinker, and finally reached Thompson a week after it was found.

To her consternation, Thompson saw that Herrod had taken just two shots, and that his three other carefully-numbered rolls of film remained unused. 'I kept thinking, it has to be fifty-fifty. Are they shots of a snowy ridge, or are they really what I wanted to see? But I still had in my mind that he wouldn't let us down – that his sheer doggedness and methodical approach to life would continue to the very end.'

Herrod's two pictures were developed that day. They were everything Thompson had hoped for. She imagined him clamping his Canon EOS-1N to his ice-axe, and adjusting its 28/105mm zoom lens with utmost precision.

'He was obsessed with composition and technical detail, and always took immense care about setting up shots.' She could see him returning to position the camera several times, particularly to obtain a sense of height.

At first, Thompson was tempted to interpret Herrod's pictures as his own final testament to his achievement, composed to perfection because he sensed it could be the last photograph he ever took. But she adds that he was always so meticulous, 'he would have done that anyway'.

Just as over the delay in Herrod's ascent, there are other puzzles. Why had Herrod taken just these two shots – which were virtually identical – all day? 'I can only think that he gave up the chance to photograph the greatest mountain panorama of his life because he was drained beyond belief.'

She was still pondering this enigma when more disturbing news arrived. She spoke by phone to Athans, who had just returned to his home in Colorado. What she heard dispelled her peaceful image of Herrod subsiding into the snow at the foot of the Hillary Step.

Athans told her that Herrod's body had been hanging from the ropes which have been fixed on the Step. The best guess was that he had toppled backwards during the descent, from either tiredness or a slip of the foot. He could have simply been unable to right himself; or, from the evidence of a head injury, had been knocked out by the fall and never regained consciousness, an explanation which Thompson prefers. Athans added that he and colleagues had cut the body from the ropes and toppled it off the ridge, so that it fell down the mountain's giant Kangshung Face. He told Thompson: 'We felt that was the most respectful solution,' which she accepts.

The revelation modified Thompson's perspective on Herrod's photograph. Whereas previously she had believed that to some extent Herrod had been reconciled to his own possible death, and took his photograph in that light, she is now certain that he was determined to reach the South Summit and survive the night there – and that it was only his mistake on the Hillary Step which cost his life.

Her overriding consolation remains. Seeing the photograph, she says, 'was the moment it suddenly all seemed all right again. I can dispel the image of his body on the Hillary Step and recapture that image of how he always looked. I felt so angry with him all year. Being able to look at the world as he saw it that day has lessened my anger. Now I feel immensely proud of what he did.'

Sue Thompson kneels by Herrod's memorial chorten at Gorak Shep, Nepal, in 1999. Seeing Herrod's summit photographs, she said after they had been found, brought her a measure of peace.

TEN TIMES TO THE SUMMIT

by Ang Rita
Interview by Wendy Brewer Lama

The Sherpas of Nepal have played an important part in the mountaineering history of Everest, proving vital to the success of visiting expeditions as well as making more ascents than any other group. In 1992, when he gave this interview, Ang Rita held the individual record with seven ascents, all achieved without using supplementary oxygen. From a family of potato farmers, Ang Rita was first a low-level porter, then a high-altitude Sherpa, finally a sirdar, leader of the entire team of Sherpas, porters and support staff. His knowledge of the mountain's mood and weather patterns, its safe camp sites and hazards, made him much in demand. Ang Rita eventually increased his tally of ascents to ten.

Ang Rita, photographed by Pertemba during the Norwegian expedition of 1985. The expedition saw both Ang Rita and Pertemba make their third ascent, Pertemba going to the summit with Chris Bonington. Ang Rita forged ahead in the next seven years, adding four more ascents. He made his tenth and final ascent in 1996. Since then, younger Sherpas have matched Ang Rita's total.

Many people wonder, 'What is Ang Rita like?' They imagine me as a big, strong successful person. But when they meet me, they see I am just a simple man. I wear a T-shirt, I live in an old stone house, and I never went to school.

I grew up in Thame along the old trade route with Tibet. My family raised potatoes but, like now, farming wasn't enough to support our family. I started working for mountaineering expeditions in order to earn some money, first as a porter, then as a member of a Base Camp kitchen staff. At that time there were no schools in Solu Khumbu. Since I had no education, I could find no other work; there aren't many paying jobs in the mountains. Soon I was carrying loads to Camp I, and eventually learned how to fix the ropes and accompany the foreign climbers to higher camps. I knew that climbing was dangerous, but I had no choice. People said that some day I wouldn't come back.

The first time I summited Everest was with the American expedition in spring 1983. I'd climbed other 8,000 metre peaks - twice to the top of Dhaulagiri. Of course I was thrilled, but always on my mind was how this would help me support my family and how I could provide them with security and status in our Sherpa community to give them a better future.

In those days expedition teams brought along good climbing equipment for the Sherpas. Nowadays it is too expensive so they give us an allowance to buy equipment in Kathmandu. Some teams have lots of money and give us a good allowance; others give us less, depending on their budget and whether they are big or small hearted. Whether I got a big allowance or not, I always worked hard for the expeditions. If I could earn a good reputation with the foreigners, they would ask me to climb with them again.

When I was climbing with the Czechoslovakians in autumn 1984 they didn't have enough money to give us good equipment. The Slovak climbers had thick down jackets, but the Sherpas' jackets had no stuffing, like something you'd wear in Kathmandu. They were attempting the South Pillar and several teams had tried for the summit but none had succeeded. They approached me at Base Camp and buttered me up to give it a try - they promised to take me to their country if we summited.

So I tried and we made it, in three days from Base Camp. Two Slovaks and I reached the top at 3 pm, and returned that day to the high camp. One of them continued down to Camp II but the older one was bone-weary and wanted to sleep. I couldn't get him to go down and yet I couldn't stay with him either. The jacket and sleeping-bag they'd given me weren't very warm and I was afraid I'd freeze if I stayed on.

He dug a place in the snow and told me to go

down if I was cold. I stayed with him until midnight and then started down in the dark, by myself with no light. It was full moon and I could barely see the other Slovak's footprints. It was bitterly cold and I knew that if I stopped I might die. My stomach was crying for food and my legs were aching with pain.

At 3 am, when I reached Camp III, I couldn't stand up any longer. I ate a little chocolate and some snow and tried to sleep in an abandoned tent. The frozen air bit through my clothes and I was slowly losing the sensation in my toes. I stumbled onward, down to Camp II. To my relief, others of my team were there and warmed me with hot drinks and body heat.

The older Slovak stayed a second night at high camp. We worried about him being alone, and were ready to go after him when a Nepalese team on their way up offered to bring him down. But they were too late. He must have started down and was too weak to make it. As the Nepalese approached they saw his body tumble down the mountain. Perhaps if I'd had better equipment I could have stayed up there with him and helped him.

When we got back to Base Camp, they again offered to take me to Czechoslovakia but I couldn't go because I had another expedition.

My third ascent was with the Norwegians in May 1985, when four of them reached the top. My fourth was with the South Koreans in a winter expedition in December 1987. That time my climbing partner and I tried for two days to reach the top. We got close twice but both days the weather turned bad and we returned to the South Col. The third day we tried again and succeeded. We took off from our high camp at 12.30 am and got to the top at 2.20 pm. It was late to start down and we only made it to the South Summit where we bivouacked. This was one of the highest bivouacs on Everest at the time.

The Korean wanted to sleep but I knew that if we did, we would freeze to death. I kept talking to him to keep him awake. I didn't want him to die or I'd have to descend alone. All I could think about was staying alive and how we were going to get down. Finally, we saw the sun coming up over the peaks and we started feeling our way down with our near-frozen legs. We made it, but suffered from frost-bitten feet.

The stamina and fortitude of the Sherpas have been vital ingredients in the success of Everest expeditions. Here, South African Cathy O'Dowd, the first woman to climb Everest by two different routes, uses oxygen as she rests at 26,900ft/8,200m en route to Camp III on 28 May 1999. The Sherpas, right to left, are Pemba Tenji, Jangbu and Phuri. Jangbu and Pemba Tenji, who went to the summit with O'Dowd, started using oxygen equipment from Camp III (27,230ft/8,300m).

Local Tibetans have also proved invaluable to Everest enterprises ever since they were hired by the British during the 1902s. In Ed Webster's photograph, taken during the US-British Kangshung Face attempt of 1988, villagers from Kharta display impressive fortitude as a blizzard sweeps across the baggage line.

Ang Rita's Ten Ascents

7 May 1983
South Col route
(American expedition)
15 October 1984
South Pillar (Slovak)
29 April 1985
South Col (Norwegian)
22 December 1987
South Col (South Korean)
14 October 1988
South Col (Catalan)
23 April 1990
South Col (Nepalese Army)
15 May 1992
South Col (Chilean)
16 May 1993
South Col (Basque)
13 May 1995
North Col (Russian)
23 May 1996
South Col (US/International)

I never use oxygen on climbs. Other climbers think that it gives them energy. What is more important is to eat nutritious food, otherwise you lose strength and can die. I always carry a thermos of hot tea, a coil of rope and a snow bar when I go for the summit. You never know what you'll encounter, or if someone will need help. I'm not really happy until everyone is back at Base Camp, there have been no accidents or problems, and everyone has got along with each other.

My fifth ascent was with the Spanish in October 1988. By now only one other person, Sungdare Sherpa, had been up Everest more times than I had. I guess it became sort of a competition. But I also realized how important the ascents were becoming to me. Perhaps here was a path to success where I didn't need an education after all. Expeditions started asking for me, and I became like a celebrity. I travelled to other countries and met important people. Because I couldn't speak English, and I didn't know much about the world, I didn't know what to day.

In 1990 I became the first person to have summitted Everest six times when I climbed with the Nepalese Army. Four of us reached the summit. My companions ran out of oxygen and we bivouacked above the South Summit, higher even than with the Koreans in 1985. Two of them had bad frost-bite but I was unharmed.

In spring 1992 I made it for a seventh time with the Chileans. The weather was very bad and many expeditions were coming to me in Base Camp asking what I thought about the climbing conditions. The Chileans trusted me 100 per cent and were successful. Now I have the experience that many other sirdars and climbing Sherpas don't have. Many people die because their sirdars don't know the weather, they don't know the mountain.

Overall, mountaineering has been good to me and I think for most of the Sherpas. It has given us jobs and the chance to meet new people. Some of us have made friends from all over the world. But it has also taken us away from the fields where we are needed, leaving our wives and children to do the work.

Now we have schools in Solu Khumbu, [those built by Sir Edmund Hillary's Himalayan Trust] where two of my four children go. More than anything else, young people need education. If they learn to read and write, they can choose what to do with their lives, whether to climb mountains or do something else. They will hold a respected place in Nepalese society.

I must keep climbing - I have no choice. I'll wait for someone to call me and I'll go. I'm getting older and people tell me to retire. But they don't understand. I must keep climbing for I know no other work. Without education, I don't know how to make something long lasting of my success. I'd like to teach mountaineering and make it safer for everyone, but I can't do it alone. I need someone to be my guide.

THE NEW STARS

The name Sherpa is derived from the Tibetan Shar-Pa, which means easterner. Originally from Tibet, a group of Sherpas crossed into Nepal around 400 years ago to settle in the upper valleys south and west of Everest. The Sherpas' first contact with mountaineers came when Dr Alexander Kellas, who made a series of mountain journeys from Sikkim before the First World War, recruited porters from the Sherpas who had settled in Darjeeling. The British employed them on the first Everest expedition in 1921, at first calling them 'coolies', a now-anachronistic term dating from the earliest days of the Raj. One of the tasks undertaken by George Mallory and Guy Bullock in 1921 was to teach a select group of porters ice-climbing and safety techniques, and elite groups of Sherpas – whom they dubbed the Tigers – were selected for high-altitude work in 1922 and 1924. At that time, Sherpas were paid a few pence a day.

Gradually, Sherpas achieved recognition in their own right: Mallory was full of praise for Nyima, a young man who made the arduous climb with him to the summit of Kartse in 1921 in the hope of obtaining a view of the approach to the North Col. Tenzing was one of the early stars, in demand by both the Swiss and the British for his unrivalled experience when they made their attempts in 1952 and 1953. Ang Rita found no shortage of work either. Originally paid a few pence a day in the 1920s, the day's rate rose to £4–5 by the early 1990s, while a Sirdar like Ang Rita could earn about £1000 per expedition. The work was often a family affair – one of Ang Rita's four children, a son in his 20s, joined his father on his first expedition in 1992.

Since Ang Rita made his tenth ascent, at the age of 49, in 1996, younger Sherpas closed in on his total. The first was the redoubtable Babu Chiri Sherpa, who made ten ascents between 1990 and 2000. Like Ang Rita, he came from a farming family in the Solu Khumbu region, and started as a trekking porter. His first major expedition was to Kanchenjunga with a large-scale Russian expedition, and he was both surprised and pleased when he was the only one of 18 Sherpas who reached the summit.

His first visit to Everest was in 1990, on an expedition led by Frenchman Marc Batard. Babu Chiri made a solo bid the day after Batard and five others had gone to the summit. 'It was really scary,' Babu Chiri said. 'I didn't know anything about the weather.' He left the South Col at midnight, was not deterred by the Hillary Step – 'it wasn't too difficult and there were ropes in place' – and reached the summit at 8 am. When he descended he was canny enough to bring down an item of equipment the French had left on the summit in order to prove his ascent.

His next four ascents were with

Babu Chiri – known formally as Babu Tshering – was one of the rising stars among the Sherpas during the 1990s, racking up ten ascents by 2000 (and achieving that total in 11 years). But even that figure was passed by Apa, who made a record eleventh ascent on 24 May 2000.

British groups climbing from the North: the Second Step, he said, was 'no problem', as there were ropes as well as the Chinese ladder. He then returned to the South Side, and on 23 May 1996 took a French client to the summit having decided judiciously to retreat on 10 May, the day of the great disasters on the South-East Ridge; the great danger of the commercial expeditions, he felt, was the 'enormous pressure from the clients' to succeed. In 1999 he set a remarkable record by bivouacking on the summit, without oxygen, for 21 hours. In May 2000, going for the summit for the tenth time, he made the fastest ascent ever, climbing from Base Camp on the Nepalese side via the South Col in just under 16 hours. It all helped to bring acclaim for him and his Kathmandu trekking company, Nomad Expeditions, while he also pledged to contribute funds to building a schoolhouse in Solu Khumbu.

In the same month, a new name entered the records, when Apa Sherpa made his eleventh ascent, leading the way to the summit for a US environmental expedition. Then 41, Apa had made his ascents in 11 years. The ever-increasing tallies of ascents reflected the growing number of expeditions to Everest, which had continued to expand since Ang Rita's day. As for Babu Chiri, then 34, with six children between the ages of two and 14, all of them girls, he reckoned he would go 'a few times more'. After that he would concentrate on his business ventures – a better future, he reckoned, than carrying on risking his life. Like most of his colleagues, Babu Chiri knew only too well that Sherpas account for just under one third of all Everest fatalities.

At the same time Apa and Babu Chiri were ready to pay tribute to the work of Ang Rita in reinforcing the Sherpas' esteem and showing the way, both as climber and as entrepreneur. He too had established a trekking and climbing company in Kathmandu. For Babu Chiri, he was a 'role model'; for Apa, a hero.

THE SAME JOYS AND SORROWS

by Conrad Anker and David Roberts

During 80 years of mountaineering history, the myths of Everest took a powerful hold. No image was more compelling than that of Mallory and Irvine disappearing into the mists shrouding the summit in June 1924. In 1999, an American expedition made a bid to discover their fate. In 1975, a Chinese climber had seen an 'English dead' – believed to be Irvine – at 26,700 feet/8,138 metres on the North Face, and the Americans, led by Eric Simonson, focused on that area. If they found Irvine's body, perhaps carrying a camera, it could help answer the key questions. Did he and Mallory reach the summit? And how did they die? Early on 1 May five climbers, among them Conrad Anker, began their search.

Conrad Anker was one of the first choices for the 1999 Mallory and Irvine Research Expedition, as it was known. An exceptional technical rock-climber and alpinist, he had not been at the highest altitudes before, but was reckoned to have a strong mountain sense. Anker's co-author, David Roberts, is one of the US's leading mountaineering and outdoor writers.

I had just sat down to take off my crampons, because the traverse across the rock band ahead would be easier without them. I drank some fluid - a carbohydrate drink I keep in my water bottle - and sucked a cough drop. At that altitude, it's essential to keep your throat lubricated. I looked out over this vast expanse. To the south and west, I could see into Nepal, with jagged peaks ranging toward the horizon. In front of me to the north stretched the great Tibetan plateau, brown and corrugated as it dwindled into the distance. The wind was picking up, and small clouds were forming below, on the lee side of some of the smaller peaks.

All of a sudden, a strong feeling came over me that something was going to happen. Something good. I usually feel content when the climb I'm on is going well, but this was different. I felt positive, happy. I was in a good place.

It was 11.45 am on 1 May. We were just below 27,000 feet on the North Face of Mount Everest. The other four guys were fanned out above me and to the east. They were in sight, but too far away to holler to. We had to use our radios to communicate.

I attached my crampons to my pack, stood up, put the pack on, and started hiking up a small corner. Then, to my left, out of the corner of my eye, I caught a glimpse of a piece of blue and yellow fabric flapping in the wind, tucked behind a boulder. I thought, I'd better go look at this. Anything that wasn't part of landscape was worth looking at.

When I got to the site, I could see that the fabric was probably a piece of tent that had been ripped loose by the wind and blown down here, where it came to rest in the hollow behind the boulder. It was modern stuff, nylon. I wasn't surprised - there are a lot of abandoned tents on Everest, and the wind just shreds them.

But as I stood there, I carefully scanned the mountain right and left. I was wearing my prescription dark glasses, so I could see really well. As I scanned right, I saw a patch of white, about a hundred feet away. I knew at once there was something unusual about it, because of the color. It wasn't the gleaming white of snow reflecting the sun. It wasn't the white of the chunks of quartzite and calcite that crop up here and there on the north of Everest. It had a kind of matte look - a light-absorbing quality, like marble.

I walked closer. I immediately saw a bare foot, sticking into the air, heel up, toes pointed downward. At that moment, I knew I had found a human body.

Then, when I got even closer, I could see from the tattered clothing that this wasn't the body of a modern climber. This was somebody very old.

It didn't really sink in at first. It was as if everything was in slow motion. Is this a dream? I wondered. *Am I really here?* But I also thought, *This is what we came here to do. This is who we're looking for. This is Sandy Irvine.*

We'd agreed beforehand on a series of coded messages for the search. Everybody on the mountain could listen in on our radio conversations. If we found something, we didn't want some other expedition breaking the news to the world.

'Boulder' was the code word for 'body'. So I sat down on my pack, got out my radio, and broadcast a message: 'Last time I went bouldering in my hobnails, I fell off.' It was the first thing that came to mind. I just threw in 'hobnails', because an old hobnailed boot - the kind that went out of style way back in the 1940s - was still laced onto the man's right foot. .

We all had our radios stuffed inside our down suits, so it wasn't easy to hear them. Of the other four guys out searching, only Jake Norton caught any part of my message, and all he heard was 'hobnails'. I could see him, some fifty yards above me and a ways to the east. Jake sat down, ripped out his radio, and broadcast back, 'What was that, Conrad?'

'Come on down,' I answered. He was looking at me now, so I started waving the ski stick I always carry at altitude. 'Let's get together for Snickers and tea.'

Jake knew I'd found something important, but the other three were still oblivious. He tried to wave and yell and get their attention, but it wasn't working. At 27,000 feet, because of oxygen deprivation, you retreat into a kind of personal shell; the rest of the world doesn't seem quite real. So I got back on the radio and put some urgency into my third message: 'I'm calling a mandatory group meeting right now!'

Where we were searching was fairly tricky terrain, downsloping shale slabs, some of them covered with a dusting of snow. If you fell in the wrong place, you'd go all the way, 7,000 feet to the Rongbuk Glacier. So it took the other guys a little while to work their way down and over to me.

I rooted through my pack to get out my camera. That morning, at Camp V, I thought I'd stuck it in my pack, but I had two nearly identical stuff sacks, and it turns out I'd grabbed my radio batteries instead. I realized I'd forgotten my camera. I thought, Oh well, if I had had the camera, I might not have found the body. That's just the way things work.

When I told a friend about this, he asked if I'd read Faulkner's novella *The Bear*. I hadn't. On reading that story, I saw the analogy. The best hunters in the deep Mississippi woods can't even catch a glimpse of Old Ben, the huge, half-mythic

bear that has ravaged their livestock for years. It's only when Ike McCaslin gives up everything he's relied on - lays down not only his rifle, but his compass and watch - that, lost in the forest, he's graced with the sudden presence of Old Ben in a clearing: 'It did not emerge, appear: it was just there, immobile, fixed in the green and windless noon's hot dappling.'

As I sat on my pack waiting for the others, a feeling of awe and respect for the dead man sprawled in front of me started to fill me. He lay face down, head uphill, frozen into the slope. A tuft of hair stuck out from the leather pilot's cap he had on his head. His arms were raised, and his fingers were planted in the scree, as if he'd tried to self-arrest with them. It seemed likely that he was still alive when he had come to rest in this position. There were no gloves on his hands; later I'd think long and hard about the implications of that fact. I took off my own gloves to compare my hands to his. I've got short, thick fingers; his were long and thin, and deeply tanned, probably from the weeks of having walked the track all the way from Darjeeling over the crest of the Himalaya to the north face of Everest.

The expedition's Camp V, pitched close to the site of the 1924 Camp V, at 25,600ft/7,800m on the North Ridge, with the summit visible beyond. The search area was some 1,500 feet higher, diagonally upwards to the left.

The winds of the decades had torn most of the clothing away from his back and lower torso. He was naturally mummified - that patch of alabaster I'd spotted from a hundred feet away was the bare, perfectly preserved skin of his back. What was incredible was that I could still see the powerful, well-defined muscles in his shoulders and back, and the blue discoloration of bruises.

Around his shoulders and upper arms, the remnants of seven or eight layers of clothing still covered him - shirts and sweaters and jackets made of wool, cotton, and silk. There was a white, braided cotton rope tied to his waist, about three eighths of an inch in diameter - many times weaker than any rope we'd use today. The rope was tangled around his left shoulder. About ten feet from his waist, I could see the frayed end where the rope had broken. So I knew at once that he'd been tied to his partner, and that he'd taken a long fall. The rope had either broken in the fall, or when his partner tried to belay him over a rock edge.

The right elbow looked as if it was dislocated or broken. It lay imbedded in the scree, bent in an unnatural position. The right scapula was a little disfigured. And above his waist on a right rib, I could see the blue contusion from an upward pull of the rope as it took the shock of the fall.

His right leg was badly broken, both tibia and fibula. With the boot still on, the leg lay at a grotesque angle. They weren't compound fractures - the bones hadn't broken the skin - but they were very bad breaks. My conclusion was that in the fall, the right side of the man's body had taken the worst of the impact. It looked as though perhaps in his last moments, the man had laid his good left leg over his broken right, as if to protect it from further harm. The left boot may have been whipped off in the fall, or it may have eroded and

fallen apart. Only the tongue of the boot was present, pinched between the bare toes of his left foot and the heel of his right foot.

Goraks - the big black ravens that haunt the high Himalaya - had pecked away at the right buttock and gouged out a pretty extensive hole, big enough for a gorak to enter. From that orifice, they had eaten out most of the internal organs, simply hollowed out the body.

The muscles of the left lower leg and the thighs had become stringy and desiccated. It's what happens, apparently, to muscles exposed for seventy-five years. The skin had split and opened up, but for some reason the goraks hadn't eaten it. After fifteen or twenty minutes, Jake Norton arrived. Then the others, one by one: first Tap Richards, then Andy Politz, then Dave Hahn. They didn't say much: just, 'Wow, good job, Conrad,' or, 'This has to be Sandy Irvine.' Later Dave said, 'I started blinking in awe,' and Tap remembered, 'I was pretty blown away. It was obviously a body, but it looked like a Greek or Roman marble statue.'

The guys took photos, shot some video, and discussed the nuances of the scene. There seemed to be a kind of taboo about touching him. Probably half an hour passed before we got up the

Climber Thom Pollard, photographed by Andy Politz, heads for the principal search zone, a sloping, exposed terrace of loose scree west of Camp VI (26,900ft/8,200m), visible in the background. Conrad Anker, going on some mountaineering instinct, headed lower down the slope.

nerve to touch him. But we had agreed that if we found Mallory or Irvine, we would perform as professional an excavation as we could under the circumstances, to see if what we found might cast any light on the mystery of their fate.

Tap and Jake did most of the excavating work. We'd planned to cut small squares out of the clothing to take down to Base Camp and analyze. Almost at once, on the collar of one of the shirts, Jake found a name tag. It read, 'G. Mallory'. Jake looked at us and said, 'That's weird. Why would Irvine be wearing Mallory's shirt?'

We didn't have all that much time to work. We'd agreed on a tentative turnaround hour of 2.00 pm to get back to Camp V while it was still daylight, and by the time we started excavating, it was past noon. There were clouds below us, but only a slight wind. As one can imagine, this was hard work at 26,700 feet (the altitude of the body, as I later calculated it). We had taken off our oxygen gear, because it was just too cumbersome to dig with it on.

Because the body was frozen into the scree, we had to chip away at the surrounding ice and rock with our ice axes. It took some vigorous swings even to dislodge little chunks, the ice was so dense. We were all experienced climbers, we were used to swinging tools, so we did the chipping pretty efficiently; only once did a pick glance off a rock and impale the man's arm. As we got closer to the body, we put down our axes and started chipping with our pocket-knives.

We were so sure this was Sandy Irvine that Jake actually sat down, took a smooth piece of shale in his lap, and started to scratch out a tombstone with Irvine's name and dates, 1902-1924. But then we found the 'G. Mallory' tag on the collar, and shortly after, Tap found another one on a seam under the arm. It read, 'G. Leigh Mallory'. We just stared at each other, stunned, as we realized this wasn't Irvine. We had found George Mallory.

As we excavated, Tap chipped away on his left side, Jake on his right. I did mostly lifting and prying. Dave and Andy took pictures and shot video. It was good fortune that George was lying on his stomach, because most of the stuff you carry when you climb is in the front pockets, so it had been protected by his body for seventy-five years. It may seem funny, or even pretentious, but we referred to him as 'George', not as 'Mallory'. All through the weeks before, we'd talked about Mallory and Irvine so much that it was as if we knew them, like old friends; they had become George and Sandy.

We left George's face where it was, frozen into the scree, but once I could lift the lower part of his

body, Tap and Jake could reach underneath him and go through the pockets. The body was like a frozen log. When I lifted it, it made that same creaky noise as when you pull up a log that's been on the ground for years.

It was disconcerting to look into the hole in the right buttock that the goraks had chewed. His body had been hollowed out, almost like a pumpkin. You could see the remains of seeds and some other food - very possibly Mallory's last meal.

We didn't go near George's head. We moved the loose rock away from it, but we didn't try to dig it out. I think that was a sort of unspoken agreement, and at the time, none of us wanted to look at his face.

Of course we were most excited about the possibility of finding the camera. Jake even thought for a minute he'd found it. George had a small bag that was lodged under his right biceps. Jake reached in there, squeezed the bag, and felt a small, square object, just about the right size. We finally had to cut the bag to get the object out, and when we did, we found it wasn't the camera after all, it was a tin of beef lozenges!

The clincher that it was Mallory came when Jake pulled out a neatly folded, new-looking silk handkerchief in which several letters had been carefully

Resting place: just before midday on 1 May 1999, Anker came upon the body of George Mallory, stretched out on the scree. Jake Norton's photograph caused controversy when it was first published in newspapers and magazines, with several leading climbers condemning its use as irreverent and ghoulish. Others argued that, in context and over time, it was a noble image encapsulating the fate of Everest's first true hero.

The most poignant items in Mallory's pockets included these notes, all but one in his hand-writing, listing supplies that were to be used to stock the camps. The note in the left foreground shows that for Camp VI, their launchpoint for the summit, Mallory and Irvine were carrying Bovril pemmican, dried pea soup, Gruyere cheese, sardines, tea and coffee. The Gamage's bill for fives equipment shows Mallory's home address: Herschel House, Cambridge. It was there that his wife Ruth received the telegram telling her he was dead.

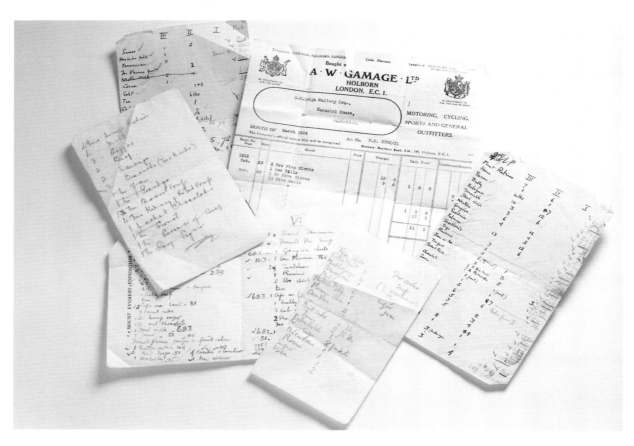

wrapped. They were addressed to Mallory. On the envelope of one of them, for instance, we read, 'George Leigh Mallory Esq., c/o British Trade Agent, Yalung Tibet'.

Besides the letters, we found a few penciled notes in other pockets. As we found out later, they were all about logistics, about bringing so many loads to Camp VI, and so on. We read them carefully, hoping Mallory might have jotted down a note about reaching the summit or turning back, but there was nothing of the sort.

One by one, Jake and Tap produced what we started calling 'the artefacts'. It seemed an odd collection of items to carry to the summit of Everest. There was a small penknife; a tiny pencil, about two and a half inches long, onto which some kind of mint cake had congealed (we could still smell the mint); a needle and thread; a small pair of scissors with a file built into one blade; a second handkerchief well used (the one he blew his nose on), woven in a red and yellow floral pattern on a blue background, with the monogram G.L.M. in yellow; a box of special matches, Swan Vestas, with extra phosphorus on the tips; a little piece of leather with a hose clamp on it that might have been a mouthpiece for the oxygen apparatus; a tube of zinc oxide, rolled partway up; a spare pair of fingerless mittens that looked like they hadn't been used.

Two other artefacts seemed particularly intrigu-

ing. Jake found a smashed altimeter in one pocket. The hand was missing from the dial, but you could see that the instrument had been specially calibrated for Everest, with a range from 20,000 feet to 30,000 feet. Inscribed on the back, in fine script, was 'M.E.E. II' - Mount Everest Expedition II. And in the vest pocket, we found a pair of goggles. The frames were bent, but the green glass was unbroken. It was Andy who came up with the possible significance of the goggles being in the pocket. To him, it argued that George had fallen after dusk. If it had been in the daytime, he would have been wearing the goggles, even on rock. He'd just had a vivid lesson in the consequences of taking them off during the day, when Teddy Norton got a terrible attack of snow blindness the night after his summit push on 4 June.

As we removed each artefact, we put it carefully in a Ziploc bag. Andy volunteered to carry the objects down to Camp V. To some people, it may seem that taking George's belongings with us was a violation. We even had a certain sense that we were disturbing the dead - I think that's why we had hesitated to begin the excavation. But this was the explicit purpose of the expedition: to find Mallory and Irvine and to retrieve the artefacts and try to solve the mystery of what had happened on 8 June 1924. I think we did the right thing.

As interesting as what we found was what we didn't find. George had no backpack on, nor any trace of the frame that held the twin oxygen bottles. His only carrying sack was the little bag we found under his right biceps. He didn't have any water bottle, or Thermos flask, which was what they used in '24. He didn't have a flashlight, because he'd forgotten to take it with him. We know this not from Odell, but from the 1933 party, who found the flashlight in the tent at the 1924 Camp VI.

And we didn't find the camera. That was the great disappointment.

It was getting late - we'd already well overstayed our 2.00 turnaround. The last thing we gathered was a DNA sample, for absolute proof of the identity of the man we had found. Simonson had received approval for this procedure from John Mallory, George's only son, who's seventy-nine and living in South Africa. I had agreed to do this job.

I cut an inch-and-a-half-square patch of skin off the right forearm. It wasn't easy. I had to use the serrated blade on Dave's knife. Cutting George's skin was like cutting saddle leather, cured and hard. Since the expedition, I've often wondered whether taking the tissue was a sacrilegious act. In Base Camp, I had volunteered for the task. On the mountain, I had no time to reflect on whether or not this was the right thing to do.

We wanted to bury George, or at least to cover him up. There were rocks lying around, but not a lot that weren't frozen. We formed a kind of bucket brigade, passing rocks down to the site.

Then Andy read, as a prayer of committal, Psalm 103: 'As his days are as grass: as a flower of the field, so he flourisheth./ For the wind passeth over it, and it is gone. . .'

We finally left at 4.00 pm. I lingered a bit after the other four. The last thing I did was to leave a small Butterfinger candy bar in the rocks nearby, like a Buddhist offering. I said a sort of prayer for him, several times over.

The other guys traversed back to Camp VI to rejoin the route down to V, but I saw that I could take a shortcut straight to V. I got there at 5.00 pm, the others forty-five minutes to an hour later.

Dave and Andy were in one tent, Tap, Jake and I in the other. Dave said later that it was only back in Camp V that what we'd really found began to sink in, that his emotions spilled out, that he was filled with satisfaction and amazement.

We had some food and tried to sleep. I was pretty tired - it had been a twelve-hour day. I slept soundly for a couple of hours then I woke up. I was on the downhill side of the tent, getting forced out of the good spot. The wind kept blowing. The rest of the night, I couldn't sleep. I just kept tossing and turning. It was miserable.

In my sleeplessness, I kept reviewing the day. Despite the broken leg and the gorak damage, at George's side I had experienced a powerful feeling that he was at peace with himself. As I had sat next to him, I thought, This man was a fellow climber. We shared the same goals and aspirations, the same joys and sorrows. Our lives were motivated by the same elemental force. When I thought of what a valiant effort George had made, to climb this high on the north side of Everest in 1924, given the equipment and clothing of his day, I was flooded with a sense of awe.

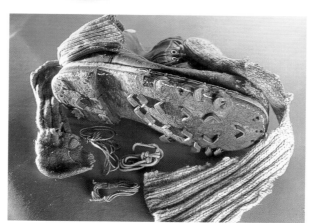

Among other items retrieved from the body were: goggles, a pocket knife and altimeter with missing hands; his leather boots, showing the climbing nails (a mix of tricounis, clinkers and an unusual vee-shaped nail) he had hammered into the sole; and fragments of his clothing, showing his name and the address of an outfitter in Godalming, where he had lived until 1923. So convinced were the Americans that they had found Irvine that they first asked themselves: 'Why was Irvine wearing Mallory's shirt?'

THE FIVE-MINUTE CLIMB

by Conrad Anker and David Roberts

I decided that the only place to climb the Step was right where the ladder had been tied in. I started to the left of the ladder, where a crack angles up and right. I left my crampons on, because it would have been too much effort to take them off, and I knew it might be icy at the top of the pitch. Besides, I felt comfortable climbing hard rock with crampons on. The exposure here was unbelievable - 8,000 feet of space down to the Rongbuk Glacier. I knew I was going to have to move fast, because that's the way to go on hard routes, especially at an altitude as high as 28,230 feet. If you rest and hang on to a hold too long, you just flame out.

I started up with an arm bar and a knee jam; then I stepped onto some tiny edges with my right foot. Dave had hoped to film my lead, but as soon as I started climbing, it was all he could do to stay alert and pay out the rope. It was in his interest to pay attention, because once I got above him, if I'd popped off and landed on him with my crampons, we could both have been badly injured. It wasn't until I got about fifteen feet above Dave that I could place my first and only piece of protection. There was a chockstone wedged in the crack, underneath which I placed a perfect hand-sized cam. As soon as I clipped my rope to the cam, I felt better. At this point, I had to step right. Now I had a hand jam with my left hand, my right hand on a sloping hold, my left foot jammed in the crack, and I was only about six inches away from the ladder. The place I needed to put my right foot was between the rungs of the ladder. It was really awkward - the ladder was in the way.

I reached my foot between the rungs, but at that point I was panting, totally winded. I just had to step on the rung and rest, just long enough to unleash a string of swear words and catch my breath. I was mad because by stepping on the rung, I'd compromised my free climb. Then I moved on up. There was one tricky move, and then the cliff sloped back. I led on up to the anchor, a coffee-table-sized boulder sitting on a ledge, backed up with several knife-blade pitons pounded into shallow, fissure-like cracks. All the fixed ropes are tied to this anchor. I tied in, gave myself some slack, crept back to the edge of the cliff, and had Dave tie in my pack so I could haul it up.

The Second Step, which obstructs the North-east Ridge at 28,200 feet, is the most formidable obstacle on the northern route. Left, Dawson Stelfox, having resolved to go for the summit alone, approaches the step across alarmingly steep ground during his ascent in 1993 – the first British climber to complete the North-east Ridge route. Right, Russian Andrei Louchnikov, photographed by Fred Barth, reaches the top of the Chinese ladder on 26 May 1999. Below, after Anker climbed the step on 17 May 1999, he and Dave Hahn (photographed) went on to the summit.

Then Dave climbed the ladder, ascending the fixed ropes. I hadn't free-climbed the Second Step. That achievement still awaits a stronger climber. I had done all but one move, yet I'd failed in what I set out to do.

Nonetheless, the effort had given me a good idea of how hard the climb was. At the time, erring on the side of caution, I tentatively graded the pitch at 5.8. Later, when I got back to the States and saw at what level I was climbing in

Yosemite and Indian Creek, Utah, I changed my mind. The Second Step is probably a solid 5.10. And that's a lot harder than anything climbers were doing in Wales, with plimsoll shoes, hemp ropes, no pitons, and a 'gentleman's belay' (with no anchor to the rock), in the early 1920s.

I got on the radio to Simo. I said right off the bat that I hadn't free-climbed the Step. I told him I'd been weak, I'd had to step on the ladder at one point. I'd done the twenty-five feet quickly, in about five minutes. It was 11.00 am now. We left the climbing rack there, an empty water bottle, a couple of other odds and ends. Before we started on, I asked Dave, 'How are you feeling? Are you psyched to go on?' I felt it was important to present him with the option. I said, 'Dave, if you want to go down, I understand. I can get to the top from here on my own. I feel comfortable on this terrain.' Right away he answered, 'Let's go for the summit.'

THE GEOLOGY OF EVEREST

by Leni Gillman

The Himalaya mountains were born of a cataclysmic collision between India and Asia which began 50 million years ago and continues today. Although you would scarcely notice it, Everest grows higher each year.

Geologists have developed tectonic plate theory over the last 40 years, which explains how this change has happened. The earth comprises an inner core, an intermediary mantle and an outer crust. The crust consists of tectonic plates, of which there are two kinds: continental plates, which are relatively light, and heavier oceanic plates. The plates are constantly moving and the crust is unstable where the two kinds of plates meet, crushing against one another to produce earthquakes and volcanoes as violent reminders of the earth's latent power. In the Himalaya the rocks continue to rupture under the massive compression caused by India's impact with Asia.

Geologists estimate that this titanic process began 200 million years ago. Previously, they believe, there was a single vast continent called Pangaea – and they find evidence for this in similarities in geological structures across now widely-separated continents, as well as in the distribution of plants and animals. Then Pangaea began to fragment, with the land masses drifting apart on their plates. In the south the area that consisted of Antarctica, Australia and India broke up, with the Indian plate moving north-east.

About 80 million years ago India had become an island continent separated from Asia by an ocean known as the Tethys Sea. India continued to migrate for another 30 million years, gradually closing the Tethys Sea and finally crashing into Asia. This impact created the Tibetan plateau and Himalayan mountains.

India's arrival unleashed massive waves of pressure and heat. The heavy rocks of the oceanic plate beneath the Tethys Sea were subducted or pushed down into the earth's mantle, eventually to be recycled. The Indus Valley now forms the visible edge of the subduction zone where the Tethys Sea vanished. The Tethys sea-bed was thrust up and as the sea closed, India was forced upward into a complex fold system – the Himalaya. This process is not over yet. Having already driven Asia some 900 miles north, India is still buckling and pushing northward and anti-clockwise into Asia by about three centimetres a year.

Visitors to the Himalaya see a breathtaking and awesome landscape. To connect this vision with the primeval forces that created it, and to understand how the rocks which climbers cling to were formed, requires a leap of the imagination. Under the massive heat and pressure resulting from the collision of continents, the rocks changed – metamorphosed – sometimes repeatedly.

The consequences are visible in the Chomolungma massif, as the four peaks of Everest, Lhotse, Nuptse and Changtse are termed. The lower levels are composed mainly of the metamorphic rocks which intruded into the base of the massif from the earth's mantle. They are schists, which are coarse-grained and crystalline and split easily into thin layers. Among the schists are gneisses and migmatites, all strongly metamorphic, bearing witness to having been wrought under profound heat and stress.

Higher up we find a huge intrusion of granite, called the Makalu granite formation, which is strikingly evident on the lower part of the Nuptse-Lhotse wall. It is light coloured and erodes characteristically in blocks. Above this are sedimentary rocks, which were laid down under the Tethys Sea and were only weakly metamorphosed. The clays, silts and chalky remains of marine animals were transformed into pelites, shale, sandstone, and limestone. Everest climbers know them as the famous 'Yellow Band'.

The Yellow Band is in two formations. The first, on Everest's South-west Face and Lhotse's South Wall, is the lower of the two. Some 1,640 feet/500 metres higher up on the north side of Everest is the Upper Yellow Band, which is about 390 feet/120 metres thick.

The Summit Pyramid of Everest, sometimes called the Sagarmatha, is a purer limestone, greyish with sandy layers and other debris. It is curious to contemplate that the highest peak of the world was formed 325 million years ago on an ancient sea bed, now extinct.

The Himalaya are young mountains; they have been through their adolescence, and still have some growing to do. The weather will always chip away at them. But as climbers gather at Base Camp they might pause to consider that in the past 100 years Everest has grown by three metres. Is it harder now to reach the top than it would have been before?

The three great faces of Everest are revealed simultaneously in this breath-taking aerial photograph, taken from over the summit at 35,000ft/10,668m. Above the summit are the sunlit snows of the Kangshung Face; below right, the South-west Face; in shadow, left, the North Face. The photograph was taken on 22 December 1984 by Swissair Photo+Surveys, based in Zurich, and was part of a sequence used by Bradford Washburn to help compile his map of Everest, reproduced on page 14.

THE FIFTEEN ROUTES

In the 47 years to the new millennium, Everest was climbed by 15 principal different routes. All 15 are shown on the aerial photograph below, and on the three main faces, starting on page 217.

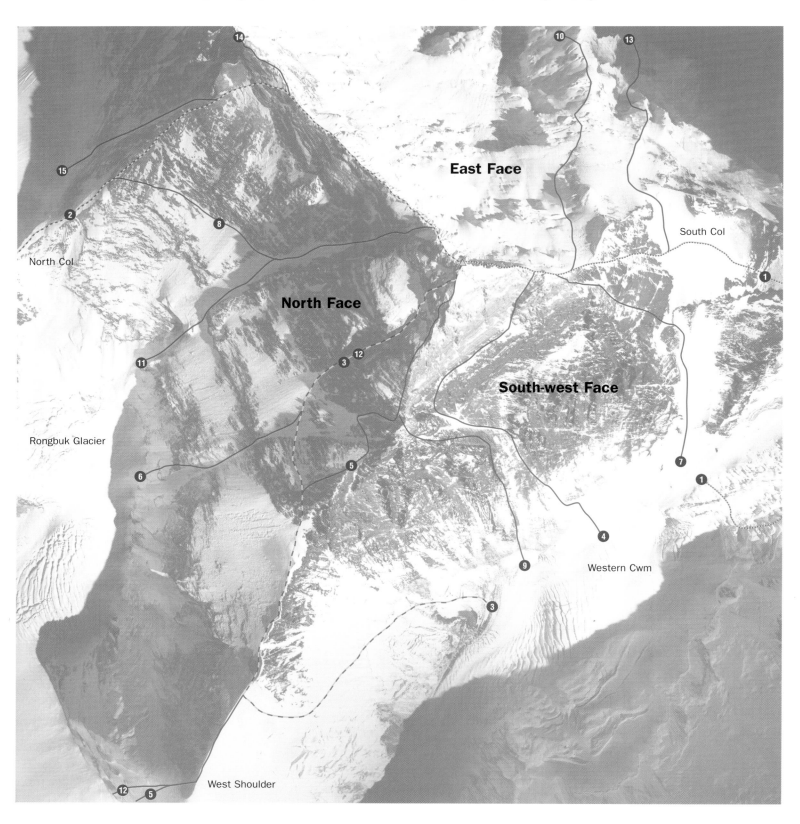

East Face

South Col

North Col

North Face

South-west Face

Rongbuk Glacier

Western Cwm

West Shoulder

216

THE SOUTH-WEST FACE

The 15 routes are numbered in chronological order covering a span of 43 years, from the first ascent by the British expedition of May 1953, to the Russians' route up the North-north-east Couloir in May 1996. The first three routes – by the British, Chinese and Americans – are shown in broken or dotted lines for clarity and emphasis. The numbers on the four diagrams are keyed to the dates and descriptions shown on the next three pages. Each item also shows the number of ascents for each route by the end of 2000.

❶ 29 MAY 1953. The first ascent, following seven failures by the British and two by the Swiss, by Edmund Hillary and Tenzing Norgay. Their route, via the Western Cwm and Lhotse Face to the South Col and up the South-east Ridge, became the standard means of ascent. Of 1318 ascents to 31 December 2000, 800 went this way. The 1953 British team zigzagged up the centre of the icefall on the Lhotse Face on their way to the South Col; there have been many variations to this part of the route. Although the 1953 expedition was British, Hillary was from New Zealand, Tenzing from India; no British climber reached the summit until 1975 (see route 4). See page 68.

❷ 25 MAY 1960. The controversial Chinese ascent, once disputed but now widely accepted. The Chinese made much of the fact that they succeeded on the route where the pre-war British failed, climbing from the North Col to the crest of the North-east Ridge. Of the summit trio, Wang Fu-chou and Chu Yin-hua were Chinese – the third, Konbu, a Tibetan. Total ascents: 377. See page 74.

❸ 22 MAY 1963. The US West Ridge ascent by Tom Hornbein and Willi Unsoeld, who also completed the first traverse of the mountain - ascending by one route, descending by another (in this case, the South-east Ridge/South Col). Although described as a West Ridge route, it is now regarded as a West Ridge/North Face ascent, since the climbers traversed leftwards into the couloir which now bears Hornbein's name. Total ascents: 2. See page 79.

❹ 24 SEPTEMBER 1975. The British ascent of the South-west Face – one of the most important climbs of the post-war years, helping to open up the great faces of the Himalaya. Above the great Central Gully, the key was a gully at 26,000 feet left of the Rock Band. Dougal Haston and Doug Scott had stunning summit views but the weather deteriorated for Pete Boardman and Pertemba the next day. Mick Burke, who disappeared on the summit ridge is widely believed to have reached the top. Total ascents: 15. See page 94.

THE NORTH FACE

5 **13 MAY 1979.** The Yugoslav ascent which 'straightened out' the West Ridge – instead of veering on to the North Face, the Yugoslavs followed the ridge all the way, accomplishing the hardest sustained rock climbing on Everest to that date. The summit climbers – headed by Andrej Stremfelj and Nejc Zaplotnik, followed by three the next day – descended via the Hornbein Couloir, although Ang Phu fell to his death. Total ascents: 13. See page 110.

6 **10 MAY 1980.** The first full ascent of the North Face, by the Japanese Tsuneoh Shigehiro and Takashi Ozaki, who ran out of oxygen several hundred feet from the summit. Starting from the Rongbuk Glacier, they took a direct line up a gully – now known as the Japanese Couloir – which led into the Hornbein Couloir. Total ascents: 7. See page 164.

7 **19 MAY 1980.** A notable Polish success, following their first winter ascent (see page 117) three months before. The Poles followed the South Pillar at the right-hand edge of the South-west Face. The Rock Band took 16 days to climb and Jerzy Kukuczka and Andrzej Czok reached the summit in a gale. There had been 14 ascents by the end of 2000, while a further 31 summit climbers followed the pillar to mid-height before traversing to the South-east Ridge route.

8 **20 AUGUST 1980.** The most formidable climb of all - Reinhold Messner's ascent, solo and without oxygen, from the north. Messner had hoped to follow the Chinese route on to the North-east Ridge but soft snow forced him to traverse on to the face. After reaching the Norton (or Great) Couloir he climbed it almost directly to the summit pyramid. Total ascents: 18. See page 120.

9 **4 MAY 1982.** The Russian ascent, made on the first Everest attempt by Soviet climbers, of the South-west Pillar, left of the Great Central Gully on the South-west Face. Including the leading pair, Eduard Myslovski and Volodya Balyberdin, 11 Soviet climbers reached the summit – the highest number on a new route. Total ascents: 11. See page 130.

10 **8 OCTOBER 1983.** The audacious US ascent of the East or Kangshung Face, following a reconnaissance in 1980 and an attempt to 22,800 feet in 1981. The route ascended a 3,500 foot buttress followed by 7,500 foot snow slopes to just below the South Summit. The summit trio of Lou Reichardt, Kim Momb and Carlos Buhler was followed by three climbers who went to the summit the next day. Total ascents: 6. See page 134.

THE EAST FACE

11 **3 OCTOBER 1984.** The bravura ascent, by an unheralded Australian team, of the North Face via the Norton Couloir. The summit pair, Tim Macartney-Snape and Greg Mortimer, became the second climbers (after Reinhold Messner) to set up a new route without supplementary oxygen; Andy Henderson turned back 150 feet short. Total ascents: 4. See page 144.

12 **20 MAY 1986.** An impressive 'double' for Canadian Sharon Wood, the first North American woman to climb Everest and the first woman to do so by a new route. The expedition climbed to the West Shoulder from the Rongbuk Glacier; although two previous expeditions had done this, neither had continued to the summit. Wood and summit partner Dwayne Congdon followed the US 1963 line by traversing to the Hornbein Couloir. They

remained the only climbers to have taken this route, although in May 1989 a Polish pair established a variant by going to the Lho La Pass from the Khumbu Glacier and then following the Canadian line. See page 160.

13 **12 MAY 1988.** The second ascent of the Kangshung Face, taking a line to the left of the 1983 route, by a US team plus the British Stephen Venables; of the three who went for the summit from the South Col, only Venables reached the top. (The broken line in the photograph indicates where the route, which met the standard South Col line, is out of sight.) This was the second new route completed solo and the third by a party without supplementary oxygen. Total ascents: 7. See page 166.

14 **11 MAY 1995.** The first and long-coveted ascent of the full North-east

Ridge from the East Rongbuk Glacier to the summit, including a traverse of the three pinnacles east of the junction with the North Ridge. A large Japanese party sieged the route in May 1995, preparing the pinnacles and then making a three-day complete ascent, placing two Japanese and four Sherpas on the summit. Total ascents: 6. See page 183.

15 **20 MAY 1996.** An astonishingly bold ascent of the North-north-east Couloir – also known as Zakharov's Couloir – which the Russians identified as a potential new route during a reconnaissance in 1995. After reaching the top of the couloir on 18 May, the Russians pressed on in atrocious conditions, reaching the summit in a blizzard. The climbing leader, Nikolai Zakharov, stopped 15 minutes below the summit in order to find a missing colleague. Total ascents: 3. See page 180.

CLIMBING EVEREST: THE COMPLETE LISTS

by Xavier Eguskitza and Eberhard Jurgalski

Between May 1953 and December 2000, there were 1,318 ascents of Everest, made by 981 climbers. The first list, starting opposite, shows (in order) the number of the ascent, the name and nationality of the climber, the date and route of their ascent, and the nationality of their expedition. Also shown, after the climber's name, is the ordinal number of their ascent if they have made more than one. The '†' symbol marks climbers who died during the descent; 'f' indicates a female climber and 'x' denotes ascents (including descents) made without supplementary oxygen. Other abbreviations are shown on page 231 and further lists begin on page 232.

Mother goddess of the earth: in the photograph by Kurt Keller of Swissair Photo+Surveys, the great ridges of Everest appear to embrace the landscape. The central feature of the mountain is the North Face, with the West Ridge descending to the right and North-east and North Ridge to the left. To the right of Everest, beyond the Western Cwm, is the Lhotse–Nuptse Ridge. The foreground is dominated by the confluence of the main Rongbuk Glacier, descending from the North Face, and the West Rongbuk Glacier, entering from the right.

Ascents of Everest, 29 May 1953 to 9 October 2000

Dates are shown as day/month/year

No.	Name	Nat	Date	Route	Exp	Leader
1	Edmund Hillary	NZ	29.05.53	S Col - SE Ridge	UK	John Hunt
2	Tenzing Norgay	Ind/Sh	29.05.53	S Col - SE Ridge	UK	John Hunt
3	Jürg Marmet	Swi	23.05.56	S Col - SE Ridge	Swi	Albert Eggler
4	Ernst Schmied	Swi	23.05.56	S Col - SE Ridge	Swi	Albert Eggler
5	Adolf Reist	Swi	24.05.56	S Col - SE Ridge	Swi	Albert Eggler
6	Hansrudolf von Gunten	Swi	24.05.56	S Col - SE Ridge	Swi	Albert Eggler
7	Wang Fu-zhou	Chn	25.05.60	N Col - NE Ridge	Chn	Shih Chan-Chun
8	Chu Yin-hua	Chn	25.05.60	N Col - NE Ridge	Chn	Shih Chan-Chun
9	Konbu	Tib	25.05.60	N Col - NE Ridge	Chn	Shih Chan-Chun
10	Jim Whittaker	US	01.05.63	S Col - SE Ridge	US	Norman Dyhrenfurth
11	Nawang Gombu (1)	Ind/Sh	01.05.63	S Col - SE Ridge	US	Norman Dyhrenfurth
12	Barry Bishop	US	22.05.63	S Col - SE Ridge	US	Norman Dyhrenfurth
13	Lute Jerstad	US	22.05.63	S Col - SE Ridge	US	Norman Dyhrenfurth
14	William Unsoeld	US	22.05.63	W Ridge from W Cwm	US	Norman Dyhrenfurth
15	Thomas Hornbein	US	22.05.63	W Ridge from W Cwm	US	Norman Dyhrenfurth
16	A. S. Cheema	Ind	20.05.65	S Col - SE Ridge	Ind	Mohan S. Kohli
17	Nawang Gombu (2)	Ind/Sh	20.05.65	S Col - SE Ridge	Ind	Mohan S. Kohli
18	Sonam Gyatso	Ind	22.05.65	S Col - SE Ridge	Ind	Mohan S. Kohli
19	Sonam Wangyal	Ind	22.05.65	S Col - SE Ridge	Ind	Mohan S. Kohli
20	C. P. Vohra	Ind	24.05.65	S Col - SE Ridge	Ind	Mohan S. Kohli
21	Ang Kami I	Ind/Sh	24.05.65	S Col - SE Ridge	Ind	Mohan S. Kohli
22	Hari Pal Singh Ahluwalia	Ind	29.05.65	S Col - SE Ridge	Ind	Mohan S. Kohli
23	Harish Chandra S. Rawat	Ind	29.05.65	S Col - SE Ridge	Ind	Mohan S. Kohli
24	Phu Dorje I	Np/Sh	29.05.65	S Col - SE Ridge	Ind	Mohan S. Kohli
25	Naomi Uemura	Jp	11.05.70	S Col - SE Ridge	Jp	Saburo Matsukata
26	Teruo Matsuura	Jp	11.05.70	S Col - SE Ridge	Jp	Saburo Matsukata
27	Katsutoshi Hirabayashi	Jp	12.05.70	S Col - SE Ridge	Jp	Saburo Matsukata
28	Chotare	Np/Sh	12.05.70	S Col - SE Ridge	Jp	Saburo Matsukata
29	Rinaldo Carrel	It	05.05.73	S Col - SE Ridge	It	Guido Monzino
30	Mirko Minuzzo	It	05.05.73	S Col - SE Ridge	It	Guido Monzino
31	Shambu Tamang (1)	Np	05.05.73	S Col - SE Ridge	It	Guido Monzino
32	Lhakpa Tenzing	Np/Sh	05.05.73	S Col - SE Ridge	It	Guido Monzino
33	Fabrizio Innamorati	It	07.05.73	S Col - SE Ridge	It	Guido Monzino
34	Virginio Epis	It	07.05.73	S Col - SE Ridge	It	Guido Monzino
35	Claudio Benedetti	It	07.05.73	S Col - SE Ridge	It	Guido Monzino
36	Sonam Gyalzen	Np/Sh	07.05.73	S Col - SE Ridge	It	Guido Monzino
37	Hisashi Ishiguro	Jp	26.10.73	S Col - SE Ridge	Jp	Michio Yuasa
38	Yasuo Kato (1)	Jp	26.10.73	S Col - SE Ridge	Jp	Michio Yuasa
39	Junko Tabei (f)	Jp	16.05.75	S Col - SE Ridge	Jp	Eiko Hisano (f)
40	Ang Tshering I	Np/Sh	16.05.75	S Col - SE Ridge	Jp	Eiko Hisano (f)
41	Phantog (f)	Tib	27.05.75	N Col - NE Ridge	Chn	Shih Chan-chun
42	Sodnam Norbu	Tib	27.05.75	N Col - NE Ridge	Chn	Shih Chan-chun
43	Lotse	Tib	27.05.75	N Col - NE Ridge	Chn	Shih Chan-chun
44	Samdrub	Tib	27.05.75	N Col - NE Ridge	Chn	Shih Chan-chun
45	Darphuntso	Tib	27.05.75	N Col - NE Ridge	Chn	Shih Chan-chun
46	Kunga Pasang	Tib	27.05.75	N Col - NE Ridge	Chn	Shih Chan-chun
47	Tsering Tobgyal	Tib	27.05.75	N Col - NE Ridge	Chn	Shih Chan-chun
48	Ngapo Khyen	Tib	27.05.75	N Col - NE Ridge	Chn	Shih Chan-chun
49	Hou Sheng-fu	Chn	27.05.75	N Col - NE Ridge	Chn	Shih Chan-chun
50	Dougal Haston	UK	24.09.75	SW Face	UK	Chris Bonington
51	Doug Scott	UK	24.09.75	SW Face	UK	Chris Bonington
52	Peter Boardman	UK	26.09.75	SW Face	UK	Chris Bonington
53	Pertemba (1)	Np/Sh	26.09.75	SW Face	UK	Chris Bonington
?	† Mick Burke	UK	26.09.75	SW Face	UK	Chris Bonington
54	John Stokes	UK	16.05.76	S Col - SE Ridge	UK	Tony Streather
55	Michael Lane	UK	16.05.76	S Col - SE Ridge	UK	Tony Streather
56	Robert Còrmack	US	08.10.76	S Col - SE Ridge	US	Philip Trimble
57	Chris Chandler	US	08.10.76	S Col - SE Ridge	US	Philip Trimble
58	Ko Sang-Don	SK	15.09.77	S Col - SE Ridge	SK	Kim Young-Do
59	Pemba Norbu (Nuru) I	Np/Sh	15.09.77	S Col - SE Ridge	SK	Kim Young-Do
60	Wolfgang Nairz	Au	03.05.78	S Col - SE Ridge	Au	Wolfgang Nairz
61	Robert Schauer (1)	Au	03.05.78	S Col - SE Ridge	Au	Wolfgang Nairz
62	Horst Bergmann	Au	03.05.78	S Col - SE Ridge	Au	Wolfgang Nairz
63	Ang Phu (1)	Np/Sh	03.05.78	S Col - SE Ridge	Au	Wolfgang Nairz
64	Reinhold Messner (1) (x)	It	08.05.78	S Col - SE Ridge	Au	Wolfgang Nairz
65	Peter Habeler (x)	Au	08.05.78	S Col - SE Ridge	Au	Wolfgang Nairz
66	Reinhard Karl	Ger	11.05.78	S Col - SE Ridge	Au	Wolfgang Nairz
67	Oswald Oelz	Au	11.05.78	S Col - SE Ridge	Au	Wolfgang Nairz
68	Franz Oppurg	Au	14.05.78	S Col - SE Ridge	Au	Wolfgang Nairz
69	Josef Mack	Ger	14.10.78	S Col - SE Ridge	Ger	Karl Herrligkoffer
70	Hubert Hillmaier	Ger	14.10.78	S Col - SE Ridge	Ger	Karl Herrligkoffer
71	Hans Engl (x)	Ger	14.10.78	S Col - SE Ridge	Ger	Karl Herrligkoffer
72	Jean Afanassieff	Fra	15.10.78	S Col - SE Ridge	Fra	Pierre Mazeaud
73	Nicolas Jaeger	Fra	15.10.78	S Col - SE Ridge	Fra	Pierre Mazeaud
74	Pierre Mazeaud	Fra	15.10.78	S Col - SE Ridge	Fra	Pierre Mazeaud
75	Kurt Diemberger	Au	15.10.78	S Col - SE Ridge	Fra	Pierre Mazeaud
76	Wanda Rutkiewicz (f)	Pol	16.10.78	S Col - SE Ridge	Ger	Karl Herrligkoffer
77	Robert Allenbach	Swi	16.10.78	S Col - SE Ridge	Ger	Karl Herrligkoffer
78	Sigi Hupfauer	Ger	16.10.78	S Col - SE Ridge	Ger	Karl Herrligkoffer
79	Wilhelm Klimek	Ger	16.10.78	S Col - SE Ridge	Ger	Karl Herrligkoffer
80	Mingma Nuru I (x)	Np/Sh	16.10.78	S Col - SE Ridge	Ger	Karl Herrligkoffer
81	Ang Dorje I (1) (x)	Np/Sh	16.10.78	S Col - SE Ridge	Ger	Karl Herrligkoffer
82	Ang Kami II (1)	Np/Sh	16.10.78	S Col - SE Ridge	Ger	Karl Herrligkoffer
83	Georg Ritter	Ger	17.10.78	S Col - SE Ridge	Ger	Karl Herrligkoffer
84	Bernd Kullmann	Ger	17.10.78	S Col - SE Ridge	Ger	Karl Herrligkoffer
85	Jernej Zaplotnik	Slo	13.05.79	W Ridge Integrale	Slo	Tone Skarja
86	Andrej Stremfelj (1)	Slo	13.05.79	W Ridge Integrale	Slo	Tone Skarja
87	Stane Belak	Slo	15.05.79	W Ridge Integrale	Slo	Tone Skarja
88	Stipe Bozic (1)	Cro	15.05.79	W Ridge Integrale	Slo	Tone Skarja
89	†Ang Phu (2)	Np/Sh	15.05.79	W Ridge Integrale	Slo	Tone Skarja
90	Gerhard Schmatz	Ger	01.10.79	S Col - SE Ridge	Ger	Gerhard Schmatz
91	Hermann Warth	Ger	01.10.79	S Col - SE Ridge	Ger	Gerhard Schmatz
92	Hans von Känel	Swi	01.10.79	S Col - SE Ridge	Ger	Gerhard Schmatz
93	Pertemba (2)	Np/Sh	01.10.79	S Col - SE Ridge	Ger	Gerhard Schmatz
94	Lhakpa Gyalzen I	Np/Sh	01.10.79	S Col - SE Ridge	Ger	Gerhard Schmatz
95	† Ray Genet	US	02.10.79	S Col - SE Ridge	Ger	Gerhard Schmatz
96	† Hannelore Schmatz (f)	Ger	02.10.79	S Col - SE Ridge	Ger	Gerhard Schmatz
97	Sungdare (1)	Np/Sh	02.10.79	S Col - SE Ridge	Ger	Gerhard Schmatz
98	Tilman Fischbach	Ger	02.10.79	S Col - SE Ridge	Ger	Gerhard Schmatz
99	Günter Kämpfe	Ger	02.10.79	S Col - SE Ridge	Ger	Gerhard Schmatz
100	Nick Banks	NZ	02.10.79	S Col - SE Ridge	Ger	Gerhard Schmatz
101	Ang Phurba I	Np/Sh	02.10.79	S Col - SE Ridge	Ger	Gerhard Schmatz
102	Ang Jangbu I	Np/Sh	02.10.79	S Col - SE Ridge	Ger	Gerhard Schmatz
103	Leszek Cichy	Pol	17.02.80	S Col - SE Ridge	Pol	Andrzej Zawada
104	Krzysztof Wielicki	Pol	17.02.80	S Col - SE Ridge	Pol	Andrzej Zawada
105	Yasuo Kato (2)	Jp	03.05.80	N Col - NE Ridge	Jp	Hyoriko Watanabe
106	Tsuneo Shigehiro	Jp	10.05.80	N Face (Hornbein C)	Jp	Hyoriko Watanabe
107	Takashi Ozaki (1)	Jp	10.05.80	N Face (Hornbein C)	Jp	Hyoriko Watanabe
108	Martín Zabaleta	Sp/B	14.05.80	S Col - SE Ridge	Sp	Juan-Ignacio Lorente
109	Pasang Temba	Np/Sh	14.05.80	S Col - SE Ridge	Sp	Juan-Ignacio Lorente
110	Andrzej Czok	Pol	19.05.80	S Pillar	Pol	Andrzej Zawada
111	Jerzy Kukuczka	Pol	19.05.80	S Pillar	Pol	Andrzej Zawada
112	Reinhold Messner (2) (x)	It	20.08.80	N Col - N Face	solo	Reinhold Messner
113	Chris Kopczynski	US	21.10.81	S Pillar - SE Ridge	US	John West
114	Sungdare (2)	Np/Sh	21.10.81	S Pillar - SE Ridge	US	John West
115	Chris Pizzo	US	24.10.81	S Pillar - SE Ridge	US	John West
116	Yong Tenzing	Np/Sh	24.10.81	S Pillar - SE Ridge	US	John West
117	Peter Hackett	US	24.10.81	S Pillar - SE Ridge	US	John West
118	Vladimir Balyberdin (1)	Rus	04.05.82	SW Pillar	Rus	Yevgeni Tamm
119	Eduard Myslovski	Rus	04.05.82	SW Pillar	Rus	Yevgeni Tamm

No.	Name	Nat	Date	Route	Exp	Leader
120	Sergei Bershov (1)	Ukr	04.05.82	SW Pillar	Rus	Yevgeni Tamm
121	Mikhail Turkevich	Ukr	04.05.82	SW Pillar	Rus	Yevgeni Tamm
122	Valentin Ivanov	Rus	05.05.82	SW Pillar	Rus	Yevgeni Tamm
123	Sergei Efimov	Rus	05.05.82	SW Pillar	Rus	Yevgeni Tamm
124	Kazbek Valiev	Kaz	08.05.82	SW Pillar	Rus	Yevgeni Tamm
125	Valeri Khrishchaty	Kaz	08.05.82	SW Pillar	Rus	Yevgeni Tamm
126	Valeri Khomutov	Rus	09.05.82	SW Pillar	Rus	Yevgeni Tamm
127	Yuri Golodov	Kaz	09.05.82	SW Pillar	Rus	Yevgeni Tamm
128	Vladimir Puchkov	Rus	09.05.82	SW Pillar	Rus	Yevgeni Tamm
129	Laurie Skreslet	Can	05.10.82	S Col - SE Ridge	Can	William March
130	Sungdare (3)	Np/Sh	05.10.82	S Col - SE Ridge	Can	William March
131	Lhakpa Dorje I (1)	Np/Sh	05.10.82	S Col - SE Ridge	Can	William March
132	Pat Morrow	Can	07.10.82	S Col - SE Ridge	Can	William March
133	Pema Dorje (1)	Np/Sh	07.10.82	S Col - SE Ridge	Can	William March
134	Lhakpa Tshering I (1)	Np/Sh	07.10.82	S Col - SE Ridge	Can	William March
135	† Yasuo Kato (3)	Jp	27.12.82	S Col - SE Ridge	Jp	Yasuo Kato
136	Peter Jamieson	US	07.05.83	S Col - SE Ridge	US	Gerhard Lenser (Ger)
137	Gerald Roach	US	07.05.83	S Col - SE Ridge	US	Gerhard Lenser (Ger)
138	David Breashears (1)	US	07.05.83	S Col - SE Ridge	US	Gerhard Lenser (Ger)
139	Ang Rita (1) (x)	Np/Sh	07.05.83	S Col - SE Ridge	US	Gerhard Lenser (Ger)
140	Larry Nielsen (x)	US	07.05.83	S Col - SE Ridge	US	Gerhard Lenser (Ger)
141	Gary Neptune	US	14.05.83	S Col - SE Ridge	US	Gerhard Lenser (Ger)
142	Jim States	US	14.05.83	S Col - SE Ridge	US	Gerhard Lenser (Ger)
143	Lhakpa Dorje II	Np/Sh	14.05.83	S Col - SE Ridge	US	Gerhard Lenser (Ger)
144	Kim Momb	US	08.10.83	E Face - SE Ridge	US	James Morrissey
145	Lou Reichardt	US	08.10.83	E Face - SE Ridge	US	James Morrissey
146	Carlos Buhler	US	08.10.83	E Face - SE Ridge	US	James Morrissey
147	Haruichi Kawamura (x)	Jp	08.10.83	S Pillar - SE Ridge	Jp	Haruichi Kawamura
148	Shomi Suzuki (x)	Jp	08.10.83	S Pillar - SE Ridge	Jp	Haruichi Kawamura
149	Haruyuki Endo (x)	Jp	08.10.83	S Col - SE Ridge	Jp	Hiroshi Yoshino
150	† Hiroshi Yoshino (x)	Jp	08.10.83	S Col - SE Ridge	Jp	Hiroshi Yoshino
151	† Hironobu Kamuro (x)	Jp	08.10.83	S Col - SE Ridge	Jp	Hiroshi Yoshino
152	George Lowe	US	09.10.83	E Face - SE Ridge	US	James Morrissey
153	Dan Reid	US	09.10.83	E Face - SE Ridge	US	James Morrissey
154	Jay Cassell	US	09.10.83	E Face - SE Ridge	US	James Morrissey
155	Takashi Ozaki (2)	Jp	16.12.83	S Col - SE Ridge	Jp	Kazuyuki Takahashi
156	Noboru Yamada (1)	Jp	16.12.83	S Col - SE Ridge	Jp	Kazuyuki Takahashi
157	Kazunari Murakami	Jp	16.12.83	S Col - SE Ridge	Jp	Kazuyuki Takahashi
158	Nawang Yonden	Np/Sh	16.12.83	S Col - SE Ridge	Jp	Kazuyuki Takahashi
159	† Hristo Ivanov Prodanov (x)	Bul	20.04.84	W Ridge	Bul	Avram Illiev Avramov
160	Ivan Valtchev	Bul	08.05.84	W Ridge, SE Ridge down	Bul	Avram Illiev Avramov
161	Metodi Stefanov Savov	Bul	08.05.84	W Ridge, SE Ridge down	Bul	Avram Illiev Avramov
162	Nicolay Petkov	Bul	09.05.84	W Ridge, SE Ridge down	Bul	Avram Illiev Avramov
163	Kiril Doskov	Bul	09.05.84	W Ridge, SE Ridge down	Bul	Avram Illiev Avramov
164	Phu Dorje II	Ind/Sh	09.05.84	S Col - SE Ridge	Ind	Darshan Kumar Khullar
165	Bachendri Pal (f)	Ind	23.05.84	S Col - SE Ridge	Ind	Darshan Kumar Khullar
166	Dorjee Lhatoo	Ind/Sh	23.05.84	S Col - SE Ridge	Ind	Darshan Kumar Khullar
167	Ang Dorje I (2) (x)	Np/Sh	23.05.84	S Col - SE Ridge	Ind	Darshan Kumar Khullar
168	Sonam Palzor	Ind	23.05.84	S Col - SE Ridge	Ind	Darshan Kumar Khullar
169	Tim Macartney-Snape (1) (x)	Aus	03.10.84	N Face (Norton C)	Aus	Geoffrey Bartram
170	Greg Mortimer (x)	Aus	03.10.84	N Face (Norton C)	Aus	Geoffrey Bartram
171	Bart Vos	NL	08.10.84	S Col - SE Ridge	NL	Herman Plugge
172	† Jozef Psotka (x)	Slk	15.10.84	S Pillar, SE Ridge down	Slk	Frantisek Kele
173	Zoltan Demjan (x)	Slk	15.10.84	S Pillar, SE Ridge down	Slk	Frantisek Kele
174	Ang Rita (2) (x)	Np/Sh	15.10.84	S Pillar, SE Ridge down	Slk	Frantisek Kele
175	Philip Ershler	US	20.10.84	N Col - N Face	US	Louis W. Whittaker
176	Björn Myrer-Lund	Nor	21.04.85	S Col - SE Ridge	Nor	Arne Naess
177	Pertemba (3)	Np/Sh	21.04.85	S Col - SE Ridge	Nor	Arne Naess
178	Ang Lhakpa Dorje	Np/Sh	21.04.85	S Col - SE Ridge	Nor	Arne Naess
179	Odd Eliassen	Nor	21.04.85	S Col - SE Ridge	Nor	Arne Naess
180	Chris Bonington	UK	21.04.85	S Col - SE Ridge	Nor	Arne Naess
181	Dawa Norbu	Np/Sh	21.04.85	S Col - SE Ridge	Nor	Arne Naess
182	Arne Naess	Nor	29.04.85	S Col - SE Ridge	Nor	Arne Naess
183	Stein Aasheim	Nor	29.04.85	S Col - SE Ridge	Nor	Arne Naess
184	Havard Nesheim	Nor	29.04.85	S Col - SE Ridge	Nor	Arne Naess
185	Ralph Höibakk	Nor	29.04.85	S Col - SE Ridge	Nor	Arne Naess
186	Sungdare (4)	Np/Sh	29.04.85	S Col - SE Ridge	Nor	Arne Naess
187	Ang Rita (3) (x)	Np/Sh	29.04.85	S Col - SE Ridge	Nor	Arne Naess
188	Pema Dorje (2)	Np/Sh	29.04.85	S Col - SE Ridge	Nor	Arne Naess
189	Chowang Rinzing	Np/Sh	29.04.85	S Col - SE Ridge	Nor	Arne Naess
190	Dick Bass	US	30.04.85	S Col - SE Ridge	Nor	Arne Naess
191	David Breashears (2)	US	30.04.85	S Col - SE Ridge	Nor	Arne Naess
192	Ang Phurba II (1)	Np/Sh	30.04.85	S Col - SE Ridge	Nor	Arne Naess
193	Oscar Cadiach (1)	Sp	28.08.85	N Col - NE Ridge	Sp	Conrad Blanch
194	Toni Sors	Sp	28.08.85	N Col - NE Ridge	Sp	Conrad Blanch
195	Carles Vallès	Sp	28.08.85	N Col - NE Ridge	Sp	Conrad Blanch
196	Ang Karma	Np/Sh	28.08.85	N Col - NE Ridge	Sp	Conrad Blanch
197	Shambu Tamang (2)	Np	28.08.85	N Col - NE Ridge	Sp	Conrad Blanch
198	Narayan Shrestha	Np	28.08.85	N Col - NE Ridge	Sp	Conrad Blanch
199	Etsuo Akutsu	Jp	30.10.85	S Col - SE Ridge	Jp	Kuniaki Yagihara
200	Satoshi Kimoto	Jp	30.10.85	S Col - SE Ridge	Jp	Kuniaki Yagihara
201	Hideji Nazuka (1)	Jp	30.10.85	S Col - SE Ridge	Jp	Kuniaki Yagihara
202	Teruo Saegusa (1)	Jp	30.10.85	S Col - SE Ridge	Jp	Kuniaki Yagihara
203	Masanori Sato	Jp	30.10.85	S Col - SE Ridge	Jp	Kuniaki Yagihara
204	Kuniaki Yagihara	Jp	30.10.85	S Col - SE Ridge	Jp	Kuniaki Yagihara
205	Noboru Yamada (2) (x)	Jp	30.10.85	S Col - SE Ridge	Jp	Kuniaki Yagihara
206	Sharon Wood (f)	Can	20.05.86	W Ridge (from Tibet)	Can	Jim Elzinga
207	Dawayne Congdon	Can	20.05.86	W Ridge (from Tibet)	Can	Jim Elzinga
208	Erhard Loretan (x)	Swi	30.08.86	N Face (Hornbein C)	Fra/Swi	Pierre Béghin (F)
209	Jean Troillet (x)	Swi	30.08.86	N Face (Hornbein C)	Fra/Swi	Pierre Béghin (F)
210	Heo Young-Ho (1)	SK	22.12.87	S Col - SE Ridge	SK	Hahm Tak-Young
211	Ang Rita (4) (x)	Np/Sh	22.12.87	S Col - SE Ridge	SK	Hahm Tak-Young
212	Noboru Yamada (3)	Jp	05.05.88	N Col - S Col Traverse	Asian	Tsuneoh Shigehiro (Jp)
213	Ang Lhakpa Nuru (1)	Np/Sh	05.05.88	N Col - S Col Traverse	Asian	Tsuneoh Shigehiro (Jp)
214	Cering Doje (1)	Tib	05.05.88	N Col - S Col Traverse	Asian	Tsuneoh Shigehiro (Jp)
215	Ang Phurba II (2)	Np/Sh	05.05.88	S Col - N Col Traverse	Asian	Kunga (Np Sherpa)
216	Rinqing Puncog	Tib	05.05.88	S Col - N Col Traverse	Asian	Kunga (Np Sherpa)
217	Da Cering	Tib	05.05.88	S Col - N Col Traverse	Asian	Kunga (Np Sherpa)
218	Susumu Nakamura	Jp	05.05.88	S Col - SE Ridge	Asian	Tsuneoh Shigehiro (Jp)
219	Shoji Nakamura	Jp	05.05.88	S Col - SE Ridge	Asian	Tsuneoh Shigehiro (Jp)
220	Teruo Saegusa (2)	Jp	05.05.88	S Col - SE Ridge	Asian	Tsuneoh Shigehiro (Jp)
221	Munehiko Yamamoto	Jp	05.05.88	N Col - NE Ridge	Asian	Tsuneoh Shigehiro (Jp)
222	Li Zhixin	Chn	05.05.88	N Col - NE Ridge	Asian	Tsuneoh Shigehiro (Jp)
223	Lhakpa Sona	Np/Sh	05.05.88	N Col - NE Ridge	Asian	Tsuneoh Shigehiro (Jp)
224	Sungdare (5)	Np/Sh	10.05.88	S Col - SE Ridge	Asian	Kunga (Np Sherpa)
225	Padma Bahadur Tamang	Np	10.05.88	S Col - SE Ridge	Asian	Kunga (Np Sherpa)
226	Stephen Venables (x)	UK	12.05.88	E Face - S Col - SE Ridge	US	Robert Anderson
227	Paul Bayne	Aus	25.05.88	S Col - SE Ridge	Aus	Austin Brooks
228	Patrick Cullinan	Aus	25.05.88	S Col - SE Ridge	Aus	Austin Brooks
229	John Muir	Aus	28.05.88	S Col - SE Ridge	Aus	Austin Brooks
230	Jean-Marc Boivin	Fra	26.09.88	S Col - SE Ridge	Fra	François Poissonnier
231	Michel Metzger (x)	Fra	26.09.88	S Col - SE Ridge	Fra	François Poissonnier
232	Jean-Pierre Frachon	Fra	26.09.88	S Col - SE Ridge	Fra	François Poissonnier
233	Gérard Vionnet-Fuasset	Fra	26.09.88	S Col - SE Ridge	Fra	François Poissonnier
234	André Georges	Swi	26.09.88	S Col - SE Ridge	Fra	François Poissonnier
235	Pasang Tshering I (1)	Np/Sh	26.09.88	S Col - SE Ridge	Fra	François Poissonnier
236	Sonam Tshering (1)	Np/Sh	26.09.88	S Col - SE Ridge	Fra	François Poissonnier
237	Ajiwa (1)	Np/Sh	26.09.88	S Col - SE Ridge	Fra	François Poissonnier
238	Kim Chang-Seon	SK	26.09.88	S Pillar - SE Ridge	SK	Choi Chang-Min
239	Pema Dorje (3)	Np/Sh	26.09.88	S Pillar - SE Ridge	SK	Choi Chang-Min
240	Um Hong-Gil	SK	26.09.88	S Pillar - SE Ridge	SK	Choi Chang-Min
241	Marc Batard (1) (x)	Fra	26.09.88	S Col - SE Ridge	solo	Marc Batard
242	Jang Bong-Wan	SK	29.09.88	S Pillar - SE Ridge	SK	Choi Chang-Min
243	Chang Byong-Ho	SK	29.09.88	S Pillar - SE Ridge	SK	Choi Chang-Min
244	Jeong Seung-Kwon	SK	29.09.88	S Pillar - SE Ridge	SK	Choi Chang-Min
245	Stacy Allison (f)	US	29.09.88	S Col - SE Ridge	US	James Frush
246	Pasang Gyalzen	Np/Sh	29.09.88	S Col - SE Ridge	US	James Frush
247	Geoffrey Tabin	US	02.10.88	S Col - SE Ridge	US	James Frush
248	Nam Sun-Woo	SK	02.10.88	S Pillar - SE Ridge	US	James Frush
249	Dawa Tshering I	Np/Sh	02.10.88	S Col - SE Ridge	US	James Frush

No.	Name	Nat	Date	Route	Exp	Leader
250	Nima Tashi (1)	Np/Sh	02.10.88	S Col - SE Ridge	US	James Frush
251	Phu Dorje (1)	Np/Sh	02.10.88	S Col - SE Ridge	US	James Frush
252	Peggy Luce (f)	US	02.10.88	S Col - SE Ridge	SK	Choi Chang-Min
253	Serge Koenig	Fra	13.10.88	S Col - SE Ridge	Fra	Serge Koenig
254	† Lhakpa Sonam	Np/Sh	13.10.88	S Col - SE Ridge	Fra	Serge Koenig
?	† Pasang Temba (II)	Np/Sh	13.10.88	S Col - SE Ridge	Fra	Serge Koenig
255	Jerónimo López	Sp	14.10.88	S Col - SE Ridge	Sp	Lluis Belvis
256	Nil Bohigas	Sp	14.10.88	S Col - SE Ridge	Sp	Lluis Belvis
257	Lluis Giner	Sp	14.10.88	S Col - SE Ridge	Sp	Lluis Belvis
258	Ang Rita (5) (x)	Np/Sh	14.10.88	S Col - SE Ridge	Sp	Lluis Belvis
259	Nima Rita (1) (x)	Np/Sh	14.10.88	S Col - SE Ridge	Sp	Lluis Belvis
260	Lydia Bradey (f) (x)	NZ	14.10.88	S Col - SE Ridge	NZ	Rob Hall
261	† Jozef Just (x)	Slk	17.10.88	SW Face	Slk	Ivan Fiala
262	Stipe Bozic (2)	Cro	10.05.89	S Col - SE Ridge	Mac	Jovan Poposki
263	† Dimitar Ilijevski	Mac	10.05.89	S Col - SE Ridge	Mac	Jovan Poposki
264	Ajiwa (2)	Np/Sh	10.05.89	S Col - SE Ridge	Mac	Jovan Poposki
265	Sonam Tshering (2) (x)	Np/Sh	10.05.89	S Col - SE Ridge	Mac	Jovan Poposki
266	Viki Groselj	Slo	10.05.89	S Col - SE Ridge	Mac	Jovan Poposki
267	Ricardo Torres	Mex	16.05.89	S Col - SE Ridge	US	Walt McConnell
268	† Phu Dorje III (2)	Np/Sh	16.05.89	S Col - SE Ridge	US	Walt McConnell
269	Ang Dannu	Np/Sh	16.05.89	S Col - SE Ridge	US	Walt McConnell
270	Adrian Burgess	UK	24.05.89	S Col - SE Ridge	US	Karen Fellerhoff (f), Pete Athans
271	Ang Lhakpa Nuru (2)	Np/Sh	24.05.89	S Col - SE Ridge	US	Fellerhoff/Athans
272	Sonam Dendu (1)	Np/Sh	24.05.89	S Col - SE Ridge	US	Fellerhoff/Athans
273	Roddy Mackenzie	Aus	24.05.89	S Col - SE Ridge	US	Fellerhoff/Athans
274	† Eugeniusz Chrobak	Pol	24.05.89	W Ridge (Hornbein C)	Pol	Eugeniusz Chrobak
275	Andrzej Marciniak	Pol	24.05.89	W Ridge (Hornbein C)	Pol	Eugeniusz Chrobak
276	Toichiro Mitani	Jp	13.10.89	S Col - SE Ridge	Jp	Ken Kanazawa
277	Hiroshi Ohnishi	Jp	13.10.89	S Col - SE Ridge	Jp	Ken Kanazawa
278	Atsushi Yamamoto	Jp	13.10.89	S Col - SE Ridge	Jp	Ken Kanazawa
279	Chiring Thebe Lama	Np	13.10.89	S Col - SE Ridge	Jp	Ken Kanazawa
280	Chuldin Dorje	Np/Sh	13.10.89	S Col - SE Ridge	Jp	Ken Kanazawa
281	Cho Kwang-Je	SK	13.10.89	S Pillar - SE Ridge	SK	Kim In-Tae
282	Carlos Carsolio (x)	Mex	13.10.89	S Col - SE Ridge	Mex	Carlos Carsolio
283	Chung Sang-Yong	SK	23.10.89	W Ridge from Nepal	SK	Lee Suk-Woo
284	Nima Rita (2)	Np/Sh	23.10.89	W Ridge from Nepal	SK	Lee Suk-Woo
285	Nuru Jangbu	Np/Sh	23.10.89	W Ridge from Nepal	SK	Lee Suk-Woo
286	Ang Rita (6) (x)	Np/Sh	23.04.90	S Col - SE Ridge	Np	Chitra Bahadur
287	Ang Kami II (2)	Np/Sh	23.04.90	S Col - SE Ridge	Np	Chitra Bahadur
288	Pasang Norbu	Np/Sh	23.04.90	S Col - SE Ridge	Np	Chitra Bahadur
289	Top Bahadur Khatri	Np	23.04.90	S Col - SE Ridge	Np	Chitra Bahadur
290	Robert Link	US	07.05.90	N Col - NE Ridge	int	Jim Whittaker
291	Steve Gall	US	07.05.90	N Col - NE Ridge	int	Jim Whittaker
292	Sergei Arsentiev (1) (x)	Rus	07.05.90	N Col - NE Ridge	int	Jim Whittaker
293	Grigori Lunyakov (x)	Kaz	07.05.90	N Col - NE Ridge	int	Jim Whittaker
294	Daqimi (1)	Tib	07.05.90	N Col - NE Ridge	int	Jim Whittaker
295	Jiabu (1)	Tib	07.05.90	N Col - NE Ridge	int	Jim Whittaker
296	Ed Viesturs (1) (x)	US	08.05.90	N Col - NE Ridge	int	Jim Whittaker
297	Mstislav Gorbenko	Ukr	08.05.90	N Col - NE Ridge	int	Jim Whittaker
298	Andrei Tselishchev (x)	Kaz	08.05.90	N Col - NE Ridge	int	Jim Whittaker
299	Ian Wade	US	09.05.90	N Col - NE Ridge	int	Jim Whittaker
300	Daqiong	Tib	09.05.90	N Col - NE Ridge	int	Jim Whittaker
301	Luoze (1)	Tib	09.05.90	N Col - NE Ridge	int	Jim Whittaker
302	Rena (1)	Tib	09.05.90	N Col - NE Ridge	int	Jim Whittaker
303	Kui Sang (1) (f)	Tib	09.05.90	N Col - NE Ridge	int	Jim Whittaker
304	Yekaterina Ivanova (f)	Rus	10.05.90	N Col - NE Ridge	int	Jim Whittaker
305	Anatoli Moshnikov (1) (x)	Rus	10.05.90	N Col - NE Ridge	int	Jim Whittaker
306	Yervand Ilyinsky	Kaz	10.05.90	N Col - NE Ridge	int	Jim Whittaker
307	Aleksandr Tokarev (x)	Rus	10.05.90	N Col - NE Ridge	int	Jim Whittaker
308	Mark Tucker	US	10.05.90	N Col - NE Ridge	int	Jim Whittaker
309	Wangjia	Tib	10.05.90	N Col - NE Ridge	int	Jim Whittaker
310	Pete Athans (1)	US	10.05.90	S Col - SE Ridge	US	Glenn Porzak
311	Glenn Porzak	US	10.05.90	S Col - SE Ridge	US	Glenn Porzak
312	Ang Jangbu II	Np/Sh	10.05.90	S Col - SE Ridge	US	Glenn Porzak
313	Nima Tashi (2)	Np/Sh	10.05.90	S Col - SE Ridge	US	Glenn Porzak
314	Dana Coffield	US	10.05.90	S Col - SE Ridge	US	Glenn Porzak
315	Brent Manning	US	10.05.90	S Col - SE Ridge	US	Glenn Porzak
316	Michael Browning	US	10.05.90	S Col - SE Ridge	US	Glenn Porzak
317	Dawa Nuru I (1)	Np/Sh	10.05.90	S Col - SE Ridge	US	Glenn Porzak
318	Peter Hillary	NZ	10.05.90	S Col - SE Ridge	NZ	Rob Hall
319	Rob Hall (1)	NZ	10.05.90	S Col - SE Ridge	NZ	Rob Hall
320	Gary Ball (1)	NZ	10.05.90	S Col - SE Ridge	NZ	Rob Hall
321	Rudy Van Snik	Bel	10.05.90	S Col - SE Ridge	NZ	Rob Hall
322	Apa (1)	Np/Sh	10.05.90	S Col - SE Ridge	NZ	Rob Hall
323	Andrew Lapkass (1)	US	11.05.90	S Col - SE Ridge	US	Glenn Porzak
324	Tim Macartney-Snape (2) (x)	Aus	11.05.90	S Col - SE Ridge	Aus	Tim Macartney-Snape
325	Mikael Reutersward	Swe	11.05.90	S Col - SE Ridge	NZ	Rob Hall
326	Oskar Khilborg	Swe	11.05.90	S Col - SE Ridge	NZ	Rob Hall
327	Alex Lowe (1)	US	04.10.90	S Col - SE Ridge	US	Hooman Aprin
328	Dan Culver	Can	04.10.90	S Col - SE Ridge	US	Hooman Aprin
329	Yves Salino	Fra	04.10.90	S Col - SE Ridge	Fra	Laurence de la Ferrière (f)
330	Hooman Aprin	US	05.10.90	S Col - SE Ridge	US	Hooman Aprin
331	Ang Temba I	Np/Sh	05.10.90	S Col - SE Ridge	US	Hooman Aprin
332	Erik Decamp	Fra	05.10.90	S Col - SE Ridge	Fra	Marc Batard
333	Nawang Thile (1)	Np/Sh	05.10.90	S Col - SE Ridge	Fra	Marc Batard
334	Sonam Dendu (2)	Np/Sh	05.10.90	S Col - SE Ridge	Fra	Marc Batard
335	Marc Batard (2) (x)	Fra	05.10.90	S Col - SE Ridge	Fra	Marc Batard
336	Christine Janin (f)	Fra	05.10.90	S Col - SE Ridge	Fra	Marc Batard
337	Pascal Tournaire	Fra	05.10.90	S Col - SE Ridge	Fra	Marc Batard
338	Bok Jin-Young	SK	06.10.90	S Col - SE Ridge	Jp/SK	Nobuo Kuwahara
339	Kim Jae-Soo	SK	06.10.90	S Col - SE Ridge	Jp/SK	Nobuo Kuwahara
340	Park Chang-Woo	SK	06.10.90	S Col - SE Ridge	Jp/SK	Nobuo Kuwahara
341	Dawa Sange	Np/Sh	06.10.90	S Col - SE Ridge	Jp/SK	Nobuo Kuwahara
342	Pemba Dorje I	Np/Sh	06.10.90	S Col - SE Ridge	Jp/SK	Nobuo Kuwahara
343	Babu Chiri (1)	Np/Sh	06.10.90	S Col - SE Ridge	Fra	Marc Batard
344	Andrej Stremfelj (2)	Slo	07.10.90	S Col - SE Ridge	Slo	Tomaz Jamnik
345	Marija Stremfelj (f)	Slo	07.10.90	S Col - SE Ridge	Slo	Tomaz Jamnik
346	Janez Jeglic	Slo	07.10.90	S Col - SE Ridge	Slo	Tomaz Jamnik
347	Lhakpa Rita I (1)	Np/Sh	07.10.90	S Col - SE Ridge	Slo	Tomaz Jamnik
348	Cathy Gibson (f)	US	07.10.90	S Col - SE Ridge	US	Hooman Aprin
349	Aleksei Krasnokutsky	Rus	07.10.90	S Col - SE Ridge	US	Hooman Aprin
350	Phinzo I (1)	Np/Sh	07.10.90	S Col - SE Ridge	US	Hooman Aprin
351	Jean-Noël Roche	Fra	07.10.90	S Col - SE Ridge	Fra	Laurence de la Ferrière (f)
352	Bertrand Roche	Fra	07.10.90	S Col - SE Ridge	Fra	Laurence de la Ferrière (f)
353	Denis Pivot	Fra	07.10.90	S Col - SE Ridge	Fra	Laurence de la Ferrière (f)
354	Alain Desez	Fra	07.10.90	S Col - SE Ridge	Fra	Laurence de la Ferrière (f)
355	René De Bos	NL	07.10.90	S Col - SE Ridge	Fra	Laurence de la Ferrière (f)
356	Ang Phurba III	Np/Sh	07.10.90	S Col - SE Ridge	Fra	Laurence de la Ferrière (f)
357	Nima Dorje I (1)	Np/Sh	07.10.90	S Col - SE Ridge	Fra	Laurence de la Ferrière (f)
358	Ang Temba II	Np/Sh	08.05.91	S Col - SE Ridge	Np	Lobsang (Sherpa)
359	Sonam Dendu (3)	Np/Sh	08.05.91	S Col - SE Ridge	Np	Lobsang (Sherpa)
360	Apa (2)	Np/Sh	08.05.91	S Col - SE Ridge	Np	Lobsang (Sherpa)
361	Pete Athans (2)	US	08.05.91	S Col - SE Ridge	US	Rick Wilcox
362	Mark Richey	US	15.05.91	S Col - SE Ridge	US	Rick Wilcox
363	Yves La Forest	Can	15.05.91	S Col - SE Ridge	US	Rick Wilcox
364	Rick Wilcox	US	15.05.91	S Col - SE Ridge	US	Rick Wilcox
365	Barry Rugo	US	15.05.91	S Col - SE Ridge	US	Rick Wilcox
366	Eric Simonson	US	15.05.91	N Col - N Face	US	Eric Simonson
367	Bob Sloezen (1)	US	15.05.91	N Col - N Face	US	Eric Simonson
368	George Dunn	US	15.05.91	N Col - N Face	US	Eric Simonson
369	Andy Politz	US	15.05.91	N Col - N Face	US	Eric Simonson
370	Lhakpa Dorje I (2)	Np/Sh	15.05.91	N Col - N Face	US	Eric Simonson
371	Ang Dawa (1)	Np/Sh	15.05.91	N Col - N Face	US	Eric Simonson
372	Ed Viesturs (2)	US	15.05.91	S Col - SE Ridge	US	Ed Viesturs/Robert Link
373	Mingma Norbu (Nuru)	Np/Sh	15.05.91	N Face (Hornbein C)	Swe	Jack Berg
374	Gyalbu (1)	Np/Sh	15.05.91	N Face (Hornbein C)	Swe	Jack Berg
375	Mike Perry	NZ	17.05.91	N Col - N Face	US	Eric Simonson
376	Battistino Bonali (x)	It	17.05.91	N Face (Norton C)	It	Oreste Forno
377	Leopold Sulovsky (x)	Cz	17.05.91	N Face (Norton C)	It	Oreste Forno

No.	Name	Nat	Date	Route	Exp	Leader
378	Lars Cronlund	Swe	20.05.91	N Face (Hornbein C)	Swe	Jack Berg
379	Mark Whetu (1)	NZ	21.05.91	N Col - N Face	US	Eric Simonson
380	Brent Okita	US	21.05.91	N Col - N Face	US	Eric Simonson
381	Babu Chiri (2)	Np/Sh	22.05.91	N Col - N Face	UK	Harry Taylor
382	Chuldin Temba (1)	Np/Sh	22.05.91	N Col - N Face	UK	Harry Taylor
383	Greg Wilson	US	24.05.91	N Col - N Face	US	Eric Simonson
384	Muneo Nukita (1)	Jp	27.05.91	N Col - N Face	Jp	Muneo Nukita
385	† Junichi Futagami	Jp	27.05.91	N Col - N Face	Jp	Muneo Nukita
386	Nima Dorje I (2)	Np/Sh	27.05.91	N Col - N Face	Jp	Muneo Nukita
387	Phinzo Norbu (1)	Np/Sh	27.05.91	N Col - N Face	Jp	Muneo Nukita
388	Francisco José Pérez	Sp	06.10.91	S Col - SE Ridge	Sp	Juan-Carlos Gómez
389	Rafael Vidaurre	Sp	06.10.91	S Col - SE Ridge	Sp	Juan-Carlos Gómez
390	José-Antonio Garcés	Sp	06.10.91	S Col - SE Ridge	Sp	Juan-Carlos Gómez
391	Antonio Ubieto	Sp	06.10.91	S Col - SE Ridge	Sp	Juan-Carlos Gómez
392	Vladimir Balyberdin (2) (x)	Rus	07.10.91	S Col - SE Ridge	Rus	Vladimir Balyberdin
393	Anatoli Boukreev (1) (x)	Kaz	07.10.91	S Col - SE Ridge	Rus	Vladimir Balyberdin
394	Roman Giutashvili	Geo	10.10.91	S Col - SE Ridge	Rus	Vladimir Balyberdin
395	Dan Mazur	US	10.10.91	S Col - SE Ridge	Rus	Vladimir Balyberdin
396	Prem Singh	Ind	10.05.92	S Col - SE Ridge	Ind	Hukam Singh
397	Sunil Dutt Sharma	Ind	10.05.92	S Col - SE Ridge	Ind	Hukam Singh
398	Kanhaiya Lal (Pokhriyal)	Ind	10.05.92	S Col - SE Ridge	Ind	Hukam Singh
399	Ned Gillette	US	12.05.92	S Col - SE Ridge	NZ	Rob Hall
400	Doron Erel	Isr	12.05.92	S Col - SE Ridge	NZ	Rob Hall
401	Cham Yick-Kai	Chn	12.05.92	S Col - SE Ridge	NZ	Rob Hall
402	Gary Ball (2)	NZ	12.05.92	S Col - SE Ridge	NZ	Rob Hall
403	Doug Mantle	US	12.05.92	S Col - SE Ridge	NZ	Rob Hall
404	Rob Hall (2)	NZ	12.05.92	S Col - SE Ridge	NZ	Rob Hall
405	Randall Danta	US	12.05.92	S Col - SE Ridge	NZ	Rob Hall
406	Guy Cotter (1)	NZ	12.05.92	S Col - SE Ridge	NZ	Rob Hall
407	Sonam Tshering (3)	Np/Sh	12.05.92	S Col - SE Ridge	NZ	Rob Hall
408	Ang Dorje II (1)	Np/Sh	12.05.92	S Col - SE Ridge	NZ	Rob Hall
409	Tashi Tshering (1)	Np/Sh	12.05.92	S Col - SE Ridge	NZ	Rob Hall
410	Apa (3)	Np/Sh	12.05.92	S Col - SE Ridge	NZ	Rob Hall
411	Ang Dawa (2)	Np/Sh	12.05.92	S Col - SE Ridge	NZ	Rob Hall
412	Ingrid Baeyens (f)	Bel	12.05.92	S Col - SE Ridge	NZ	Rob Hall
413	Ronald Naar	NL	12.05.92	S Col - SE Ridge	NL	Ronald Naar
414	Edmond Öfner	NL	12.05.92	S Col - SE Ridge	NL	Ronald Naar
415	Dawa Tashi (1)	Np/Sh	12.05.92	S Col - SE Ridge	NL	Ronald Naar
416	Nima Temba I	Np/Sh	12.05.92	S Col - SE Ridge	NL	Ronald Naar
417	Aleksandr Gerasimov	Rus	12.05.92	S Col - SE Ridge	Rus	Vyacheslav Volkov
418	Andrei Volkov	Rus	12.05.92	S Col - SE Ridge	Rus	Vyacheslav Volkov
419	Ilia Sabelnikov	Rus	12.05.92	S Col - SE Ridge	Rus	Vyacheslav Volkov
420	Ivan Dusharin	Rus	12.05.92	S Col - SE Ridge	Rus	Vyacheslav Volkov
421	Skip Horner	US	12.05.92	S Col - SE Ridge	US	Todd Burleson
422	Louis Bowen	US	12.05.92	S Col - SE Ridge	US	Todd Burleson
423	Vernon Tejas	US	12.05.92	S Col - SE Ridge	US	Todd Burleson
424	Dawa Temba (1)	Np/Sh	12.05.92	S Col - SE Ridge	US	Todd Burleson
425	Ang Gyalzen I	Np/Sh	12.05.92	S Col - SE Ridge	US	Todd Burleson
426	Lobsang	Ind/Sh	12.05.92	S Col - SE Ridge	Ind	Hukam Singh
427	Santosh Yadav (1) (f)	Ind	12.05.92	S Col - SE Ridge	Ind	Hukam Singh
428	Mohan Singh (Gunjyal)	Ind	12.05.92	S Col - SE Ridge	Ind	Hukam Singh
429	Sange Mudok (1)	Ind/Sh	12.05.92	S Col - SE Ridge	Ind	Hukam Singh
430	Wangchuk	Ind/Sh	12.05.92	S Col - SE Ridge	Ind	Hukam Singh
431	Sergei Penzov	Rus	14.05.92	S Col - SE Ridge	Rus	Vyacheslav Volkov
432	Vladimir Zakharov	Rus	14.05.92	S Col - SE Ridge	Rus	Vyacheslav Volkov
433	Yevgeni Vinogradsky (1)	Rus	14.05.92	S Col - SE Ridge	Rus	Vyacheslav Volkov
434	Fedor Konyukhov	Rus	14.05.92	S Col - SE Ridge	Rus	Vyacheslav Volkov
435	Cristián García-Huidobro	Chl	15.05.92	E Face - S Col - SE Ridge	Chl	Rodrigo Jordán
436	Rodrigo Jordán	Chl	15.05.92	E Face - S Col - SE Ridge	Chl	Rodrigo Jordán
437	Juan-Sebastián Montes	Chl	15.05.92	E Face - S Col - SE Ridge	Chl	Rodrigo Jordán
438	Pete Athans (3)	US	15.05.92	S Col - SE Ridge	US	Todd Burleson
439	Lhakpa Rita I (2)	Np/Sh	15.05.92	S Col - SE Ridge	US	Todd Burleson
440	Keith Kerr	UK	15.05.92	S Col - SE Ridge	US	Todd Burleson
441	Todd Burleson (1)	US	15.05.92	S Col - SE Ridge	US	Todd Burleson
442	Hugh Morton	US	15.05.92	S Col - SE Ridge	US	Todd Burleson
443	Man Bahadur Tamang (1)	Np	15.05.92	S Col - SE Ridge	US	Todd Burleson
444	Dorje I (1)	Np/Sh	15.05.92	S Col - SE Ridge	US	Todd Burleson
445	Francisco Gan	Sp	15.05.92	S Pillar - SE Ridge	Sp	Francisco Soria
446	Alfonso Juez	Sp	15.05.92	S Pillar - SE Ridge	Sp	Francisco Soria
447	Ramón Portilla	Sp	15.05.92	S Pillar - SE Ridge	Sp	Francisco Soria
448	Lhakpa Nuru I (1)	Np/Sh	15.05.92	S Pillar - SE Ridge	Sp	Francisco Soria
449	Pemba Norbu (Nuru) II (1)	Np/Sh	15.05.92	S Pillar - SE Ridge	Sp	Francisco Soria
450	Mauricio Purto	Chl	15.05.92	S Col - SE Ridge	Chl	Mauricio Purto
451	Ang Rita (7) (x)	Np/Sh	15.05.92	S Col - SE Ridge	Chl	Mauricio Purto
452	Ang Phuri	Np/Sh	15.05.92	S Col - SE Ridge	Chl	Mauricio Purto
453	Jonathan Pratt	UK	15.05.92	S Col - SE Ridge	Cz	Miroslav Smid
454	Juan-María Eguillor	Sp/B	25.09.92	S Col - SE Ridge	Sp	Pedro Tous
455	Francisco Fernández	Sp/B	25.09.92	S Col - SE Ridge	Sp	Pedro Tous
456	Alberto Iñurrategi (x)	Sp/B	25.09.92	S Col - SE Ridge	Sp	Pedro Tous
457	Félix Iñurrategi (x)	Sp/B	25.09.92	S Col - SE Ridge	Sp	Pedro Tous
458	Giuseppe Petigax	It	28.09.92	S Col - SE Ridge	It	Agostino Da Polenza
459	Lorenzo Mazzoleni	It	28.09.92	S Col - SE Ridge	It	Agostino Da Polenza
460	Mario Panzeri (x)	It	28.09.92	S Col - SE Ridge	It	Agostino Da Polenza
461	Pierre Royer	Fra	28.09.92	S Col - SE Ridge	It	Agostino Da Polenza
462	Lhakpa Nuru I (2)	Np/Sh	28.09.92	S Col - SE Ridge	It	Agostino Da Polenza
463	Benoît Chamoux	Fra	29.09.92	S Col - SE Ridge	It	Agostino Da Polenza
464	Oswald Santin	It	29.09.92	S Col - SE Ridge	It	Agostino Da Polenza
465	Abele Blanc	It	30.09.92	S Col - SE Ridge	It	Agostino Da Polenza
466	Giampietro Verza	It	30.09.92	S Col - SE Ridge	It	Agostino Da Polenza
467	Iosu Bereziartua	Sp/B	01.10.92	S Col - SE Ridge	Sp	Pedro Tous
468	Eugène Berger	Lux	01.10.92	S Col - SE Ridge	Fra	Bernard Muller
469	Mikel Repáraz	Sp/B	03.10.92	S Col - SE Ridge	Sp	Pedro Tous
470	Pedro Tous	Sp/B	03.10.92	S Col - SE Ridge	Sp	Pedro Tous
471	Juan Tomás	Sp	03.10.92	S Col - SE Ridge	Sp	Pedro Tous
472	Ralf Dujmovits	Ger	04.10.92	S Col - SE Ridge	Ger	Ralf Dujmovits
473	Sonam Tshering (4)	Np/Sh	04.10.92	S Col - SE Ridge	Ger	Ralf Dujmovits
474	Michel Vincent	Fra	07.10.92	S Col - SE Ridge	Fra	Michel Vincent
475	Wally Berg (1)	US	09.10.92	S Col - SE Ridge	US	Wally Berg
476	Augusto Ortega (1)	Per	09.10.92	S Col - SE Ridge	US	Wally Berg
477	Alfonso de la Parra	Mex	09.10.92	S Col - SE Ridge	US	Wally Berg
478	Apa (4)	Np/Sh	09.10.92	S Col - SE Ridge	US	Wally Berg
479	Kaji (1)	Np/Sh	09.10.92	S Col - SE Ridge	US	Wally Berg
480	Philippe Grenier	Fra	09.10.92	S Col - SE Ridge	Fra	Michel Pellé
481	Michel Pellé	Fra	09.10.92	S Col - SE Ridge	Fra	Michel Pellé
482	Thierry Defrance	Fra	09.10.92	S Col - SE Ridge	Fra	Michel Pellé
483	Alain Roussey	Fra	09.10.92	S Col - SE Ridge	Fra	Michel Pellé
484	Pierre Aubertin	Fra	09.10.92	S Col - SE Ridge	Fra	Michel Pellé
485	Scott Darsney	US	09.10.92	S Pillar - SE Ridge	Fra	Michel Vincent
486	Heo Young-Ho (2)	SK	13.04.93	N Col - S Col Traverse	SK	Oh In-Hwan
487	Ngati	Np/Sh	13.04.93	N Col - S Col Traverse	SK	Oh In-Hwan
488	Dawa Tashi (2)	Np/Sh	22.04.93	S Col - SE Ridge	Np	Pasang Lhamu (f)
489	† Pasang Lhamu (f)	Np/Sh	22.04.93	S Col - SE Ridge	Np	Pasang Lhamu (f)
490	Pemba Norbu (Nuru) II (2)	Np/Sh	22.04.93	S Col - SE Ridge	Np	Pasang Lhamu (f)
491	† Sonam Tshering (5)	Np/Sh	22.04.93	S Col - SE Ridge	Np	Pasang Lhamu (f)
492	Lhakpa Nuru I (3)	Np/Sh	22.04.93	S Col - SE Ridge	Np	Pasang Lhamu (f)
493	Nawang Thile (2)	Np/Sh	22.04.93	S Col - SE Ridge	Np	Pasang Lhamu (f)
494	Qimi	Tib	05.05.93	N Col - NE Ridge	Chn/Tai	Zeng Shu-Sheng
495	Jia Chuo	Tib	05.05.93	N Col - NE Ridge	Chn/Tai	Zeng Shu-Sheng
496	Kai Zhong (1)	Tib	05.05.93	N Col - NE Ridge	Chn/Tai	Zeng Shu-Sheng
497	Pu Bu	Tib	05.05.93	N Col - NE Ridge	Chn/Tai	Zeng Shu-Sheng
498	Wang Yong-feng	Chn	05.05.93	N Col - NE Ridge	Chn/Tai	Zeng Shu-Sheng
499	Wu Chin-Hsiung	Tai	05.05.93	N Col - NE Ridge	Chn/Tai	Zeng Shu-Sheng
500	Alex Lowe (2)	US	10.05.93	S Col - SE Ridge	US	Todd Burleson
501	John Helenek	US	10.05.93	S Col - SE Ridge	US	Todd Burleson
502	John Dufficy	US	10.05.93	S Col - SE Ridge	US	Todd Burleson
503	Wally Berg (2)	US	10.05.93	S Col - SE Ridge	US	Todd Burleson
504	Michael Sutton	Can	10.05.93	S Col - SE Ridge	US	Todd Burleson
505	Apa (5)	Np/Sh	10.05.93	S Col - SE Ridge	US	Todd Burleson
506	Dawa Nuru I (2)	Np/Sh	10.05.93	S Col - SE Ridge	US	Todd Burleson
507	Chuldin Temba (2)	Np/Sh	10.05.93	S Col - SE Ridge	US	Todd Burleson

No.	Name	Nat	Date	Route	Exp	Leader
508	Kim Soon-Jo (f)	SK	10.05.93	S Col - SE Ridge	SK	Ji Hyun-Ok (f)
509	Ji Hyun-Ok (f)	SK	10.05.93	S Col - SE Ridge	SK	Ji Hyun-Ok (f)
510	Choi Oh-Soon (f)	SK	10.05.93	S Col - SE Ridge	SK	Ji Hyun-Ok (f)
511	Ang Dawa (3)	Np/Sh	10.05.93	S Col - SE Ridge	SK	Ji Hyun-Ok (f)
512	Ang Tshering II	Np/Sh	10.05.93	S Col - SE Ridge	SK	Ji Hyun-Ok (f)
513	Sonam Dendu (4)	Np/Sh	10.05.93	S Col - SE Ridge	SK	Ji Hyun-Ok (f)
514	Rinzin	Np/Sh	10.05.93	S Col - SE Ridge	SK	Ji Hyun-Ok (f)
515	Michael Groom (1) (x)	Aus	10.05.93	S Col - SE Ridge	Aus/Ind	Tashi Wangchuk Tenzing
516	† Lobsang Tshering	Ind	10.05.93	S Col - SE Ridge	Aus/Ind	T W Tenzing
517	Harry Taylor	UK	10.05.93	S Col - SE Ridge	UK	John Barry
518	Dicky Dolma (f)	Ind	10.05.93	S Col - SE Ridge	Ind/Np	Bachendri Pal (f)
519	Santosh Yadav (2) (f)	Ind	10.05.93	S Col - SE Ridge	Ind/Np	Bachendri Pal (f)
520	Kunga Bhutia (f)	Ind	10.05.93	S Col - SE Ridge	Ind/Np	Bachendri Pal (f)
521	Baldev Kunwer	Ind	10.05.93	S Col - SE Ridge	Ind/Np	Bachendri Pal (f)
522	Ongda Chiring (1)	Np/Sh	10.05.93	S Col - SE Ridge	Ind/Np	Bachendri Pal (f)
523	Na Temba (1)	Np/Sh	10.05.93	S Col - SE Ridge	Ind/Np	Bachendri Pal (f)
524	Kusang Dorje (1)	Ind/Sh	10.05.93	S Col - SE Ridge	Ind/Np	Bachendri Pal (f)
525	Dorje I (2)	Np/Sh	10.05.93	S Col - SE Ridge	Ind/Np	Bachendri Pal (f)
526	Dolly Lefever (f)	US	10.05.93	S Col - SE Ridge	US	Paul Pfau, Michael Sinclair
527	Mark Selland	US	10.05.93	S Col - SE Ridge	US	Pfau/Sinclair
528	Charles Armatys	US	10.05.93	S Col - SE Ridge	US	Pfau/Sinclair
529	Pemba Temba	Np/Sh	10.05.93	S Col - SE Ridge	US	Pfau/Sinclair
530	Moti Lal Gurung	Np	10.05.93	S Col - SE Ridge	US	Pfau/Sinclair
531	Veikka Gustafsson (1)	Fin	10.05.93	S Col - SE Ridge	NZ	Rob Hall
532	Jan Arnold (f)	NZ	10.05.93	S Col - SE Ridge	NZ	Rob Hall
533	Rob Hall (3)	NZ	10.05.93	S Col - SE Ridge	NZ	Rob Hall
534	Jonathan Gluckman	NZ	10.05.93	S Col - SE Ridge	NZ	Rob Hall
535	Ang Chumbi	Np/Sh	10.05.93	S Col - SE Ridge	NZ	Rob Hall
536	Ang Dorje II (2)	Np/Sh	10.05.93	S Col - SE Ridge	NZ	Rob Hall
537	Norbu (Nuru) (1)	Np/Sh	10.05.93	S Col - SE Ridge	NZ	Rob Hall
538	Vladas Vitkauskas	Lit	10.05.93	S Col - SE Ridge	Lat	Vladas Vitkauskas
539	Aleksei Mouravlev	Rus	10.05.93	S Col - SE Ridge	Rus	Aleksander Volgin
540	Vladimir Yanochkin	Rus	15.05.93	S Col - SE Ridge	Rus	Aleksander Volgin
541	Vladimir Bashkirov (1) (x)	Rus	16.05.93	S Col - SE Ridge	Rus	Aleksander Volgin
542	Josep Pujante	Sp	16.05.93	S Col - SE Ridge	Sp	Lluis Belvis
543	Ang Phurba II (3)	Np/Sh	16.05.93	S Col - SE Ridge	Sp	Lluis Belvis
544	Joxe María Oñate	Sp/B	16.05.93	S Col - SE Ridge	Sp	Josu Feijoo
545	Alberto Zerain	Sp/B	16.05.93	S Col - SE Ridge	Sp	Josu Feijoo
546	José Ramón Agirre	Sp/B	16.05.93	S Col - SE Ridge	Sp	Josu Feijoo
547	Jangbu I	Np/Sh	16.05.93	S Col - SE Ridge	Sp	Josu Feijoo
548	Ang Rita (8) (x)	Np/Sh	16.05.93	S Col - SE Ridge	Sp	Josu Feijoo
549	Jan Harris	US	16.05.93	S Col - SE Ridge	US	Keith Brown
550	Keith Brown	US	16.05.93	S Col - SE Ridge	US	Keith Brown
551	Park Young-Seok	SK	16.05.93	S Col - SE Ridge	SK	Lee Jong-Ryang
552	† An Jin-Seob	SK	16.05.93	S Col - SE Ridge	SK	Lee Jong-Ryang
553	Kim Tae-Kon	SK	16.05.93	S Col - SE Ridge	SK	Lee Jong-Ryang
554	Kaji (2)	Np/Sh	16.05.93	S Col - SE Ridge	SK	Lee Jong-Ryang
555	Michael Sinclair	US	16.05.93	S Col - SE Ridge	US	Pfau/Sinclair
556	Mark Rabold	US	16.05.93	S Col - SE Ridge	US	Pfau/Sinclair
557	Phinzo I (2)	Np/Sh	16.05.93	S Col - SE Ridge	US	Pfau/Sinclair
558	Dorje II	Np/Sh	16.05.93	S Col - SE Ridge	US	Pfau/Sinclair
559	Durga Tamang	Np	16.05.93	S Col - SE Ridge	US	Pfau/Sinclair
560	Radha Devi Thakur (f)	Ind	16.05.93	S Col - SE Ridge	Ind/Np	Bachendri Pal (f)
561	Rajiv Sharma	Ind	16.05.93	S Col - SE Ridge	Ind/Np	Bachendri Pal (f)
562	Deepu Sharma (f)	Ind	16.05.93	S Col - SE Ridge	Ind/Np	Bachendri Pal (f)
563	Savita Martolia (f)	Ind	16.05.93	S Col - SE Ridge	Ind/Np	Bachendri Pal (f)
564	Nima Norbu Dolma	Ind	16.05.93	S Col - SE Ridge	Ind/Np	Bachendri Pal (f)
565	Suman Kutiyal (f)	Ind	16.05.93	S Col - SE Ridge	Ind/Np	Bachendri Pal (f)
566	Nima Dorje I (3)	Np/Sh	16.05.93	S Col - SE Ridge	Ind/Np	Bachendri Pal (f)
567	Tenzing (1)	Np/Sh	16.05.93	S Col - SE Ridge	Ind/Np	Bachendri Pal (f)
568	Lobsang Jangbu (1)	Np/Sh	16.05.93	S Col - SE Ridge	Ind/Np	Bachendri Pal (f)
569	Nga Temba (1)	Np/Sh	16.05.93	S Col - SE Ridge	Ind/Np	Bachendri Pal (f)
570	Vladimir Koroteev	Rus	17.05.93	S Col - SE Ridge	Rus	Aleksander Volgin
571	Oscar Cadiach (2) (x)	Sp	17.05.93	S Col - SE Ridge	Sp	Lluis Belvis
572	Rebecca Stephens (f)	UK	17.05.93	S Col - SE Ridge	UK	John Barry
573	Ang Pasang I (1)	Np/Sh	17.05.93	S Col - SE Ridge	UK	John Barry
574	Kami Tshering (1)	Np/Sh	17.05.93	S Col - SE Ridge	UK	John Barry
575	Dawson Stelfox	Ire	27.05.93	N Col - NE Ridge	Ire	Dawson Stelfox
576	Park Hyun-Jae	SK	06.10.93	N Col - NE Ridge	SK	Lim Hyung-Chil
577	Panuru (1)	Np/Sh	06.10.93	N Col - NE Ridge	SK	Lim Hyung-Chil
578	François Bernard	Fra	06.10.93	S Col - SE Ridge	Fra	Alain Estève
579	Antoine Cayrol	Fra	06.10.93	S Col - SE Ridge	Fra	Alain Estève
580	Eric Grammond (x)	Fra	06.10.93	S Col - SE Ridge	Fra	Alain Estève
581	Gyalbu (2)	Np/Sh	06.10.93	S Col - SE Ridge	Fra	Alain Estève
582	Dawa Tashi (3)	Np/Sh	06.10.93	S Col - SE Ridge	Fra	Alain Estève
583	Juanito Oiarzabal	Sp/B	07.10.93	S Pillar	Sp	Juanito Oiarzabal
584	Ongda Chiring (2)	Np/Sh	07.10.93	S Pillar	Sp	Juanito Oiarzabal
585	Ginette Harrison (f)	UK	07.10.93	S Col - SE Ridge	UK	Steve Bell
586	Gary Pfisterer	US	07.10.93	S Col - SE Ridge	UK	Steve Bell
587	Ramón Blanco	Sp	07.10.93	S Col - SE Ridge	UK	Steve Bell
588	Graham Hoyland	UK	07.10.93	S Col - SE Ridge	UK	Steve Bell
589	Steve Bell	UK	07.10.93	S Col - SE Ridge	UK	Steve Bell
590	Scott McIvor	UK	07.10.93	S Col - SE Ridge	UK	Steve Bell
591	Na Temba (2)	Np/Sh	07.10.93	S Col - SE Ridge	UK	Steve Bell
592	Pasang Kami I (1)	Np/Sh	07.10.93	S Col - SE Ridge	UK	Steve Bell
593	Dorje I (3)	Np/Sh	07.10.93	S Col - SE Ridge	UK	Steve Bell
594	Alain Estève	Fra	09.10.93	S Col - SE Ridge	Fra	Alain Estève
595	Hubert Giot (x)	Fra	09.10.93	S Col - SE Ridge	Fra	Alain Estève
596	Norbu (Nuru) (2)	Np/Sh	09.10.93	S Col - SE Ridge	Fra	Alain Estève
597	Nima Gombu (1)	Np/Sh	09.10.93	S Col - SE Ridge	Fra	Alain Estève
598	Martin Barnicott	UK	09.10.93	S Col - SE Ridge	UK	Steve Bell
599	David Hempleman-Adams	UK	09.10.93	S Col - SE Ridge	UK	Steve Bell
600	Lee Nobmann	US	09.10.93	S Col - SE Ridge	UK	Steve Bell
601	Tenzing (2)	Np/Sh	09.10.93	S Col - SE Ridge	UK	Steve Bell
602	Nga Temba (2)	Np/Sh	09.10.93	S Col - SE Ridge	UK	Steve Bell
603	Lhakpa Gelu (1)	Np/Sh	09.10.93	S Col - SE Ridge	UK	Steve Bell
604	Ang Pasang II	Np/Sh	09.10.93	S Col - SE Ridge	UK	Steve Bell
605	Maciej Berbeka	Pol	09.10.93	N Col - NE Ridge	UK	Jon Tinker
606	Lhakpa Nuru I (4)	Np/Sh	09.10.93	N Col - NE Ridge	UK	Jon Tinker
607	Jon Tinker	UK	10.10.93	N Col - NE Ridge	UK	Jon Tinker
608	Babu Chiri (3)	Np/Sh	10.10.93	N Col - NE Ridge	UK	Jon Tinker
609	Hideji Nazuka (2)	Jp	18.12.93	SW Face	Jp	Kuniaki Yagihara
610	Fumiaki Goto	Jp	18.12.93	SW Face	Jp	Kuniaki Yagihara
611	Osamu Tanabe	Jp	20.12.93	SW Face	Jp	Kuniaki Yagihara
612	Shinsuke Ezuka	Jp	20.12.93	SW Face	Jp	Kuniaki Yagihara
613	Yoshio Ogata	Jp	22.12.93	SW Face	Jp	Kuniaki Yagihara
614	Ryushi Hoshino	Jp	22.12.93	SW Face	Jp	Kuniaki Yagihara
615	Kiyohiko Suzuki	Jp	08.05.94	S Pillar	Jp	Mitsuyoshi Hongo
616	Wataru Atsuta	Jp	08.05.94	S Pillar	Jp	Mitsuyoshi Hongo
617	Nima Dorje I (4)	Np/Sh	08.05.94	S Pillar	Jp	Mitsuyoshi Hongo
618	Dawa Tshering II (1)	Np/Sh	08.05.94	S Pillar	Jp	Mitsuyoshi Hongo
619	Na Temba (3)	Np/Sh	08.05.94	S Pillar	Jp	Mitsuyoshi Hongo
620	Lhakpa Nuru I (5)	Np/Sh	08.05.94	S Pillar	Jp	Mitsuyoshi Hongo
621	† Shih Fang-Fang	Tai	08.05.94	N Col - NE Ridge	Tai	Chang Jui-Kong
622	Lobsang Jangbu (2) (x)	Np/Sh	09.05.94	S Col - SE Ridge	US	Steven Goryl
623	Rob Hess (x)	US	09.05.94	S Col - SE Ridge	US	Steven Goryl
624	Scott Fischer (1) (x)	US	09.05.94	S Col - SE Ridge	US	Steven Goryl
625	Brent Bishop	US	09.05.94	S Col - SE Ridge	US	Steven Goryl
626	Sonam Dendu (5)	Np/Sh	09.05.94	S Col - SE Ridge	US	Steven Goryl
627	Ang Dorje II (3)	Np/Sh	09.05.94	S Col - SE Ridge	NZ	Rob Hall
628	Hall Wendel	US	09.05.94	S Col - SE Ridge	NZ	Rob Hall
629	Hellmut Seitzl	Ger	09.05.94	S Col - SE Ridge	NZ	Rob Hall
630	David Keaton	US	09.05.94	S Col - SE Ridge	NZ	Rob Hall
631	Ekke Gundelach	Ger	09.05.94	S Col - SE Ridge	NZ	Rob Hall
632	Rob Hall (4)	NZ	09.05.94	S Col - SE Ridge	NZ	Rob Hall
633	Ed Viesturs (3)	US	09.05.94	S Col - SE Ridge	NZ	Rob Hall
634	Nima Gombu (2)	Np/Sh	09.05.94	S Col - SE Ridge	NZ	Rob Hall
635	Norbu (Nuru) (3)	Np/Sh	09.05.94	S Col - SE Ridge	NZ	Rob Hall

No.	Name	Nat	Date	Route	Exp	Leader		No.	Name	Nat	Date	Route	Exp	Leader
636	David Taylor	US	09.05.94	S Col - SE Ridge	NZ	Rob Hall		701	Dan Aguilar	US	14.05.95	N Col - NE Ridge	US/Aus	Paul Pfau
637	Erling Kagge	Nor	09.05.94	S Col - SE Ridge	NZ	Rob Hall		702	Wangchu	Np/Sh	14.05.95	N Col - NE Ridge	US/Aus	Paul Pfau
638	Tomiyasu Ishikawa	Jp	13.05.94	S Pillar	Jp	Mitsuyoshi Hongo		703	Luc Jourjon	Fra	14.05.95	N Col - NE Ridge	int	Jon Tinker
639	Nima Temba II	Np/Sh	13.05.94	S Pillar	Jp	Mitsuyoshi Hongo		704	Babu Chiri (4)	Np/Sh	14.05.95	N Col - NE Ridge	int	Jon Tinker
640	Dawa Tashi (4)	Np/Sh	13.05.94	S Pillar	Jp	Mitsuyoshi Hongo		705	Josef Hinding (x)	Au	14.05.95	N Col - NE Ridge	Au	Willi Bauer
641	Pasang Tshering I (2)	Np/Sh	13.05.94	S Pillar	Jp	Mitsuyoshi Hongo		706	Bradford Bull	US	15.05.95	S Col - SE Ridge	int	Bob Hoffman
642	Steven Goryl	US	13.05.94	S Col - SE Ridge	US	Steven Goryl		707	Tommy Heinrich	Arg	15.05.95	S Col - SE Ridge	int	Bob Hoffman
643	Lhakpa Rita I (3)	Np/Sh	13.05.94	S Col - SE Ridge	US	Todd Burleson		708	Apa (7)	Np/Sh	15.05.95	S Col - SE Ridge	int	Bob Hoffman
644	Chuwang Nima (1)	Np/Sh	13.05.94	S Col - SE Ridge	US	Todd Burleson		709	Arita (1)	Np/Sh	15.05.95	S Col - SE Ridge	int	Bob Hoffman
645	Man Bahadur Tamang (2)	Np	13.05.94	S Col - SE Ridge	US	Todd Burleson		710	Nima Rita (3)	Np/Sh	15.05.95	S Col - SE Ridge	int	Bob Hoffman
646	Kami Rita I (1)	Np/Sh	13.05.94	S Col - SE Ridge	US	Todd Burleson		711	Phinzo I (3)	Np/Sh	16.05.95	N Col - NE Ridge	US/Aus	Paul Pfau
647	Dorje I (4)	Np/Sh	13.05.94	S Col - SE Ridge	US	Todd Burleson		712	Colin Lynch	US	16.05.95	N Col - NE Ridge	US/Aus	Paul Pfau
648	Ryszard Pawlowski (1)	Pol	13.05.94	S Col - SE Ridge	US	Todd Burleson		713	Jay Budnik	US	16.05.95	N Col - NE Ridge	US/Aus	Paul Pfau
649	Robert Cedergreen	US	13.05.94	S Col - SE Ridge	US	Todd Burleson		714	Steve Reneker	US	16.05.95	N Col - NE Ridge	US/Aus	Paul Pfau
650	Paul Morrow	US	13.05.94	S Col - SE Ridge	US	Todd Burleson		715	Kurt Wedberg	US	16.05.95	N Col - NE Ridge	US/Aus	Paul Pfau
651	Pete Athans (4)	US	13.05.94	S Col - SE Ridge	US	Todd Burleson		716	Jangbu II (1)	Np/Sh	16.05.95	N Col - NE Ridge	US/Aus	Paul Pfau
652	Todd Burleson (2)	US	13.05.94	S Col - SE Ridge	US	Todd Burleson		717	Tony Tonsing	US	16.05.95	N Col - NE Ridge	US/Per	Thor Kieser
653	Dave Hahn (1)	US	19.05.94	N Col - NE Ridge	US	Eric Simonson		718	Musal Kazi Tamang	Np	16.05.95	N Col - NE Ridge	US/Per	Thor Kieser
654	Steve Swenson (x)	US	25.05.94	N Col - NE Ridge	US	Eric Simonson		719	Graham Ratcliffe (1)	UK	17.05.95	N Col - NE Ridge	int	Henry Todd
655	Mark Whetu (2)	NZ	26.05.94	N Col - NE Ridge	US	Eric Simonson		720	Anatoli Boukreev (2) (x)	Kaz	17.05.95	N Col - NE Ridge	int	Henry Todd
656	† Michael Rheinberger	Aus	26.05.94	N Col - NE Ridge	US	Eric Simonson		721	Nikolai Sitnikov	Rus	17.05.95	N Col - NE Ridge	int	Henry Todd
657	Bob Sloezen (2)	US	31.05.94	N Col - NE Ridge	US	Eric Simonson		722	Constantin Lacatusu	Rom	17.05.95	N Col - NE Ridge	int	Russell Brice
658	Muneo Nukita (2)	Jp	10.10.94	S Col - SE Ridge	Jp	Takashi Miyahara		723	George Kotov	Rus	17.05.95	N Col - NE Ridge	int	Jon Tinker
659	Apa (6)	Np/Sh	10.10.94	S Col - SE Ridge	Jp	Takashi Miyahara		724	Nasuh Mahruki	Tur	17.05.95	N Col - NE Ridge	int	Henry Todd
660	Chuwang Nima (2)	Np/Sh	10.10.94	S Col - SE Ridge	Jp	Takashi Miyahara		725	Michael Jörgensen	Den	23.05.95	N Col - NE Ridge	int	Henry Todd
661	Dawa Tshering III (1)	Np/Sh	10.10.94	S Col - SE Ridge	Jp	Takashi Miyahara		726	Crag Jones	UK	23.05.95	N Col - NE Ridge	int	Henry Todd
662	Charlie Hornsby	UK	11.10.94	S Col - SE Ridge	UK/US	Simon Curran		727	Jeff Shea	US	24.05.95	N Col - NE Ridge	int	Jon Tinker
663	Roddy Kirkwood	UK	11.10.94	S Col - SE Ridge	UK/US	Simon Curran		728	Lhakpa Gelu (2)	Np/Sh	24.05.95	N Col - NE Ridge	int	Jon Tinker
664	Dorje I (5)	Np/Sh	11.10.94	S Col - SE Ridge	UK/US	Simon Curran		729	Tshering Dorje I (1)	Np/Sh	24.05.95	N Col - NE Ridge	int	Jon Tinker
665	Dawa Temba (2)	Np/Sh	11.10.94	S Col - SE Ridge	UK/US	Simon Curran		730	Patrick Hache	Fra	26.05.95	N Col - NE Ridge	int	Jon Tinker
666	Lobsang Jangbu (3) (x)	Np/Sh	07.05.95	S Col - SE Ridge	NZ	Rob Hall		731	Robert Hempstead	US	26.05.95	N Col - NE Ridge	int	Jon Tinker
667	Kiyoshi Furuno	Jp	11.05.95	NE Ridge complete	Jp	Tadao Kanzaki		732	Lama Jangbu (1)	Np/Sh	26.05.95	N Col - NE Ridge	int	Jon Tinker
668	Shigeki Imoto	Jp	11.05.95	NE Ridge complete	Jp	Tadao Kanzaki		733	Babu Chiri (5)	Np/Sh	26.05.95	N Col - NE Ridge	int	Jon Tinker
669	Dawa Tshering II (2)	Np/Sh	11.05.95	NE Ridge complete	Jp	Tadao Kanzaki		734	Greg Child	Aus	26.05.95	N Col - NE Ridge	int	Russell Brice
670	Pasang Kami I (2)	Np/Sh	11.05.95	NE Ridge complete	Jp	Tadao Kanzaki		735	Karsang (1)	Np/Sh	26.05.95	N Col - NE Ridge	int	Russell Brice
671	Lhakpa Nuru I (6)	Np/Sh	11.05.95	NE Ridge complete	Jp	Tadao Kanzaki		736	Lobsang Temba (1)	Np/Sh	26.05.95	N Col - NE Ridge	int	Russell Brice
672	Nima Dorje I (5)	Np/Sh	11.05.95	NE Ridge complete	Jp	Tadao Kanzaki		737	Mike Smith (1)	UK	27.05.95	N Col - NE Ridge	int	Jon Tinker
673	Vladimir Shataev	Rus	11.05.95	N Col - NE Ridge	Rus	Kazbek Khamitsayev		738	Pat Falvey	Ire	27.05.95	N Col - NE Ridge	int	Jon Tinker
674	Iria Projaev	Rus	11.05.95	N Col - NE Ridge	Rus	Kazbek Khamitsayev		739	James Allen	Aus	27.05.95	N Col - NE Ridge	int	Jon Tinker
675	Fedor Shuljev	Rus	11.05.95	N Col - NE Ridge	Rus	Kazbek Khamitsayev		740	Jo Young-Il	SK	14.10.95	N Col - NE Ridge	SK	Kim Jong-Ho
676	Piotr Pustelnik	Pol	12.05.95	N Col - NE Ridge	It/Pol	Marco Bianchi (It)		741	† Zangbu	Np/Sh	14.10.95	N Col - NE Ridge	SK	Kim Jong-Ho
677	Ryszard Pawlowski (2)	Pol	12.05.95	N Col - NE Ridge	int	Henry Todd		742	Han Hwang-Yong	SK	14.10.95	N Col - NE Ridge	SK	Lee Dong-Ho
678	Cheng Kuo-Chun	Tai	12.05.95	N Col - NE Ridge	Tai	Liang Ming-Pen		743	Hong Sung-Taek	SK	14.10.95	N Col - NE Ridge	SK	Lee Dong-Ho
679	Chiang Hsiu-Chen (f)	Tai	12.05.95	N Col - NE Ridge	Tai	Liang Ming-Pen		744	Tashi Tshering (2)	Np/Sh	14.10.95	N Col - NE Ridge	SK	Lee Dong-Ho
680	Mingma Tshering (1)	Np/Sh	12.05.95	N Col - NE Ridge	Tai	Liang Ming-Pen		745	Park Jung-Hun	SK	14.10.95	SW Face	SK	Cho Hyung-Gyu
681	Lhakpa Dorje III (1) (x)	Np/Sh	12.05.95	N Col - NE Ridge	Tai	Liang Ming-Pen		746	Kim Young-Tae	SK	14.10.95	SW Face	SK	Cho Hyung-Gyu
682	Tenzing Nuru (1) (x)	Np/Sh	12.05.95	N Col - NE Ridge	Tai	Liang Ming-Pen		747	Kipa (1)	Np/Sh	14.10.95	SW Face	SK	Cho Hyung-Gyu
683	Kazbek Khamitsayev	Rus	13.05.95	N Col - NE Ridge	Rus	Kazbek Khamitsayev		748	Ang Dawa Tamang (1)	Np	14.10.95	SW Face	SK	Cho Hyung-Gyu
684	Yevgeni Vinogradsky (2)	Rus	13.05.95	N Col - NE Ridge	Rus	Kazbek Khamitsayev		749	Anatoli Boukreev (3) (x)	Kaz	10.05.96	S Col - SE Ridge	US	Scott Fischer
685	Sergei Bogomolov	Rus	13.05.95	N Col - NE Ridge	Rus	Kazbek Khamitsayev		750	Neal Beidleman	US	10.05.96	S Col - SE Ridge	US	Scott Fischer
686	Vladimir Korenkov	Rus	13.05.95	N Col - NE Ridge	Rus	Kazbek Khamitsayev		751	Martin Adams	US	10.05.96	S Col - SE Ridge	US	Scott Fischer
687	Ang Rita (9) (x)	Np/Sh	13.05.95	N Col - NE Ridge	Rus	Kazbek Khamitsayev		752	Klev Schoening	US	10.05.96	S Col - SE Ridge	US	Scott Fischer
688	Marco Bianchi (x)	It	13.05.95	N Col - NE Ridge	It/Pol	Marco Bianchi (It)		753	Charlotte Fox (f)	US	10.05.96	S Col - SE Ridge	US	Scott Fischer
689	Christian Kuntner (x)	It	13.05.95	N Col - NE Ridge	It/Pol	Marco Bianchi (It)		754	Tim Madsen	US	10.05.96	S Col - SE Ridge	US	Scott Fischer
690	Alison Hargreaves (f) (x)	UK	13.05.95	N Col - NE Ridge	int	Russell Brice		755	Sandy Hill Pittman (f)	US	10.05.96	S Col - SE Ridge	US	Scott Fischer
691	Mozart Catao	Bra	14.05.95	N Col - NE Ridge	int	Henry Todd		756	† Scott Fischer (2)	US	10.05.96	S Col - SE Ridge	US	Scott Fischer
692	Waldemar Niclevicz	Bra	14.05.95	N Col - NE Ridge	int	Henry Todd		757	Lene Gammelgaard (f)	Den	10.05.96	S Col - SE Ridge	US	Scott Fischer
693	Reinhard Patscheider (x)	It	14.05.95	N Col - NE Ridge	Lat/It	T. Kirsis/R. Patscheider		758	Lobsang Jangbu (4) (x)	Np/Sh	10.05.96	S Col - SE Ridge	US	Scott Fischer
694	Teodors Kirsis	Lat	14.05.95	N Col - NE Ridge	Lat/It	T. Kirsis/R. Patscheider		759	Nawang Dorje (1)	Np/Sh	10.05.96	S Col - SE Ridge	US	Scott Fischer
695	Imants Zauls	Lat	14.05.95	N Col - NE Ridge	Lat/It	T. Kirsis/R. Patscheider		760	Tenzing (3)	Np/Sh	10.05.96	S Col - SE Ridge	US	Scott Fischer
696	Ongda Chiring (3)	Np/Sh	14.05.95	N Col - NE Ridge	US/Aus	Paul Pfau		761	Tashi Tshering (3)	Np/Sh	10.05.96	S Col - SE Ridge	US	Scott Fischer
697	George Mallory	Aus	14.05.95	N Col - NE Ridge	US/Aus	Paul Pfau		762	Jon Krakauer	US	10.05.96	S Col - SE Ridge	NZ	Rob Hall
698	Jeffrey Hall	US	14.05.95	N Col - NE Ridge	US/Aus	Paul Pfau		763	† Andrew Harris	NZ	10.05.96	S Col - SE Ridge	NZ	Rob Hall
699	Kaji (3)	Np/Sh	14.05.95	N Col - NE Ridge	US/Aus	Paul Pfau		764	Michael Groom (2)	Aus	10.05.96	S Col - SE Ridge	NZ	Rob Hall
700	Jim Litch	US	14.05.95	N Col - NE Ridge	US/Aus	Paul Pfau		765	† Rob Hall (5)	NZ	10.05.96	S Col - SE Ridge	NZ	Rob Hall

No.	Name	Nat	Date	Route	Exp	Leader
766	† Yasuko Namba (f)	Jp	10.05.96	S Col - SE Ridge	NZ	Rob Hall
767	† Doug Hansen	US	10.05.96	S Col - SE Ridge	NZ	Rob Hall
768	Ang Dorje II (4)	Np/Sh	10.05.96	S Col - SE Ridge	NZ	Rob Hall
769	Norbu (Nuru) (4)	Np/Sh	10.05.96	S Col - SE Ridge	NZ	Rob Hall
770	Gau Ming-Ho	Tai	10.05.96	S Col - SE Ridge	Tai	Gau Ming-Ho
771	Nima Gombu (3)	Np/Sh	10.05.96	S Col - SE Ridge	Tai	Gau Ming-Ho
772	Mingma Tshering (2)	Np/Sh	10.05.96	S Col - SE Ridge	Tai	Gau Ming-Ho
773	† Tsewang Smanla	Ind	10.05.96	N Col - NE Ridge	Ind	Mohinder Singh
774	† Tsewang Paljor	Ind	10.05.96	N Col - NE Ridge	Ind	Mohinder Singh
775	† Dorje Morup	Ind	10.05.96	N Col - NE Ridge	Ind	Mohinder Singh
776	Hiroshi Hanada	Jp	11.05.96	N Col - NE Ridge	Jp	Mitsuo Uematsu
777	Eisuke Shigekawa	Jp	11.05.96	N Col - NE Ridge	Jp	Mitsuo Uematsu
778	Pasang Tshering I (3)	Np/Sh	11.05.96	N Col - NE Ridge	Jp	Mitsuo Uematsu
779	Pasang Kami I (3)	Np/Sh	11.05.96	N Col - NE Ridge	Jp	Mitsuo Uematsu
780	Ang Gyalzen II (1)	Np/Sh	11.05.96	N Col - NE Ridge	Jp	Mitsuo Uematsu
781	Mamoru Kikuchi	Jp	13.05.96	N Col - NE Ridge	Jp	Mitsuo Uematsu
782	Hirotaka Sugiyama	Jp	13.05.96	N Col - NE Ridge	Jp	Mitsuo Uematsu
783	Nima Dorje I (6)	Np/Sh	13.05.96	N Col - NE Ridge	Jp	Mitsuo Uematsu
784	Chuwang Nima (3)	Np/Sh	13.05.96	N Col - NE Ridge	Jp	Mitsuo Uematsu
785	Dawa Tshering III (2)	Np/Sh	13.05.96	N Col - NE Ridge	Jp	Mitsuo Uematsu
786	Sange Mudok (2)	Ind/Sh	17.05.96	N Col - NE Ridge	Ind	Mohinder Singh
787	Hira Ram	Ind	17.05.96	N Col - NE Ridge	Ind	Mohinder Singh
788	Tashi Ram	Ind	17.05.96	N Col - NE Ridge	Ind	Mohinder Singh
789	Nadra Ram	Ind	17.05.96	N Col - NE Ridge	Ind	Mohinder Singh
790	Kusang Dorje (2)	Ind/Sh	17.05.96	N Col - NE Ridge	Ind	Mohinder Singh
791	Hirotaka Takeuchi	Jp	17.05.96	S Col - SE Ridge	Jp	Koji Yamazaki
792	Pemba Tshering I	Np/Sh	17.05.96	S Col - SE Ridge	Jp	Koji Yamazaki
793	Na Temba (4)	Np/Sh	17.05.96	S Col - SE Ridge	Jp	Koji Yamazaki
794	Sven Gangdal	Nor	17.05.96	N Col - NE Ridge	int	Jon Gangdal (Nor)
795	Olav Ulvund	Nor	17.05.96	N Col - NE Ridge	int	Jon Gangdal (Nor)
796	Dawa Tashi (5)	Np/Sh	17.05.96	N Col - NE Ridge	int	Jon Gangdal (Nor)
797	Dawa Tshering II (3)	Np/Sh	17.05.96	N Col - NE Ridge	int	Jon Gangdal (Nor)
798	Morten Rostrup	Nor	18.05.96	N Col - NE Ridge	int	Jon Gangdal (Nor)
799	Josef Nezerka	Cz	18.05.96	N Col - NE Ridge	int	Jon Gangdal (Nor)
800	Fausto De Stefani	It	18.05.96	N Col - NE Ridge	int	Jon Gangdal (Nor)
801	Gyalbu (3)	Np/Sh	18.05.96	N Col - NE Ridge	int	Jon Gangdal (Nor)
802	Alan Hinkes	UK	19.05.96	N Col - NE Ridge	int	Simon Lowe
803	Matt Dickinson	UK	19.05.96	N Col - NE Ridge	int	Simon Lowe
804	Mingma Dorje	Np/Sh	19.05.96	N Col - NE Ridge	int	Simon Lowe
805	Lhakpa Gelu (3)	Np/Sh	19.05.96	N Col - NE Ridge	int	Simon Lowe
806	Phur Gyalzen	Np/Sh	19.05.96	N Col - NE Ridge	int	Simon Lowe
807	Peter Kuznetzov	Rus	20.05.96	NNE Couloir	Rus	Sergei Antipine
808	Valeri Kohanov	Rus	20.05.96	NNE Couloir	Rus	Sergei Antipine
809	Grigori Semikolenkov	Rus	20.05.96	NNE Couloir	Rus	Sergei Antipine
810	Koji Yamazaki	Jp	21.05.96	N Col - NE Ridge	Jp	Koji Yamazaki
811	Thierry Renard	Fra	23.05.96	S Col - SE Ridge	Fra	Thierry Renard
812	Babu Chiri (6)	Np/Sh	23.05.96	S Col - SE Ridge	Fra	Thierry Renard
813	Dawa I (1)	Np/Sh	23.05.96	S Col - SE Ridge	Fra	Thierry Renard
814	Ed Viesturs (4) (x)	US	23.05.96	S Col - SE Ridge	int	David Breashears
815	David Breashears (3)	US	23.05.96	S Col - SE Ridge	int	David Breashears
816	Robert Schauer (2)	Au	23.05.96	S Col - SE Ridge	int	David Breashears
817	Jamling Tenzing Norgay	Ind/Sh	23.05.96	S Col - SE Ridge	int	David Breashears
818	Araceli Segarra (f)	Sp	23.05.96	S Col - SE Ridge	int	David Breashears
819	Lhakpa Dorje III (2) (x)	Np/Sh	23.05.96	S Col - SE Ridge	int	David Breashears
820	Dorje III (1)	Np/Sh	23.05.96	S Col - SE Ridge	int	David Breashears
821	Jangbu II (2)	Np/Sh	23.05.96	S Col - SE Ridge	int	David Breashears
822	Muktu Lhakpa	Np/Sh	23.05.96	S Col - SE Ridge	int	David Breashears
823	Thilen	Np/Sh	23.05.96	S Col - SE Ridge	int	David Breashears
824	Göran Kropp (1) (x)	Swe	23.05.96	S Pillar - SE Ridge	Swe	Göran Kropp
825	Ang Rita (10) (x)	Np/Sh	23.05.96	S Pillar - SE Ridge	Swe	Göran Kropp
826	Jesús Martínez (x)	Sp	23.05.96	S Pillar - SE Ridge	Sp	Jose Antonio Martínez
827	Hans Kammerlander (x)	It	24.05.96	N Col - NE Ridge	It	Hans Kammerlander
828	Yuri Contreras (1)	Mex	24.05.96	N Col - NE Ridge	int	Peter Kowalzik
829	Héctor Ponce De León	Mex	24.05.96	N Col - NE Ridge	int	Peter Kowalzik
830	Ian Woodall (1)	UK/SA	25.05.96	S Col - SE Ridge	SA	Ian Woodall
831	Cathy O'Dowd (1) (f)	SA	25.05.96	S Col - SE Ridge	SA	Ian Woodall
832	† Bruce Herrod	UK	25.05.96	S Col - SE Ridge	SA	Ian Woodall
833	Pemba Tenji (1)	Np/Sh	25.05.96	S Col - SE Ridge	SA	Ian Woodall
834	Ang Dorje III	Np/Sh	25.05.96	S Col - SE Ridge	SA	Ian Woodall
835	Lama Jangbu (2)	Np/Sh	25.05.96	S Col - SE Ridge	SA	Ian Woodall
836	Clara Sumarwati (f)	RI	26.09.96	N Col - NE Ridge	RI	Clara Sumarwati (f)
837	Kaji (4)	Np/Sh	26.09.96	N Col - NE Ridge	RI	Clara Sumarwati (f)
838	Gyalzen I (1)	Np/Sh	26.09.96	N Col - NE Ridge	RI	Clara Sumarwati (f)
839	Ang Gyalzen II (2)	Np/Sh	26.09.96	N Col - NE Ridge	RI	Clara Sumarwati (f)
840	Dawa Tshering III (3)	Np/Sh	26.09.96	N Col - NE Ridge	RI	Clara Sumarwati (f)
841	Chuwang Nima (4)	Np/Sh	26.09.96	N Col - NE Ridge	RI	Clara Sumarwati (f)
842	Choi Jong-Tai	SK	11.10.96	S Col - SE Ridge	SK	Lim Hyung-Chil
843	Shin Kwang-Chal	SK	11.10.96	S Col - SE Ridge	SK	Lim Hyung-Chil
844	Panuru (2)	Np/Sh	11.10.96	S Col - SE Ridge	SK	Lim Hyung-Chil
845	Kipa (2)	Np/Sh	11.10.96	S Col - SE Ridge	SK	Lim Hyung-Chil
846	Ang Dawa Tamang (2)	Np	11.10.96	S Col - SE Ridge	SK	Lim Hyung-Chil
847	Apa (8)	Np/Sh	26.04.97	S Col - SE Ridge	RI	Edhie Wibowo
848	Anatoli Boukreev (4)	Kaz	26.04.97	S Col - SE Ridge	RI	Edhie Wibowo
849	Dawa Nuru II (1)	Np/Sh	26.04.97	S Col - SE Ridge	RI	Edhie Wibowo
850	Vladimir Bashkirov (2)	Rus	26.04.97	S Col - SE Ridge	RI	Edhie Wibowo
851	Asmujiono	RI	26.04.97	S Col - SE Ridge	RI	Edhie Wibowo
852	Vladimir Frolov	Kaz	02.05.97	N Col - NE Ridge	Rus/Kaz	Yervand Ilinski
853	Andrei Molotov	Kaz	02.05.97	N Col - NE Ridge	Rus/Kaz	Yervand Ilinski
854	Sergei Ovsharenko	Kaz	02.05.97	N Col - NE Ridge	Rus/Kaz	Yervand Ilinski
855	Vladimir Suviga (x)	Kaz	02.05.97	N Col - NE Ridge	Rus/Kaz	Yervand Ilinski
856	† Ivan Plotnikov	Rus	07.05.97	N Col - NE Ridge	Rus/Kaz	Yervand Ilinski
857	† Nikolai Chevtchenko	Rus	02.05.97	N Col - NE Ridge	Rus/Kaz	Yervand Ilinski
858	Lee In	SK	07.05.97	N Col - NE Ridge	SK	Lee Dong-Yon
859	Ang Dawa Tamang (3)	Np	07.05.97	N Col - NE Ridge	SK	Lee Dong-Yon
860	Antoine de Choudens (x)	Fra	08.05.97	N Col - NE Ridge	Fra/Bul	Antoine de Choudens
861	Stephane Cagnin	Fra	08.05.97	N Col - NE Ridge	Fra/Bul	Antoine de Choudens
862	Konstantin Farafonov	Kaz	20.05.97	N Col - NE Ridge	Rus/Kaz	Yervand Ilinski
863	Sergei Lavrov	Kaz	20.05.97	N Col - NE Ridge	Rus/Kaz	Yervand Ilinski
864	Dmitri Grekov	Kaz	20.05.97	N Col - NE Ridge	Rus/Kaz	Yervand Ilinski
865	Dmitri Sobolev	Kaz	20.05.97	N Col - NE Ridge	Rus/Kaz	Yervand Ilinski
866	Dmitri Mouravev	Kaz	20.05.97	N Col - NE Ridge	Rus/Kaz	Yervand Ilinski
867	Lyudmila Savina (f)	Kaz	20.05.97	N Col - NE Ridge	Rus/Kaz	Yervand Ilinski
868	Doytchin Vassilev	Bul	20.05.97	N Col - NE Ridge	Fra/Bul	Antoine de Choudens
869	Nick Kekus	UK	21.05.97	S Col - SE Ridge	UK/Ice	Jon Tinker
870	Björn Olafsson	Ice	21.05.97	S Col - SE Ridge	UK/Ice	Jon Tinker
871	Hallgrimur Magnusson	Ice	21.05.97	S Col - SE Ridge	UK/Ice	Jon Tinker
872	Einar Stefansson	Ice	21.05.97	S Col - SE Ridge	UK/Ice	Jon Tinker
873	Babu Chiri (7)	Np/Sh	21.05.97	S Col - SE Ridge	UK/Ice	Jon Tinker
874	Dawa I (2)	Np/Sh	21.05.97	S Col - SE Ridge	UK/Ice	Jon Tinker
875	Danuri	Np/Sh	21.05.97	S Col - SE Ridge	Np	Bhakta Bahadur Thakuri
876	Andy Evans	Can	22.05.97	N Col - NE Ridge	Rus/Kaz	Yervand Ilinski
877	Franc Pepevnic	Slo	22.05.97	N Col - NE Ridge	Slo/Cro	Darko Berljak
878	Tashi Tenzing	Aus/Sh	23.05.97	S Col - SE Ridge	int	Guy Cotter
879	Guy Cotter (2)	NZ	23.05.97	S Col - SE Ridge	int	Guy Cotter
880	Ed Viesturs (5)	US	23.05.97	S Col - SE Ridge	int	Guy Cotter
881	David Carter	US	23.05.97	S Col - SE Ridge	int	Guy Cotter
882	Veikka Gustafsson (2) (x)	Fin	23.05.97	S Col - SE Ridge	int	Guy Cotter
883	Ang Dorje II (5)	Np/Sh	23.05.97	S Col - SE Ridge	int	Guy Cotter
884	Mingma Tshering (3)	Np/Sh	23.05.97	S Col - SE Ridge	int	Guy Cotter
885	David Breashears (4)	US	23.05.97	S Col - SE Ridge	US	David Breashears
886	Pete Athans (5)	US	23.05.97	S Col - SE Ridge	US	David Breashears
887	Jangbu II (3)	Np/Sh	23.05.97	S Col - SE Ridge	US	David Breashears
888	Dorje III (2)	Np/Sh	23.05.97	S Col - SE Ridge	US	David Breashears
889	Kami (1)	Np/Sh	23.05.97	S Col - SE Ridge	US	David Breashears
890	Alan Hobson	Can	23.05.97	S Col - SE Ridge	Can/US	Jason Edwards
891	Jamie Clarke	Can	23.05.97	S Col - SE Ridge	Can/US	Jason Edwards
892	Lhakpa Tshering I (2)	Np/Sh	23.05.97	S Col - SE Ridge	Can/US	Jason Edwards
893	Gyalbu (4)	Np/Sh	23.05.97	S Col - SE Ridge	Can/US	Jason Edwards
894	Tashi Tshering (4)	Np/Sh	23.05.97	S Col - SE Ridge	Can/US	Jason Edwards
895	Kami Tshering (2)	Np/Sh	23.05.97	S Col - SE Ridge	Can/US	Jason Edwards

No.	Name	Nat	Date	Route	Exp	Leader
896	Mark Warham	UK	23.05.97	S Col - SE Ridge	UK/Ice	Jon Tinker
897	Lhakpa Gelu (4)	Np/Sh	23.05.97	S Col - SE Ridge	UK/Ice	Jon Tinker
898	Andrés Delgado	Mex	23.05.97	S Col - SE Ridge	int	Mal Duff
899	Tenzing (4)	Np/Sh	23.05.97	S Col - SE Ridge	int	Mal Duff
900	Eric Blakeley	UK	23.05.97	S Col - SE Ridge	UK/Ice	Jon Tinker
901	Mohandas Nagappan	Mal	23.05.97	S Col - SE Ridge	Mal	Nor RamlleSulaiman
902	Magendran Munisamy	Mal	23.05.97	S Col - SE Ridge	Mal	Nor RamlleSulaiman
903	Na Temba (5)	Np/Sh	23.05.97	S Col - SE Ridge	Mal	Nor RamlleSulaiman
904	Dawa Temba (3)	Np/Sh	23.05.97	S Col - SE Ridge	Mal	Nor RamlleSulaiman
905	Gyalzen I (2)	Np/Sh	23.05.97	S Col - SE Ridge	Mal	Nor RamlleSulaiman
906	Ang Phuri Gyalzen	Np/Sh	23.05.97	S Col - SE Ridge	Mal	Nor RamlleSulaiman
907	Fura Dorje (1)	Np/Sh	23.05.97	S Col - SE Ridge	Mal	Nor RamlleSulaiman
908	Dawa Tenzi (1)	Np/Sh	23.05.97	S Col - SE Ridge	UK/Ice	Jon Tinker
909	Pavle Kozjek (x)	Slo	23.05.97	N Col - NE Ridge	Slo/Cro	Darko Berljak
910	Hugo Rodríguez (1)	Mex	23.05.97	S Col - SE Ridge	UK/Ice	Jon Tinker
911	Aleksander Zelinski	Rus	24.05.97	N Col - NE Ridge	Rus	Kazbek Khamitsayev
912	Sergei Sokolov	Rus	24.05.97	N Col - NE Ridge	Rus	Kazbek Khamitsayev
913	Wally Berg (3)	US	25.05.97	S Col - SE Ridge	US/UK	Todd Burleson
914	Ang Pasang I (2)	Np/Sh	25.05.97	S Col - SE Ridge	US/UK	Todd Burleson
915	Pemba Tenji (2)	Np/Sh	25.05.97	S Col - SE Ridge	US/UK	Todd Burleson
916	Mingma Chiri (1)	Np/Sh	25.05.97	S Col - SE Ridge	US/UK	Todd Burleson
917	Nima Tashi (3)	Np/Sh	25.05.97	S Col - SE Ridge	US/UK	Todd Burleson
918	Lhakpa Rita I (4)	Np/Sh	25.05.97	S Col - SE Ridge	US/UK	Todd Burleson
919	Kami Rita I (2)	Np/Sh	25.05.97	S Col - SE Ridge	US/UK	Todd Burleson
920	† Tenzing Nuru (2)	Np/Sh	25.05.97	S Col - SE Ridge	US/UK	Todd Burleson
921	Yuri Contreras (2)	Mex	25.05.97	S Col - SE Ridge	int	Henry Todd
922	Ilgvars Pauls	Lat	27.05.97	S Col - SE Ridge	int	Henry Todd
923	Dawa Sona (1)	Np/Sh	27.05.97	S Col - SE Ridge	int	Henry Todd
924	Brigitte Muir (f)	Aus	27.05.97	S Col - SE Ridge	int	Mal Duff*
925	Kipa (3)	Np/Sh	27.05.97	S Col - SE Ridge	int	Mal Duff
926	Dorje I (6)	Np/Sh	27.05.97	S Col - SE Ridge	int	Mal Duff
927	Russell Brice (1)	NZ	29.05.97	N Col - NE Ridge	NZ	Russell Brice
928	Richard Price	NZ	29.05.97	N Col - NE Ridge	NZ	Russell Brice
929	Daqimi (2)	Tib	29.05.97	N Col - NE Ridge	Tib	Da Chimyi
930	Tenzing Doji	Tib	29.05.97	N Col - NE Ridge	Tib	Da Chimyi
931	Kai Zhong (2)	Tib	29.05.97	N Col - NE Ridge	Tib	Da Chimyi
932	Surendra Chavan	Ind	18.05.98	N Col - NE Ridge	Ind	Hrishikesh Yadav
933	Dawa Tashi (6)	Np/Sh	18.05.98	N Col - NE Ridge	Ind	Hrishikesh Yadav
934	Dawa Nuru II (2)	Np/Sh	18.05.98	N Col - NE Ridge	Ind	Hrishikesh Yadav
935	Thomting (1)	Np/Sh	18.05.98	N Col - NE Ridge	Ind	Hrishikesh Yadav
936	Nawang Tenzing I (1)	Np/Sh	18.05.98	N Col - NE Ridge	Ind	Hrishikesh Yadav
937	Shoji Abe	Jp	18.05.98	N Col - NE Ridge	Jp	Hitoshi Onodera
938	Toshiya Nakajima	Jp	18.05.98	N Col - NE Ridge	Jp	Hitoshi Onodera
939	Pasang Kami I (4)	Np/Sh	18.05.98	N Col - NE Ridge	Jp	Hitoshi Onodera
940	Na Temba (6)	Np/Sh	18.05.98	N Col - NE Ridge	Jp	Hitoshi Onodera
941	Ang Gyalzen II (3)	Np/Sh	18.05.98	N Col - NE Ridge	Jp	Hitoshi Onodera
942	Hidetoshi Kurahashi	Jp	18.05.98	N Col - NE Ridge	Jp	Kazuyoshi Kondo
943	Masaru Sato	Jp	18.05.98	N Col - NE Ridge	Jp	Kazuyoshi Kondo
944	Koichi Nagata	Jp	18.05.98	N Col - NE Ridge	Jp	Kazuyoshi Kondo
945	Hisashi Hashimoto	Jp	18.05.98	N Col - NE Ridge	Jp	Kazuyoshi Kondo
946	Shoji Sakamoto	Jp	18.05.98	N Col - NE Ridge	Jp	Kazuyoshi Kondo
947	Ang Mingma (1)	Np/Sh	18.05.98	N Col - NE Ridge	Jp	Kazuyoshi Kondo
948	Aleksei Bolotov	Rus	18.05.98	N Col - NE Ridge	Rus/Fra	Boris Sedusov
949	Valeri Pershin	Rus	18.05.98	N Col - NE Ridge	Rus/Fra	Boris Sedusov
950	Sergei Timofeev	Rus	18.05.98	N Col - NE Ridge	Rus/Fra	Boris Sedusov
951	Yevgeni Vinogradsky (3)	Rus	18.05.98	N Col - NE Ridge	Rus/Fra	Boris Sedusov
952	Viktor Kulbachenko	By	18.05.98	N Col - NE Ridge	Rus/By	Vladimir Shataev (Rus)
953	Hitoshi Onodera	Jp	19.05.98	N Col - NE Ridge	Jp	Hitoshi Onodera
954	Hiromichi Kamimura	Jp	19.05.98	N Col - NE Ridge	Jp	Hitoshi Onodera
955	Chuwang Nima (5)	Np/Sh	19.05.98	N Col - NE Ridge	Jp	Hitoshi Onodera
956	Dawa Tshering III (4)	Np/Sh	19.05.98	N Col - NE Ridge	Jp	Hitoshi Onodera
957	Loveraj Dharmshaktu	Ind	19.05.98	N Col - NE Ridge	Ind	Hrishikesh Yadav
958	Phinzo Norbu (2)	Np/Sh	19.05.98	N Col - NE Ridge	Ind	Hrishikesh Yadav
959	Nima Gyalzen (1)	Np/Sh	19.05.98	N Col - NE Ridge	Ind	Hrishikesh Yadav
960	Peter Hamor	Slk	19.05.98	N Col - NE Ridge	Slk/Chn	Pavol Lazar, Luo Chen
961	Vladimir Zboja	Slk	19.05.98	N Col - NE Ridge	Slk/Chn	Pavol Lazar, Luo Chen
962	Vladimir Plulik (x)	Slk	19.05.98	N Col - NE Ridge	Slk/Chn	Pavol Lazar, Luo Chen
963	Noriyuki Muraguchi	Jp	19.05.98	N Col - NE Ridge	Jp	Noriyuki Muraguchi
964	Minoru Sawada	Jp	19.05.98	N Col - NE Ridge	Jp	Noriyuki Muraguchi
965	Mingma Tshering (4)	Np/Sh	19.05.98	N Col - NE Ridge	Jp	Noriyuki Muraguchi
966	Tshering Dorje II	Np/Sh	19.05.98	N Col - NE Ridge	Jp	Noriyuki Muraguchi
967	Pasang Kitar (1)	Np/Sh	19.05.98	N Col - NE Ridge	Jp	Noriyuki Muraguchi
968	Radek Jaros (x)	Cz	19.05.98	N Col - NE Ridge	Cz	Zdenek Hruby
969	Vladimir Nosek (x)	Cz	19.05.98	N Col - NE Ridge	Cz	Zdenek Hruby
970	Toshiaki Yano	Jp	20.05.98	N Col - NE Ridge	Jp	Kazuyoshi Kondo
971	Yoshinori Kawahara	Jp	20.05.98	N Col - NE Ridge	Jp	Kazuyoshi Kondo
972	Gyalzen I (3)	Np/Sh	20.05.98	N Col - NE Ridge	Jp	Kazuyoshi Kondo
973	Bob Hoffman	US	20.05.98	S Col - SE Ridge	US	Bob Hoffman
974	Donald Beavon	US	20.05.98	S Col - SE Ridge	US	Bob Hoffman
975	Pasquale Scaturro	US	20.05.98	S Col - SE Ridge	US	Bob Hoffman
976	Charles Demarest	US	20.05.98	S Col - SE Ridge	US	Bob Hoffman
977	Mark Cole	US	20.05.98	S Col - SE Ridge	US	Bob Hoffman
978	Apa (9)	Np/Sh	20.05.98	S Col - SE Ridge	US	Bob Hoffman
979	Pemba Norbu III (1)	Np/Sh	20.05.98	S Col - SE Ridge	US	Bob Hoffman
980	Nima Rita (4)	Np/Sh	20.05.98	S Col - SE Ridge	US	Bob Hoffman
981	Gyalzen II	Np/Sh	20.05.98	S Col - SE Ridge	US	Bob Hoffman
982	Chuldin Nuru	Np/Sh	20.05.98	S Col - SE Ridge	US	Bob Hoffman
983	Ang Pasang III (1)	Np/Sh	20.05.98	S Col - SE Ridge	US	Bob Hoffman
984	Arita (2)	Np/Sh	20.05.98	S Col - SE Ridge	US	Bob Hoffman
985	Jalal Cheshmeh Ghasabani	Irn	20.05.98	S Col - SE Ridge	Irn	Sadegh Aghajani Kalkhran
986	Mohammad Hassan Najarian	Irn	20.05.98	S Col - SE Ridge	Irn	Sadegh Aghajani Kalkhran
987	Hamid Reza Olanj	Irn	20.05.98	S Col - SE Ridge	Irn	Sadegh Aghajani Kalkhran
988	Mohammad Oraz	Irn	20.05.98	S Col - SE Ridge	Irn	Sadegh Aghajani Kalkhran
989	Dawa Tenzi (2)	Np/Sh	20.05.98	S Col - SE Ridge	Irn	Sadegh Aghajani Kalkhran
990	Chuldim	Np/Sh	20.05.98	S Col - SE Ridge	Irn	Sadegh Aghajani Kalkhran
991	Pemba Rinzi (1)	Np/Sh	20.05.98	S Col - SE Ridge	Irn	Sadegh Aghajani Kalkhran
992	Jeffrey Rhoads (1)	US	20.05.98	S Col - SE Ridge	US	Tom Whittaker
993	Tashi Tshering (5)	Np/Sh	20.05.98	S Col - SE Ridge	US	Tom Whittaker
994	Wally Berg (4)	US	20.05.98	S Col - SE Ridge	US	Wally Berg
995	Anatoli Moshnikov (2)	Rus	21.05.98	N Col - NE Ridge	Rus/Fra	Boris Sedusov
996	Gilles Roman	Fra	21.05.98	N Col - NE Ridge	Rus/Fra	Boris Sedusov
997	Kazuyoshi Kondo	Jp	22.05.98	N Col - NE Ridge	Jp	Kazuyoshi Kondo
998	Dawa II	Np/Sh	22.05.98	N Col - NE Ridge	Jp	Kazuyoshi Kondo
999	† Francys Arsentiev (f) (x)	US	22.05.98	N Col - NE Ridge	Rus/Fra	Boris Sedusov
1000	† Sergei Arsentiev (2) (x)	Rus	22.05.98	N Col - NE Ridge	Rus/Fra	Boris Sedusov
1001	Rustam Radjapov	Uzb	22.05.98	N Col - NE Ridge	Uzb	Anatoly Shabanov
1002	Svetlana Baskakova (f)	Uzb	23.05.98	N Col - NE Ridge	Uzb	Anatoly Shabanov
1003	Sergei Sokolov	Uzb	23.05.98	N Col - NE Ridge	Uzb	Anatoly Shabanov
1004	Marat Usaev	Uzb	23.05.98	N Col - NE Ridge	Uzb	Anatoly Shabanov
1005	Oleg Grigoriev	Uzb	23.05.98	N Col - NE Ridge	Uzb	Anatoly Shabanov
1006	Andrei Fedorov	Uzb	23.05.98	N Col - NE Ridge	Uzb	Anatoly Shabanov
1007	Aleksei Dukukin	Uzb	24.05.98	N Col - NE Ridge	Uzb	Anatoly Shabanov
1008	Ilyas Tukhvatullin	Uzb	24.05.98	N Col - NE Ridge	Uzb	Anatoly Shabanov
1009	Andrei Zaikin	Uzb	24.05.98	N Col - NE Ridge	Uzb	Anatoly Shabanov
1010	Khaniv Balmagambetov	Uzb	24.05.98	N Col - NE Ridge	Uzb	Anatoly Shabanov
1011	Roman Mats	Uzb	24.05.98	N Col - NE Ridge	Uzb	Anatoly Shabanov
1012	Lama Jangbu (3)	Np/Sh	24.05.98	N Col - NE Ridge	SA	Ian Woodall
1013	Lhakpa Gelu (5)	Np/Sh	24.05.98	N Col - NE Ridge	SA	Ian Woodall
1014	Luo Ci	Tib	24.05.98	N Col - NE Ridge	Slk/Chn	Pavol Lazar, Luo Chen
1015	Bernardo Guarachi	Bol	25.05.98	S Col - SE Ridge	Bol	Bernardo Guarachi
1016	Siew Cheok-Wai	Mal	25.05.98	S Col - SE Ridge	Sin/Mal	David Lim
1017	Khoo Swee-Chiow	Mal	25.05.98	S Col - SE Ridge	Sin/Mal	David Lim
1018	Kami Rita I (3)	Np/Sh	25.05.98	S Col - SE Ridge	Sin/Mal	David Lim
1019	Dorje III (3)	Np/Sh	25.05.98	S Col - SE Ridge	Sin/Mal	David Lim
1020	Fura Dorje (2)	Np/Sh	25.05.98	S Col - SE Ridge	Sin/Mal	David Lim
1021	Nawang Phurba	Np/Sh	25.05.98	S Col - SE Ridge	Sin/Mal	David Lim
1022	Sundeep Dhillon	UK	25.05.98	S Col - SE Ridge	int	David Walsh
1023	David Walsh	UK	25.05.98	S Col - SE Ridge	int	David Walsh
1024	Nima Gombu (4)	Np/Sh	25.05.98	S Col - SE Ridge	int	David Walsh
1025	Kusang Dorje (3)	Ind/Sh	25.05.98	S Col - SE Ridge	int	David Walsh

Mal Duff still shown as leader following his death

No.	Name	Nat	Date	Route	Exp	Leader
1026	Nima Dorje II (1)	Np/Sh	25.05.98	S Col - SE Ridge	int	David Walsh
1027	Russell Brice (2)	NZ	25.05.98	N Col - NE Ridge	NZ/Jp	Russell Brice
1028	Sumiyo Tsuzuki (f)	Jp	25.05.98	N Col - NE Ridge	NZ/Jp	Russell Brice
1029	Karsang (2)	Np/Sh	25.05.98	N Col - NE Ridge	NZ/Jp	Russell Brice
1030	† Mark Jennings	UK	25.05.98	N Col - NE Ridge	UK	Mark Jennings
1031	Nima Wangchu (1)	Np/Sh	25.05.98	N Col - NE Ridge	UK	Mark Jennings
1032	Craig John	US	25.05.98	N Col - NE Ridge	US	David Hahn
1033	Dawa Nuru III	Np/Sh	25.05.98	N Col - NE Ridge	US	David Hahn
1034	Lhakpa Rita II	Np/Sh	25.05.98	N Col - NE Ridge	US	David Hahn
1035	Alan Silva	Aus	26.05.98	S Col - SE Ridge	int	Henry Todd
1036	Neil Laughton	UK	26.05.98	S Col - SE Ridge	int	Henry Todd
1037	Bear Grylls	UK	26.05.98	S Col - SE Ridge	int	Henry Todd
1038	Pasang Dawa (1)	Np/Sh	26.05.98	S Col - SE Ridge	int	Henry Todd
1039	Pasang Tshering II (1)	Np/Sh	26.05.98	S Col - SE Ridge	int	Henry Todd
1040	Heinz Rockenbauer	Au	26.05.98	N Col - NE Ridge	Ger/Au	Heinz Rockenbauer
1041	Jeffrey Rhoads (2)	US	27.05.98	S Col - SE Ridge	US	Tom Whittaker
1042	Tashi Tshering (6)	Np/Sh	27.05.98	S Col - SE Ridge	US	Tom Whittaker
1043	Tom Whittaker	US	27.05.98	S Col - SE Ridge	US	Tom Whittaker
1044	Norbu (Nuru) (5)	Np/Sh	27.05.98	S Col - SE Ridge	US	Tom Whittaker
1045	Lhakpa Tshering I (3)	Np/Sh	27.05.98	S Col - SE Ridge	US	Tom Whittaker
1046	Dawa Sona (2)	Np/Sh	27.05.98	S Col - SE Ridge	US	Tom Whittaker
1047	Richard Alpert	US	27.05.98	N Col - NE Ridge	US	David Hahn
1048	Bob Sloezen (3)	US	27.05.98	N Col - NE Ridge	US	David Hahn
1049	Panuru (3)	Np/Sh	27.05.98	N Col - NE Ridge	US	David Hahn
1050	Carlos Pitarch	Sp	15.10.98	S Col - SE Ridge	Sp	Carlos Pitarch
1051	Kaji (5)	Np/Sh	17.10.98	S Col - SE Ridge	Sp	Carlos Pitarch
1052	Tashi Tshering (7)	Np/Sh	17.10.98	S Col - SE Ridge	Sp	Carlos Pitarch
1053	Pete Athans (6)	US	05.05.99	S Col - SE Ridge	US/UK	Pete Athans
1054	William Crouse	US	05.05.99	S Col - SE Ridge	US/UK	Pete Athans
1055	Chuwang Nima (6)	Np/Sh	05.05.99	S Col - SE Ridge	US/UK	Pete Athans
1056	Phu Tashi (1)	Np/Sh	05.05.99	S Col - SE Ridge	US/UK	Pete Athans
1057	Dorje I (7)	Np/Sh	05.05.99	S Col - SE Ridge	US/UK	Pete Athans
1058	Gyalzen I (4)	Np/Sh	05.05.99	S Col - SE Ridge	US/UK	Pete Athans
1059	Na Temba (7)	Np/Sh	05.05.99	S Col - SE Ridge	US/UK	Pete Athans
1060	Graham Ratcliffe (2)	UK	05.05.99	S Col - SE Ridge	int	Henry Todd
1061	Ray Brown	Aus	05.05.99	S Col - SE Ridge	int	Henry Todd
1062	Elsa Avila (f)	Mex	05.05.99	S Col - SE Ridge	int	Henry Todd
1063	Andrew Lapkass (2)	US	05.05.99	S Col - SE Ridge	int	Henry Todd
1064	Pasang Tshering II (2)	Np/Sh	05.05.99	S Col - SE Ridge	int	Henry Todd
1065	Renata Chlumska (f)	Swe	05.05.99	S Col - SE Ridge	Swe	Göran Kropp
1066	Göran Kropp (2)	Swe	05.05.99	S Col - SE Ridge	Swe	Göran Kropp
1067	Mingma Tshering (5)	Np/Sh	05.05.99	S Col - SE Ridge	Swe	Göran Kropp
1068	Kami (2)	Np/Sh	05.05.99	S Col - SE Ridge	Swe	Göran Kropp
1069	Ang Chiri	Np/Sh	05.05.99	S Col - SE Ridge	Swe	Göran Kropp
1070	Bernard Voyer	Can	05.05.99	S Col - SE Ridge	Can	Bernard Voyer
1071	Dorje III (4)	Np/Sh	05.05.99	S Col - SE Ridge	Can	Bernard Voyer
1072	Chhongra Nuru	Np/Sh	05.05.99	S Col - SE Ridge	Can	Bernard Voyer
1073	Babu Chiri (8) (x)	Np/Sh	06.05.99	S Col - SE Ridge	Swe	Thomas & Tina Sjögren
1074	Dawa I (3)	Np/Sh	06.05.99	S Col - SE Ridge	Swe	Thomas & Tina Sjögren
1075	Nima Dorje II (2)	Np/Sh	06.05.99	S Col - SE Ridge	Swe	Thomas & Tina Sjögren
1076	† Vasili Kopytko (x)	Ukr	08.05.99	N Col - NE Ridge	Ukr	Mstislav Gorbenko
1077	Vladislav Terzeoul (x)	Ukr	08.05.99	N Col - NE Ridge	Ukr	Mstislav Gorbenko
1078	Vladimir Gorbach (x)	Ukr	08.05.99	N Col - NE Ridge	Ukr	Mstislav Gorbenko
1079	Guillermo Benegas	Arg	12.05.99	S Col - SE Ridge	int	Jon Tinker, Nick Kekus
1080	Joby Ogwyn	US	12.05.99	S Col - SE Ridge	int	David Hamilton
1081	Tenzing (5)	Np/Sh	12.05.99	S Col - SE Ridge	int	David Hamilton
1082	Nima Gombu (5)	Np/Sh	12.05.99	S Col - SE Ridge	int	David Hamilton
1083	Lev Sarkisov	Geo	12.05.99	S Col - SE Ridge	Geo/Aze	Benedict Kashakashvili
1084	Afi Gigani	Geo	12.05.99	S Col - SE Ridge	Geo/Aze	Benedict Kashakashvili
1085	Bidzina Gujabidze	Geo	12.05.99	S Col - SE Ridge	Geo/Aze	Benedict Kashakashvili
1086	Benedict Kashakashvili	Geo	12.05.99	S Col - SE Ridge	Geo/Aze	Benedict Kashakashvili
1087	Chewang Dorje (1)	Np/Sh	12.05.99	S Col - SE Ridge	Geo/Aze	Benedict Kashakashvili
1088	Nawang Tenzing II	Np/Sh	12.05.99	S Col - SE Ridge	Geo/Aze	Benedict Kashakashvili
1089	Michael Trueman	UK	13.05.99	S Col - SE Ridge	int	Henry Todd
1090	Pasang Dawa (2)	Np/Sh	13.05.99	S Col - SE Ridge	int	Henry Todd
1091	Augusto Ortega (2)	Per	13.05.99	S Col - SE Ridge	int	Jon Tinker, Nick Kekus
1092	Constantine Niarchos	Swi	13.05.99	S Col - SE Ridge	int	Jon Tinker, Nick Kekus
1093	David Rodney	Can	13.05.99	S Col - SE Ridge	int	Jon Tinker, Nick Kekus
1094	Katja Staartjes (f)	NL	13.05.99	S Col - SE Ridge	int	Jon Tinker, Nick Kekus
1095	Chris Brown	UK	13.05.99	S Col - SE Ridge	int	Jon Tinker, Nick Kekus
1096	Martin Doyle	UK	13.05.99	S Col - SE Ridge	int	Jon Tinker, Nick Kekus
1097	Mike Smith (2)	UK	13.05.99	S Col - SE Ridge	int	Jon Tinker, Nick Kekus
1098	† Michael Matthews	UK	13.05.99	S Col - SE Ridge	int	Jon Tinker, Nick Kekus
1099	Lhakpa Gelu (6)	Np/Sh	13.05.99	S Col - SE Ridge	int	Jon Tinker, Nick Kekus
1100	Nima Gyalzen (2)	Np/Sh	13.05.99	S Col - SE Ridge	int	Jon Tinker, Nick Kekus
1101	Kami Rita I (4)	Np/Sh	13.05.99	S Col - SE Ridge	int	Jon Tinker, Nick Kekus
1102	Pasang Kitar (2)	Np/Sh	13.05.99	S Col - SE Ridge	int	Jon Tinker, Nick Kekus
1103	Tshering Dorje I (2)	Np/Sh	13.05.99	S Col - SE Ridge	int	Jon Tinker, Nick Kekus
1104	Pemba Rinzi (2)	Np/Sh	13.05.99	S Col - SE Ridge	int	Jon Tinker, Nick Kekus
1105	Dawa Nurbu (1)	Np/Sh	13.05.99	S Col - SE Ridge	int	Jon Tinker, Nick Kekus
1106	Ken Noguchi	Jp	13.05.99	S Col - SE Ridge	Jp	Ken Noguchi
1107	Dawa Tshering III (5)	Np/Sh	13.05.99	S Col - SE Ridge	Jp	Ken Noguchi
1108	Nima Wangchu (2)	Np/Sh	13.05.99	S Col - SE Ridge	Jp	Ken Noguchi
1109	Nawang Wangchu (1)	Np/Sh	13.05.99	S Col - SE Ridge	Jp	Ken Noguchi
1110	Krishna Bahadur Tamang	Np	13.05.99	S Col - SE Ridge	Jp	Ken Noguchi
1111	Conrad Anker	US	17.05.99	N Col - NE Ridge	int	Eric Simonson
1112	Dave Hahn (2)	US	17.05.99	N Col - NE Ridge	int	Eric Simonson
1113	Charles Corfield	UK	18.05.99	S Col - SE Ridge	US/UK	Pete Athans
1114	Chuwang Nima (7)	Np/Sh	18.05.99	S Col - SE Ridge	US/UK	Pete Athans
1115	Nima Tashi (4)	Np/Sh	18.05.99	S Col - SE Ridge	US/UK	Pete Athans
1116	Dawa Sona (3)	Np/Sh	18.05.99	S Col - SE Ridge	US/UK	Pete Athans
1117	Jacek Maselko	Pol	18.05.99	N Col - NE Ridge	int	Ryszard Pawlowski (Pol)
1118	† Tadeusz Kudelski	Pol	18.05.99	N Col - NE Ridge	int	Ryszard Pawlowski (Pol)
1119	Ryszard Pawlowski (3)	Pol	18.05.99	N Col - NE Ridge	int	Ryszard Pawlowski (Pol)
1120	Joao Garcia (x)	Por	18.05.99	N Col - NE Ridge	int	Pascal Debrouwer (Bel)
1121	† Pascal Debrouwer	Bel	18.05.99	N Col - NE Ridge	int	Pascal Debrouwer (Bel)
1122	Thomas Sjögren	Swe	26.05.99	S Col - SE Ridge	Swe	Thomas & Tina Sjögren
1123	Tina Sjögren (f)	Swe	26.05.99	S Col - SE Ridge	Swe	Thomas & Tina Sjögren
1124	Babu Chiri (9) (x)	Np/Sh	26.05.99	S Col - SE Ridge	Swe	Thomas & Tina Sjögren
1125	Dawa I (4)	Np/Sh	26.05.99	S Col - SE Ridge	Swe	Thomas & Tina Sjögren
1126	Nima Dorje II (3)	Np/Sh	26.05.99	S Col - SE Ridge	Swe	Thomas & Tina Sjögren
1127	Dawa Temba (4)	Np/Sh	26.05.99	S Col - SE Ridge	Swe	Thomas & Tina Sjögren
1128	Carlos Guevara	Mex	26.05.99	S Col - SE Ridge	Mex	Hugo Rodríguez
1129	Hugo Rodríguez (2)	Mex	26.05.99	S Col - SE Ridge	Mex	Hugo Rodríguez
1130	Lhakpa Nuru II	Np/Sh	26.05.99	S Col - SE Ridge	Mex	Hugo Rodríguez
1131	Mingma Chiri (2)	Np/Sh	26.05.99	S Col - SE Ridge	Mex	Hugo Rodríguez
1132	Pemba	Np/Sh	26.05.99	S Col - SE Ridge	Mex	Hugo Rodríguez
1133	Apa (10)	Np/Sh	26.05.99	N Col - NE Ridge	US	Gheorghe Dijmarescu
1134	Nanda Dorje	Np/Sh	26.05.99	N Col - NE Ridge	US	Fred Barth
1135	Andrei Lushnikov	Rus	26.05.99	N Col - NE Ridge	Rus/Bul	Viatsheslav Skripko
1136	Gheorghe Dijmarescu (1)	US	26.05.99	N Col - NE Ridge	US	Gheorghe Dijmarescu
1137	Fred Barth	US	26.05.99	N Col - NE Ridge	US	Fred Barth
1138	Merab Khabazi	Geo	26.05.99	N Col - NE Ridge	Geo	Gia Tortladze
1139	Irakli Ugulava	Geo	26.05.99	N Col - NE Ridge	Geo	Gia Tortladze
1140	Mamuka Tsikhiseli	Geo	26.05.99	N Col - NE Ridge	Geo	Gia Tortladze
1141	Man Bahadur Tamang (3)	Np	26.05.99	N Col - NE Ridge	Geo	Gia Tortladze
1142	Sergio Martini	It	26.05.99	N Col - NE Ridge	int	Sergio Martini (It)
1143	María-Jesús Lago (f)	Sp	26.05.99	N Col - NE Ridge	int	Sergio Martini (It)
1144	Samdu	Np/Sh	26.05.99	N Col - NE Ridge	int	Sergio Martini (It)
1145	Geoffrey Robb	Aus	27.05.99	N Col - NE Ridge	int	Russell Brice
1146	Helga Hengge (f)	Ger	27.05.99	N Col - NE Ridge	int	Russell Brice
1147	Kazuhiko Kozuka	Jp	27.05.99	N Col - NE Ridge	int	Russell Brice
1148	Karsang (3)	Np/Sh	27.05.99	N Col - NE Ridge	int	Russell Brice
1149	Lobsang Temba (2)	Np/Sh	27.05.99	N Col - NE Ridge	int	Russell Brice
1150	Phurba Tashi	Np/Sh	27.05.99	N Col - NE Ridge	int	Russell Brice
1151	Iván Vallejo (x)	Ecu	27.05.99	N Col - NE Ridge	int	Iván Loredo (Mex)
1152	Heber Orona (x)	Arg	27.05.99	N Col - NE Ridge	int	Iván Loredo (Mex)
1153	Karla Wheelock (f)	Mex	27.05.99	N Col - NE Ridge	int	Iván Loredo (Mex)
1154	Fura Dorje (3)	Np/Sh	27.05.99	N Col - NE Ridge	int	Iván Loredo (Mex)
1155	Ari Piela	Fin	28.05.99	N Col - NE Ridge	int	Iván Loredo (Mex)

No.	Name	Nat	Date	Route	Exp	Leader
1156	Antti Maniken	Fin	28.05.99	N Col - NE Ridge	int	Iván Loredo (Mex)
1157	Jiabu (2)	Tib	28.05.99	N Col - NE Ridge	Tib	Samdrub
1158	Luoze (2)	Tib	28.05.99	N Col - NE Ridge	Tib	Samdrub
1159	Bianba Zaxi	Tib	28.05.99	N Col - NE Ridge	Tib	Samdrub
1160	Rena (2)	Tib	28.05.99	N Col - NE Ridge	Tib	Samdrub
1161	Akbu	Tib	28.05.99	N Col - NE Ridge	Tib	Samdrub
1162	Kui Sang (2) (f)	Tib	28.05.99	N Col - NE Ridge	Tib	Samdrub
1163	Jiji (f)	Tib	28.05.99	N Col - NE Ridge	Tib	Samdrub
1164	Cering Doje (2)	Tib	28.05.99	N Col - NE Ridge	Tib	Samdrub
1165	La Ba	Tib	28.05.99	N Col - NE Ridge	Tib	Samdrub
1166	Zaxi Cering	Tib	28.05.99	N Col - NE Ridge	Tib	Samdrub
1167	Amar Prakash	Ind	28.05.99	E Face - S Col - SE Ridge	Ind	Santosh Yadav (f)
1168	Kusang Dorje (4)	Ind/Sh	28.05.99	E Face - S Col - SE Ridge	Ind	Santosh Yadav (f)
1169	Sange Mudok (3)	Ind/Sh	28.05.99	E Face - S Col - SE Ridge	Ind	Santosh Yadav (f)
1170	Cathy O'Dowd (2) (f)	SA	29.05.99	N Col - NE Ridge	SA	Ian Woodall
1171	Ian Woodall (2)	UK/SA	29.05.99	N Col - NE Ridge	SA	Ian Woodall
1172	Lama Jangbu (4)	Np/Sh	29.05.99	N Col - NE Ridge	SA	Ian Woodall
1173	Pemba Tenji (3)	Np/Sh	29.05.99	N Col - NE Ridge	SA	Ian Woodall
1174	Ivan Aristov	Rus	15.05.00	N Col - NE Ridge	Rus	Ivan Aristov
1175	Nikolai Kadoshnikov	Rus	15.05.00	N Col - NE Ridge	Rus	Ivan Aristov
1176	Aleksander Fukolov	Rus	15.05.00	N Col - NE Ridge	Rus	Ivan Aristov
1177	Andrei Alexandrov	Rus	15.05.00	N Col - NE Ridge	Rus	Ivan Aristov
1178	Jordi Bayona	Sp	16.05.00	S Col - SE Ridge	Sp	Antoni Bahi
1179	Joan Belmonte	Sp	16.05.00	S Col - SE Ridge	Sp	Antoni Bahi
1180	Thomting (2)	Np/Sh	16.05.00	S Col - SE Ridge	Sp	Antoni Bahi
1181	Nima Nuru	Np/Sh	16.05.00	S Col - SE Ridge	Sp	Antoni Bahi
1182	Mo Sang-Hyun	SK	16.05.00	S Col - SE Ridge	SK	Son Joong-Ho
1183	Park Heon-Ju	SK	16.05.00	S Col - SE Ridge	SK	Son Joong-Ho
1184	John Barry	UK	16.05.00	S Col - SE Ridge	UK	Gavin Bate
1185	Andrew Salter	UK	16.05.00	S Col - SE Ridge	UK	Gavin Bate
1186	Polly Murray (f)	UK	16.05.00	S Col - SE Ridge	UK	Gavin Bate
1187	Lama Jangbu (5)	Np/Sh	16.05.00	S Col - SE Ridge	UK	Gavin Bate
1188	Pemba Gyalzen I	Np/Sh	16.05.00	S Col - SE Ridge	UK	Gavin Bate
1189	Sergei Bershov (2)	Ukr	17.05.00	N Col - NE Ridge	Rus	Ivan Aristov
1190	Andrei Iakimov	Rus	17.05.00	N Col - NE Ridge	Rus	Ivan Aristov
1191	Oleg Kravchenko	Rus	17.05.00	N Col - NE Ridge	Rus	Ivan Aristov
1192	Vladimir Nedelkin	Rus	17.05.00	N Col - NE Ridge	Rus	Ivan Aristov
1193	Karl Kobler	Swi	17.05.00	N Col - NE Ridge	int	Karl Kobler
1194	Josef Hurschler	Swi	17.05.00	N Col - NE Ridge	int	Karl Kobler
1195	Nawang Thile (3)	Np/Sh	17.05.00	N Col - NE Ridge	int	Karl Kobler
1196	Koichi Ezaki	Jp	17.05.00	N Col - NE Ridge	Jp	Koichi Ezaki
1197	Hiroshi Kudo	Jp	17.05.00	N Col - NE Ridge	Jp	Koichi Ezaki
1198	Ruchia Takahashi (f)	Jp	17.05.00	N Col - NE Ridge	Jp	Koichi Ezaki
1199	Phinzo II	Np/Sh	17.05.00	N Col - NE Ridge	Jp	Koichi Ezaki
1200	Palden Namgye	Np/Sh	17.05.00	N Col - NE Ridge	Jp	Koichi Ezaki
1201	Ben Webster	Can	17.05.00	S Col - SE Ridge	Can	Ben Webster
1202	Nazir Sabir	Pak	17.05.00	S Col - SE Ridge	int	Christine Boskoff (f)
1203	Dorje I (8)	Np/Sh	17.05.00	S Col - SE Ridge	int	Christine Boskoff (f)
1204	Dawa Nurbu (2)	Np/Sh	17.05.00	S Col - SE Ridge	int	Christine Boskoff (f)
1205	Dorje III (5)	Np/Sh	17.05.00	S Col - SE Ridge	int	Christine Boskoff (f)
1206	Lhakpa Gelu (7)	Np/Sh	17.05.00	S Col - SE Ridge	int	Christine Boskoff (f)
1207	Frits Vrijlandt	NL	17.05.00	N Col - NE Ridge	int	David Allason-Pritt
1208	Paul Walters	UK	17.05.00	N Col - NE Ridge	int	David Allason-Pritt
1209	Nobuo Matsumoto	Jp	17.05.00	N Col - NE Ridge	Jp/Aus	Tosio Nakamura
1210	Roman Rosenbaum	Aus	17.05.00	N Col - NE Ridge	Jp/Aus	Tosio Nakamura
1211	Mingma Tshering (6)	Np/Sh	17.05.00	N Col - NE Ridge	Jp/Aus	Tosio Nakamura
1212	Pemba Gyalzen II	Np/Sh	17.05.00	N Col - NE Ridge	Jp/Aus	Tosio Nakamura
1213	Akinori Hosaka	Jp	17.05.00	N Col - NE Ridge	Jp	Hiroshi Yashima
1214	Takashi Kodama	Jp	17.05.00	N Col - NE Ridge	Jp	Hiroshi Yashima
1215	Hiroshi Yashima	Jp	17.05.00	N Col - NE Ridge	Jp	Hiroshi Yashima
1216	Nima Gyalzen (3)	Np/Sh	17.05.00	N Col - NE Ridge	Jp	Hiroshi Yashima
1217	Pemba Dorje II	Np/Sh	17.05.00	N Col - NE Ridge	Jp	Hiroshi Yashima
1218	Yuji Ogio	Jp	18.05.00	N Col - NE Ridge	Jp/Aus	Tosio Nakamura
1219	Tenzing (6)	Np/Sh	18.05.00	N Col - NE Ridge	Jp/Aus	Tosio Nakamura
1220	Norbu (Nuru) (6)	Np/Sh	18.05.00	N Col - NE Ridge	Jp/Aus	Tosio Nakamura
1221	Lhakpa (f)	Np/Sh	18.05.00	S Col - SE Ridge	Np	Lhakpa (f)
1222	Ang Pasang III (2)	Np/Sh	18.05.00	S Col - SE Ridge	Np	Lhakpa (f)
1223	Ang Mingma (2)	Np/Sh	18.05.00	S Col - SE Ridge	Np	Lhakpa (f)
1224	Ang Phurba IV	Np/Sh	18.05.00	S Col - SE Ridge	Np	Lhakpa (f)
1225	Mark James	UK	18.05.00	N Col - NE Ridge	UK	Ian Anderson
1226	Dan White	UK	18.05.00	N Col - NE Ridge	UK	Ian Anderson
1227	Na Temba (8)	Np/Sh	18.05.00	N Col - NE Ridge	UK	Ian Anderson
1228	Nikolai Zakharov	Rus	19.05.00	N Col - NE Ridge	Rus	Ivan Aristov
1229	Boris Sedusov	Rus	19.05.00	N Col - NE Ridge	Rus	Ivan Aristov
1230	Aleksei Bokov	Ukr	19.05.00	N Col - NE Ridge	Rus	Ivan Aristov
1231	Oleg Afanassiev	Rus	19.05.00	N Col - NE Ridge	Rus	Ivan Aristov
1232	Bernhard Fahrner	Swi	19.05.00	N Col - NE Ridge	int	Karl Kobler
1233	Pemba Doma (f)	Np/Sh	19.05.00	N Col - NE Ridge	int	Karl Kobler
1234	Toshio Yamamoto	Jp	19.05.00	N Col - NE Ridge	Jp/Aus	Tosio Nakamura
1235	Pasang Kitar (3)	Np/Sh	19.05.00	N Col - NE Ridge	Jp/Aus	Tosio Nakamura
1236	Nawang Dorje (2)	Np/Sh	19.05.00	N Col - NE Ridge	Jp/Aus	Tosio Nakamura
1237	Juichi Kobayashi	Jp	19.05.00	N Col - NE Ridge	Jp	Hiroshi Yashima
1238	Kazuya Konno	Jp	19.05.00	N Col - NE Ridge	Jp	Hiroshi Yashima
1239	Toshio Tanaka	Jp	19.05.00	N Col - NE Ridge	Jp	Hiroshi Yashima
1240	Tateo Yamashita	Jp	19.05.00	N Col - NE Ridge	Jp	Hiroshi Yashima
1241	Nawang Tenzing I (2)	Np/Sh	19.05.00	N Col - NE Ridge	Jp	Hiroshi Yashima
1242	Gyalu Lama	Np/Sh	19.05.00	N Col - NE Ridge	Jp	Hiroshi Yashima
1243	Pasang Kami II	Np/Sh	19.05.00	N Col - NE Ridge	Jp	Hiroshi Yashima
1244	Gheorghe Dijmarescu (2) (x)	US	19.05.00	N Col - NE Ridge	US	Gheorghe Dijmarescu
1245	Mads Granlien	Den	20.05.00	S Pillar - SE Ridge	Den	Henrik Hansen
1246	Asmus Norreslet	Den	20.05.00	S Pillar - SE Ridge	Den	Henrik Hansen
1247	Dawa Chiri	Np/Sh	20.05.00	S Pillar - SE Ridge	Den	Henrik Hansen
1248	Dawa Temba (5)	Np/Sh	20.05.00	S Pillar - SE Ridge	Den	Henrik Hansen
1249	Nima Dawa	Np/Sh	21.05.00	S Pillar - SE Ridge	Den	Henrik Hansen
1250	Babu Chiri (10)	Np/Sh	21.05.00	S Col - SE Ridge	Np	Babu Chiri
1251	Dawa I (5)	Np/Sh	21.05.00	S Col - SE Ridge	Np	Babu Chiri
1252	Byron Smith	Can	21.05.00	S Col - SE Ridge	Can	Byron Smith
1253	Lhakpa Tshering II	Np/Sh	21.05.00	S Col - SE Ridge	Can	Byron Smith
1254	Ang Dorje II (6)	Np/Sh	21.05.00	S Col - SE Ridge	Can	Byron Smith
1255	Mingma Tenzing	Np/Sh	21.05.00	S Col - SE Ridge	Can	Byron Smith
1256	Mingma	Np/Sh	21.05.00	S Col - SE Ridge	Can	Byron Smith
1257	Tenzing Dorje	Np/Sh	21.05.00	S Col - SE Ridge	Can	Byron Smith
1258	Nuru Wangchu	Np/Sh	21.05.00	S Col - SE Ridge	Can	Byron Smith
1259	Karchen Dawa	Np/Sh	21.05.00	S Col - SE Ridge	Can	Byron Smith
1260	† Yan Gen-hua	Chn	21.05.00	N Col - NE Ridge	Chn	Yan Gen-hua
1261	Lhakpa Tshering I (4)	Np/Sh	21.05.00	N Col - NE Ridge	Chn	Yan Gen-hua
1262	Dave Hahn (3)	US	22.05.00	S Col - SE Ridge	US	Robert Link
1263	Charles Brown	US	22.05.00	S Col - SE Ridge	US	Robert Link
1264	Kami Tshering (3)	Np/Sh	22.05.00	S Col - SE Ridge	US	Robert Link
1265	Tashi Tshering (8)	Np/Sh	22.05.00	S Col - SE Ridge	US	Robert Link
1266	Phu Tashi (2)	Np/Sh	22.05.00	S Col - SE Ridge	US	Robert Link
1267	Juan José Garra	Sp	22.05.00	S Col - SE Ridge	Sp	Manuel González
1268	Manuel González	Sp	22.05.00	S Col - SE Ridge	Sp	Manuel González
1269	Iván Jara	Sp	22.05.00	S Col - SE Ridge	Sp	Manuel González
1270	Anna Czerwinska (f)	Pol	22.05.00	S Col - SE Ridge	Pol	Anna Czerwinska (f)
1271	Pasang Tshering III	Np/Sh	22.05.00	S Col - SE Ridge	Pol	Anna Czerwinska (f)
1272	Saeed Toossi	US	22.05.00	S Col - SE Ridge	US	Saeed Toossi
1273	Chewang Dorje (2)	Np/Sh	22.05.00	S Col - SE Ridge	US	Saeed Toossi
1274	Chuwang Nima (8)	Np/Sh	23.05.00	S Col - SE Ridge	US/Can	Vernon Tejas
1275	Mingma Chiri	Np/Sh	23.05.00	S Col - SE Ridge	US/Can	Vernon Tejas
1276	Kami Rita I (5)	Np/Sh	23.05.00	S Col - SE Ridge	US/Can	Vernon Tejas
1277	Christine Boskoff (f)	US	24.05.00	S Col - SE Ridge	int	Christine Boskoff (f)
1278	Nawang Wangchu (2)	Np/Sh	24.05.00	S Col - SE Ridge	int	Christine Boskoff (f)
1279	Apa (11)	Np/Sh	24.05.00	S Col - SE Ridge	US	Bob Hoffman
1280	Lhakpa Tshering III	Np/Sh	24.05.00	S Col - SE Ridge	US	Bob Hoffman
1281	Kami Rita II	Np/Sh	24.05.00	S Col - SE Ridge	US	Bob Hoffman
1282	Lily Leonard (f)	US	24.05.00	S Col - SE Ridge	US	Bob Hoffman
1283	Pemba Tshering II	Np/Sh	24.05.00	S Col - SE Ridge	US	Bob Hoffman
1284	Pemba Chuti	Np/Sh	24.05.00	S Col - SE Ridge	US	Bob Hoffman
1285	James Williams	US	24.05.00	S Col - SE Ridge	US	Bob Hoffman

No.	Name	Nat	Date	Route	Exp	Leader
1286	Arita (3)	Np/Sh	24.05.00	S Col - SE Ridge	US	Bob Hoffman
1287	Pasang Tharke	Np/Sh	24.05.00	S Col - SE Ridge	US	Bob Hoffman
1288	Nima (Ang Nima)	Np/Sh	24.05.00	S Col - SE Ridge	US	Bob Hoffman
1289	Francis Slakey	US	24.05.00	S Col - SE Ridge	US	Bob Hoffman
1290	Pemba Norbu III (2)	Np/Sh	24.05.00	S Col - SE Ridge	US	Bob Hoffman
1291	Dawa Jangbu	Np/Sh	24.05.00	S Col - SE Ridge	US	Bob Hoffman
1292	Andrew Lock	Aus	24.05.00	S Col - SE Ridge	int	Andrew Lock
1293	Paul Giorgio	US	24.05.00	S Col - SE Ridge	int	Andrew Lock
1294	Nima Gombu (6)	Np/Sh	24.05.00	S Col - SE Ridge	int	Andrew Lock
1295	Simone Moro	It	24.05.00	S Col - SE Ridge	It/Kaz	Simone Moro
1296	Denis Urubko (x)	Kaz	24.05.00	S Col - SE Ridge	It/Kaz	Simone Moro
1297	Michael Down	Can	26.05.00	S Col - SE Ridge	int	Henry Todd
1298	Tim Cowen	US	26.05.00	S Col - SE Ridge	int	Henry Todd
1299	Richard Stone	US	26.05.00	S Col - SE Ridge	int	Henry Todd
1300	Patrick Kenny	US	26.05.00	S Col - SE Ridge	int	Henry Todd
1301	Richard Allen	UK	26.05.00	S Col - SE Ridge	int	Henry Todd
1302	Dragan Jacimovic	Yu	26.05.00	S Col - SE Ridge	int	Henry Todd

No.	Name	Nat	Date	Route	Exp	Leader
1303	Mingma Nuru II	Np/Sh	26.05.00	S Col - SE Ridge	int	Henry Todd
1304	Juan Carlos González	Sp	27.05.00	N Col - NE Ridge	Sp/Arg	Guillermo Banales
1305	Lhakpa Gyalzen II	Np/Sh	27.05.00	N Col - NE Ridge	Sp/Arg	Guillermo Banales
1306	Viktor Volodin	Rus	28.05.00	N Col - NE Ridge	Rus/UK	Viatcheslav Skripko
1307	Kim Hwan-Koo	SK	04.10.00	S Col - SE Ridge	SK	Kim Young-Moon
1308	Kim Seong-Cheol	SK	04.10.00	S Col - SE Ridge	SK	Kim Young-Moon
1309	Kim Woong-Sik	SK	04.10.00	S Col - SE Ridge	SK	Yoon Hong-Keun
1310	Hong Sun-Dok	SK	04.10.00	S Col - SE Ridge	SK	Yoon Hong-Keun
1311	Cho Cheol-Hee	SK	04.10.00	S Col - SE Ridge	SK	Yoon Hong-Keun
1312	Davo Karnicar	Slo	07.10.00	S Col - SE Ridge	Slo	Davorin Karnicar
1313	Franc Oderlap	Slo	07.10.00	S Col - SE Ridge	Slo	Davorin Karnicar
1314	Ang Dorje II (7)	Np/Sh	07.10.00	S Col - SE Ridge	Slo	Davorin Karnicar
1315	Pasang Tenzing	Np/Sh	07.10.00	S Col - SE Ridge	Slo	Davorin Karnicar
1316	Tadej Golob	Slo	09.10.00	S Col - SE Ridge	Slo	Davorin Karnicar
1317	Matej Flis	Slo	09.10.00	S Col - SE Ridge	Slo	Davorin Karnicar
1318	Gregor Lacen	Slo	09.10.00	S Col - SE Ridge	Slo	Davorin Karnicar

ABBREVIATIONS FOR CLIMBERS' NATIONALITIES
– shown in order of appearance

NZ New Zealand, **Ind** India, **Sh** Sherpa, **Swi** Switzerland, **Chn** China, **Tib** Tibet, **US** United States, **Np** Nepal, **Jp** Japan, **It** Italy, **UK** United Kingdom, **SK** South Korea, **Au** Austria, **Ger** Germany, **Fra** France, **Pol** Poland, **Slo** Slovenia, **Cro** Croatia, **Sp** Spain, **Rus** Russia, **Ukr** Ukraine, **Kaz** Kazakhstan, **Can** Canada, **Bul** Bulgaria, **Aus** Australia, **NL** Netherlands, **Slk** Slovakia, **Nor** Norway, **Mac** Macedonia, **Mex** Mexico, **Bel** Belgium, **Swe** Sweden, **Cz** Czech Republic, **Geo** Georgia, **Isr** Israel, **Chl** Chile, **Lux** Luxembourg, **Per** Peru, **Tai** Taiwan, **Fin** Finland, **Lit** Lithuania, **Ire** Ireland, **Bra** Brazil, **Lat** Latvia, **Arg** Argentina, **Rom** Romania, **Tur** Turkey, **Den** Denmark, **SA** South Africa, **RI** Indonesia, **Ice** Iceland, **Mal** Malaysia, **By** Belarus, **Irn** Iran, **Uzb** Uzbekistan, **Bol** Bolivia, **Por** Portugal, **Ec** Ecuador, **Pak** Pakistan, **Yu** Yugoslavia.

Two additional nationalities appear in the list of expeditions: **Sin** Singapore, **Aze** Azerbaijan. **Int** signifies international, and includes some commercial expeditions. Where national identities are concerned, the list makes the following

distinctions. Sherpa climbers are shown with the abbreviation **Sh** after their nationality. Tibetans are listed as such, rather than as Chinese. Climbers and expeditions from the former USSR are indicated with their post-Soviet identities. Those from the former Yugoslavia and the former Czechoslovakia follow the same principles. Expeditions from West Germany before 1990 are shown as German. The letter **B** denotes Spanish climbers from the Basque region.

ASCENTS IN ORDER OF CLIMBERS' NATIONALITY

Nepal **456**; US **154**; Japan **84**; Russia **59**; UK **53**; India **49**; China (including Tibet) **44**; Spain **39**; France **37**; South Korea **36**; New Zealand **22**; Italy, Kazakhstan **21**; Australia **19**; Germany **17**; Canada, Poland **15**; Slovenia **14**; Switzerland **13**; Mexico **12**; Uzbekistan **11**; Austria, Norway **10**; Georgia, Sweden, Ukraine **8**; Bulgaria, Netherlands, Slovakia **6**; Taiwan **5**; Chile, Czech Republic, Denmark, Finland, Iran, Malaysia **4**; Argentina, Belgium, Iceland, Latvia **3**; Brazil, Croatia, Indonesia, Ireland, Peru, South Africa **2**; Israel, Luxembourg, Lithuania, Macedonia, Turkey, Romania, Belarus, Bolivia, Portugal, Ecuador, Pakistan, Yugoslavia **1**.

The 1318 ascents have been made by 981 individual climbers. Heading the list for repeat ascents is Apa with 11, followed by Ang Rita and Babu Tshering with 10 each (see pages 202-205). Among non-Sherpa climbers, the highest number of ascents is 6 by Pete Athans (US), followed by Ed Viesturs (US) and Rob Hall (New Zealand) with 5. Hall died while descending from the summit in May 1996. The highest number of ascents in a year is 145, in 2000, followed by 1993 (129) and 1998 and 1999 (both 121). The most recent year with no ascents is 1974.

The list contains two non-proven entries. These are Mick Burke (26 September 1975) and Pasang Temba (13 October 1988). In each case there is no absolute proof that they reached the summit, although their colleagues are convinced that they did. In the strict accounting of Everest statistics, their presumed ascents have not been included in the final total. There are a very few other cases where climbers' summit claims have been privately doubted, but this list follows the customary practice of accepting claims at face value unless conclusively proved otherwise.

The lists have been assembled through a remarkable collaborative effort by three people. First is the redoubtable Liz Hawley, an American journalist based in Kathmandu, who became the authoritative source for all information about Everest expeditions, as well as those to other Himalayan peaks in Nepal. For 40 years she searched out teams on their way to Everest and on their way back, quizzing the leaders about their intentions and their achievements in order to compose definitive lists. In compiling her records she worked closely with Xavier Eguskitza, a Spanish Basque, residing in England, who started collecting Everest statistics in 1974 and provided information for many publications since. In 1997 Eguskitza joined forces with Eberhard Jurgalski, a German who first researched mountaineering statistics in 1981 and computerised his lists in 1989.

DEATHS ON EVEREST

No.	Name	Nat	Date	Exp	Location	Cause
1	Norbu	Ind/Sh	07.06.22	UK	Below N Col	Avalanche
2	Lhakpa	Ind/Sh	07.06.22	UK	Below N Col	Avalanche
3	Pasang	Ind/Sh	07.06.22	UK	Below N Col	Avalanche
4	Pema	Ind/Sh	07.06.22	UK	Below N Col	Avalanche
5	Sange	Ind/Sh	07.06.22	UK	Below N Col	Avalanche
6	Dorje	Ind/Sh	07.06.22	UK	Below N Col	Avalanche
7	Temba	Ind/Sh	07.06.22	UK	Below N Col	Avalanche
8	Shamsherpun	Np	13.05.24	UK	Above Rongbuk BC	Frostbite, brain haem.
9	Manbahadur	Ind	17.05.24	UK	At Rongbuk BC	Frostbite, pneumonia
10	George Mallory	UK	08.06.24	UK	NE Ridge	Fall
11	Andrew Irvine	UK	08.06.24	UK	NE Ridge	Disappeared
12	Maurice Wilson	UK	??.06.34	solo	E Rongbuk Glacier	Exhaustion
13	Mingma Dorje	Np/Sh	31.10.52	Swi	Lhotse Face	Falling ice
14	Wang Ji	Tib	??.05.60	Chn	Camp III, 6400m	Pulmonary oedema
15	Nawang Tshering	Np/Sh	28.04.62	Ind	Lhotse Face	Falling rocks
16	John Breitenbach	US	23.03.63	US	Icefall	Falling serac
17	Shao Shi-ching	Chn	01.04.64	Chn	Camp IV, 7050m	Heart attack
18	Ma Gao-shu	Chn	01.05.66	Chn	On descent from 7790m	Fall
19	Phu Dorje I	Np/Sh	18.10.69	Jp	Icefall	Collapsed snow bridge
20	Mima Norbu	Np/Sh	05.04.70	Jp	Icefall	Avalanche
21	Nima Dorje	Np/Sh	05.04.70	Jp	Icefall	Avalanche
22	Tshering Tarkey	Np/Sh	05.04.70	Jp	Icefall	Avalanche
23	Pasang	Np/Sh	05.04.70	Jp	Icefall	Avalanche
24	Kunga Norbu	Np/Sh	05.04.70	Jp	Icefall	Avalanche
25	Kami Tshering	Np/Sh	05.04.70	Jp	Icefall	Avalanche
26	Kyak Tshering	Np/Sh	09.04.70	Jp	Icefall	Falling seracs
27	Kiyoshi Narita	Jp	21.04.70	Jp	Camp I (Icefall)	Heart attack
28	Harsh Bahuguna	Ind	18.04.71	int	W Ridge, 6900m	Cold, exhaustion
29	Tony Tighe	Aus	16.11.72	UK	Icefall	Falling serac
30	Jangbu	Np/Sh	12.10.73	Jp	SW Face	Avalanche
31	Gérard Devouassoux	Fra	09.09.74	Fra	W Shoulder, 6400m	Avalanche
32	Lhakpa	Np/Sh	09.09.74	Fra	W Shoulder, 6400m	Avalanche
33	Sanu Wongal	Np/Sh	09.09.74	Fra	W Shoulder, 6400m	Avalanche
34	Pemba Dorje	Np/Sh	09.09.74	Fra	W Shoulder, 6400m	Avalanche
35	Nawang Lutuk	Np/Sh	09.09.74	Fra	W Shoulder, 6400m	Avalanche
36	Nima Wangchu	Np/Sh	09.09.74	Fra	W Shoulder, 5800m	Avalanche
37	Wu Tsung-yue	Chn	04.05.75	Chn	NE Ridge, 8500m	Exhaustion, fall
38	Mick Burke	UK	26.09.75	UK	Near summit	Disappeared
39	Terry Thompson	UK	10.04.76	UK	Western Cwm	Fall into crevasse
40	Dawa Nuru	Np/Sh	18.04.78	Au	Icefall	Fall into crevasse
41	Shi Ming-ji	Chn	??.05.78	Chn/Irn	E Rongbuk Glacier, 5700m	Cerebral haem.
42	Ang Phu	Np/Sh	16.05.79	Slo	Hornbein Couloir	Fall
43	Ray Genet	US	03.10.79	Ger	SE Ridge, 8400m	Cold, exhaustion
44	Hannelore Schmatz (f)	Ger	03.10.79	Ger	SE Ridge, 8400m	Cold, exhaustion
45	Wang Hong-bao	Chn	12.10.79	Chn/Jp	Below N Col	Avalanche
46	Lou San	Chn	12.10.79	Chn/Jp	Below N Col	Avalanche
47	Nima Tashi	Tib	12.10.79	Chn/Jp	Below N Col	Avalanche
48	Akira Ube	Jp	02.05.80	Jp	N Face, 7900m	Avalanche
49	Nawang Kersang	Np/Sh	06.09.80	It/Np	Icefall	Fall
50	Mario Piana	It	22.09.80	It/Np	Lhotse Face	Falling seracs
51	Noboru Takenaka	Jp	12.01.81	Jp	Western Cwm, 6900m	Fall
52	Marty Hoey (f)	US	15.05.82	US	N Face, 8000m	Fall
53	Peter Boardman	UK	17.05.82	UK	NE Ridge, 8200m	Exhaustion
54	Joe Tasker	UK	17.05.82	UK	NE Ridge, 8200m	Disappeared
55	Pasang Sona	Np/Sh	31.08.82	Can	Icefall	Avalanche
56	Ang Chuldim	Np/Sh	31.08.82	Can	Icefall	Avalanche
57	Dawa Dorje	Np/Sh	31.08.82	Can	Icefall	Avalanche
58	Blair Griffiths	Can	02.09.82	Can	Icefall	Falling seracs
59	Lhakpa Tshering	Np/Sh	27.09.82	Sp	W Ridge, 6770m	Internal haemorrhage
60	Nima Dorje	Np/Sh	14 .10.82	Sp	W Ridge, 8300m	Fall
61	Yasuo Kato	Jp	27.12.82	Jp	S Summit area	Disappeared
62	Toshiaki Kobayashi	Jp	27.12.82	Jp	S Summit area	Disappeared
63	Pasang Temba	Np/Sh	08.10.83	Jp	SE Ridge, 8600m	Fall
64	Hironobu Kamuro	Jp	08.10.83	Jp	Hillary Step	Fall
65	Hiroshi Yoshino	Jp	08.10.83	Jp	Hillary Step	Fall
66	Ang Rinji	Np/Sh	26.03.84	Ind	Icefall	Avalanche
67	Tony Swierzy	UK	03.04.84	UK	N Face, 6150m	Avalanche
68	Hristo Ivanov Prodanov	Bul	21.04.84	Bul	W Ridge, 8500m	Exhaustion
69	Craig Nottle	Aus	09.10.84	Aus	Hornbein Couloir	Fall
70	Fred From	Aus	09.10.84	Aus	Hornbein Couloir	Fall
71	Jozef Psotka	Slo	16.10.84	Slo	Lhotse Face	Fall
72	Ang Dorje I	Np/Sh	24.10.84	Np	SE Ridge, 8400m	Fall
73	Yogendra Thapa	Np	24.10.84	Np	SE Ridge, 8400m	Fall
74	Juanjo Navarro	Sp	12.05.85	Sp	N Ridge, 7300m	Fall
75	Shinichi Ishii	Jp	17.09.85	Jp	Below N Col	Avalanche
76	Kiran Inder Kumar	Ind	07.10.85	Ind	SE Ridge, 8500m	Fall
77	Vijay Pal Singh Negi	Ind	11.10.85	Ind	S Col	Exposure
78	Ranjeet Singh Bakshi	Ind	11.10.85	Ind	S Col	Exposure
79	Jai Bahugana	Ind	11.10.85	Ind	S Col	Exposure
80	M.U. Bhaskar Rao	Ind	11.10.85	Ind	S Col	Exposure
81	Víctor Hugo Trujillo	Chl	16.08.86	Chl	Below N Col	Avalanche
82	Simon Burkhardt	Swi	28.09.86	Swi	Lhotse Face	Avalanche
83	Gyalu	Np/Sh	04.10.86	Swi	Icefall	Falling seracs
84	Dawa Norbu	Np/Sh	17.10.86	US	Below N Col	Avalanche
85	Tsuttin Dorje	Np/Sh	30.01.87	SK	SW Face, 7700m	Fall
86	Roger Marshall	Can	21.05.87	solo	Hornbein Couloir	Fall
87	Masao Yokoyama	Jp	02.09.87	Jp	E Rongbuk Glacier	Drowned
88	Mangal Singh	Np	20.10.87	UK	Above Rongbuk BC	Avalanche
89	Hidetaka Mizukoshi	Jp	21.04.88	Jp	Base Camp	Heart attack
90	Michel Parmentier	Fra	20.09.88	int	N Face, 7700m	Exposure
91	Narayan Shrestha	Np	21.09.88	Sp	W Ridge, 7200m	Avalanche
92	Lhakpa Sonam	Np/Sh	13.10.88	Fra	SE Ridge, 8200m	Fall
93	Pasang Temba (II)	Np/Sh	13.10.88	Fra	SE Ridge, 8200m	Fall
94	Dusan Becik	Slo	17.10.88	Cz	SE Ridge	Disappeared
95	Peter Bozic	Slo	17.10.88	Cz	SE Ridge	Disappeared
96	Jaroslav Jasko	Slo	17.10.88	Cz	SE Ridge	Disappeared
97	Jozef Just	Slo	17.10.88	Cz	SE Ridge	Disappeared
98	Ang Lhakpa Dorje	Np/Sh	23.12.88	Bel	S Col	Cerebral thrombosis
99	Dimitar Ilijevski	Mac	10.05.89	Mac	SE Ridge	Fall
100	Phu Dorje III	Np/Sh	16.05.89	US	SE Ridge	Fall
101	Miroslaw Dasal	Pol	27.05.89	Pol	Lho La area	Avalanche
102	Miroslaw Gardzielewski	Pol	27.05.89	Pol	Lho La area	Avalanche
103	Waclaw Otreba	Pol	27.05.89	Pol	Lho La area	Avalanche
104	Zygmunt Heinrich	Pol	27.05.89	Pol	Lho La area	Avalanche
105	Eugeniusz Chrobak	Pol	28.05.89	Pol	Lho La area	Avalanche
106	Ang Pinjo	Np/Sh	12.12.89	SK	Western Cwm	Altitude sickness
107	Rafael Gómez-Menor	Sp	12.09.90	Sp	Below N Col	Avalanche
108	Ang Sona	Np/Sh	12.09.90	Sp	Below N Col	Avalanche
109	Badrinath Ghising	Np	12.09.90	Sp	Below N Col	Avalanche
110	Ham Sang-Hun	SK	07.10.90	SK	SE Ridge	Fall
111	Rüdiger Lang	Ger	03.05.91	Au	NNE Facet, 7850m	Exposure
112	Junichi Futagami	Jp	27.05.91	Jp	NE Ridge, 8700m	Fall
113	Deepak Kulkarni	Ind	02.05.92	Ind	Below S Col	Exposure
114	Raymond Jacob	Ind	02.05.92	Ind	Below S Col	Exposure
115	Subba Singh	Np	11.05.92	Sp	Base Camp	Heart attack
116	Sher Singh	Ind	22.05.92	Ind	Icefall	Fall
117	Manabu Hoshi	Jp	23.05.92	Jp	NE Ridge, 8350m	Disappeared
118	Ang Tshering	Np/Sh	15.01.93	Sp	Western Cwm	Fall into crevasse

No.	Name	Nat	Date	Exp	Location	Cause
119	Pasang Lhamu (f)	Np/Sh	23.04.93	Np	SE Ridge, 8750m	Exposure
120	Sonam Tshering	Np/Sh	23.04.93	Np	SE Ridge	Fall
121	Lobsang Tshering	Ind	10.05.93	Ind	SE Ridge	Fall
122	Nam Won-Woo	SK	16.05.93	SK	SW Face, 8450m	Fall
123	An Jin-Seob	SK	17.05.93	SK	SW Face, foot	Fall
124	Karl Henize	US	05.10.93	UK	Rongbuk ABC	Cerebral oedema
125	Antonio Miranda	Sp	07.10.93	Sp	SE Ridge, 8100m	Fall
126	Prem Thapa	Np	06.04.94	Ger	Rongbuk BC	Cerebral oedema
127	Shih Fang-Fang	Tai	09.05.94	Tai	W Ridge to NE Ridge	Disappeared
128	Giuseppe Vigani	It	18.05.94	It	N Face	Fall
129	Mike Rheinberger	Aus	27.05.94	int	NE Ridge, 8500m	Cerebral oedema, fall
130	Mingma Norbu	Np/Sh	12.09.94	Nor	Below N Col	Avalanche
131	Kami Rita	Np/Sh	06.05.95	US	SE Ridge	Fall
132	Lhakpa Nuru I	Np/Sh	10.09.95	SK	NE Ridge, 6900m	Avalanche
133	Zangbu	Np/Sh	14.10.95	SK	Descending Great Couloir	Fall
134	Yu Nam-Cheng	Tai	09.05.96	Tai	Lhotse Face	Fall
135	Doug Hansen	US	11.05.96	NZ	S Summit	Exhaustion, exposure
136	Andrew Harris	NZ	11.05.96	NZ	NE Ridge	Disappeared
137	Yasuko Namba (f)	Jp	11.05.96	NZ	S Col area	Exhaustion
138	Scott Fischer	US	11.05.96	US	SE Ridge, 8400m	Exhaustion, exposure
139	Rob Hall	NZ	11.05.96	NZ	Near S Summit	Exhaustion, exposure
140	Dorje Morup	Ind	11.05.96	Ind	NE to N Ridge	Disappeared
141	Tsewang Paljor	Ind	11.05.96	Ind	NE to N Ridge	Disappeared
142	Tsewang Smanla	Ind	11.05.96	Ind	NE to N Ridge	Disappeared
143	Reinhard Wlasich	Au	19.05.96	Au	N Face, 8300m	Altitude sickness

No.	Name	Nat	Date	Exp	Location	Cause
144	Bruce Herrod	UK	25.05.96	SA/UK	Hillary Step	Fall
145	Nawang Dorje	Np/Sh	06.06.96	US	Camp II	Coma, died in hospital
146	Yves Bouchon	Fra	21.09.96	int	Lhotse Face, 7400m	Avalanche
147	Lobsang Jangbu	Np/Sh	21.09.96	Jp	Lhotse Face, 7400m	Avalanche
148	Dawa	Np/Sh	21.09.96	SK	Lhotse Face, 7400m	Avalanche
149	Mal Duff	UK	23.04.97	UK	Base Camp	Heart attack
150	Nima Rinzi	Np/Sh	06.05.97	Mal	Lhotse Face	Fall
151	Aleksandr Torochin	Rus	07.05.97	Rus	NE Ridge	Fall
152	Ivan Plotnikov	Rus	07.05.97	Rus	NE Ridge	Illness
153	Nikolai Chevtchenko	Rus	07.05.97	Rus	NE Ridge	Illness
154	Mingma	Np	07.05.97	SK	NE Ridge	Fall
155	Peter Kowalzik	Ger	08.05.97	Pol	NE Ridge	Disappeared
156	Tenzing Nuru	Np/Sh	25.05.97	US	SE Ridge	Disappeared
157	Choi Byung-Soo	SK	08.09.97	SK	Below N Col	Avalanche
158	Sergei Arsentiev	Rus	23.05.98	Rus/Fra	NE Ridge	Illness and fall?
159	Francys Arsentiev (f)	US	24.05.98	Rus/Fra	NE Ridge	Exhaustion
160	Mark Jennings	UK	25.05.98	UK	NE Ridge	Exhaustion?
161	Roger Buick	NZ	26.05.98	NZ	NE Ridge	Cold, exhaustion
162	Vasili Kopytko	Ukr	08.05.99	Ukr	NE Ridge	Disappeared
163	Michael Matthews	UK	13.05.99	int	SE Ridge	Disappeared
164	Tadeusz Kudelski	Pol	18.05.99	int	NE Ridge	Disappeared
165	Pascal Debrouwer	Bel	18.05.99	int	NE Ridge	Fall
166	Jeppe Stoltz	Den	20.05.00	Den	NE Ridge	Fall
167	Yan Gen-hua	Chn	21.05.00	Chn	NE Ridge	Fall

The list shows all deaths to climbers at or above base camps. Heights of fatal incidents on non-specific locations are given where known. Avalanches caused most deaths (49) followed by falls (40). Deaths in the notorious Khumbu Icefall have fallen dramatically, with 18 occurring up to 1986, but only one since. The group incurring most deaths are Sherpas, with 55. Among non-Sherpa nations, the highest totals are Japan, 13, and the UK, 12. The US total is 7. There were deaths in every year since 1969, apart from 1977. The worst year was 1996, with 15. Since 1982, the lightest years were 1991 and 2000, with 2 deaths each.

The most chilling figure shows that 41 climbers who reached the summit died during their descent (4.2% of all successful climbers). The most poignant of these were the Russian Sergei Arsentiev and his US wife Francys, who on 22 May 1998 made the 999th and 1,000th ascents together. Francys collapsed during the descent. Sergei died in a fall while trying to fetch help and Francys is believed to have died the following day. One cause has been revised since 1993: George Mallory, who was previously described as having disappeared, is now known to have died in a fall.

OLDEST EVEREST CLIMBERS

No.	Name	Nat	Birth Date	Ascent	Age
1	Tenzing Norgay	Ind/Sh	??.05.14	29.05.53	39 years
2	Sonam Gyatso	Ind	??.11.22	22.05.65	42 years 6 months
3	Pierre Mazeaud	Fra	24.08.29	15.10.78	49 years 52 days
4	Gerhard Schmatz	Ger	05.06.29	01.10.79	50 years 118 days
5	Jozef Psotka	Slo	12.01.34	15.10.84	50 years 246 days

No.	Name	Nat	Birth Date	Ascent	Age
6	Chris Bonington	UK	06.08.34	21.04.85	50 years 258 days
7	Dick Bass	US	21.12.29	30.04.85	55 years 130 days
8	Ramón Blanco	Sp	30.04.33	07.10.93	60 years 160 days
9	Lev Sarkisov	Geo	02.12.38	12.05.99	60 years 161 days
10	Toshio Yamamoto	Jp	13.07.36	19.05.00	63 years 311 days

YOUNGEST EVEREST CLIMBERS

No.	Name	Nat	Birth Date	Ascent	Age
1	Edmund Hillary	NZ	20.07.19	29.05.53	33 years 313 days
2	Jürg Marmet	Swi	14.09.27	23.05.56	28 years 252 days
3	Hansrudolf von Gunten	Swi	12.12.28	24.05.56	27 years 164 days

No.	Name	Nat	Birth Date	Ascent	Age
4	Chu Yin-hua	Chn	31.03.35	25.05.60	25 years 55 days
5	Sonam Wangyal	Ind	08.01.42	22.05.65	23 years 134 days
6	Shambu Tamang (1)	Np	1954/1955	05.05.73	18 years approx.
7	Bertrand Roche	Fra	04.03.73	07.10.90	17 years 217 days

The 'Oldest' and 'Youngest' lists are progressive, showing how the age of the oldest Everest climber has advanced, while that of the youngest climber has decreased. The shortest tenure was Jürg Marmet's, whose 'youngest' record lasted one day. The youngest climber by 2000, Frenchman Bertrand Roche, went to the summit with his father Jean-Noël – the first father/son pair to succeed.

EVEREST WITHOUT ARTIFICIAL OXYGEN

No.	Name	Nat	Date	Route
1	Reinhold Messner (1)	It	08.05.78	S Col - SE Ridge
2	Peter Habeler	Au	08.05.78	S Col - SE Ridge
3	Hans Engl	Ger	14.10.78	S Col - SE Ridge
4	Mingma Nuru	Np/Sh	16.10.78	S Col - SE Ridge
5	Ang Dorje I (1)	Np/Sh	16.10.78	S Col - SE Ridge
6	Reinhold Messner (2)	It	20.08.80	N Col - N Face
7	Ang Rita (1)	Np/Sh	07.05.83	S Col - SE Ridge
8	Larry Nielson	US	07.05.83	S Col - SE Ridge
9	Haruichi Kawamura	Jp	08.10.83	S Pillar - S Col
10	Shomi Suzuki	Jp	08.10.83	S Pillar - S Col
11	Haruyuki Endo	Jp	08.10.83	S Col - SE Ridge
12	†Hiroshi Yoshino	Jp	08.10.83	S Col - SE Ridge
13	†Hironobu Kamuro	Jp	08.10.83	S Col - SE Ridge
14	†Hristo Ivanov Prodanov	Bul	20.04.84	W Ridge
15	Ang Dorje I (2)	Np/Sh	23.05.84	S Col - SE Ridge
16	Tim Macartney-Snape (1)	Aus	03.10.84	N Face (Norton Couloir)
17	Greg Mortimer	Aus	03.10.84	N Face (Norton Couloir)
18	†Jozef Psotka	Slk	15.10.84	S Pillar
19	Zoltan Demjan	Slk	15.10.84	S Pillar
20	Ang Rita (2)	Np/Sh	15.10.84	S Pillar
21	Ang Rita (3)	Np/Sh	29.04.85	S Col - SE Ridge
22	Noboru Yamada	Jp	30.10.85	S Col - SE Ridge
23	Erhard Loretan	Swi	30.08.86	N Face (Hornbein Couloir)
24	Jean Troillet	Swi	30.08.86	N Face (Hornbein Couloir)
25	Ang Rita (4)	Np/Sh	22.12.87	S Col - SE Ridge
26	Stephen Venables	UK	12.05.88	E Face - S Col - SE Ridge
27	Michel Metzger	Fra	26.09.88	S Col - SE Ridge
28	Marc Batard (1)	Fra	26.09.88	S Col - SE Ridge
29	Ang Rita (5)	Np/Sh	14.10.88	S Col - SE Ridge
30	Nima Rita	Np/Sh	14.10.88	S Col - SE Ridge
31	Lydia Bradey (f)	NZ	14.10.88	S Col - SE Ridge
32	†Jozef Just	Slk	17.10.88	SW Face
33	Sonam Tshering	Np/Sh	10.05.89	S Col - SE Ridge
34	Carlos Carsolio	Mex	13.10.89	S Col - SE Ridge
35	Ang Rita (6)	Np/Sh	23.04.90	S Col - SE Ridge
36	Sergei Arsentiev (1)	Rus	07.05.90	N Col - NE Ridge
37	Grigori Lunyakov	Kaz	07.05.90	N Col - NE Ridge
38	Ed Viesturs (1)	US	08.05.90	N Col - NE Ridge
39	Andrei Tselishchev	Kaz	08.05.90	N Col - NE Ridge
40	Anatoli Moshnikov	Rus	10.05.90	N Col - NE Ridge
41	Aleksandr Tokarev	Rus	10.05.90	N Col - NE Ridge
42	Tim Macartney-Snape (2)	Aus	11.05.90	S Col - SE Ridge
43	Marc Batard (2)	Fra	05.10.90	S Col - SE Ridge
44	Battistino Bonali	It	17.05.91	N Face (Norton Couloir)
45	Leopold Sulovsky	Cz	17.05.91	N Face (Norton Couloir)
46	Vladimir Balyberdin	Rus	07.10.91	S Col - SE Ridge
47	Anatoli Boukreev (1)	Kaz	07.10.91	S Col - SE Ridge
48	Ang Rita (7)	Np/Sh	15.05.92	S Col - SE Ridge
49	Alberto Iñurrategi	Sp/B	25.09.92	S Col - SE Ridge
50	Félix Iñurrategi	Sp/B	25.09.92	S Col - SE Ridge
51	Mario Panzeri	It	28.09.92	S Col - SE Ridge
52	Michael Groom	Aus	10.05.93	S Col - SE Ridge
53	Vladimir Bashkirov	Rus	16.05.93	S Col - SE Ridge
54	Ang Rita (8)	Np/Sh	16.05.93	S Col - SE Ridge
55	Oscar Cadiach	Sp	17.05.93	S Col - SE Ridge
56	Eric Grammond	Fra	06.10.93	S Col - SE Ridge
57	Hubert Giot	Fra	09.10.93	S Col - SE Ridge
58	Lobsang Jangbu (1)	Np/Sh	09.05.94	S Col - SE Ridge
59	Rob Hess	US	09.05.94	S Col - SE Ridge
60	Scott Fischer	US	09.05.94	S Col - SE Ridge
61	Steve Swenson	US	25.05.94	N Col - NE Ridge
62	Lobsang Jangbu (2)	Np/Sh	07.05.95	S Col - SE Ridge
63	Lhakpa Dorje III (1)	Np/Sh	12.05.95	N Col - NE Ridge
64	Tenzing Nuru	Np/Sh	12.05.95	N Col - NE Ridge
65	Ang Rita (9)	Np/Sh	13.05.95	N Col - NE Ridge
66	Marco Bianchi	It	13.05.95	N Col - NE Ridge
67	Christian Kuntner	It	13.05.95	N Col - NE Ridge
68	Alison Hargreaves (f)	UK	13.05.95	N Col - NE Ridge
69	Reinhard Patscheider	It	14.05.95	N Col - NE Ridge
70	Josef Hinding	Au	14.05.95	N Col - NE Ridge
71	Anatoli Boukreev (2)	Kaz	17.05.95	N Col - NE Ridge
72	Anatoli Boukreev (3)	Kaz	10.05.96	S Col - SE Ridge
73	Lobsang Jangbu (3)	Np/Sh	10.05.96	S Col - SE Ridge
74	Ed Viesturs (2)	US	23.05.96	S Col - SE Ridge
75	Lhakpa Dorje III (2)	Np/Sh	23.05.96	S Col - SE Ridge
76	Göran Kropp	Swe	23.05.96	S Col - SE Ridge
77	Ang Rita (10)	Np/Sh	23.05.96	S Col - SE Ridge
78	Jesús Martínez	Sp	23.05.96	S Col - SE Ridge
79	Hans Kammerlander	It	24.05.96	N Col - NE Ridge
80	Vladimir Suviga	Kaz	02.05.97	N Col - NE Ridge
81	Antoine de Choudens	Fra	08.05.97	N Col - NE Ridge
82	Veikka Gustafsson	Fin	23.05.97	S Col - SE Ridge
83	Pavle Kozjek	Slo	23.05.97	N Col - NE Ridge
84	Vladimir Plulik	Slk	19.05.98	N Col - NE Ridge
85	Radek Jaros	Cz	19.05.98	N Col - NE Ridge
86	Vladimir Nosek	Cz	19.05.98	N Col - NE Ridge
87	†Francys Arsentiev (f)	US	22.05.98	N Col - NE Ridge
88	†Sergei Arsentiev (2)	Rus	22.05.98	N Col - NE Ridge
89	Babu Chiri (1)	Np/Sh	06.05.99	S Col - SE Ridge
90	†Vasili Kopytko	Ukr	08.05.99	N Col - NE Ridge
91	Vladislav Terzeoul	Ukr	08.05.99	N Col - NE Ridge
92	Vladimir Gorbach	Ukr	08.05.99	N Col - NE Ridge
93	Joao Garcia	Por	18.05.99	N Col - NE Ridge
94	Babu Chiri (2)	Np/Sh	26.05.99	S Col - SE Ridge
95	Iván Vallejo	Ecu	27.05.99	N Col - NE Ridge
96	Heber Orona	Arg	27.05.99	N Col - NE Ridge
97	Gheorghe Dijmarescu	US	19.05.00	N Col - NE Ridge
98	Denis Urubko	Kaz	24.05.00	S Col - SE Ridge

In 1984, the British Alpine Club expert Peter Lloyd observed that Everest was precisely the right height to test a climber's strength and endurance. 'Were it 1,000 feet lower it would have been climbed in 1924. Were it 1,000 feet higher it would have been an engineering problem.' So it proved. The issue of using supplementary oxygen provoked controversy from the start. George Mallory was at first opposed, on the grounds that it was improper and an encumbrance: 'When I think of mountaineering with four cylinders of oxygen on one's back and a mask over one's face – well, it loses its charm.' In the end, he and Sandy Irvine used supplementary oxygen on their final attempt. A few days before, Edward Norton and Howard Somervell had reached 28,000 feet without it. In 1961, Sir Edmund Hillary predicted: 'Even the summit of Everest is not beyond the capacity of an unassisted man. But the risks are enormous.' In 1965, Tom Hornbein was clear about its benefits. Without it, 'each step at great height is virtually a maximal effort' with nothing in reserve; while using oxygen brought 'a striking sensation of release, a spring in the step'. One of the supreme moments of mountaineering came in 1978, when Reinhold Messner and Peter Habeler reached the summit without it: 'I am nothing more than a single narrow gasping lung, floating over the mists and the summits,' Messner declared. According to information supplied by expedition leaders to Liz Hawley, there were 98 ascents without oxygen by the end of 2000, made by 77 individuals. Just one was made in winter: by the remarkable Ang Rita, on 22 December 1987.

ASCENTS BY WOMEN

No.	Name	Nat	Date	Route	Leader
1	Junko Tabei	Jp	16.05.75	S Col - SE Ridge	Eiko Hisano (f)
2	Phantog	Tib	27.05.75	N Col - NE Ridge	Shih Chan-chun
3	Wanda Rutkiewicz	Pol	16.10.78	S Col - SE Ridge	Karl Herrligkoffer
4	† Hannelore Schmatz	Ger	02.10.79	S Col - SE Ridge	Gerhard Schmatz
5	Bachendri Pal	Ind	23.05.84	S Col - SE Ridge	Darshan K. Khullar
6	Sharon Wood	Can	20.05.86	W Ridge (from Tibet)	Jim Elzinga
7	Stacy Allison	US	29.09.88	S Col - SE Ridge	James Frush
8	Peggy Luce	US	02.10.88	S Col - SE Ridge	James Frush
9	Lydia Bradey (x)	NZ	14.10.88	S Col - SE Ridge	Rob Hall
10	Kui Sang (1)	Tib	09.05.90	N Col - NE Ridge	Jim Whittaker
11	Yekaterina Ivanova	Rus	10.05.90	N Col - NE Ridge	Jim Whittaker
12	Christine Janin	Fra	05.10.90	S Col - SE Ridge	Marc Batard
13	Marija Stremfelj	Slo	07.10.90	S Col - SE Ridge	Andrej Stremfelj
14	Catherine Gibson	US	07.10.90	S Col - SE Ridge	Hooman Aprin
15	Ingrid Baeyens	Bel	12.05.92	S Col - SE Ridge	Rob Hall
16	Santosh Yadav (1)	Ind	12.05.92	S Col - SE Ridge	Hukam Singh
17	† Pasang Lhamu	Np/Sh	22.04.93	S Col - SE Ridge	Pasang Lhamu (f)
18	Kim Soon-Jo	SK	10.05.93	S Col - SE Ridge	Ji Hyun-Ok (f)
19	Ji Hyun-Ok	SK	10.05.93	S Col - SE Ridge	Ji Hyun-Ok (f)
20	Choi Oh-Soon	SK	10.05.93	S Col - SE Ridge	Ji Hyun-Ok (f)
21	Dicky Dolma	Ind	10.05.93	S Col - SE Ridge	Bachendri Pal (f)
22	Santosh Yadav (2)	Ind	10.05.93	S Col - SE Ridge	Bachendri Pal (f)
23	Kunga Bhutia	Ind	10.05.93	S Col - SE Ridge	Bachendri Pal (f)
24	Dolly Lefever	US	10.05.93	S Col - SE Ridge	Paul Pfau/Michael Sinclair
25	Jan Arnold	NZ	10.05.93	S Col - SE Ridge	Rob Hall
26	Radha Devi Thakur	Ind	16.05.93	S Col - SE Ridge	Bachendri Pal (f)
27	Deepu Sharma	Ind	16.05.93	S Col - SE Ridge	Bachendri Pal (f)
28	Savita Martolia	Ind	16.05.93	S Col - SE Ridge	Bachendri Pal (f)
29	Suman Kutiyal	Ind	16.05.93	S Col - SE Ridge	Bachendri Pal (f)
30	Rebecca Stephens	UK	17.05.93	S Col - SE Ridge	John Barry
31	Ginette Harrison	UK	07.10.93	S Col - SE Ridge	Stephen Bell
32	Chiang Hsiu-Chen	Tai	12.05.95	N Col - NE Ridge	Liang Ming-Pen
33	Alison Hargreaves (x)	UK	13.05.95	N Col - NE Ridge	Russell Brice
34	Charlotte Fox	US	10.05.96	S Col - SE Ridge	Scott Fischer
35	Sandy Hill Pittman	US	10.05.96	S Col - SE Ridge	Scott Fischer
36	Lene Gammelgaard	Den	10.05.96	S Col - SE Ridge	Scott Fischer
37	† Yasuko Namba	Jp	10.05.96	S Col - SE Ridge	Rob Hall
38	Araceli Segarra	Sp	23.05.96	S Col - SE Ridge	David Breashears
39	Cathy O'Dowd (1)	SA	25.05.96	S Col - SE Ridge	Ian Woodall
40	Clara Sumarwati	RI	26.09.96	N Col - NE Ridge	Clara Sumarwati (f)
41	Lyudmila Savina	Kaz	20.05.97	N Col - NE Ridge	Yervand Ilinski
42	Brigitte Muir	Aus	27.05.97	S Col - SE Ridge	Mal Duff
43	† Francys Arsentiev (x)	US	22.05.98	N Col - NE Ridge	Boris Sedusov
44	Svetlana Baskakova	Uzb	23.05.98	N Col - NE Ridge	Anatoly Shabanov
45	Sumiyo Tsuzuki	Jp	25.05.98	N Col - NE Ridge	Russell Brice
46	Elsa Avila	Mex	05.05.99	S Col - SE Ridge	Henry Todd
47	Renata Chlumska	Swe	05.05.99	S Col - SE Ridge	Göran Kropp
48	Katja Staartjes	NL	13.05.99	S Col - SE Ridge	Jon Tinker/Nick Kekus
49	Tina Sjögren	Swe	26.05.99	S Col - SE Ridge	Thomas & Tina Sjögren (f)
50	María-Jesús Lago	Sp	26.05.99	N Col - NE Ridge	Sergio Martini
51	Helga Hengge	Ger	27.05.99	N Col - NE Ridge	Russell Brice
52	Karla Wheelock	Mex	27.05.99	N Col - NE Ridge	Ivan Loredo
53	Kui Sang (2)	Tib	28.05.99	N Col - NE Ridge	Samdrub
54	Jiji	Tib	28.05.99	N Col - NE Ridge	Samdrub
55	Cathy O'Dowd (2)	SA	29.05.99	N Col - NE Ridge	Ian Woodall
56	Polly Murray	UK	16.05.00	S Col - SE Ridge	Gavin Bate
57	Ruchia Takahashi	Jp	17.05.00	N Col - NE Ridge	Koichi Ezaki
58	Lhakpa	Np/Sh	18.05.00	S Col - SE Ridge	Lhakpa (f)
59	Pemba Doma	Np/Sh	19.05.00	N Col - NE Ridge	Karl Kobler
60	Anna Czerwinska	Pol	22.05.00	S Col - SE Ridge	Anna Czerwinska (f)
61	Christine Boskoff	US	24.05.00	S Col - SE Ridge	Christine Boskoff (f)
62	Lily Leonard	US	24.05.00	S Col - SE Ridge	Bob Hoffman

With 62 ascents out of 1318, women account for 4.7% of the overall total. Kui Sang (China), Santosh Yadav (India) and Cathy O'Dowd (South Africa) have made two ascents, and O'Dowd is the only woman to have done so by different routes – the South Col route in 1996, followed by the North Col route in 1999. Just two made ascents without using supplementary oxygen: Lydia Bradey (New Zealand) in 1988 and the British climber Alison Hargreaves in 1995. Bradey's ascent was initially disputed, but is now accepted. Although formally part of an expedition led by Russell Brice, Hargreaves climbed unsupported from the East Rongbuk Glacier to the summit, declining assistance – even a cup of tea – from any other climbers.

Hargreaves herself never claimed she had made a solo ascent, since she had not been alone on the mountain, although others did on her behalf. Hers was the third British ascent, following Rebecca Stephens and Ginette Harrison in 1993. The fourth – and the first by a Scotswoman – was by Polly Murray in 2000. Marija Stremfelj (Slovenia) and her husband Andrej were the first married couple to make an ascent together, on 7 October 1990; they were followed moments later by Cathy Gibson (US) and her Russian husband, Aleksei Krasnokutsky. Among nationalities, the US and India top the list, with 9 ascents each. Four women died after reaching the summit; five women have died on Everest in all. See pages 104-105.

HEIGHTS OF EVEREST LANDMARKS

	Feet	Metres		Feet	Metres
Khumbu Icefall (foot)	18,000	5,486	South Col	26,200	7,986
Lho La	19,705	6,006	Third Pinnacle (crest)	27,630	8,422
Western Cwm (lip)	20,200	6,157	First Step	27,880	8,498
Lhotse Face (foot)	23,000	7,010	Second Step	28,200	8,595
North Col	23,000	7,010	South Summit	28,750	8,763
West Shoulder	23,800	7,254	Summit (pre-1999 figure)	29,028	8,848
First Pinnacle (foot)	25,920	7,900	Summit (1999 revision)	29,035	8,850

Sources and Acknowledgements

We gratefully acknowledge all those who gave permission for written material to appear in this book. In the list, texts are sourced as follows: title and author as appearing in this anthology/original source (author/s or editor shown if different from author of extract) plus first publication date (published in London unless otherwise shown)/permission and/or copyright holder (whether for 1993 or 2001 editions) with current editions listed where appropriate. We have made every endeavour to trace copyright holders but if errors or omissions are brought to our notice we shall be pleased to publish corrections in future editions.

We have established the way by George Mallory/library of Magdalene College, Cambridge/Mallory and Millikan families and Master and Fellows of Magdalene College, Cambridge

The tortures of Tantalus by George Finch/*The Assault on Mount Everest 1922* Charles Bruce (ed), Arnold 1923/Dr and Mrs R. Scott Russell

The Lama's tale/*Kailash, a Journal of Himalayan Studies* Vol 1 No 3, Kathmandu 1973/Alexander W MacDonald

Two frail mortals by T Howard Somervell/*After Everest*, Hodder & Stoughton 1936/Somervell family and Hodder & Stoughton

Pursuing the dream by Peter and Leni Gillman/*The Wildest Dream*, Headline 1999 (US: Mountaineers, Seattle 1999)/authors and Headline

My nastiest moment by Jack Longland/*Tight Corners* Sir A. Cobham (Ed.), Allen and Unwin 1940/author

Mirages at 28,000 feet by Frank Smythe/*Everest 1933* Hugh Ruttledge, Hodder & Stoughton 1934/Smythe family

One day Mount Everest will be climbed by Eric Shipton/*Upon That Mountain*, Hodder & Stoughton 1943/Shipton family (republished in *Eric Shipton – The Six Mountain-Travel Books*, Bâton Wicks 1999, US: Mountaineers, Seattle 1999)

A new world by Raymond Lambert/*Forerunners to Everest* by René Dittert, Gabriel Chavelley and Raymond Lambert, Allen and Unwin 1954/author

It seemed like a lifetime by Edmund Hillary/*The Ascent of Everest* John Hunt, Hodder & Stoughton 1953/author and Mount Everest Foundation

The great mystery by Tenzing Norgay/*Tiger of the Snows* J. R. Ullman, Harrap 1955/Chambers, Edinburgh

How we climbed Chomolungma by Wang Fu-chou and Chu Yin-hua/*Mountain Craft* summer 1961

Promises to keep by Tom Hornbein/*Everest: the West Ridge* Tom Hornbein, Sierra Club (San Francisco) 1965/author (Mountaineers, Seattle 1999)

I was in heaven by Sonam Gyatso and Sonam Wangyal/*Nine Atop Everest* M. S. Kohli, Orient Longmans (Bombay) 1969/Capt. M. S. Kohli

Sorry, Harsh, you've had it by Murray Sayle/*Sunday Times* 2 May 1971/ © Times Newspapers Ltd 1971

All the winds of Asia by Peter Boardman/*Mountain Life* January 1976/Hilary Boardman

A breath of fresh air by Doug Scott/*Mountain* Jan–Feb 1976/author

The loneliest people in the world by Peter Habeler/*Everest, Impossible Victory*, Arlington 1979/author and Arlington

No sacrifice could be big enough by Nejc Zaplotnik/*Everest* by Tone Skarja, Mladinska (Ljubljana) 1981/Nejc Zaplotnik and Tone Skarja

The summit at 40° below by Andrzej Zawada/*Alpine Journal* 1981/author

A partner in myself by Nena Holguin/*Mountain* (Sheffield) July–Aug 1981/author

To spend eternity by Maria Coffey/*Fragile Edge* by Maria Coffey, Chatto & Windus 1989/author (Harbour Publishing, British Columbia 1999; US: Mountaineers, Seattle 2000)

A new star to follow by Eduard Myslovski/*Everest 1982* by Jiri Rost, Fizkultura & Sport (Moscow) 1984/author

A fine day for me by Carlos Buhler/unpublished diaries/author

Sweet and sour by Andy Henderson/*Mountain* July–August 1985/author

Avalanche! by Brummie Stokes/*Soldiers and Sherpas*, Michael Joseph 1988/author

Absent friends by Chris Bonington/adapted from *The Everest Years*, Hodder & Stoughton 1986/author

A dangerous day by Mal Duff/*Alpine Journal* 1986/author

'Ya gotta want it!' by Sharon Wood/*Vancouver* magazine March 1988/author

Get down or die by Stephen Venables/*Everest Kangshung Face*, Hodder & Stoughton 1989/author (republished as *Everest – Alone at the Summit*, Odyssey Books, Bath 1996; US: Balliett and Fitzgerald, New York 1999)

Our last chance by Rebecca Stephens/*Financial Times 29 May 1993*/author

The North-east Ridge complete adapted from report by Nihon University Mt Everest Expedition 1995, translated by Harold Solomon

The Russians are crazy by Nikolai Zakharov/original/author

The longest night by Charlotte Fox/*American Alpine Journal* 1997/author

Like a mirage by Anatoli Boukreev and G. Weston DeWalt (© 1997)/*The Climb*, St Martin's Press, New York 1997/St Martin's Press, LLC

In the nick of time by Jon Krakauer (© 1997)/*Into Thin Air*, Villard Books, New York 1997; UK: Macmillan 1997/Villard Books, a division of Random House, Inc.

The final picture by Peter Gillman/*Daily Telegraph* 14 June 1997/author

Ten times to the summit – interview with Ang Rita by Wendy Brewer Lama/original/Wendy Brewer Lama

The same joys and sorrows/The five-minute climb by Conrad Anker and David Roberts (© 1999)/*The Lost Explorer*, Simon & Schuster, New York 1999; UK: Constable & Robinson 2000/authors, Simon & Schuster, Constable & Robinson Publishing Ltd

The geology of Everest by Leni Gillman/original/author

Ascent lists © 2001 Xavier Eguskitza and Eberhard Jurgalski

NOTE: Most of the texts have been extracted from books or from longer articles as indicated above. Original texts, written for this collection, are shown as such. All uncredited articles are by Peter Gillman apart from Women on Top, which was written jointly with Audrey Salkeld. Of the 37 by-lined extracts and articles in the 1993 edition, five have been omitted, with regrets, on grounds of space, while a further seven have been added. Some texts have been slightly trimmed for reasons of space. Others have been subject to minor editing but only in the case of living authors and with their consent. We have endeavoured to make proper names consistent but have left other stylistic variations intact. On the question of conversion between feet and metres, we have given specific heights in both measures in captions and standfirsts. We have not converted references to approximate heights, and we have retained the authors' preference in their texts. Everest's height was revised from 29,028 feet/8,848 metres to 29,035 feet/8,850 metres between the two editions (see page 13), but we have kept references to the former figure as that was believed to be the height at the time.

The Mount Everest Foundation

After the first ascent of Everest in 1953, the Himalayan Committee of the Alpine Club and Royal Geographical Society had to decide what to do with the proceeds of the official book and film of the expedition. It set up the Mount Everest Foundation with the aim of encouraging climbing, exploration and scientific research in the mountain regions. By 2000, the MEF had dispensed more than £700,000 in grants to around 1350 expeditions, mostly from Britain and New Zealand. It assisted first ascents and new routes both on major mountains such as Kangchenjunga and Everest and on other remote and lesser-known peaks. It favours exploratory and innovative ventures, and aims to protect mountain peoples and wild life, with strict environmental criteria for all its projects. The foundation remains keen to attract funds. Potential donors and applicants for grants should contact the MEF at the Royal Geographical Society, 1 Kensington Gore, London SW7 2AR.

The Royal Geographical Society

The Royal Geographical Society has more than 5,000 photographs from the 1953 Everest expedition in its Picture Library at the society's headquarters in Kensington, London. They range from street scenes in Kathmandu to Sir Edmund Hillary's celebrated shot of Tenzing Norgay on the summit on 29 May 1953 (see page 73). These pictures form part of the 20,000 images which comprise the society's Everest Collection, recording all seven British Everest attempts of the 1920s and 1930s, as well as the 1951 reconnaissance and the 1953 ascent. The collection includes George Mallory's photographs, together with others by such climbers as Sandy Irvine, Frank Smythe and Eric Shipton. The library has around half a million images in all, recording all aspects of travel and exploration and dating back to the first days of photography in the 1830s. As for the MEF, the picture library can be contacted at the RGS, 1 Kensington Gore, London SW7 2AR.

PHOTOGRAPHERS AND PICTURE SOURCES

Our gratitude, again, to all those who supplied pictures for use in this book, as listed below, with the modern source and/or copyright holder shown after the photographer's name where appropriate. Apologies too to those whose submissions we were unable to use. As with the texts, we have made every effort to trace copyright holders but if errors or omissions are brought to our notice we will be pleased to make corrections in future editions of this book.

Abbreviations: a (above), b (below), l (left), m (middle), r (right); NGS (National Geographic Society, Washington), RGS (Royal Geographical Society, London)

Cover Galen Rowell/Mountain Light **1** Roger Mear **2** Doug Scott **6** Chris Curry/Hedgehog House **7**(UK) David Ogle/Chris Bonington Picture Library **7**(US) Peter Gillman **8/9** Galen Rowell/Mountain Light **10/13** Science Museum (London) and RGS **14** Bradford Washburn/NGS **15** Claude White/India Office Library, British Museum **16/17** Noel Odell/Peter Odell **18** Salkeld Collection **21** Millikan family **22/23** Charles Howard-Bury/RGS **24** Map Gary Cooke **25** A.F.R.Wollaston/RGS **26/27** Alpine Club **28** George Finch/Mrs R Scott Russell **29** John Noel Photographic Collection **30** George Mallory/RGS **31** George Finch/Scott Russell **32** Arthur Wakefield/Diadem Collection **33** George Finch/Mrs R Scott Russell **35** Captain C.J.Morris/RGS **36/37** Odell portrait: John Noel Photographic Collection. *All other pictures:* Noel Odell/Peter Odell **38** John Noel Photographic Collection **39** Howard Somervell/Somervell family **40**l Tom Holzel **40**r Howard Somervell/Somervell family **41** Howard Somervell **42** Millikan family **44** Salkeld Collection **45**a Noel Odell/Peter Odell **45**b Sandy Irvine/The Sandy Irvine Trust **46** Noel Odell/Peter Odell **47** Noel Odell/Peter Odell **48** Ed Webster; diagram Alan James, Rockfax **49** S.R. Bonnett/RGS **51/54** *All pictures* Frank Smythe/RGS **55** Salkeld Collection **56** Roger Mear **57** Charles Warren/Salkeld Collection **58/59** Galen Rowell/Mountain Light **60/61** Eric Shipton/RGS **61**r 1951 Everest reconnaissance/RGS **62**l Pilots of 684 Squadron/RGS **62**r 1951 Everest reconnaissance/RGS **62**b Map Gary Cooke **63**l&r Eric Shipton/RGS **64** Doug Scott **65** Salkeld Collection **66/67** Swiss Foundation for Alpine Research **68** Tom Bourdillon/RGS **69** Alfred Gregory/RGS **70** George Band/RGS **71**l George Lowe/RGS **72**r Alfred Gregory/RGS **73** Edmund Hillary/RGS **74**l&r Salkeld Collection **75** Gillman Collection **76** Diadem Collection **78** Dr Barry C. Bishop/© NGS **79** Thomas J. Abercrombie/NGS **80/81** Al Auten **82** Dr Barry C. Bishop/© NGS **83** Willi Unsoeld/Jolene Unsoeld **84** Al Auten **85**a Dr Barry C. Bishop/© NGS **85**b Thomas J. Abercrombie/© NGS **86**a&b Salkeld Collection **87**a&b Indian Mountaineering Federation **88/89** Doug Scott **90-93** *All pictures* John Cleare **94** Doug Scott **95** Doug Scott **96** Chris Ralling **97** Doug Scott **98/99** *All pictures* Doug Scott **100** Peter Boardman **100/101** Doug Scott

102 Peter Boardman **103** Doug Scott **104**a Mountain Camera Collection **104**m Salkeld Collection **104**b Pasang Gyalzen Sherpa **105**a Nigel Gifford **105**m Free to Decide **105**b Leo Dickinson **107** Leo Dickinson **108** Dickinson Collection **109** Dickinson Collection **110** Tone Skarja **111**a Tone Skarja **111**b Bojan Pollak **112** Nejc Zaplotnik **114/115** Ed Webster **116** Andrzej Zawada **119** Andrzej Zawada **120/121** Nena Holguin **122** Reinhold Messner **123** Reinhold Messner **124** Chris Bonington **125** Dag Goering **126** Chris Bonington Picture Library **127** Chris Bonington **129** Chris Bonington **130/133** *All pictures* 1982 USSR Everest expedition **134** David Cheesmond **135** George Lowe **136** Carlos Buhler **137** Carl Tobin **138** George Lowe **139** George Lowe **140** Lou Reichardt **140/141** Carlos Buhler **142** Lou Reichardt **143** Lou Reichardt **144** Colin Monteath/Hedgehog House **145/150** *All pictures* Lincoln Hall **151**a&b Colin Monteath/Hedgehog House **152** John English Collection **153** Ed Webster **154** Stephen Venables **155** Bjorn Myrer-Lund **157** Chris Bonington **159** Ed Webster **161** Sharon Wood **162/163** Dwayne Congdon **164**a John Cleare **164**b Yasuo Kato **165** Kazuo Akimoto/Yomiuri **166** Ed Webster **167** Ed Webster **168** Stephen Venables **169** Ed Webster **170/171** Ed Webster **173** Ed Webster **174/175** Neal Beidleman **176** Dave Halton **177** Rebecca Stephens **178** Tchering Zhambu **179** Dave Halton **180**l Alexander Kuznetzov **180**r Nikolai Zakharov **181** Nikolai Zakharov **182** Peter Kuznetzov **183/185** *All pictures* Kiyoshi Furuno **186** Klev Schoening **187** Neal Beidleman/Woodfin Camp Associates **188** Scott Fischer/Woodfin Camp Associates **189** Neal Beidleman/Woodfin Camp Associates **190**a ©2000 Collection of Linda Wylie and A. Boukreev **190** Scott Fischer/Woodfin Camp Associates **191** Scott Fischer/Woodfin Camp Associates **192/193** Neal Beidleman/Woodfin Camp Associates **194** Tom Kelly/Woodfin Camp Associates **195** Tom Kelly/Woodfin Camp Associates **196/198** Bruce Herrod/Sue Thompson **201** Rich Lee/Sue Thompson **202** Pertemba **203** Free to Decide **204** Ed Webster **205** Peter Gillman **206** Jake Norton **207** Jake Norton **208** Andy Politz **209** Jake Norton **210/211** *All pictures* Jim Fagiolo/Mallory & Irvine Research Expedition **212** Jim Nugent **213**a Fred Barth **213**b Conrad Anker **215/216** Kurt Keller/Swissair Photo+Surveys **217** Chris Bonington Picture Library **218** Ed Webster **219** Ed Webster **220** Kurt Keller/Swissair Photo+Surveys **Back cover** (top to bottom): Ed Webster, Fred Barth, Ed Webster, Chris Bonington Picture Library

Fred Barth's photograph (back cover) *shows climbers on the North-east Ridge approaching the summit at 9.30 am on 26 May 1999. Climbers (from nearest to camera) are: Andrei Lushnikov, Gheorghe Dijmarescu and Apa Sherpa.*

EDITOR'S THANKS

In addition to the authors, photographers and others named in the sources and acknowledgements, I wish to register my immense gratitude to the large number of people who gave their assistance in preparing both the 1993 and 2001 editions of this anthology, who are listed below. Where the 2001 edition is concerned, I should like to record special thanks to the following: John Cleare, for his usual good-hearted help on a diverse range of topics; Liz Hawley, Xavier Eguskitza and Eberhard Jurgalski for their meticulous devotion to the statistics of Everest; Tom Hornbein, for his patience and alacrity in solving a range of transatlantic problems; Alan James of Rockfax, for his route diagrams; Jon Krakauer, for his generosity and for easing several paths on my behalf; Fran Loft, American Alpine Club library, for her help with research; Bill and Flura Sumner for their diligence in obtaining and translating Nikolai Zakharov's account of his 1995 ascent; Ed Webster, for assistance on so many matters apart from his own superb photographs; Ken Wilson, for his encouragement and advice. I also wish to thank Audrey Salkeld, the most assiduous mountaineering historian and researcher, for her enormous contribution to the 1993 edition, which is of course reflected in the updated version.

Tetsuya Akiyama/Yomiuri Shimbun, Alex and Rachel Alexiev, Rick Allen, Werner Altherr/Swissair Photo+Surveys, John Barry, George Band, Peter Bayley, Steve Bell, Geoff Birtles, Justin Black/Mountain Light Photography, Conrad Blanch, Dorothy Boardman, Margaret Body, John Boyle, Martin Bryant, Woody Camp, Peter Clark/RGS, Charlie Clarke, Naomi Coke, Andrew Cook/India Office Library, Gary Cooke, Gary Crabbe/Mountain Light Photography, Frances Daltrey/Chris Bonington picture library, Ingeborga Doubrawa-Cochlin, Ed Douglas, Rachel Duncan/RGS, Norman Dyhrenfurth, Margaret Ecclestone/Alpine Club Library, Aude Fitzsimons/Magdalene College Library Cambridge, Hilary Foakes, John and Andrew Frost, Dr Eugene Gippenreiter, Phil Green, Alf Gregory, Dave Hahn, Sheila Harrison/Alpine Club, Andy Harvard, Clive Hayball, Jochen Hemmleb, Sir Edmund Hillary, Claudia Hill-Norton, Roger Houghton, Peter Humphrey, Jane Insley/Science Museum, Pat Katterhorn/India Office Library, Captain M. S. Kohli, Kunga Sherpa, Karma D. Lama, Bob Lawford, George Lowe, Col. K. S. Mall/Indian Mountaineering Federation, John Mallory, George Martin/ Everestnews.com, Rick Millikan, Colin Monteath, Greg Mortimer, Bernard Newman, Mike Nicholson, Ralph Nodder, Sandra Noel, Peter Odell, Sue Parsons, Jo Ralling, Lou Reichardt, Dr and Mrs R. Scott Russell, Bill Ruthven, Tseten Sandup, Joanna Scadden and Nicky Sherrif/RGS picture library, Nick Shipton, Eric Simonson, Tone Skarja, Ian Smith, Tony Smythe, Jim Somervell, Julie Summers, Katherine and Pierre Tardivel, Sue Thompson, Charles Warren, A. Warrington/Swiss Foundation for Alpine Research, Bradford Washburn, Peter Wickman, Steve Wilson, Louise Wilson, and Linda Wylie. Particular thanks to our editor, Rachel Connolly, for her coolness under fire; to Clare Pemberton and Julia Charles at Little Brown; and Mary Metz and Mark Thompson at Mountaineers.

INDEX